Peterson's
SUCCESS
WITH
WORDS

Peterson's
SUCCESS
WITH
WORDS

Joan Davenport Carris

Peterson's Guides

Princeton, New Jersey

Excerpt from *The Troubled People Book,* copyright 1985, by Crossroad/ Continuum Publishing Company, New York, NY.

Excerpt from *Germany: 2000 Years,* copyright 1961, by Crossroad/Continuum/ Ungar Publishing, New York, NY.

Excerpts from *Black Women Writers at Work,* copyright 1985, and *The Tongue-Tied American,* copyright 1980, by Continuum Publishing Company, New York, NY.

Excerpts from *Celtic Mysteries,* copyright 1975, and *To Secure the Blessings of Liberty,* copyright 1985, by Crossroad Publishing Company, New York, NY.

Excerpts from "Fire and Ice" and "Provide, Provide" from *The Poetry of Robert Frost,* copyright 1969, by Holt, Rinehart and Winston. Additional copyrights 1962, by Robert Frost, and 1975, by Lesley Frost Ballantine. Used with permission of Henry Holt and Company, Inc.

Excerpt from "Mad Dogs and Englishmen" by Noel Coward, copyright 1932, by Chappell Music Ltd. Copyright renewed; international copyright secured; all rights reserved. Used by permission.

Library of Congress Cataloging-in-Publication Data

Carris, Joan Davenport.
    Peterson's success with words.

    Includes index.
    Summary: A workbook for building vocabulary, with definitions, usage examples, and exercises in such areas as foreign words, words with prefixes, medical terms, and antonyms. Includes a unit on standardized tests such as the PSAT and SAT.
    1. Vocabulary. [1. Vocabulary] I. Peterson's Guides, inc. II. Title. III. Title: Success with words.
PE1449.C34   1987   428.1   87-29202
ISBN 0-87866-536-6

Composition and design by Peterson's Guides

Printed in the United States of America

10   9   8   7   6   5   4   3   2   1

For information about other Peterson's publications, please see the listing at the back of this volume.

Contents

UNIT IV/YOUR BEST ON THE TEST

THE ANSWER SECTION

Acknowledgments

I was urged by the modest folk at Peterson's who edited, proofread, and designed *Peterson's Success with Words* to leave their thank-you until the end or to omit it entirely. "After all," they said, "this is what we are supposed to do. You don't have to put *us* in—you wrote the book."

But as every author knows, especially workbook authors, a book's editing and design make a critical difference. I will always be grateful for the long hours, the scrutiny, and the thoughtful attention given to *Success with Words* by so many members of the Peterson's staff. And the thanks belong up front.

Any educational book has the possibility of ranging over many areas, and this is particularly true of a vocabulary book. As authorities to verify facts and quotations, I am indebted to *Merriam-Webster's Ninth New Collegiate Dictionary,* which also provided the pronunciation key used in the text; to the *Oxford Dictionary of English Etymology,* edited by C. T. Onions (Oxford University Press, 1966); to the *Dictionary of Phrase and Fable,* by E. C. Brewer (Galley Press, 1984 printing); to *Bartlett's Familiar Quotations,* by John Bartlett (125th Anniversary Edition, 1980); to the *Oxford Dictionary of Quotations* (Oxford University Press, 1954); to *Peter's Quotations,* compiled by L. J. Peter (William Morrow & Co., 1977); to *The Penguin Dictionary of Quotations,* edited by J. M. and M. J. Cohen (Penguin, 1960); to *A Second Browser's Dictionary,* by John Ciardi (Harper & Row, 1983); to *O Thou Improper, Thou Uncommon Noun,* by Willard Espy (Clarkson N. Potter, Inc., 1978); to *The People's Almanac,* by David Wallechinsky and Irving Wallace (Bantam, 1978); to *A Handbook to Literature,* by Thrall, Hibbard, and Holman (Odyssey Press, 1960); to *A Glossary of Literary Terms,* by M. H. Abrams (Holt, Rinehart and Winston, 1981); to *Introduction to Satire,* by Leonard Feinberg (Iowa State University Press, 1967); and to the *Dictionary of English Word-Roots,* by Robert W. L. Smith (Littlefield, Adams & Co., 1966).

For permission to quote from Robert Frost's poems "Fire and Ice" and "Provide, Provide," I

In the SAT/PSAT preparation unit, I needed passages to parallel the reading matter found on those two exams. I found appropriate selections in *The Troubled People Book,* by Paul G. Quinnett (Crossroad/Continuum Publishing Company, 1985); in *Germany: 2000 Years,* by Kurt Reinhardt (Crossroad/Continuum/Ungar Publishing, 1961); in *Black Women Writers at Work,* edited by Claudia Tate (Continuum Publishing Company, 1985); in *The Tongue-Tied American,* by Paul Simon (Continuum Publishing Company, 1980); in *Celtic Mysteries,* by John Sharkey (Crossroad Publishing Company, 1975); and in *To Secure the Blessings of Liberty,* by William C. Shepherd (Crossroad Publishing Company, 1985). I thank the publishers for permission to use these excerpted passages.

I am especially grateful to three English teachers who spent time with the unedited manuscript before final editing, so that the completed text could benefit from their years of experience in the classroom. (Added to my years it's a scary number and we're all being very quiet about it.) Warmest thanks to James Kerr of The Hun School of Princeton, to Betty Lies of Stuart Country Day School of the Sacred Heart, and to Sally Gilbert of Princeton Day School.

Joan Davenport Carris

Introduction

Do any of the following statements apply to you?

- You need a bigger vocabulary to raise your verbal score on standardized tests like the PSAT, SAT, ACT, or GRE.
- You hope to increase your vocabulary and general language skills so that you can get a better job. After all, most employers are looking for people with strong verbal skills.
- You wish for a broad vocabulary because you enjoy knowing what words mean, or because you realize that strong language skills make a good impression on other people.

If you said Yes! to any of the above, please continue reading.

Peterson's Success with Words can help you to reach any or all of those goals. It teaches vocabulary, and how to use vocabulary effectively and correctly. The exercises are varied. They will encourage you to use your imagination, because some are quite difficult. I urge you to ask a friend, parent, or teacher for help whenever you're stumped. It is not necessary to struggle alone to learn words.

If you want to learn to think logically, if you dislike repeating information like a parrot and would rather reason out an answer, if you want greater facility with words, this book can help. It compels you to use logic and reasoning—skills critical for every area of your life.

I especially hope you will enjoy the humor. You may even find some of the exercises a trifle zany; learning new words shouldn't be boring.

Why a Workbook Format?

You know the saying "Use it or lose it." This is especially true of vocabulary.

With this book's workbook format you will read each new word several times and use it even more times. You will work with the words in context most of the time, not as isolated units. To keep a word, you must use it—and not just once or twice. By the end of every lesson, you will have read or used each new word at least six times.

Frequent review lessons help to fix the words in mind before too many run together in a hopeless jumble. After every four lessons of new material, you will review and use again all the words and roots taught in those lessons.

Vocabulary and the PSAT, SAT, and ACT

Few tests explore the depth and understanding of your vocabulary as well as the College Board's Preliminary Scholastic Aptitude Test (PSAT), taken by high school juniors, and Scholastic Aptitude Test (SAT), taken by college-bound high school seniors.

The PSAT is composed of former SAT questions and comes to most juniors as a distinct shock. The possible scores range from 20—given to anyone who can write his or her name correctly on the form—to 80, the highest score. On the verbal section, the average score in 1986 was 40.9; the average math score was 45. The same relative averages hold for the SAT, which has a range of 200 to 800. In 1987, the average SAT verbal score was 430, with an average score of 476 for the math section.

Since 50 on a PSAT or 500 on an SAT indicates a score of 50 percent, or half correct, anyone can see that these averages are dismal. Students' attitudes toward these tests are often correspondingly dismal.

Questions on the PSAT and SAT involve sentence completions, antonyms, analogies, and reading comprehension. *While these appear to be different types of questions, they often are not.* Whenever the vocabulary in a sentence-completion or reading-comprehension question is demanding—and it often is—the entire question becomes dependent on vocabulary knowledge. You may understand the question perfectly yet not recognize some of the words or phrases given as answer choices.

The math portions of the PSAT and SAT also call for strong verbal skills, especially reading comprehension.

The ACT Assessment exam, prepared by American College Testing, demands a level of achievement similar to that of the SAT. Questions on grammar and usage test English skills. Students need strong reading comprehension skills to answer questions about social studies and natural sciences. This test has no antonym or analogy questions. (Math problems on an ACT resemble those on a PSAT or SAT, although students often feel that the math portion of an ACT is more difficult.)

All of these college entrance exams require just what current students appear to lack: good working vocabularies. Any test that lasts for 3 hours, like the SAT, can do a good job of pinpointing people with weak vocabularies.

Because of the particular demands of these tests, and because students are intimidated by them, I have included a special unit titled "Your Best on the Test." This unit explains how to approach the various PSAT and SAT questions and suggests techniques that lead to correct answers. Many practice questions follow, so that any test taker will know exactly what to expect on the Big Day. Practice in answering the reading comprehension questions should be especially helpful if you're preparing for the ACT.

Enhancing Vocabulary When School Is Over

Whether you simply enjoy words or have a need to increase your language skills, I hope that you have fun with the following pages. That's right, *fun*. You will delight in knowing crossword-puzzle words that had formerly eluded you. You'll love the look on your boss's face when you volunteer to give a speech, write a brochure, or make a presentation. As you add new vocabulary, word skills, and language mastery to your life, you will find that this knowledge enriches nearly everything you do. Words are an expression of ideas, after all, and who does not enjoy being rich in ideas?

And now, take a look at Unit I, "What You Already Know." You bring a substantial fund of knowledge with you—more than you may realize. This knowledge is the basis for the next step in learning, and I wish you success.

How to Use This Book . . . As a Student

You can work well with this book alone, without a teacher or classroom full of other students. The best way to achieve your goal of a bigger, better vocabulary is to set a schedule that suits your life. *Regular study sessions,* planned in advance, always bring you greater rewards than a haphazard approach.

You should begin by checking the abbreviation key on the last page of this book because these abbreviations will be used throughout the text. Then *look at the table of contents* briefly for an outline of your course, and check out the handy index at the back of the book. Whenever you have a question about a word's meaning, the index will tell you what pages to read for definition and usage. The page number in **bold type** indicates which page has the fullest explanation of the word in question.

Unit I is called "What You Already Know." Do it first, as it's a great confidence builder. You really do have a good head on your shoulders, and this unit will prove it. Follow the directions for each separate section, and check your answers with the answer key on pp. 328–367. *Always check to see how many you got right. And how many wrong, too. You may learn the most from what you missed.* Taking time to write the correct answers in place of the wrong ones is an excellent idea. Writing fixes words in mind.

Unit II, "Vocabulary In and Out of Context," will set you up for the rest of the book by teaching you how to derive the meaning of a strange word from its context or surroundings. With practice, you will get better and better at this critical skill. Again, *always* check your answers with the answer key, and correct any that you missed.

Unit III is the major portion of this book. It consists of twenty-four teaching lessons and six review lessons. Each lesson is somewhat different, so you won't get bored.

For each lesson in Unit III, do the practice work *in the order presented.* Take a stab at figuring out the words' meanings from their use in context *before* you study their definitions. Next, work the exercises in order, as they become progressively more difficult. Make flash cards if learning words is difficult for you. Ask other people to help whenever you're stumped. But *don't give up.* Anyone holding a job will tell you that a strong vocabulary is a valuable asset in the workplace and a joy to its owner.

Unit IV is preparation for standardized tests, specifically the PSAT and SAT. If you're preparing for the ACT, you will want to do the section on reading comprehension for sure. Although not as lengthy as my book, *SAT Success,* this unit includes the test tips you will need to better your score on the SAT and PSAT. Practice exercises follow the suggested strategies for each question type, and they are demanding questions—just like those on the PSAT and SAT. It would be no kindness to offer simple exercises and delude you into thinking that an SAT is a piece of cake. If you do well on the exercises in this unit, you will do just as well on an actual exam.

The last unit of the text is a book list. The titles in it were recommended by high school students over a period of many years. There are few "classics" in the list, because lists of them are all over the place. (If you're preparing for college, you will want to be familiar with major authors' works and should obtain a list for college-bound students from your high school or local library.) If you need books "for fun" that will build your vocabulary, you will find them in the list in this book.

If you're in class, with this text as assigned material, I hope it will increase your vocabulary pleasurably. I made as many crazy exercises as I could—and still be considered "serious" about teaching vocabulary. I'm intensely serious about words, but a steady diet of we-must-take-this-seriously is BORING.

How to Use This Book . . . As a Teacher

As a teacher, you may flip through this text and quickly get ideas about its use for your students. My comments are offered strictly as suggestions, and as a way of sharing experience with others in my field. Your comments would be welcome; Peterson's Guides will see that I receive all letters.

This text is meant to help you teach vocabulary as easily and effectively as possible. English teachers have so much to teach—writing, understanding of good literature, grammar, speech— that we'd like to have our students for a couple of hours a day, not a measly 45 minutes. We know from talking to pupils and seeing their test scores that their vocabularies are often pitifully limited. The problem is how to enlarge their storehouse of words *without* spending hours on lesson plans and too much time in a class that *never* has enough time. (Have you ever been wildly jealous of the chem or bio teacher who gets extra time for labs? I have!)

Because this book is self-teaching, it should allow you to add a full course in vocabulary development with minimal time and teacher commitment. All the instructions are in the text, including many hints to promote better writing. The answers to exercises are included; of course, you may choose to remove them at the beginning of the year.

Unit I, "What You Already Know," is meant to get the year off to an encouraging start. Students are usually amazed at their own knowledge of roots and prefixes. This unit can be completed as quickly as you want, depending on class ability.

Unit II is called "Vocabulary In and Out of Context." It explains how to derive the meaning of an unknown word from its context and offers many practice exercises. Throughout the book, students will meet new words in context first, so that they will learn to glean meaning from context by year's end. (Only on tests do we tend to see words in isolation.) As with Unit I, you can complete the work as rapidly as the class permits.

The major portion of the text is Unit III, which consists of twenty-four vocabulary lessons and six review lessons. A review appears after every four vocabulary lessons, for a total of thirty lessons. You may want to pull these reviews from the book and use them as unit tests.

The vocabulary lessons group words by type, as you can see from their titles. You may wish to invite professionals into the classroom at appropriate times to ask them what *they* would suggest teaching as necessary vocabulary for the general public. Lawyers, medical doctors and psychologists, artists and playwrights, help to give life to the words for the week. Most business or professional people are happy to give 20 minutes of their time to promote education.

Learning Latin and Greek roots is essential for any study of English, which is 60–70 percent derivative. Long lists of roots are boring to learn, however, and hard to remember. This text presents them in small, manageable groups of four or five, appended to the vocabulary lists.

The practice exercises give students many chances to use the new words and roots. Exercises tend to increase in difficulty, with the most demanding ones near the end. Analogy problems are posed to teach the words in the lesson, not to imitate PSAT or SAT analogies. (The analogies most imitative of test questions are in the unit "Your Best on the Test.") Throughout Unit 3, Exercise VI, "Word Analysis," may be omitted if students' time is insufficient, but it is the most thought-provoking of the lot, and for some people the most fun.

If you give quizzes on each week's list, you may want to consider student-written quizzes. The pupil who writes and helps to grade the quiz does not have to take it that week. As you know, the one who creates the test usually learns more than those who take it.

Also, students may make giant flash cards of the weekly list . . . with the reward of an extra plus in the grade book. As the class settles down at the beginning of a period, you run through the flash cards. This takes only a few minutes and serves a dual purpose: a brisk beginning to the class and a necessary repetition of the words you're teaching.

Unit IV is designed to help students do better on PSAT and SAT exams. Help for the ACT is mainly in the section on reading comprehension, as half of an ACT consists of questions based on reading passages. All questions in Unit IV are designed to be as nearly like SAT and PSAT questions as possible. Class needs will dictate how much time you decide to spend on this unit.

Knowledgeable instructors are what students need most when they're preparing for college entrance exams. If you are not familiar with recent exams, please examine *10 SATs* (available at most bookstores) or past ACTs, obtainable from American College Testing, Iowa City,

Iowa. School libraries should have several test copies available, and so should guidance departments. *Lack of familiarity with the test format penalizes our students as much as lack of knowledge.*

Last, you should know that this is not a formal textbook but a rather informal one. I learn and teach better when I can laugh occasionally.

UNIT I

What You Already Know

The Root of It All
REVIEWING THE ORIGINS OF OUR LANGUAGE

You already know over sixty Latin and Greek roots, plus half as many prefixes. This unit will prove that to you. You have absorbed these language tidbits over time, just as easily as you learned the words and tune to "Happy Birthday."

Roots and prefixes are the guts of language—basic bits of information you use without thinking. That the basics are Latin and Greek should come as no surprise. You learned in history class that the Latin-speaking Romans occupied Britain for a number of years. They left behind not only mosaics, hypocausts, and walls but much of their language as well. (And Latin had already been influenced by Greek.)

Remember 1066, when William the Conqueror won the Battle of Hastings and became ruler of Britain? William spoke French, a Romance language, so-called because it came from the Romans. William's French became the legal language of Britain until the fourteenth century, and French is roughly 85 percent descended from Latin. (See how circular this is? We can't escape Latin.)

So it happens that today's English is a blend of the Anglo-Saxon original with Latin and Greek, plus French overtones. It's a linguistic stew, richer in flavor and variety than the old Britons could ever have dreamed.

Reminding yourself that you know many of these language roots is reassuring proof that your brain hasn't been fried to a potato chip by the summer sun. As you go through this unit, *you should be encouraged by the extent of what you already know.*

Lesson A. Basic Roots

Below are some old friends, some basic roots of our language. As a helpful memory aid, write their meanings on the lines provided.

1. An *Aqua-lung*™ is a device that lets a scuba diver breathe under water. An *aquarium* is a water-bearing container for fish or marine life. An *aqueduct* is a conduit for flowing water.

   AQUA/AQU means _____ .

2. A *hydrant,* also called a fireplug, is connected to the water mains. A *hydrate* is a compound or complex ion formed by the union of water with another substance. Travelers on the desert, where there is no water, often worry about *dehydration*.

   HYDR means _____ .

3. *Biology* is the science of living organisms and life processes. A *biopsy* examines tissues, cells, or fluids from the living body. A *biography* is the story of someone's life.

   BIO means _____ .

4. *Kodachrome* is a brand name of film used for color photography. Certain small, brightly colored African fish are termed *chromides*. The portion of the cell nucleus that stains well with dyes (assuming various basic colors) is the *chromatin*.

   CHROM means _____ .

5. A person with a sizable, bulky body may be described as *corpulent*. A *corps* such as the Marine *Corps* is an organized body of people. A *corporation* is an association or body of people organized as a legal entity for the purpose of conducting business.

CORP means _____ .

6. An *egoist* (or *egotist*) uses the word "I" frequently. Your *alter ego* is your "other self," one who shares your beliefs and personality to an amazing degree. An *egocentric* person concentrates on himself and his own interests.

EGO means _____ .

7. *Geology* is the science and history of the earth, especially as revealed in rocks. *Geometry* comes from a Greek root meaning to measure the earth. *Geophysics* concentrates on the physics of the earth and includes hydrology, meteorology, and other sciences.

GE/GEO means _____ .

8. One type of *bibliography* is a list of sources (books, articles, tapes, personal interviews) consulted by the author of a book. *Bibliophiles* are crazy about books. The French word for library is *bibliothèque*.

BIBLI/BIBLIO means _____ .

9. If you want to study management of soils, fields, and crop production, enroll in a course in *agronomy*. A broader term, *agriculture,* includes the study of crops, fields, and soils and the raising of livestock. The old Roman *agricola*, bowed over his hoe in the field, farmed the soil.

AGR means _____ .

10. Parents gaze at their newborns with fond *maternal* and *paternal* glances. Mothers are the rulers in a *matriarchal* society, whereas fathers dominate in *patriarchal* ones. Known for his *patriotism*, Abraham Lincoln believed that his fatherland must be a unified country.

MATER and MATRI mean _____ .

PATER and PATRI mean _____ .

Lesson B. No Surprises

You will recognize these roots and their derivative words just as you did those in Lesson A. Write their meanings on the lines provided.

1. An *audible* signal is one you can hear. *Auditorium, auditory, inaudible,* and *audience* also derive from the same root.

AUD/AUDIT means _____ _____ .

2. To be *cognizant* is to know or be aware. Related words include *recognize, cognitive, incognito,* and *cognate.*

COGN means _____ .

3. When I *dictate* words, I'm saying them aloud. Some other members of this giant family are *diction, predict, dictionary, abdicate, benediction,* and *dictator.*

DICT/DIC means _____ .

4. _Dormant_ talents are asleep, waiting to be discovered. Relatives include _dormitory, dormer_ (originally a bedroom window), and _dormouse,_ the one who snoozed at the Mad Hatter's tea party.

      DORM means _____ .

5. To _err_ is to wander astray or make a mistake, as when answering a Trivial Pursuit question. _Erroneous, error, errant, erratic,_ and _aberration_ belong to this word family.

      ERR means _____ .

6. Knees bend or _flex,_ a common muscle action, just as _inflection,_ literally a bending or curving of the voice, is common in speech. Derived from the same root are _deflect, inflexible, circumflex,_ and _reflection._

      FLECT and FLEX mean _____ .

7. A sentence of five years at hard _labor_ means that tough work lies ahead. _Laboratory, laborious, belabored,_ and _elaborate_ come from this root.

      LABOR means _____ .

8. A _science_ is a body of knowledge, normally systematized. The same useful root is buried in _omniscient, conscious, prescient,_ and _unscientific_ and gives the key to their meanings.

      SCI means _____ .

9. A _scribbled_ signature that resembles chicken tracks is not as easy to read as one in fine _script._ Well-known relatives include _scripture, inscription, description,_ and _prescription._

      SCRIB and SCRIPT mean _____ .

10. _Video_ is a fairly modern word directly related to _visible._ Also in this family are _vision, envision, provide, revise,_ and _visit._

      VID and VIS mean _____ .

11. To _sense_ something is to feel it, sometimes without any obvious reason. A _presentiment_ is the inexplicable feeling that something will happen. _Sensitive, resent, sensual, consent,_ and _dissent_ are derived from the same root.

      SENS and SENT mean _____ .

Lesson C. More Roots You Know

Yes, you will know this list of roots, too. This time, you isolate the root and write it on the line, followed by its meaning.

1. _synchronize_—to bring or happen together in time, as _to synchronize watches_
   chronological—arranged in order of time
   chronometer—an exceptionally accurate timepiece

      The root _____ means _____ .

2. _cosmic_—like the great and comprehensive universe
   microcosm—a tiny world, typical of the larger one
   cosmopolitan—worldwide in scope; sophisticated, worldly

      The root _____ means _____ .

3. *civil*—of the state or its citizens; polite, mannerly
   civilization—the state of cultural development
   civic—of citizens or a city, e.g., *civic concerns*

   The root _____ means _____.

4. *pedal*—a foot lever, as on a piano or wheeled cycle
   podiatrist—a professional who cares for feet
   pedometer—a walker's recording instrument to measure distance

   The Latin roots _____ and _____ mean

   _____.

5. *psychiatry*—a branch of medicine dealing with the health of the mind
   psyche—the mind or innermost soul or self
   psychosomatic—referring to the interaction between mind and body (usually refers to a
   mental conflict that results in physical symptoms)

   The root _____ means _____.

6. *pediatrician*—physician who cares for children and teens
   pedagogue—originally a slave who walked children to school; now a teacher or instructor
   pedant—from the word *pedagogue;* now a nitpicking teacher or educated show-off

   The Greek root _____ means _____.

7. *via*—by way of or by means of
   viaduct—a road or railway bridge supported by pilings
   trivial—insignificant, unimportant; literally *three ways*

   The root _____ means _____.

8. *urban*—referring to a city
   suburbs—outlying yet attached areas of a city
   urbane—sophisticated, suave, as a city dweller is apt to be

   The root _____ means _____.

9. *tempo*—pace; rate of motion or speed, as in music
   temporary—of limited duration (not permanent)
   contemporary—simultaneous; existing or occurring at the present time; also, n., someone
   near your age

   The root _____ means _____.

10. *zoo*—an assortment of animals for display
    zoology—the science of the animal kingdom
    Protozoa—a subkingdom of acellular or single-celled animals; primitive animals

    The root _____ means _____.

11. *equine*—referring to horses; horselike
    equestrian—one who rides horses; adj., referring to horses, as *her equestrian skills*
    equerry—one who cares for horses

    The root _____ means _____.

Lesson D. Roots One More Time

Over thirty roots already and you're still going strong, right? This time, complete the
matching portion of each question by writing the number of the definition in the blank opposite
the appropriate word; then write the root and its meaning on the lines provided.

1. _____ a. tricycle   (1) storm revolving around a center

     _____ b. Cyclops   (2) three-wheeled vehicle with pedals

     _____ c. cyclone   (3) mythical giant with one large, circular eye

     The root _____ means _____ .

2. _____ a. false   (1) erroneous idea

     _____ b. fallacy   (2) untrue; not correct

     _____ c. infallible   (3) without error; certain or sure

     The roots _____ and _____

     mean _____ .

3. _____ a. grave (adj.)   (1) to worsen; to intensify

     _____ b. gravity   (2) serious, weighty, somber, important

     _____ c. aggravate   (3) seriousness; great weight, as "the earth's gravity"

     The root _____ means _____ .

4. _____ a. amity   (1) filled with love

     _____ b. amicable   (2) strong friendship or accord

     _____ c. enamored   (3) friendly, peaceable, congenial

     The roots _____ and _____

     mean _____ and _____ .

5. _____ a. negative   (1) self-denial, renunciation; denial

     _____ b. neglect (v.)   (2) characterized by denial or prohibition

     _____ c. abnegation   (3) to ignore, pay no attention to

     The root _____ means _____ .

6. _____ a. novel (adj.)   (1) beginner, novice

     _____ b. innovate   (2) to attempt something new

     _____ c. neophyte   (3) element in air, used in electric lamps

     _____ d. neon   (4) original, fresh, new

     The roots _____ and _____

     mean _____ .

7. _____ a. vacuum (n.)   (1) space totally empty of matter

     _____ b. evacuate   (2) empty or dully foolish

     _____ c. vacuous   (3) to remove or empty the contents of

     The root _____ means _____ .

8. ____ a. equate   (1) lack of equality

    ____ b. inequality   (2) unclear as to meaning, almost as if voicing several opinions

    ____ c. equivocal

                    (3) to make equal; to treat as the same

The root _____ means _____ .

9. ____ a. fragile   (1) portion or piece of the whole

    ____ b. fracture (v.)   (2) delicate, easily broken

    ____ c. refractory   (3) stubborn, difficult to manage

    ____ d. fragment (n.)   (4) to break, destroy, or shatter

The roots _____ and _____

mean _____ .

10. ____ a. minus   (1) insignificant, of minor import

    ____ b. minuscule   (2) less, without, subtracted from

    ____ c. minimal   (3) tiny, almost immeasurable

    ____ d. minimize   (4) to reduce in importance; to diminish

The roots _____ and _____

mean _____ .

Using the Words

Yes, you know the roots. But do you remember those words given as examples? You will want to know all of the words in this unit, so here is a quick self-test.

Exercise I. Fill-ins. Select the most appropriate word from the choices offered, based on clues in context. The word form or capitalization may need changing. Each word is used only once. Key words in each sentence that point you toward the answer are shown in italics.

hydroponics	dormant	matron	novice
collaborate	temporal	pedant	biopsy
dissension	amorous	podium	trivial
corpulent	fraction	audience	

1. *Once* a *scrawny* kitten, Marigold *has become* lazy and _____ because she interrupts her naps only to *eat*.

2. The _____, *plaintive howls* of neighboring *tomcats* have often disturbed our sleep since the *lovely Marigold* joined our family.

3. This cat has been the subject of much _____ in our household—*some* of us *arguing in favor* of her charms, the *others decrying* her faults.

4. When Marigold was under anesthetic, the veterinarian did a routine _____ on the *growth* he *removed from her neck*.

5. Contrasting her once youthful figure with her current shape, Mom said, "Darn it. I never planned on looking like a _____."

6. The popular game _____ Pursuit poses many questions about basic, useful knowledge—not solely items *of minor importance,* as its name suggests.

7. The visible *tip* of an iceberg is *but a(n)* _____ of the *vaster bulk* that lies hidden underwater.

8. The practice of *growing* plants *in liquid* nutrient as opposed to cultivation in soil is called _____.

9. The _____ bulbs that *rest underground most of the year* emerge when the season is right, and we are ready to appreciate them all over again.

10. "Can everyone in the _____ *hear* me?" asked the *speaker.*

11. We raised enough money to donate an oak _____ for our orchestra director, who needs the extra height this *platform* gives her.

12. My friend Brian is a(n) _____ at directing, *but* with the band director's help he's *becoming more professional* every day.

13. *Brian and* the band *director* have _____ on a new arrangement of the school's fight song to play for the opening game of the season. (Use sentence logic as another key.)

14. Ministers of all faiths often urge their congregations to concentrate on spiritual matters rather than the _____ ones of our current *time.*

15. A(n) _____ who *prided himself on his knowledge* of cats would delight in telling you that a group of cats is a "clowder" and a litter of kittens a "kindle."

Exercise II. Antonyms. Find an antonym or contrasting expression in the right column for each word in the left column. As a help, remember to identify the root in each word you are considering.

_____ 1. **urbane**   (a) patriarchal

_____ 2. **negligence**   (b) impolite

_____ 3. **civil**   (c) unsophisticated

_____ 4. **vacuous**   (d) attentive care

_____ 5. **minuscule**   (e) correct

_____ 6. **fallacious**   (f) huge or vast

_____ 7. **omniscient**   (g) ignorant

_____ 8. **cosmic**   (h) regular, dependable

_____ 9. **matriarchal**   (i) bright, intelligent

_____ 10. **erratic**   (j) narrow in scope

Exercise III. Fill-ins. Select the most appropriate word from the choices offered. Each word is used once. Key words are shown in italics. And again, pay attention to those roots.

agrarian	dictatorial	equivocal	envision
patrimony	deflect	anachronism	grave
precognition	psychology	geological	cyclic
polychrome	equestrian	inscription	protozoans
egotistical			

1. something *out of place in time*, a(n) _____ like the hourglass or a steam locomotive

2. thorough _____ *surveys* of the *oil fields*

3. her hard-won _____ skills at *show jumping*

4. a(n) _____ *tone of voice, not appreciated* even in business boardrooms

5. wasted the vast _____ left to him by his *father*

6. beyond her ability to _____ *life in the next century* (Also, use sentence logic.)

7. lectured on *weighty* matters in a(n) _____ tone

8. brightly *colored* pottery known as _____ ware

9. wise _____ policies to preserve *farmlands*

10. combining studies of *physiology with* _____ to ensure a *total picture*

11. *psychic* whose skill at _____ is controversial

12. a(n) _____ answer that *dodged the issue,* as if she were refusing to *voice* her actual opinion

13. the *regular,* _____ *pattern* of the seasons

14. a humorous, memorable _____ on the *tombstone*

15. study of the earth's *early life forms,* the _____

16. using a garbage can lid to _____ the *snowballs*

17. the _____ answer: "*I* always know what's right for *me!*"

Figure It Out
REVIEWING NUMBER ROOTS

Life would be infinitely happier if we could only be born at the age of eighty and gradually approach eighteen.
        —Mark Twain

The significant words in Twain's comment are numbers. With each of those numbered ages come vivid mental pictures. Obviously, numbers are used for more than math problems.

Lesson E. *Demi* to *Dec*

1. A *demitasse* cup is half the size of a normal one. A *semicolon* is half a colon, with the bottom half a comma to indicate that the sentence continues. The Northern *Hemisphere* refers to the northern half of the world. Something *medium* is halfway, or in the middle.

    DEMI, SEMI, HEMI, and MED/MEDI mean _____ .

2. A one-wheeled cycle is a *unicycle*. Speaking in a *monotone* is talking on one pitch. You play *solitaire* alone—in *solitude,* perhaps.

    UNI, MONO, and SOL mean _____ .

3. A *sesquicentennial* is a 150th anniversary, or one centennial plus half of another. Anyone who has a *sesquipedalian* vocabulary uses words a foot and a half long!

    SESQUI means _____ .

4. "Two roads *diverged* in a wood," wrote Robert Frost. A *biplane* has two sets of wings. *Duplicity* is false double-dealing. It takes two people for a *duo* or a performing *duet*. A *diploma* was originally folded over double.

    DI, BI, DU/DUO, and DIPLO mean _____ .

5. Any school on the *trimester* system has three divisions to its school year. A *tertiary* treatment is the third stage of treatment.

    TRI and TER mean _____ .

6. We who walk on two legs are bipeds; *quadrupeds* walk on four. A *tetrarchy* is a government run by four equally powerful heads, each one referred to as a *tetrarch*.

    QUADR and TETR mean _____ .

7. The *pentathlete* must compete in five different events. A *quintuplet* is one of five children born in a single birth. A period of five years is a *quinquennium*.

    PENTA, QUINT, and QUINQUE mean _____ .

8. A *sextet* has six members, just as a *hexagon* has six sides.

    SEX and HEX mean _____ .

9. *September* was originally the seventh month of the year in the Roman calendar. Any line of verse with seven metrical feet is called *heptameter*.

    SEPT and HEPT mean _____ .

10. In the original Roman calendar the eighth month was *October*. An *octave* is one scale of eight notes. Eight muscular arms characterize the *octopus*.

     OCT/OCTA/OCTO means _____ .

11. A figure with nine sides and nine angles is a *nonagon*. *November,* formerly the ninth month, and *novena,* a nine days' devotion in the Catholic church, share the same root. Any group of nine is an *ennead*.

     NON, NOVEM, and ENNEA mean _____ .

12. *December* used to be the tenth month of the year. Ten track and field events made up the *decathlon*.

     DEC means _____ .

Lesson F. *Duodec* to *Omni/Pan/Panto*

The following list of roots that give number, amount, or quantity are less well known, so it's time to pay attention. You'll be familiar with most of them, and writing your answers on the lines will help to fix even the strangers in your mind.

1. The roots DUODEC and DODEC have added the prefixes _____ and

   _____ to the root DEC, which means _____ . Since

   10 + 2 = 12, DUODEC and DODEC mean _____ .

   A *dodecahedron* is a solid with _____ faces.

2. All of the teenage years are expressed as one number plus the suffix -TEEN, e.g., *sixteen, seventeen*.

   Ten and is written _____ .

3. *Twenty, thirty, forty,* and so on are numbers that include the suffix -TY, meaning *times ten*.

   Times ten is written _____ .

4. A *centennial* is a one-hundred-year celebration. Someone who is a hundred years old or older is a *centenarian*. One hundred meters is a *hectometer*. Today, *hecatomb* means a great slaughter; in ancient Greece it was the sacrifice of 100 oxen.

   CENT, HECTO, and HECATO mean _____ .

5. *Million, millimeter,* and *milligram* share the root that means thousand. The Greek form KILO is found in *kilowatt, kilogram,* and *kiloliter*.

   MILLI and KILO mean _____ .

6. The root MYRIA means 10,000—or rather, it used to. Today, a *myriad* of items is a large but not specific number of things.

   MYRIA means _____ or _____ .

7. *Megaphone* and *megalomaniac* share the root meaning million. It also means great or large, so that earning *megabucks* doesn't necessarily mean earning a million dollars. A *megacycle* is a million cycles in a measured sequence, not a giant motorbike.

   MEG/MEGA means _____ or _____ .

8. *Archaeology* often reveals facts about the lives of *primitive* people, some of whom are said to have dwelt in the forest *primeval*. *Principal*, first-in-line in school administration, and *prototype*, the first of its kind, have the same prefix meaning.

    ARCH, PRIM, PRIN, and PROTO mean _____.

9. An *ambidextrous* person uses both hands with equal skill. A good *amphitheater* offers fine acoustics for both sides of its audience, or all around the circular shape.

    AMBI and AMPHI mean _____.

10. Countries have rarely been ruled by an *oligarchy*—a group of a few people. The Latin form of this root appears in *paucity*, meaning few or scanty in number.

    OLIGO and PAUCI mean _____.

11. We'd all like a *multitude* of friends, a *myriad* of pleasures, and the joy of being a *polymath*, someone with wide and varied knowledge.

    MULTI, MYRIA, and POLY mean _____.

12. *Omnivorous* readers read everything they can find. A *pandemic* illness may occur throughout an entire population, in all areas. A mime show that is all mime, no talking, is called *pantomime*.

    OMNI and PAN/PANTO mean _____.

Figure It Out

Exercise I. Matching. Select the correct definition for each of the numbered words or phrases. Again, you must use the example words to fix them in mind. As you work the following exercises, be sure to identify each word root.

_____ 1. omnipresent

_____ 2. -ty

_____ 3. digraph

_____ 4. hecatomb

_____ 5. archetype

_____ 6. fourteen

_____ 7. quincentenary

_____ 8. hemiplegia

_____ 9. sesquipedalian orator

_____ 10. monolith

_____ 11. Heptateuch

_____ 12. paucity

(a) speaker using lengthy words

(b) one great stone, or a single impressive structure

(c) 500th anniversary

(d) first seven books of the Bible

(e) times ten

(f) scanty quantity

(g) in all places all the time

(h) a great slaughter

(i) model or prototype

(j) four plus ten

(k) two letters pronounced as one sound, e.g., *ch*orus, br*ea*d

(l) paralysis of one side of the body

Exercise II. Fill-ins. In this admittedly crazy story, please insert the appropriate words based on clues in context. (Hint: *Read the entire story first,* than go back and fill in the missing words.)

ennead	decennial	megalomaniac	dodecahedron
sextet	ambivalent	principal	millipedes
triad	omnivorous	pandemonium	one
octet	solitude	myriad	multitudinous

Once there lived a fellow with a passion for grandiose things—a true

_____ who collected _____ strange and usually worthless
  1   2

objects. This man's international residences—a _____ of homes in Hawaii,
                                                      3

Tibet, and Peoria, Illinois—were stuffed with his possessions. In Hawaii he kept half a dozen

peacocks, which _____ he flamboyantly termed an ostentation of peacocks.
                       4

There also he drilled his insect army of _____, those said to have a thousand
                                                5

legs. For entertainment he listened to a simian _____ made up of four
                                                        6

gorillas on drums and four chimps on clarinet. Of course, the peacocks chased the insect army

and the monkeys bedeviled the peacocks, so that the resulting _____ drove
                                                                      7

him to his mountainous retreat in Tibet.

He felt somewhat _____ about Tibet. At times he adored the peaceful
                        8

_____ of the area; at other times he loathed being alone. Still, there were his
  9

treasures to supervise, and as he was a(n) _____ collector, the Tibetan
                                                  10

residence was also crowded. A gaggle of geese honked underneath the feet of his nine llamas,

a(n) _____ that needed daily brushing to be presentable. His
         11

_____ objets d'art had to be polished, washed, and arranged on their
  12

shelves. When he wearied of the labor and the loneliness, he hied himself to Peoria, his

birthplace and _____ home.
                     13

His dwelling in Peoria was a multisided mansion, a(n) _____ designed to
                                                              14

show off his twelve major collections. In the year of his _____, after he had
                                                                  15

remained in Peoria for ten solid years, his fellow Peorians gave him a _____-
                                                                              16

way ticket back to Tibet.

Exercise III. Logic. Answer the questions and complete the statements by decoding the italicized words.

1. How old is an *octogenarian?* _____

2. Given the nature of human beings, why have there been so few *oligarchies* in the history of

   world governments? _____

   _____

   _____

3. A *pentavalent* element would have a valence of _____ .

4. The extensor muscle of the front thigh, called the *quadriceps,* is divided into

   _____ parts.

5. What is the problem with an *ambiguous* answer? _____

   _____

6. The root TER or TERR means land. How do you suppose the *Mediterranean* Sea got its

   name? _____

   _____

7. The slur "She's so _____!" could be applied to a woman guilty of

   duplicity.

8. Virgil's *Aeneid* was written in dactylic *hexameter,* so we know that there are

   _____ metrical feet to each line.

9. A *millennium* is a period of _____ years.

10. A series of _____ folding panels, often with artistic decoration, is called

    a *triptych.* The support for a movie camera is termed a _____ .

In the Beginning...
REVIEWING SOME ESSENTIAL PREFIXES

As you know, a prefix is a small group of letters tacked on to the beginning of a word. Prefixes are chock-full of information that can be extremely helpful when you're decoding a mystery word.

For example, the word *prefix* breaks down to PRE + FIX. You know what *fix* means, and the idea in *pre* is *going before* or *ahead*. So, a prefix must be something fixed on or attached before (in front of) something else.

The following two groups of prefixes are ones you will quickly recognize because you use them all the time.

Lesson G. Prefixes

1. RE-, RETRO-, and POST- give us the ideas of *back* (in place or time), or *after,* just as the *postscript* (P.S.) in a letter comes after the body of the letter.

    a. To *review* means _____ .

    b. To *replace* means _____ .

    c. A *retro-rocket* fires in which direction compared to the aircraft? _____

    d. Considering past events is looking at them _____*spectively*.

    e. To *postpone* a meeting is to _____ .

    f. A *postbellum* Southern mansion was built _____ the Civil War.

2. The prefixes ANTI- and ANT-, MIS- and MAL-, UN- and NON-, and CONTRA- and COUNTER- convey the ideas of *not, against,* or *bad(ly).* Using this information, define the following:

    a. unsocial or antisocial _____

    b. antiaircraft _____

    c. antithesis _____

    d. misfortune _____

    e. nonsense _____

    f. uneasy _____

    g. counteract _____

    h. malfunction _____

    i. nonallergenic _____

    j. contradict _____

3. Well-known opposites are MICRO- meaning *small, miniature,* or *tiny* and MAGNA- meaning *great* or *large.*

    a. Something of considerable *magnitude* is _____ .

b. A *magnifying* glass _____ .

c. A *microscope* allows us to examine objects that are _____

_____ .

d. *Microbes* are _____ organisms or germs.

4. The prefix PRO- means *before, for* (in favor of), or *forward*.

a. *Progress* is movement in a _____ direction.

b. If you *promote* an idea, you are _____ .

c. Anyone *pro-liberal* is _____ .

5. A familiar Greek prefix is AUTO- meaning *self*.

a. An _____*didact* is someone who has taught himself or herself.

b. The prefix _____ is a synonym for car, which is self-propelled.

c. Any business operating independent of outside control is an
_____*nomous* concern.

Lesson H. Yes, More Prefixes

I know prefixes aren't exciting, but they are useful. Often they'll give you the clue to a strange word's meaning. Write the completing words on the lines provided.

1. The prefix CIRCUM- meaning *around* is found in

a. *circumference* meaning _____

b. *circumnavigate* meaning _____

c. *circumvent* meaning _____

2. INTRO- or INTRA- means *inside* or *within*. Using this knowledge, assemble the word parts into known words.

a. Intro + spective = _____ (looking within oneself).

b. Intra + mural = _____ (activity within a community, such as between classes in a school).

c. Intra + molecular = _____ (within the molecule).

d. Intro + vert = _____ (self-contained, as opposed to being outgoing or extroverted).

3. PRE- and FORE- mean *before* or *ahead* (in time or place).

a. *Forewarned* means _____ .

b. A scene in the *foreground* is _____ .

c. *Foregoing* means _____ .

d. To *predict* an event is to _____ .

e. An idea that takes *precedence* over another does what? _____

_____ .

4. The prefixes EXTRA-, EXTRO-, and EXTER- mean *outside* or *beyond*.

a. Something *extraordinary* is _____ .

b. An _____ problem is the opposite of an internal problem.

c. An *introvert* is the opposite of an _____.

d. *Extrasensory* perception (ESP) refers to _____

_____.

5. The meaning of INTER- is *among* or *between*.

a. The *interregnum* period in a monarchy is the period _____ the reigns of two monarchs.

b. *International* dialogue is talk _____ nations.

c. An *interlude* may be a lull _____ one activity and the next.

6. The prefixes OVER-, HYPER-, SUPER-, SUPRA-, and SUR- give us the ideas of *over, above, excessive,* or *extra.*

a. Over + cooked = _____ (cooked too much).

b. Over + lord = _____ (a ruler over others).

c. Hyper + active = _____ (excessively active).

d. Hyper + bole = _____ (greatly exaggerated speech or writing).

e. Super + impose = _____ (to place one thing on top of or above another).

f. Supra + national = _____ (beyond or outside the boundaries of national interest).

g. Sur + mount = _____ (to overcome).

7. ULTR- and OUTR- mean *beyond, as an* ultramodern *shopping center is beyond what we expected, appearing to be the most modern center possible.*

a. An *outrage* is _____.

b. *Ultrapure* water is _____.

c. If her clothing is *outré*, it is _____.

Using Prefixes

Exercise I. Antonyms. Find an antonym or opposing phrase for each word or phrase in the left column.

____ 1. **toxic**   (a) prospect

____ 2. **progress**   (b) normal

____ 3. **contradict**   (c) preliminary study

____ 4. **retrospect**   (d) outré

____ 5. **postgraduate work**   (e) antagonist

____ 6. **protagonist**   (f) dependent on others

____ 7. **usual, customary**   (g) agree with

____ 8. **supernatural**   (h) regress

_____ 9. **autonomous** (i) antitoxic

_____ 10. **ultraism** (j) conservatism

Exercise II. Chart Completion. Enter the missing items in the chart. The first one serves as an example.

	PREFIX	+	ROOT	=	WORD	DEFINITION
1.	pro	+	long	=	prolong	to lengthen in time
2.	mis	+	begotten	=	_____	illegitimate; deserving contempt
3.	_____	+	vene	=	contravene	_____
4.	_____	+	reader	=	_____	one who does not or cannot read
5.	intra	+	_____	=	_____	within one galaxy
6.	_____	+	_____	=	microcosm	_____
7.	magni	+	loquent	=	_____	_____
8.	_____	+	adroit	=	_____	awkward, clumsy
9.	_____	+	_____	=	circumscribe	_____
10.	hyper	+	_____	=	_____	exaggerated speech or writing

Exercise III. Fill-ins. Select the most appropriate word from the choices offered based on clues in context.

extrajudicial	misnomer	recurrent	foregone
counteract	unassuming	postmortem	profusely
malevolent	superhuman		

1. Malaria has been called the disease that never gives up; it is a _____ problem for the victim, who must cope with successive bouts of illness.

2. The _____ examination performed on the body of an ancient Chinese woman was surely one of the more unusual scientific inquiries into the past.

3. Carrie's allergy medication made her sleepy, but she drank enough strong coffee while studying for exams for the caffeine to _____ the medicine and she wasn't groggy.

4. The wicked fairy Maleficent in *Sleeping Beauty* cast several _____ glances at the infant Aurora, so that the film audience knew trouble was brewing.

5. When Rory spilled his chocolate milk shake on Jan's new skirt, he apologized _____, but his repeated, elaborate apologies only made Jan lose her temper.

6. Superman is known for his fantastic, _____ efforts to uphold the law and foil dastardly criminals.

7. The judge kept his _____ opinions on legal cases to himself, rarely revealing his thoughts to family or colleagues.

8. Calling that scrawny, hairless dog Fluffy is the funniest _____ I've heard in ages.

9. The seniors' vote in favor of a day off was a _____ conclusion; everyone knew what the outcome would be before the actual voting.

10. Brian's talents and intelligence could have been intimidating to others, but his quiet, _____ manner earned him many friends.

UNIT II

Vocabulary In and Out of Context

You've Got to Know the Territory

STUDYING CONTEXT AS A KEY TO THE MEANING OF WORDS

Vocabulary . . .

Your vocabulary is more than the words you know—it is your storehouse of ideas. Each word represents an idea or concept. Some are straightforward and simple, like *horse*. You know what a horse is. Other words, such as *democracy,* express fairly involved concepts.

Words open the door to the world of ideas. That's why it is worthwhile to have a large vocabulary. People rich in ideas are the ones who get the most out of life—in personal enjoyment as well as material benefits.

. . . and Context

Context is environment. The context of a word includes the other words in the same sentence as well as the sentences before and after. When the context changes, so may the word's meaning change.

People make changes just as words do—if only we alter their environment or context. For a minute, think about a close friend. Would he or she behave one way at school and another way at a beach party? One way at home and another way on a camping trip?

Context makes an enormous difference—to words and to people. Consider the verb *to fire* in the following sentences, and note how its meaning changes as the context does. Jot down its different meanings in the blanks.

MEANING

1. Roger was *fired* from his job last Friday.

    _____

2. Jan *fired* one shot after another at the basket, scoring 20 points in as many minutes.

    _____

3. We were so *fired up* after the victory that we jumped to our feet to sing the school song.

    _____

4. One match *fired* the kindling, which in turn lit the brush pile.

    _____

5. We hope to keep peace without *firing* a single shot.

    _____

6. "I promise I'll listen," Dad assured Andy. "*Fire away* and I won't interrupt."

    _____

Obviously you can use the context of a word to determine its meaning in the sentence. Often the logic of the sentence will tell you what a strange word means, even if you've never seen the word before.

Example: As they gathered around their fallen leader, the eerie *keening* of the tribe rose above the clearing, penetrating the night with a mournful chorus.

What sort of sound is *keening?* _____

Given the context of the sentence, it can only be a sound of sorrow, and a creepy sound at that. It's described as *eerie* and *a mournful chorus*. Also, it *penetrates* the night, giving us the idea of shrillness and/or loudness. It is definitely not a sad, soft sigh.

Sometimes the context of the sentence actually offers a **definition of the word** you are trying to puzzle out.

Some sentences contain **synonyms or synonymous phrases** that point the way to meaning.

Others may offer an **antonym or contrasting idea,** which tells you that your mystery word means just the opposite of those words you recognize.

This text refers to all of these hints or clues to the meaning of words in context as **KEY WORDS.** Practice in locating key words will make you good at it. You will learn to depend on context to reveal the meaning of a mystery word.

Key Words in Context

Using Logic or Common Sense

Remember to use the entire meaning of each sentence to point toward the probable meaning of the word in italics. Occasionally you may see a nearly synonymous word that will help. *Read for the overall tone of the sentence*. If stumped, substitute a word you know for the italicized word. Does the sentence make good sense with your word? If so, you're in the right neighborhood!

Now, take a thoughtful look at these sentences before you fill in each of the blanks.

1. The *dank* odor of the swamp filled his nostrils, reminding him how he hated anything damp or moldy.

   Key words _____

   Dank probably means _____ .

2. All around her rose the *puling* sounds of starving infants, children without hope who cried as if they knew.

   Key words _____

   Puling probably means _____ .

3. His appearance told the story: ill-fitting clothes hung on his slender body. *Lank,* dark hair framed a face as devoid of liveliness as the rest of him.

   Key words _____

   Lank probably means _____ .

4. The River Itchen in southwest England is famous for its clear waters *teeming* with trout.

   Key words _____

   Teeming probably means _____ .

5. The *rift* between Jan and Ed is obvious. She will no longer go anywhere that Ed is apt to appear.

   Key words _____

   Rift probably means _____ .

6. "Just pay and be done with it," Mom advised us. "This isn't a marketplace where you can *haggle* over price."

   Key words _____

   Haggle probably means _____ .

7. "He's got a lot of *chutzpah* asking me to work more hours," Carrie exclaimed indignantly, "when I've already worked more than anyone else!"

   Key words _____

   Chutzpah probably means _____ .

8. Sheepishly, Sara put her dime in the collection plate and hoped that no one would notice what she felt was a *paltry* offering.

   Key words _____

   Paltry probably means _____ .

9. Old Merlin was a gray yet impressive figure, his *hoary* beard mingling almost indistinguishably with the silver cloak draped over his stooped shoulders.

   Key words _____

   Hoary probably means _____ .

10. Tim's summer job was so *lucrative* that he saved enough to pay for all books and allowance money his first year in college.

    Key words _____

    Lucrative probably means _____ .

Double Check: How close were you?

1. dank	*wet, damp*
2. puling	*whining, whimpering*
3. lank	*lean, lifeless*
4. teeming	*abounding*
5. rift	*break, breach*
6. haggle	*to wrangle, argue*
7. chutzpah	*gall, nerve*
8. paltry	*trivial*
9. hoary	*gray with age*
10. lucrative	*monetarily rewarding*

Finding a Definition in Context

This time you are looking for a fairly explicit definition of your mystery word within the sentence itself. Enter your answers before checking those that follow this practice.

1. The *sinuous* road curved narrowly up the mountain, winding in and around like a long black serpent.

   Context definition _____

   Sinuous probably means _____ .

2. Matt hoped fervently that Clyde's insensitive remarks and rude gestures would be lost in the party hubbub, because such *crass* behavior would cost them both.

   Context definition _____

   Crass probably means _____ .

3. Aunt Dolly's *effusive* praise washed over me in a flood, making me wonder why she had to rave on and on about my every achievement.

   Context definition _____

   Effusive probably means _____ .

4. The *piquant* sauce is my favorite—a sauce that will tickle the palate and add zesty flavor to food.

   Context definition _____

   Piquant probably means _____ .

5. "He's only a *stripling*," my older cousin said, trying to get a rise out of me by suggesting that I was barely a teenager, years away from college.

   Context definition _____

   Stripling probably means _____ .

6. When he was younger, Andy thought of Santa Claus as someone *ubiquitous*, a presence that was everywhere at all times.

   Context definition _____

   Ubiquitous probably means _____ .

7. She turned a *vapid* face to us and we gave up, knowing we would learn nothing from a countenance lacking life and intelligence.

   Context definition _____

   Vapid probably means _____ .

8. As only a few small items were stolen, the theft was considered *petty* crime.

   Context definition _____

   Petty probably means _____ .

9. Bess's poem titled *"Reverie"* attempted to describe that dreamlike state of thought and memory into which we all escape at times.

   Context definition _____

   Reverie probably means _____ .

10. A *pestilence* swept through the tiny town, ravaging each household with an infectious disease later named the bubonic plague.

Context definition _____

Pestilence probably means _____ .

Double Check: You should be right on target this time.

1. sinuous	*winding, snakelike*
2. crass	*rude, vulgar, boorish*
3. effusive	*gushing*
4. piquant	*zesty, spicy*
5. stripling	*youth, boy*
6. ubiquitous	*ever-present*
7. vapid	*empty, flat, dull*
8. petty	*minor* (also means *low* or *mean-spirited*)
9. reverie	*dream*
10. pestilence	*plague, disease*

Using the Words

Use the meanings you have learned for the foregoing twenty words to work the following exercises.

Exercise I. Antonyms. Find at least one antonym or contrasting definition for each word on the left.

_____ 1. **crass**	(a) major, important
_____ 2. **paltry**	(b) refined, sensitive, polite
_____ 3. **chutzpah**	(c) straight (not winding)
_____ 4. **piquant**	(d) restrained
_____ 5. **hoary**	(e) full of body, springy
_____ 6. **ubiquitous**	(f) timidity, lack of nerve
_____ 7. **lank**	(g) noticeably bright or interesting
_____ 8. **sinuous**	(h) youthful
_____ 9. **effusive**	(i) lacking zest or flavor
_____ 10. **vapid**	(j) absent

Exercise II. Logic. Here are some of the first twenty study words as they are apt to appear in writing. With logic, common sense, and imagination as your aids, write the answers where indicated. If you're still stumped, ask a friend, parent, or teacher.

1. Reword the phrase *a petty act, unworthy of her.*

_____

2. Why is the phrase *lank hair* not a compliment?

_____

3. A brain *teeming* with ideas is _____ .

4. Besides *stripling*, what other words can you think of that use the suffix *-ling* to indicate *little*? _____

_____

5. At certain times, could you describe five children—all underfoot and under 5—as a pestilence? _____

Exercise III. Fill-ins. From the choices offered, select the most appropriate word for each sentence. The word form may need changing.

dank	haggle	sinuous	ubiquitous
puling	chutzpah	crass	vapid
lank	paltry	effusive	pestilence
teeming	hoary	piquant	reverie
rift	lucrative	stripling	petty

1. Overjoyed at his promotion, Alan informed his parents that his new position was _____ enough for him to afford his own apartment now.

2. Long ago, serfs were accustomed to little and could quickly pack up their _____ belongings for a move.

3. The director told his actors, "It's no use _____ over minor changes, especially when you know that I'm going to win the arguments."

4. Hoping to mend the _____ in their relationship, Ed sent Jan a dozen red carnations.

5. *Give me your tired, your poor,*
Your huddled masses yearning to breathe free,

    The wretched refuse of your _____ *shore.*
Send these, the homeless, tempest-tost to me,
I lift my lamp beside the golden door!
        —Emma Lazarus, "The New Colossus," poem on pedestal of the Statue of Liberty

6. The anxious, _____ sounds of hungry animals resounded through the kennels each day at feeding times.

7. A remembered phrase from Edgar Allan Poe's creative gloominess describes a "deep, _____ tarn," which helps readers to picture a scummy old pond or swampy area.

8. *Incens'd with indignation Satan stood*
Unterrifi'd, and like a comet . . .
. . . and from his horrid hair

    Shakes _____ *and war.*
        —Milton, *Paradise Lost*, Bk. ii

9. Peppermint Patty is often lost in _____, but Marcie sits behind her in school and politely (or otherwise) wakes her up from time to time.

10. Mom reminded my sister Carrie that tattling was a(n) _____, mean-spirited action calculated to make the rest of us despise her.

11. Huck Finn's father loathed "the guvmint," believing it to be _____– ever present and inescapable.

12. In *A Day No Pigs Would Die,* Rob is only a _____ when his father dies and Rob becomes the man of the family.

13. Marigold rejected the advances of a scruffy tomcat whom she considered a(n) _____, loutish fellow, and mated instead with a refined Siamese from across the street.

14. The _____ movements of the hula dancers kept my dad's attention throughout their performance.

15. The calculus teacher was distressed to see all of us gazing _____ at the blackboard after he'd explained the new problem set.

Help! Hollered the Puzzled Reader

FINDING SYNONYMS OR ANTONYMS IN CONTEXT AS KEYS TO THE MEANING OF WORDS

Using Synonyms in Context

Now try finding synonyms or synonymous phrases within the context of each sentence. The meaning of the italicized word will be close to the key words that you identify.

1. Our family always wonders what *bizarre* apparel Aunt Dolly will appear in next, because the oddities of her clothing make guests feel uneasy.

    Key words _____

    Bizarre probably means _____ .

2. Roger behaved as though he were completely stupid on stage—an utter *dolt* without a memory.

    Key words _____

    Dolt probably means _____ .

3. Parts of London were *razed* by wartime bombing, yet the destruction was overcome by a city eager to rebuild.

    Key words _____

    To raze probably means _____ .

4. Knowing that Marigold had *filched* two of our tropical fish from the aquarium, we were on guard to see that our marauding feline stole no more midnight snacks.

    Key words _____

    To filch probably means _____ .

5. "You've drawn a *dour* face on Macbeth," the art teacher commented. "Was he all that gloomy and harsh, or was he more tortured in his soul?"

    Key words _____

    Dour probably means _____ .

6. Aunt Dolly's new hat is a *pert* navy pillbox that gives her a jaunty, saucy look instead of the outlandish appearance she usually affects.

    Key words _____

    Pert probably means _____ .

7. Marigold's good behavior on Saturday was only a *ruse*. No one was fooled by her deception, especially on Sunday when she resumed aquarium fishing.

Key words _____

Ruse probably means _____ .

8. Marigold's kitten, Poucette, is herself a fishing *tyro* who, as a beginner, has yet to make her first catch.

Key words _____

Tyro probably means _____ .

9. The *chagrin* on Andy's face was obvious, although he tried to cover his embarrassment by whistling nonchalantly.

Key words _____

Chagrin probably means _____ .

10. College students *scrutinize* each semester's list of course offerings, examining each selection carefully before making their new schedules.

Key words _____

Scrutinize probably means _____ .

Double Check: Did you find those synonyms?

1.	bizarre	*outlandish, odd*
2.	dolt	*clod, dumb person*
3.	raze	*to tear down, destroy*
4.	filch	*to steal something minor or small*
5.	dour	*gloomy, harsh*
6.	pert	*saucy, perky*
7.	ruse	*deception, stratagem*
8.	tyro	*novice, beginner*
9.	chagrin	*embarrassment*
10.	scrutinize	*to examine*

Using Antonyms or Opposing Ideas in Context

Time to find those antonyms. Remember that an antonym is an opposite. It shows contrast. Watch for the contrast set up in each sentence. (Usually there is only one antonym or opposing phrase. Otherwise, English would be filled with bulky sentences.)

1. "Why do we always haggle over curfews?" Dad asked. "Can't you two just *acquiesce* for once?"

Opposing word(s) _____

Acquiesce probably means _____ .

2. Classes on drug abuse emphasize not only the danger from a pure drug but also the deadly potential of an *adulterated* one.

Opposing word(s) _____

Adulterated probably means _____ .

3. The trouble with my younger brother Andy in a family picture-taking session is the broad *smirk* he adopts instead of his normal smile.

Opposing word(s) _____

Smirk probably means _____ .

(**Note:** *Instead* indicates an opposing idea.)

4. Because Joe couldn't make a firm decision, he *vacillated* between agreeing with our plan and rejecting it.

   Opposing word(s) _____

   To vacillate probably means _____ .

5. If pessimism and a dour outlook are bad for our health, let's concentrate on the *salutary* benefits of humor and an optimistic attitude.

   Opposing word(s) _____

   Salutary probably means _____ .

6. "Is Dad going to continue being stubborn about our curfew," my sister Jan asked, "or will he *capitulate?*"

   Opposing word(s) _____

   Capitulate probably means _____ .

   (**Note:** *Or* indicates an opposing idea.)

7. Terry's tendency to *dissemble* rather than reveal his true personality confuses nearly everyone he meets.

   Opposing word(s) _____

   Dissemble probably means _____ .

   (**Note:** *Rather than* indicates an opposing idea.)

8. The coach said, "Regular workouts and tough practices will make this team tops. *Indolence* never won a medal."

   Opposing word(s) _____

   Indolence probably means _____ .

9. The legendary Brave Little Tailor knew he should tell the truth about killing "seven at one blow"; nevertheless, he *prevaricated*.

   Opposing word(s) _____

   Prevaricated probably means _____ .

   (**Note:** *Nevertheless* indicates an opposing idea.)

10. "Those vapid, mournful looks won't do," cried our play director. "It's a look of *rapture* we need, not clinical depression!"

    Opposing word(s) _____

    Rapture probably means _____ .

    Double Check: How close were you?
    1. acquiesce   *to agree, say yes*
    2. adulterate   *to add impurities*

3. smirk	*sickeningly sweet grin*
4. vacillate	*to waver*
5. salutary	*promoting health*
6. capitulate	*to yield, give in to*
7. dissemble	*to pretend*
8. indolence	*laziness*
9. prevaricate	*to lie, tell an untruth*
10. rapture	*extreme joy*

Using the Words

Exercise I. Fill-ins. Select the best word from the choices given, based on clues in context.

pert	filching	smirk	vacillating
rapture	bizarre	capitulation	tyro
razed	scrutiny		

1. entire block that needed to be _____

2. the FDA's _____ of each new drug prior to approval

3. easy _____, rather than lengthy debate

4. her _____, sassy retort that irritated Mom

5. obviously a professional, not a _____

6. an unpleasant _____ of smug self-satisfaction

7. a feeling of _____ as he heard his own symphony performed for the first time

8. _____ a couple quarters, and pretending that it wasn't important

9. a _____ account that sounded highly unlikely

10. made a choice and stopped _____ at last

Exercise II. Thinking About the Words. Use common sense and logical reasoning to help in answering the following questions. If your knowledge is thin in spots, consult a dictionary.

1. Will the second-ranked senior give a *salutary* or *salutatory* address at graduation? _____

2. How would you rank the following adjectives in order of degree, beginning with contentment as the lowest degree? contentment, rapture, delight, happiness, exultation

3. *Dissemble, semblance,* and *resemble* make up a word family. In the phrase "only a semblance of her former self," what does *semblance* most probably mean? _____

4. One good synonym for indolence is *sloth*. Why is that an appropriate name for the animal who bears it? _____

5. How many synonyms can you find for *ruse*? _____

_____

6. In sentence 4 of "Using Synonyms in Context," what does the word *marauding* have to

mean? _____

Exercise III. Antonyms. Suggest an antonym or contrasting phrase for the following words.

1. bizarre _____

2. dolt _____

3. capitulate _____

4. sloth _____

5. salubrious _____

6. vacillate _____

7. raze _____

8. prevaricate _____

9. dissembler _____

10. dour _____

11. adulterant _____

12. pert _____

13. acquiescence _____

14. rapture _____

15. scrutinize _____

Review List of Words Taught in Unit II

Unit II presented forty words, with only six exercises as practice. Its purpose was to offer practice in deducing meaning from context, *not* mastery of vocabulary. According to learning specialists, you must see a word or work with it six or seven times in order to fix it in your mind for sure. That is why the vocabulary mastery portion of your book will stress repeated usage of the words being taught.

But before we leave this unit, please write a synonym or brief definition beside the words we've covered. If you miss one, flip back to find its meaning and write it on the correct line. *The act of writing is a powerful memory tool.*

1. dank _____   8. paltry _____

2. puling _____   9. hoary _____

3. lank _____   10. lucrative _____

4. teeming _____   11. sinuous _____

5. rift _____   12. crass _____

6. haggle _____   13. effusive _____

7. chutzpah _____   14. piquant _____

15. stripling _____

16. ubiquitous _____

17. vapid _____

18. petty _____

19. reverie _____

20. pestilence _____

21. bizarre _____

22. dolt _____

23. raze _____

24. filch _____

25. dour _____

26. pert _____

27. ruse _____

28. tyro _____

29. chagrin _____

30. scrutinize _____

31. acquiesce _____

32. adulterate _____

33. smirk _____

34. vacillate _____

35. salutary _____

36. capitulate _____

37. dissemble _____

38. indolence _____

39. prevaricate _____

40. rapture _____

UNIT III

The Vocabulary Lists

Look, Jane, Look!
VERBS, THE ACTION WORDS

In Context. Before studying the definitions, try reasoning out the meaning of each word, using context as your guide.

1. Hoping to *atone* for waking Dad up, Andy promised, "I'll be very quiet the next time you take a nap, okay?"

   Key: Logic   **Atone** means _____ .

2. My folks said they planned to spend spring weekends watching their garden seedlings *burgeon* healthily in response to love, weeding, and fertilizer.

   Key: Logic   **Burgeon** means _____ .

3. "You can't *coerce* me into going," Jan teased, "but you could persuade me."

   Key: Opposing word   **Coerce** means _____ .

4. Aware that the enemy was about to *defile* the sacred Ark of the Covenant, Indiana Jones warned his companion not to look for fear of what would follow the Ark's desecration.

   Key: Synonymous idea   **Defile** means _____ .

5. After I hooted at Jan's attempts to drive our old stick-shift Ford, she stormed indoors, shouting, "I'm telling Dad! You've *disparaged* my driving for the last time!"

   Key: Synonymous idea   **Disparage** means _____ .

6. Trailing a catnip mouse behind him, Andy *enticed* Poucette and Figment into the garage for the night.

   Key: Logic   **Entice** means _____ .

7. Marigold *evinced* no interest in the catnip lure and settled herself determinedly on my bed for the night.

   Key: Logic   **Evince** means _____ .

8. "Repent and be saved!" was what the street-corner preacher *exhorted* the crowd to do.

   Key: Logic   **Exhort** means _____ .

9. When we call Marigold, she *feigns* deafness if she doesn't want to come in, but she never pretends to be hard of hearing when the dinner bell rings.

   Key: Synonym   **Feign** means _____ .

10. Jan told Dad, "It would have been okay if Jeff had just *intimated* that I had a little trouble shifting, but he kept announcing it to everyone in the car!"

    Key: Opposing word   **Intimate** means _____ .

11. When Andy started raising gerbils, he *nurtured* them with the care of a practiced, tender parent.

    Keys: Logic, partial definition   **Nurture** means _____ .

12. The fun of reading an Agatha Christie murder mystery, or any modern whodunit, is deducing who *perpetrated* the crime.

    Key: Logic   **Perpetrate** means _____ .

13. My folks observed that it is impossible to *redress* the wrongs of war, because there can't be any compensation to parents for the death of their child.

    Key: Synonymous idea   **Redress** means _____ .

14. Poucette and Figment fight over possession of the catnip mouse, each trying to get the other to *relinquish* it.

    Key: Logic   **Relinquish** means _____ .

15. In Hale's story written to inspire patriotism, Philip Nolan was *stigmatized* as "the man without a country"—a man condemned to live aboard a ship that roamed the seas until he died.

    Key: Logic   **Stigmatize** means _____ .

16. "No use *truckling* to me, thinking I'm so soft in the head I'll give you more allowance," Mom warned Andy. "I can tell when somebody's buttering me up."

    Key: Synonymous phrase   **Truckle** means _____ .

Word Study

With any luck at all, you were able to get a fair idea of what each word in this list means. You plucked each meaning from the context, because the sense of a sentence depends more on the verb than on any other part of speech. The verb is IT, in other words.

A seventh-grader (eager to make points with his teacher as they both surveyed his poorly written essay) said not long ago, "Gee, I wish I had great verbs."

This list contains some "great verbs" to help your writing come alive. Consult the list of abbreviations on the last page of this book for the names of foreign languages from which these verbs are derived.

1. **atone** (ə-ˈtōn) v.   To satisfy or appease by making amends; to make up for a wrong or a deficiency; originally, *at one* in harmony

    No memory of having starred
    Atones *for later disregard,*
    Or keeps the end from being hard.
        —Robert Frost, "Provide, Provide"

    Relative: *atonement*
    Synonym: *expiate*

2. **burgeon** (ˈbər-jən) v.   To grow, often rapidly (said of people, conditions, plants); to exhibit growth such as buds or sprouts; from L. *burra,* shaggy cloth

    Now fades the last long streak of snow
    Now burgeons *every maze of quick*
    About the flowering squares and thick
    By ashen roots the violets blow.
        —Alfred, Lord Tennyson, "In Memoriam"

Synonyms: *flourish, bloom, sprout, blossom* (none exact)
Antonyms: *wither, dwindle, shrink*

3. **coerce** (kō-'ərs) v.   To dominate by force or threats; to bring about by superior strength; from L. *coercere,* to enclose, shut up

Although they didn't like the idea, we *coerced* our cats into staying in the basement while a crew cleaned our downstairs carpeting.

Relatives: *coercion, coercive, coercible, coercively*
Synonym: *force*

4. **defile** (di-fī[ə]l) v.   To make impure or unclean—anything from sanctuaries (with an unholy act or word) to new books (with suggestive notes or drawings); to corrupt, befoul, or debase; from F. *défouler,* to trample

Nor one feeling of vengeance presume to defile,
The cause, or the men, of the Emerald Isle.
      —William Drennan, "Erin"

Relatives: *defiler, defilement*
Synonyms: *contaminate, sully, dishonor, befoul, debase, besmirch, corrupt, deflower*
         (denude of chastity), *violate*
Antonyms: *honor, exalt, respect*

5. **disparage** (dis-'par-ij) v.   To belittle or minimize another's skill or accomplishments; to degrade someone, from F. *despargier,* to marry beneath one's class

"I don't want to *disparage* your achievement, dear," Mom told Carrie, "but I wonder how you can mess up the whole living room just by sewing one costume!"

Relatives: *disparagement, disparager, disparagingly*
Synonyms: *belittle, denigrate, downgrade, depreciate, decry*
Antonyms: *applaud, cheer* (for), *laud*

6. **entice** (in-'tīs) v.   To tempt or lure onward in a clever, artful manner; from L. *in + titio,* firebrand

My son, if sinners entice *thee, consent thou not.*
      —The Bible, Prov. 1:10

Relatives: *enticement, enticingly*
Synonyms: *lure, tempt, allure*
Antonyms: *scare, frighten, alarm*

7. **evince** (i-'vin[t]s) v.   To show or display clearly; from L. *evincere,* to conquer, vanquish

The tour guide warned his group not to *evince* a speck of interest in the beggars who might tag along at major tourist sights in Paris.

Relative: *evincible*
Synonyms: *reveal, display, show*
Antonyms: *conceal, hide*

8. **exhort** (ig-'zò[ə]rt) v.   To rouse and urge onward, as *the leader exhorts his troops to step up the pace;* to warn or advise urgently; from L. *exhortari,* to incite

We bent rhythmically forward and back in the racing shell, determined that our crew would be first, while the onlookers *exhorted* us to "Pull, pull!"

Relatives: *exhortation, exhortative, exhortatory*
Synonyms: *urge, press, spur* (first meaning); *admonish, caution* (second meaning)

9. **feign** ('fān) v.   To pretend or dissemble, as *he feigned illness;* from L. *fingere,* to shape, mold, conceive

Not wanting Dad to know he'd been reading by flashlight under the covers, Andy curled up and *feigned* sleep when Dad peeked into his room.

Relatives: *feigned* (adj., not genuine), *feigner*
Synonyms: *pretend, dissemble, assume*

10. **intimate** ('int-ə-,māt) v.   To suggest indirectly or hint in a delicate, subtle way; from L. *intimus,* innermost

"Sally makes me so angry," Jan said. "Yesterday she hinted that I dyed my hair, and today she *intimated* that it could use a touch-up, but this is my real hair!"

Relatives: *intimater, intimate* (adj., private, personal), *intimate* (n., close personal friend)
Synonyms: *suggest, hint; imply* and *insinuate* (usually negative in connotation)
Antonyms: *proclaim, announce*

11. **nurture** ('nər-chər) v.   To foster growth and development by giving food, education, emotional support, etc.; from L. *nutrire,* to suckle or nourish

Of the American Revolution, Samuel Morison wrote, "Independence was no conscious goal, secretly *nurtured* in cellar or jungle by bearded conspirators, but a reluctant last resort, to preserve 'life, liberty, and the pursuit of happiness.' "

(Note past participial form, used as an adjective.)

Relatives: *nurturer, nurturance, nurture* (n.)
Synonyms: *nourish, foster, feed*
Antonym: *starve* (deprive of nourishment)

12. **perpetrate** ('pər-pə-,trāt) v.   To cause to happen, as *he perpetrated the crime;* to commit; from L. *per + patrare,* to accomplish

Pointing to the empty cookie jar, Mom said, "I'd give a pretty penny to know who *perpetrated* our latest theft."

Relatives: *perpetrator, perpetration*
Synonym: *commit*

13. **redress** (ri-'dres) v.   To right a wrong by offering compensation or by removing the cause for complaint; to avenge or exact reparation; from F. *redrecier,* to make straight

There is no grievance that is a fit object of redress *by mob law.*
    —Abraham Lincoln, address delivered in Illinois, 1838

Relatives: *redress* (n.), *redresser*
Synonyms: *compensate, rectify, correct* (first meaning); *avenge* (second meaning)

14. **relinquish** (ri-'liŋ-kwish) v.   To give up or renounce, usually with regret; to cease holding on, or to yield control of; from L. *relinquere,* to leave behind

Time does not relinquish *its rights, either over human beings or over monuments.*
    —Goethe, *Elective Affinities*

Relative: *relinquishment*
Synonyms: *yield, surrender, abandon, resign, waive*
Antonyms: *keep, retain, maintain*

15. **stigmatize** ('stig-mə-,tīz) v.   To brand or mark, either physically or verbally, in a severely negative way; to disgrace utterly; from Gr. and L. *stigma,* brand or mark of a pointed instrument

Aaron Burr, who undoubtedly had some good qualities, managed to *stigmatize* himself forever as a traitor to his country.

Relatives: *stigma, stigmatic, stigmatism, stigmatization*
Synonyms: *brand, mark, denounce*
Antonyms: *honor, decorate, laud, cite* (for service, bravery, etc.)

Derivation: Romans and Greeks used to brand a slave on the forehead with red-hot irons. Colored matter was then rubbed into the wound, and from then on the slave was called a *stigmatic*.

The plural term *stigmata* often refers to the marks on Christ's body made by the crown of thorns and the nails driven through his feet and hands. Since that time, similar marks have been thought by devout Christian believers to have appeared on the bodies of certain people, notably St. Francis of Assisi. Religious paintings of the Renaissance era often show holy figures marked by stigmata.

The eye dysfunction called *astigmatism* comes from this same root and refers to a defect of the refractive system of the eye, often an irregularity of the cornea.

16. **truckle** ('trək-əl) v.   To behave as a lowly servant in an obsequious, fawning manner; from L. *trochlea,* block of pulleys

Disappointed and bitterly frustrated, Jonathan Swift wrote of the Irish people in 1731: "A servile race in folly nursed, / Who *truckle* most when treated worst."

Relative: *truckler*
Synonyms: *toady, grovel, fawn*

Derivation: A *truckle bed* was a child's trundle bed, customarily trundled out of sight during the day and hidden under the higher bed. The idea of truckling comes from the lowly position of the bed itself.

Root Study

A short list of word roots follows each Word Study section in this unit. It is boring to memorize long lists of roots—and hard to remember them—but tucking four or five into your memory at a time is relatively easy. It is worth doing, too, as knowledge of a root meaning will often help you to puzzle out the meaning of a strange word.

Usually, one or more of the roots is related to a word or words in the study list. When an "oddball" appears, it's because he was too important to leave out, and he had to appear somewhere.

Read the example words for each root slowly and carefully. And say them aloud as well. They will appear as quiz items in some of the exercises. Yes, you need to include these words in your growing vocabulary.

1. EV (AEV) means age or time.
     longevity—long life
     primeval—of the earliest known ages or times
     medieval (or *mediaeval*)—referring to the Middle Ages, also called the Dark Ages, from the late fifth century to the late fifteenth century when the Renaissance began in western Europe, printing was invented, and Columbus discovered America

2. PHIL means love of.
     philosophy—the love of wisdom
     philosopher—lover of wisdom
     philologist—lover of words
     philatelist—collector (and lover) of stamps
     Anglophile—lover of England and things English
     Francophile—lover of France and things French

3. ANTHROP means humankind.
   anthropology—the study of humankind's cultural development
   anthropomorphism—attributing human characteristics to nonhumans
   philanthropist—one who loves and helps human beings
   misanthrope—one who hates people

4. VINC and VICT mean to conquer.
   invincible—unconquerable
   convince—to persuade strongly; to assure, prove, satisfy
   Vincent, Victor, and *Victoria*—conqueror
   victorious—conquering, triumphant

Using the Words

Using the Words is the practice segment of each lesson. By this point in a lesson you will have seen the words of the basic list at least three times. Now, operating on the principle of "Use it or lose it," you need to use those words. Work through each exercise carefully, but don't go gray if you miss a few items. If you're going to miss something, this is the place to do it. This is practice time. And if you make yourself do the practice conscientiously, you can approach the perfection we'd all like to achieve.

List 1 Review

atone	disparage	feign	redress
burgeon	entice	intimate	relinquish
coerce	evince	nurture	stigmatize
defile	exhort	perpetrate	truckle

Exercise I. Definitions. Without looking back at the list you've just studied, try to write the vocabulary words beside their definitions. The first letter of the correct word is given as a hint.

1. to brand or mark in a negative way   s_____

2. to commit   p_____

3. to renounce with regret   r_____

4. to behave in a fawning manner   t_____

5. to nourish, educate, or foster   n_____

6. to show clearly   e_____

7. to suggest or to hint indirectly   i_____

8. to corrupt, befoul, or debase   d_____

9. to pretend or dissemble   f_____

10. to tempt or lure onward   e_____

If you missed one or two, look back at the definitions and enter the missing word(s) in the proper location.

Exercise II. Switcheroo—verbs become nouns. Although the words in List 1 were explained as verbs, most have noun forms as well. Match the noun forms with their correct meanings.

_____ 1. **coercion**   (a) reparation or satisfaction

_____ 2. **enticement**   (b) downgrading

_____ 3. **exhortation**   (c) one who profanes or desecrates

_____ 4. **intimation**   (d) brand of infamy

_____ 5. **atonement**   (e) lure

_____ 6. **perpetrator**   (f) urgent appeal

_____ 7. **disparagement**   (g) force

_____ 8. **redress**   (h) compensation or correction

_____ 9. **stigma**   (i) one who commits a foul deed

_____ 10. **defiler**   (j) hint, suggestion

Exercise III. Analogies. Complete the analogies with the best pair possible, using words from List 1 and Roots. (Note: If you're unfamiliar with how analogies work, see the section entitled "How to Answer Analogy Questions," beginning on page 294.)

The analogies given in Lists 1–24 are offered for practice in logical reasoning and vocabulary mastery. They are meant to help teach the words. Analogy questions on standardized tests have the same format but are often more difficult, as they test your knowledge of trickier implied relationships.

_____ 1. wax : wane ::
    (a) moon : crescent   (c) bud : flower
    (b) burgeon : wither   (d) redress : wrong

_____ 2. nurture : growth ::
    (a) improvise : rehearsal   (c) exhort : action
    (b) entice : lure   (d) defile : reputation

_____ 3. philosopher : wisdom ::
    (a) philologist : logistics   (c) chlorophyll : plants
    (b) books : bibliophile   (d) Anglophile : England

_____ 4. disparage : praise ::
    (a) truckle : command   (c) denigrate : decry
    (b) stigmatize : brand   (d) intimate : entice

_____ 5. evince : interest ::
    (a) truckle : toady   (c) perpetrate : benefit
    (b) redress : wrong   (d) nurture : parent

Exercise IV. Fill-ins. Find the most appropriate word for each phrase from the words in List 1 and Roots. The word form may need changing.

1. seeking _____ for grievous wrong

2. a _____ attitude totally inappropriate to modern life

3. obsequious employees who _____ to the manager

4. Aaron Burr, _____ forever with the name traitor

5. resigned gracefully, thereby _____ his control of the company

6. noted _____, whose love of words showed in his vocabulary

7. an offer so tempting we were _____ into going after all

8. a warship we christened *The* _____ because we hoped it would be unconquerable

9. hate being _____ into doing something I dislike

10. wondering who _____ the theft of his tapes

Exercise V. Antonyms. Select the correct opposites, one for each word on the left. (Note: Not many words have exact antonyms. Choose the best one of the choices offered.)

_____ 1. **stigma**
    (a) accusation   (b) citation   (c) cicatrix
    (d) fixation

_____ 2. **misanthrope**
    (a) arthropod   (b) philosopher
    (c) philanthropist   (d) anthropologist

_____ 3. **primeval**
    (a) futuristic   (b) ancient
    (c) archaeological   (d) postwar

_____ 4. **evince**
    (a) reveal   (b) display   (c) devolve
    (d) conceal

_____ 5. **coerce**
    (a) urge   (b) please   (c) better   (d) cajole

_____ 6. **nurture**
    (a) stunt   (b) nourish   (c) mother   (d) delay

_____ 7. **feign**
    (a) seem wary   (b) appear willing   (c) be
    truthful   (d) feel depressed

_____ 8. **defile**
    (a) benefit   (b) encourage   (c) respect
    (d) arrange

_____ 9. **longevity**
    (a) declivity   (b) brevity   (c) activity
    (d) nativity

_____ 10. **intimate**
    (a) proclaim   (b) personal   (c) apparel
    (d) preclude

Exercise VI. Word Analysis. This set of exercises is the place to exercise your brain cells. Let logic and reason do some mental calisthenics for you. If you're temporarily stumped, holler for help. Also, you can always check a good dictionary.

    But don't give up. "Word Analysis" is meant to expand your consciousness about words.

1. Many acclaimed books and movies feature *anthropomorphic* characters. They have been given the characteristics of humankind. (Remember the scary trees in the forest of the *Snow White* movie?) You know Peter Rabbit, Wilbur the pig, and Ferdinand the bull, who loved to sit under his cork tree smelling the flowers. How many characters, book titles, or movie titles can you list in which *anthropomorphism* is evident?

_____

_____

_____

2. Context profoundly affects word meaning. In the following pairs of sentences, note the different meanings on the appropriate lines.

_____ a. (1) *"The* hardly *fought election had put him in the limelight."*
                —Agatha Christie, *Sparkling Cyanide*

_____ (2) In the last round he *hardly* fought at all.

_____ b. (1) Don't *depress* me with any more bad news.

_____ (2) Remember to *depress* the clutch first.

_____ c. (1) The trail *inclined* steeply and left us breathless.

_____ (2) Is he *inclined* to go hiking each summer?

_____ d. (1) After marriage, the couple will *cleave* together as one.

_____ (2) Don't attempt to *cleave* the diamond until you have examined it thoroughly.

_____ e. (1) You're just *plumb* crazy if you think I will go!

_____ (2) We'll *plumb* the complexities of that book in class discussion.

_____ f. (1) Did he *intimate* that I was acting foolish?

_____ (2) "*'Twas one of my most* intimate *enemies.*"
—D. G. Rossetti, "Fragment"

3. How is the derivation for *atone,* "at one in harmony," consistent with our modern usage of the word?

_____

_____

4. Synonyms for *relinquish* include *yield, surrender, abandon, resign,* and *waive,* yet the **connotation** (the feeling) of each is slightly different. Try to explain the connotative meanings of the different synonyms. For instance, if you *abandon* a ship, how is that different from *relinquishing* it?

_____

_____

_____

_____

_____

5. Explain this sentence. "He *insinuated* himself into our group and made himself at home."

_____

_____

LIST 2

Excuse My Onomatopoeia

TERMS FROM THE ARTS

In Context. Before studying the definitions, try reasoning out the meaning of each word, using context as your guide.

1. After reading *Animal Farm*, everyone in our class wrote a paper about that *allegory*, discussing the human personality type and philosophy that each animal represented.

   Keys: Near definition, logic   **Allegory** means _____ .

2. "I'm not fond of the *baroque* in either art or music," Mom announced. "The art and architecture are overdecorated—entirely too elaborate for my taste—and the music is cluttered with improvisations so that I lose track of the theme."

   Keys: Synonymous phrases,
   examples   **Baroque** means _____ .

3. *Burlesque*, a form of comedy that often mocks by caricature, is a favorite technique of gifted actor Harvey Korman.

   Key: Definition   **Burlesque** means _____ .

4. You like only *classical* styles, Mom," Jan said. "You drool over the clean lines of Greek architecture, and listen to Haydn and Mozart. You're such a classicist I can't believe it!"

   Keys: Definition, examples   **Classical** means _____ .

5. I enjoy the slapstick buffoonery of Eddie Murphy as well as subtler *comedy* that isn't trying for a laugh every other line.

   Key: Logic   **Comedy** means _____ .

6. "I never know 'whodunit' until the *denouement*," Carrie complained as she closed her mystery novel. "The author always has to explain everything, telling me what wonderful clues were planted if only I'd been bright enough to spot them."

   Key: Definition   **Denouement** means _____ .

7. Because our family loves a good *farce*, we enjoy the broadly comic, slapstick movies of Mel Brooks, such as *Blazing Saddles* and *High Anxiety*.

   Keys: Synonymous phrases,
   examples   **Farce** means _____ .

8. Our entire English class thought that writing a poem in *free verse* would be simple, but we discovered that free verse, even though it hasn't a fixed meter or rhyme, takes planning and hard work to sound right.

   Key: Definition   **Free verse** means _____ .

9. My favorite literary *genre* this year is fantasy, but last year I read only westerns, and when I was a kid I liked detective stories.

        Keys: Logic, examples   **Genre** means _____ .

10. Jan and Carrie like *Gothic* novels that are set in castles or other romantic spots and have plots stuffed with mysterious characters, haunted rooms, and village folk hinting that the dark past is about to overtake the present.

        Key: Definition   **Gothic** means _____ .
                                                  (here applied to literature only)

11. In *My Family and Other Animals,* Gerald Durrell ridicules his sister Margo and brothers Larry and Leslie in a series of hilarious, memorable *lampoons*.

        Key: Synonymous phrase   **Lampoon** means _____ .

12. Each year hundreds of *parodies* for the International Imitation Hemingway Competition are submitted to judges who must decide which author has imitated Hemingway's style most faithfully and achieved the most ridiculous result.

        Keys: Definition, logic   **Parody** means _____ .

13. As the *protagonist* in many films, John Wayne was a classic hero, surmounting all odds to triumph in the end.

        Keys: Synonym, example   **Protagonist** means _____ .

14. Decorated in the eighteenth century, many rooms of the Viennese royal summer palace are *rococo* in design, featuring pierced wood or metal sculpture, highly elaborate ceilings, and ornamental wall coverings and carpets.

        Key: Definitive phrases   **Rococo** means _____ .

15. Justly famous for his gentle *satire,* Stephen Leacock wrote one essay, "Boarding-House Geometry," that always makes us laugh. Using his own axioms and postulates, Leacock satirizes life in an early twentieth century boarding house. (E.g., "Any two meals at a boarding house are together less than two square meals.")

        Keys: Synonymous word,
            example   **Satire** means _____ .

16. Renowned Welsh *thespian* Richard Burton acted in Shakespearean productions as well as Hollywood movies.

        Key: Synonymous word   **Thespian** means _____ .

17. "This is a *travesty* of justice!" my dad exclaimed over the paper this morning. "Sentencing a criminal to jail and releasing him only months later is a mockery of the entire penal system."

        Key: Synonym   **Travesty** means _____ .

Word Study

    Literary, dramatic, and architectural terms number in the thousands. (Aren't you glad that this is a drastically reduced list?) Many terms you already know, such as *prose* and *poetry.* You've probably studied the Greek word *onomatopoeia* for our use of words that sound like what they mean: *meow, dingdong,* and Poe's famous "bells, bells, bells." You remember that a *tragedy* is a work in which the main character's downfall results from a fatal character flaw. The soap opera, popularized now in "Dallas" and "Dynasty," features characters who are either mainly good or really rotten—and usually get what they deserve—in this *melodramatic* form.

These terms are easy to deal with because they are clear-cut and known to us all. Other general terms, more difficult to grasp, form this lesson.

1. **allegory** ('al-ə-,gōr-ē) n.   A story using figurative characters and language to make an idea more interesting or persuasive; from Gr. *allegoria,* to speak figuratively

   Bunyan's *Pilgrim's Progress* is an early religious *allegory* relating the wearisome progress of the hero, Christian, from the City of Destruction to the Celestial City.

   Relatives: *allegorical, allegorist, allegorization, allegorize*

2. **baroque** (bə-'rōk) adj.   Referring to the elaborate artistic style of expression most popular in the seventeenth century: in art and architecture, by curved and highly ornamental, extravagant design; in music, by improvisation, the use of contrast, and "powerful tensions" (Webster); in literature, by the use of complex and inventive yet often unclear imagery and form; from Pg. *barocco,* irregularly shaped pearl, through F.

   Visitors to Hampton Court, the "country palace" where King Henry VIII courted Anne Boleyn, are fascinated by the *baroque* gilt and plaster ornamentation embellishing many rooms.

   Relative: *baroquely*

3. **burlesque** ([,]bər-'lesk) n.   A comedic form that makes people, actions, or literary works seem ridiculous through incongruous imitation; mockery through caricature; from Sp. *burla,* joke, through It. and F.

   Carol Burnett's exaggerated portrayal of Scarlett O'Hara in a *burlesque* of *Gone with the Wind* is memorable for anyone who loves to laugh.

   Relatives: *burlesque* (adj.), *burlesquely*
   Synonym: *caricature* (not exact)

4. **classical** ('klas-i-kəl) adj.   Referring to ancient Greek and Roman cultures, especially their art, music, literature, and architecture; from L. *classicus,* highest class of Roman citizen

   Colleges are naturally interested in what *classical* works of literature incoming freshmen have studied.

   Relatives: *classic* (n. and adj.), *classicist, classicism, classical, classically*
   Synonyms: *Attic* (referring to Athens and the Greek civilization)
   Antonyms: *modern, up-to-date, contemporary*

5. **comedy** ('käm-əd-ē) n.   A literary work/production designed to amuse and to end well for the main characters; from Gr. *komos,* revel, + *aeidein,* to sing

   My favorite TV situation *comedy* is "The Cosby Show," starring Bill Cosby as an obstetrician and the father of five.

   Relatives: *comedian* (male), *comedienne* (female), *comedic*
   Synonym: *humor*
   Antonym: *tragedy*

6. **denouement** (,dā-,nü-'mä^n) n.   The "unknotting" or unraveling of the plot of a literary or dramatic work; the outcome or result of a chain of events; from L. *nodus,* knot, through F. *desnouer,* to untie

   A reader would feel cheated of both answers and literary satisfaction without a *denouement* to resolve any questions raised by the narrative.

7. **farce** ('färs) n.   Comedy featuring rowdy, sometimes violent, action, with audience laughter as the main goal; slapstick comedy, often not logical or realistic; from L. *farsus,* savory stuffing, forcemeat

Following in the footsteps of farcical comedians Charlie Chaplin, Jerry Lewis, and Fanny Brice, Goldie Hawn portrayed Private Benjamin in a lighthearted movie *farce.*
Relatives: *farcical, farceur* (a writer or actor of farce)
Synonym: *mockery* (close but not exact)

8. **free verse** ('frē 'vərs) n.   Verse more rhythmic than prose yet written without a regular metric pattern, usually lacking rhyme; from L. *versus,* turn, line, line of writing, verse

The poems of Walt Whitman, Carl Sandburg, and E. E. Cummings are typical examples of *free verse* that read almost like prose.

9. **genre** ('zhän-rə) n.   Kind, sort, or type; a category in art, music, or literature recognizable by its particular form, content, or style (e.g., science fiction is one literary *genre*); from F. *genre,* kind, gender

Favorite authors in the satiric *genre* include Mark Twain, Sinclair Lewis, Dorothy Parker, Stephen Leacock, and the more contemporary Nora Ephron and Peter deVries.

10. **Gothic** ('gäth-ik) adj.   A medieval architectural style popular in western Europe till the late 1500s, characterized by slim, upright supports (plus extra buttresses) to bear carefully calculated weight and stress, pointed arches, rather narrow windows, and vaulted ceilings. In literature,Gothic style features desolate, typically romantic settings (castles, dungeons) and macabre or sensational plots with ghosts or seemingly supernatural occurrences.

Familiar classic *Gothic* tales include Mary Shelley's *Frankenstein,* Poe's short stories, and Emily Brontë's *Wuthering Heights,* all models for today's authors creating novels in this genre.

11. **lampoon** (lam-'pün) n.   A (usually lengthy) verbal picture thoroughly ridiculing an individual; may be lighter, mocking satire; from F. *lampons,* let us drink

Lampoons vary from the rather fond, teasing appraisal of family members by Gerald Durrell in *My Family and Other Animals,* to the biting, scurrilous approach of less-restrained authors.
Relative: *lampoon* (v.)
Synonym: *ridicule*

12. **parody** ('par-əd-ē) n.   A form of high burlesque that ridicules a particular literary work or style by copying its major features and applying them to trivial or unrelated matters; from Gr. *para + aeidein,* to sing

If you were to imitate *Macbeth* and depict the victims as ants instead of people yet maintain a grave seriousness throughout, you would be creating a *parody* of the famous Shakespearean tragedy.
Relative: *parody* (v.)
Synonym: *caricature* (see *burlesque*)

13. **protagonist** (prō-'tag-ə-nəst) n.   The leading part (in drama) or main character; from Gr. *prot + agonistes,* competitor at games, actor

The uninhibited audiences in Shakespeare's time cheered for the *protagonist,* who aroused their sympathies, and pelted the antagonist with rotten fruits and vegetables.

14. **rococo** (rə-'kō-[ˌ]kō) adj.   Extremely ornate or fancifully intricate, as more elaborately baroque; referring to an eighteenth century architectural style featuring fancy carved

designs and pierced ornamental work; in music (also eighteenth century), a light, happy ornamentation different from typical baroque music; from F. *rocaille,* rockwork

The term *rococo* has acquired the connotation of "too elaborate to be tasteful," yet in its day that style was probably a logical development of the preceding baroque period.

Relative: *rococo* (n.)
Antonyms: *classic, simple, unadorned*

15. **satire** ('sa-tī[ə]r) n.   Comedy using laughter as a weapon, to evoke attitudes of contempt and scorn along with amusement; biting humor or sarcasm to expose human failings; from L. *satur,* sated, enough

Swift's *Gulliver's Travels* derides all mankind, just as Twain's *Huckleberry Finn* exposes the stupidity and narrow-mindedness of middle America in the late 1800s. Both are famous, frequently studied examples of *satire*.

Relatives: *satiric, satirical, satirize, satirically, satirist*

16. **thespian** ('thes-pē-ən) n.   An actress or actor

Most *thespians* would leap at the chance to perform on the world's major stages, such as those in London or New York.

Relative: *thespian* (adj., dramatic)
Synonyms: *actor, actress, performer*
Derivation: Supposedly, the first actor to speak lines separate from the Greek chorus was *Thespis,* who was awarded a prize for tragedy around 534 B.C. Since then, *thespian* has been synonymous with actor or actress.

17. **travesty** ('trav-ə-stē) n.   Humor that mocks its serious or lofty subject by treating it in lowly or grotesque terms; a low, inferior, warped imitation, as *a travesty of justice;* from L. *trans + vestis,* dress or garment

If you were to rewrite *Hamlet,* putting crude or silly expressions in the mouths of those noble characters, your result would be a *travesty* of Shakespeare's original drama.

Relative: *travesty* (v., often synonymous with the verb *parody*)

Root Study

You will recognize the first three roots as the bases for words in List 2. The fourth may be an old friend; after all, who does not like a *bonus?*

1. GEN means kind (or type), birth, race, cause.
    ingenue—innocent, unsophisticated young woman
    ingenuous—innocent, open, candid, natural
    ingenuity—inventiveness, cleverness, or skill
    genesis—birth, origin; coming into being
    engender—to cause or produce; to beget; to cause to develop

2. AGON means struggle.
    agony—anguish, torture, intense pain or distress
    antagonist—adversary, opponent (of the *protagonist* perhaps)

3. VERS and VERT mean turn, line, line of writing, or verse.
    verse—one line of metrical writing; language having meter, poetry
    divert—to deflect or turn from one course to another; also, to amuse or distract from something unpleasant
    versatile—turning easily from one thing to another; all-around
    reverse—v., to change in a contrary manner, literally to turn back; adj., the opposite of normal, as *reverse order*

diverse—unlike or different; also, possessed of various shapes or characteristics; v.,
  diversify

4. BON and BENE mean good or well.

bonus—an extra payment or reward (above what was promised or expected)
bonny—appealingly attractive; excellent
bonhomie—comfortable geniality, warmth, friendliness (the hail-fellow-well-met
  attitude)
beneficent—producing good, as an act of charity; *beneficial*
benevolent—kindly, marked by goodwill and high intentions

Using the Words

List 2 Review

allegory	parody	classic	Gothic
burlesque	satire	denouement	protagonist
comedy	travesty	free verse	rococo
farce	baroque	genre	thespian
lampoon			

Exercise I. Fill-ins. Select the most appropriate word from List 2, based on clues in context. Word form may need changing.

1. a delightfully scary _____ tale, replete with supernatural events

2. preferring _____, that poetry unfettered by meter

3. admired the _____ lines of Greek and Roman architecture

4. foolish production of *Othello,* a _____ of that impressive tragedy

5. Poe's "The Murders in the Rue Morgue," a first in the detective _____ of mystery fiction

6. expected an interesting _____ that would unravel the plot's complexities

7. the _____, who was actually an antihero for the first half of the book

8. her skills as a _____ desperately needed in a demanding role

9. _____ design even more elaborate than baroque ornamentation

10. a vicious _____ of the mayor that stopped just short of libel

Exercise II. Matching. Match the List 2 words with their definitions or synonyms. Remember that several study words have multiple meanings.

_____ 1. **baroque**   (a) the opposite of tragedy

_____ 2. **Gothic**   (b) illogical, often unrealistic slapstick comedy

_____ 3. **allegory**   (c) a medieval architectural style

_____ 4. **comedy**   (d) wit used as a weapon to evoke scorn or
                                            contempt

_____ 5. **burlesque**   (e) low or distorted imitation of the real thing

_____ 6. **farce**   (f) ridiculing verbal portrait of a person

_____ 7. **satire**

(g) high burlesque ridiculing a literary work or well-known literary style

_____ 8. **travesty**

(h) elaborate seventeenth-century artistic style

_____ 9. **lampoon**

(i) mockery through caricature

_____ 10. **parody**

(j) a tale using figurative characters and language

Exercise III. Analogies. Complete each analogy with the best possible pair.

_____ 1. thespian : comedienne ::
    (a) teacher : instructor
    (b) apple : fruit
    (c) doctor : pediatrician
    (d) obstetrician : mortician

_____ 2. Notre Dame Cathedral : Gothic ::
    (a) rococo : Pentagon
    (b) Parthenon : classical
    (c) Paris : capitol
    (d) Smithsonian : museum

_____ 3. classical : Attic ::
    (a) cluttered : basement
    (b) baroque : current
    (c) lampoon : tragedy
    (d) genre : category

_____ 4. prologue : denouement ::
    (a) beginning : culmination
    (b) thespian : tragedian
    (c) free verse : poetry
    (d) comedy : satire

_____ 5. comedy : amusement ::
    (a) tragedy : drama
    (b) satire : contempt
    (c) smile : humor
    (d) farce : frown

Exercise IV. Identify "the famous" by matching them with the appropriate vocabulary word from Lesson 2. (Hint: Ask a friend or teacher if you're stumped.)

_____ 1. *Huckleberry Finn*

_____ 2. Paul Newman

_____ 3. *Animal Farm*

_____ 4. Winchester Cathedral

_____ 5. *Revenge of the Pink Panther*

_____ 6. *The Hobbit*

_____ 7. *Watership Down*

_____ 8. Juliet or Romeo

_____ 9. a Greek or Roman temple

_____ 10. *Leaves of Grass*, by Walt Whitman

_____ 11. Beethoven's Fifth Symphony

_____ 12. *The Once and Future King*

_____ 13. "Chicago" by Carl Sandburg

_____ 14. a navy business suit

_____ 15. Sir Laurence Olivier

_____ 16. *Wuthering Heights*

_____ 17. Hester Prynne (of *The Scarlet Letter*)

_____ 18. "The Nutcracker" ballet

_____ 19. *Candide*, by Voltaire

_____ 20. flying buttresses

Exercise V. Word Analysis. Remember that this section is to stretch your ability to work with words. If at sea, don't hesitate to ask someone else's opinion.

1. One useful synonym for a literary classic is the French term *belles lettres*. Look up the dictionary translation and definition for this term. Can popular, current fiction appropriately be classed as *belles lettres?*

   _____

2. The Latin root **gen** meaning *kind, race, birth,* or *cause,* has at least fifty derived English words. From the clues below, try to build a few of those words. Each dash indicates a missing letter.

   a. shown to good advantage in a
      photograph   p _ _ _ _ GEN _ c

   b. a major class or kind   GENu _

   c. a refined, "well-born" man   GEN _ _ _ m _ _

   d. someone born brilliant   GEN _ _ _

   e. birth or beginning   GEN _ _ i _

   f. that which passes on hereditary traits GEN _

   g. relating to heredity   GEN _ _ _ c

   h. to beget, foster   _ _ GENd _ _

   i. native, not imported   _ _ d _ GEN _ _ _

   j. open, simple, naive girl   i _ GEN _ _

3. Antonyms abound in the arts world. See how many sets of opposites you can match.

   _____ 1. **protagonist**   (a) romanticism

   _____ 2. **tragedy**   (b) honest representation

   _____ 3. **assonance**   (c) finale

   _____ 4. **realism**   (d) antagonist

   _____ 5. **hyperbole**   (e) dissonance

   _____ 6. **travesty**   (f) sophisticate

   _____ 7. **overture**   (g) comedy

   _____ 8. **ancient**   (h) classical

   _____ 9. **ingenue**   (i) modern

   _____ 10. **rococo**   (j) understatement

4. *Divers* and *diverse* are a plagued pair of words that people frequently confuse. With the help of a dictionary, define them and use each in a sentence of your own.

   _____

   _____

   _____

   _____

   _____

5. Keeping *good* or *well* in mind as the meanings of **bon/bene,** put the following derivatives into their proper phrases.

bona fide	bonhomie	bon voyage	benefactor
beneficiary	bons mots	benediction	benefit

a. the genuine article, a _____ Ming dynasty vase

b. my _____, a generous aunt who sends me a regular allowance

c. hilarious comments, or _____, that keep us chuckling

d. waving good-bye, hollering _____ in cheerful voices

e. his kindly blessing, a _____ we all waited to hear

f. radiating _____ and friendly warmth in an irresistible way

g. been the _____ of so much kindness from others

h. a long lecture, supposedly for my _____

6. **How does the meaning of "struggle" for agon** fit in the modern words *protagonist* and *antagonist?*

_____

_____

Exercise VI. Think of some current movies, TV programs, or literary examples of the following terms: *farce, burlesque, parody, satire, travesty,* and *gothic,* and compare your list with one your parent or teacher can give you.

_____

_____

_____

_____

_____

_____

_____

Four-Letter Words
SHORT WORDS FULL OF MEANING

In Context. Before studying the definitions, try reasoning out the meaning of each word, using context as your guide.

1. Rory's desk *abuts* mine when we work on our biology lab project, and that way we don't disturb the rest of the class.

    Key: Logic **Abut** means _____.

2. When asked how she felt about having four children, Mom *averred* sincerely that she wouldn't take a million dollars for any one of us.

    Key: Logic **Aver** means _____.

3. Listening to the *cant* of some politicans is discouraging. Their mindless repetition of trite phrases is so obviously hypocritical.

    Key: Definition **Cant** means _____.

4. With a violent or unexpected *coup,* a well-organized army of rebels can overthrow a shaky government.

    Keys: Synonymous idea, logic **Coup** means _____.

5. "I don't care who the tomcat was," Mom said with exasperation. "The *crux* of the matter is whether or not Marigold is going to have more kittens!"

    Key: Logic **Crux** means _____.

6. Our family loves the minty chocolate Girl Scout cookies, so we *dole* them out one by one, wishing they'd last longer.

    Keys: Example, logic **Dole** means _____.

7. It's not so easy to *dupe* Andy now that he's eight, but when he was younger he was such a perfect pigeon that we fooled him constantly.

    Key: Synonymous ideas **Dupe** means _____.

8. The Lord might have said, *"Fiat lux"* (Let there be light), but today's *fiat* could never be such a sweeping decree.

    Key: Synonym **Fiat** means _____.

9. One of the more grisly torture methods was *flaying* the victim alive, a process whereby the skin was pulled off in strips.

    Key: Definition **Flay** means _____.

10. Jan responded to my *gibes* about her inept gear shifting by becoming an expert driver, thus forcing me to praise her after all.

    Keys: Logic, opposing phrase **Gibe** means _____.

11. "Don't get *mired* down in details on your report," the history teacher warned us. "If you get sucked into that bog, you might fail to present the overall historical significance of your topic."

        Keys: Synonymous idea, logic   **Mire** means _____ .

12. Andy's a *rank* beginner at fishing, but he shows real aptitude for the sport.

        Keys: Opposing idea, logic   **Rank** means _____ .

13. A basic tenet of the religious *sect* termed Shakers is celibacy. Once that *sect* numbered 16,000 followers; fewer than 10 survive today.

        Key: Logic   **Sect** means _____ .

14. Jan's pearl necklace is a *sham,* of course, because a necklace that long composed of genuine pearls would cost lots of money.

        Keys: Antonym, logic   **Sham** means _____ .

15. The last chem exam was a killer, so for this one I'm *wary* enough to spend extra time studying.

        Key: Logic   **Wary** means _____ .

16. "It doesn't make a *whit* of difference," Jan moaned, "whether you study for the chem test or not. You'll beat me anyway."

        Key: Logic   **Whit** means _____ .

17. One celebrated World War I spy, known for her feminine *wiles* and deceptions, was the dancer Mata Hari, who was executed by the French in 1917.

        Key: Synonym   **Wile** means _____ .

Word Study

Short words, often Anglo-Saxon in origin, are good words to know. They have a vigor and punch that the longer, Latinate words lack. Writers Ernest Hemingway and E. B. White openly preferred the small word that does a big job.

*"Do not be tempted by a twenty-dollar word when there is a
ten-center handy, ready and able."*
    —Strunk and White, *The Elements of Style*

1. **abut** (ə-'bət) v.   To border, or have a common, touching boundary, as *their property abuts on ours;* to end at a contact point; terminate on or against; from L. *ad + bout,* blow, end, and F. *abuter,* to come to an end

Where the yard next door *abuts* on my folks' vegetable garden, it forms a meeting-point for my parents to discuss local news with the neighbors.

Relative: *abutter*
Synonyms: *touch, border*

2. **aver** (ə-'vər) v.   To state, assert, affirm in a positive way; to declare as true; from L. *ad + verus,* true

Asked why he had stayed after school, Andy *averred* that he'd been helping his teacher voluntarily, not as punishment for misbehavior.

Relative: *averment*

Synonyms: *declare, attest, assert, affirm, state, avow*
Antonyms: *disavow, disclaim* (neither exact)

3. **cant** ('kant) n.   Hypocritical talk, especially trite religious sayings; dialect of a particular group or jargon; trite talk; from L. *cantare,* to chant or sing

A lawyer friend, frequently on business in prisons, says that he cannot comprehend the *cant* of prisoners.

Relatives: *cant* (v., to lean or slope at an angle or to pitch to one side, as *that table cants off oddly*); *cant* (n., a slanting surface)
Synonyms: *argot* (jargon of the underworld), *dialect, jargon*

4. **coup** ('kü) n.   A successful, sudden act or stroke; an upset or overturning; from F. *couper,* to cut

Carrie felt that she had scored a *coup* by winning the gymnastics competition when she was a freshman.

Synonyms: *upset, overthrow*

5. **crux** ('krəks) n.   The major, vital point, as *the crux of the situation;* an unresolved problem or question; plural: *cruxes, cruces;* from L. *cruc-, crux,* cross, torture

"I don't mind getting a puppy," Mom said, "but who will care for it? That's the *crux* of the problem."

(Note: The *crux* family includes *crucifix, crucible, crusade, crucifier,* and *excruciating.*)

6. **dole** ('dōl)   n. A ration or allotment portioned out in regular amounts; a grant of money (or something distributed) to the poor or unemployed.   v. (With *out)* To apportion or distribute, from OE *dāl,* portion.

We have warned all the family to *dole* out Marigold's food sparingly, as that cat will eat whatever she's allotted.

Synonyms: *ration* (n., v.), *parcel (out), distribute*

7. **dupe** ('d[y]üp)   n. Someone easily fooled, deceived, cheated.   v. To fool, deceive, cheat (see "Derivation").

Every night, without realizing they're being *duped,* Poucette and Figment chase into the garage after Andy, who trails a catnip mouse behind him as the lure.

Synonyms: *gull* (v., remember *gullible?*), *trick* (v.), *fool* (v.), *hoax* (v.), *pigeon* (n.)
Derivation: Of French origin, *dupe* has meant someone easily fooled since the 1300s. Although there's doubt, etymologists think that *dupe* comes from the hoopoe bird and his stupid appearance. It is *cant*—a slang form of *hoopoe.*

8. **fiat** ('fē-ət) n.   A decree or similar arbitrary command; an authoritative sanction; from L. *fieri. Fiat* is a complete Latin sentence meaning, "Let it be done."

Americans have never been fond of government by *fiat,* preferring instead that duly elected representatives debate and vote on issues.

Relative: *fiat money* (paper currency decreed legal by government, not backed by gold or silver)
Synonyms: *decree, edict*

9. **flay** ('flā) v.   To pull off the skin in strips; to strip of possessions or to fleece; to criticize verbally in a severe, harsh manner; from ON *flā,* to flay

When Jan and I arrived home late, the folks nearly *flayed* us alive with their blistering lecture.

Synonyms: *fleece; excoriate* (last meaning)
Antonyms: *praise, commend, compliment* (all for last meaning)

10. **gibe** ('jīb)   n. A taunt or scornful comment.   v. To taunt, deride, or tease in a scornful manner; from F. *giber,* to shake or handle roughly.

    After my team lost the basketball game, Andy *gibed* at me until I locked him out of my room to shut him up.

    Relative: *giber*
    Synonyms: *scoff* (n., v.), *taunt* (n., v.), *sneer* (n., v.)

11. **mire** ('mī[ə]r)   n. Marsh or bog; wet, soggy slush or mud.   v. To drag down or entangle as in deep mud or marshy terrain; to be bogged down, as if by mire; from OE *mōs,* marsh or moss.

    We had to walk home from our last hayride, because the wagon became *mired* in the deep mud of the country road.

    Relative: *miry*
    Synonyms: *marsh* (n.), *bog* (n.); *entangle* (v.)

12. **rank** ('raŋk) adj.   (1) Healthy, even excessive, growth, as *the rank outcropping of weeds took over the park;* (2) disgustingly crude, gross, foul; (3) highly noticeable in a negative sense, flagrant, as *rank disobedience;* (4) complete (an intensive), as *a rank amateur;* (5) disgusting in taste or odor, rancid; from OE *ranc,* overbearing, strong

    On our return to the lake this spring, we were appalled at the *rank* growth of lawn threatening to engulf our little cabin.

    Relatives: *rankly, rankness*
    Synonyms: (1) *excessive;* (2) *foul, gross;* (3) *flagrant;* (4) *complete, total;* (5) *rancid, malodorous, putrid*
    Antonyms: (1) *minimal, slight;* (2 and 5) *appealing, luscious, praiseworthy;* (3) *hidden, unnoticeable*

    [Note: Remember the other *ranks,* as *to rank in order of preference,* to rate (v.), and *a member in the ranks of common soldiers* (n.)]

13. **sect** ('sekt) n.   A group unified by beliefs; a religious denomination; from L. *sequi,* to follow

    The religious *sect* called the Puritans settled America; today, a *sectarian* is someone thought to have a narrow viewpoint.

    Relatives: *sectarian, sectarianize, sectary, nonsectarian*
    Synonyms: *party, faction*

14. **sham** ('sham)   n. Fake, imposture; hypocrisy; an imitation or simulation of the real thing.   v. To deliberately mislead, delude, or feign; perhaps from E. *shame.*

    Their pretense of being interested was such an obvious *sham* that we weren't surprised when they left the exhibit early.

    Relatives: *sham* (adj.), *shammer*
    Synonyms: (n.) *imposture, hoax, pretense, hypocrisy;* (v.) *feign, assume, pretend*
    Antonyms: *truth, veracity*

15. **wary** ('wa[ə]r-ē) adj.   Characterized by wisdom and awareness of possible danger; prudently keen, alert; from OE *waer,* careful, aware, wary

    Marigold and her kittens are exceedingly *wary* of the big black Newfoundland across the street.

    Relatives: *warily, wariness*

Synonyms: *cautious, circumspect*
Antonyms: *foolhardy, rash, bold, brash*

16. **whit** ('hwit) n.   The tiniest particle or bit imaginable; from E. *wiht, wight,* creature, thing, bit

Jan said she didn't care a *whit* about her former boyfriend; but she is shamming, and we know she still cares.

Synonyms: *bit, particle*

17. **wile** ('wī[ə]l)   n. Trick or clever stratagem for deceitful purposes; or a charmingly playful trick.   v. To entice or lure; to pass time pleasurably, as *to wile away the hours* (in this sense, *while* is a synonym); from OE *wigle,* divination, witch.

Marigold instinctively uses her feline *wiles* to sneak up on an unwary bird.

Relative: *wily* (Remember Wile E. Coyote of "The Roadrunner"?)
Synonyms: (n.) *trick, guile*
              (v.) *entice, lure*

Root Study

This group of roots is basic to your understanding of the English language and nearly 100 words, although only *ver* is related to List 3. Four-letter words are often the roots themselves, surviving with minor spelling changes.

1. ANIMA means spirit, soul, mind, or nature.
    animus—disposition, nature; sometimes ill-will, malevolence
    animal—living being that is not a human being or plant; mammal
    animated—lively, vivacious; endowed with life, as *animated cartoons*
    equanimity—evenness of disposition; a calm temperament, composure, self-possession

2. CRED means believe or trust.
    credible—believable, trustworthy
    credit—bank balance; time allotted for payment; reliance on the truth of something; esteem
    credential—testimonial, certificate, diploma
    credo—set of beliefs
    credence—acceptance as true or real

3. SEQU and SECUT mean follow.
    sequence—a series, its order in space and time
    consecutive—succeeding in regular order
    persecute—to pursue persistently, often with bad intent
    execute—to carry out (a plan); to inflict capital punishment
    sequel—one development that follows another; an installment

4. VER means truth.
    verify—to confirm or establish accuracy, truth, or reality
    verdict—judgment after a trial, opinion
    veracity—truthfulness
    veracious—truthful, honest
    verisimilitude—the appearance of truth or genuineness; literally, *similar to the truth*

Using the Words

List 3 Review

abut	dole	gibe	sham
aver	dupe	mire	wary
cant	fiat	rank	whit
coup	flay	sect	wile
crux			

Exercise I. Fill-ins. Select the most appropriate word from List 3, based on clues in context. The form of the word may change.

1. When Oliver first joined Fagin's gang of pickpockets, he was the perfect

    _____, innocent and easily fooled.

2. A _____ calling themselves Scientologists has recently been the subject

    of investigation and media probing.

3. "Three at a crack!" Carrie informed us. "A brilliant _____ with my

    invincible flyswatter."

4. The nearest large dock _____ the shore at Devils Point, right by our lake

    cabin.

5. We felt stripped and raw, _____ as we were by the coach's stinging half-

    time rebuke.

6. The hyena circled his newly discovered meal _____, alert for any sound

    or scent of the predator returning to the kill.

7. The _____ of any murder case is typically motive plus opportunity.

8. We ignored Lee's taunts, figuring that his repeated _____ only revealed

    how envious he was of our school's success.

9. Convicted of _____ insubordination, the sergeant was reduced to a

    private.

10. "It matters not a _____ that you mean well," Mom lectured Carrie,

    "unless you do something to prove it."

Exercise II. Synonyms. Choose two for each vocabulary word. Write their letters on the lines provided.

_____ 1. **aver**   (a) avoid   (b) attest   (c) avow   (d) deny

_____ 2. **cant**   (a) jargon   (b) contradiction   (c) argot
(d) talk

_____ 3. **dole**   (a) senator   (b) put   (c) distribute
(d) parcel (out)

_____ 4. **mire**   (a) bog   (b) mush   (c) briar   (d) entangle

____ 5. **rank**   (a) gross   (b) excessive   (c) score   (d) lack

____ 6. **sham**   (a) feign   (b) spread   (c) mellow
(d) hypocrisy

____ 7. **wile**   (a) during   (b) guile   (c) entice   (d) guilt

____ 8. **fiat**   (a) decree   (b) edict   (c) auto   (d) design

____ 9. **sect**   (a) crowd   (b) belief   (c) faction   (d) party

____ 10. **rank**   (a) bottom   (b) complete   (c) lever
(d) flagrant

Exercise III. Analogies. Complete each analogy with the best pair possible, using words from List 3 and Roots.

____ 1. truth : sham ::
    (a) abut : border   (c) cant : jargon
    (b) honesty : guile   (d) wariness : caution

____ 2. gull : dupe ::
    (a) coup : state   (c) touch : abut
    (b) pigeon : robin   (d) parcel : gift

____ 3. sect : political ::
    (a) execution : death   (c) fiat : command
    (b) averment : declaration   (d) verdict : guilty

____ 4. coup : downfall ::
    (a) veracity : falsehood   (c) sequel : chapter
    (b) stillness : animation   (d) credentials : employment

____ 5. noticeable : rank ::
    (a) wily : ingenious   (c) whit : particle
    (b) enticing : appealing   (d) bold : wary

Exercise IV. Famous Fill-ins. From the choices offered, select the correct word to insert in each of the following quotations.

shamming	wiles	flayed	verisimilitude
gibes	cant	mire	rank
coup			

1. *Oh! Death will find me long before I tire*
Of watching you; and swing me suddenly
Into the shade and loneliness and _____
Of the last land!
    —Rupert Brooke, "Oh! Death will find me" (sonnet)

2. Asking about the fiendishly clever Odysseus (Ulysses):

    "Tell me, Muse, of the man of many _____.*"*
    —Alexander Pope (trans.), Homer's *Odyssey*

3. *"I see it says that Dennis Radclyffe is seriously ill also."*

    "Probably _____, *the dirty blackguard."*
    —Agatha Christie, *Partners in Crime*

4. *"Wife, spouse, my dear, joy, jewel, love, sweet-heart and the rest of that nauseous*

    _____, *in which men and their wives are so fulsomely familiar."*
    —William Congreve, *The Way of the World*

5. "O! my offence is _____, it smells to heaven."
   —Shakespeare, *Hamlet*

6. *Though I've belted you an'* _____ *you,*
   By the livin' Gawd that made you,
   You're a better man than I am, Gunga Din!
        —Rudyard Kipling, "Gunga Din"

7. *"Merely corroborative detail, intended to give artistic* _____ *to an*
   otherwise bald and unconvincing narrative."
        —W. S. Gilbert, *The Mikado*

8. Hamlet, to the skull of Yorick, in Act V:

   "Where be your _____ *now? your gambols? your songs? your flashes of*
   merriment that were wont to set the table on a roar?"
        —Shakespeare, *Hamlet*

9. *"You've got it, sir. . . . we haven't been able to get a clue to it. This is a fine*

   _____ *of yours, sir."*
        —Agatha Christie, *Partners in Crime*

Exercise V. Antonyms. Find an antonym or opposing phrase for each word on the left.

____ 1. **excoriate**	(a) circumspect
____ 2. **equanimity**	(b) praise
____ 3. **wary**	(c) large amount
____ 4. **aver**	(d) reality
____ 5. **crux**	(e) disclaim
____ 6. **rash**	(f) commend
____ 7. **deride, taunt**	(g) unbelievable
____ 8. **sham**	(h) nervousness
____ 9. **whit**	(i) extraneous detail
____ 10. **credible**	(j) foolhardy

Exercise VI. Word Analysis

1. What happens to words derived from **cred** (belief, trust) when the prefixes *in-* and *dis-* are
   attached (e.g., *incredible, discredit*)?

   _____

   _____

2. We have several musical terms from the Latin *cantare,* to sing. With a dictionary's help,
   match the derived words with their meanings.

____ a. cantata	(1) one segment of a long poem
____ b. cantabile	(2) a singer or chanter in a synagogue
____ c. canticle	(3) musical direction: in a singing manner
____ d. canto	(4) sacred choral music, usually with accompaniment
____ e. cantor	(5) a religious song from the Bible

3. What link does **crux** have with the meaning of the word *excruciating?* (Hint: Webster knows.)

_____

_____

4. The word *crusade,* from **crux,** can be used in different contexts. Write two sentences illustrating the modern use of *crusade.* What does *Crusade* mean when capitalized?

_____

_____

_____

_____

5. The French word *couper* (cut) has given us some of our most colorful and useful modern expressions. How many can you match with their corresponding meanings?

_____ a. coup d'état   (1) two-door automobile

_____ b. coup de grace   (2) to deal with successfully

_____ c. coupe   (3) detachable ticket, certificate

_____ d. coup de theatre   (4) a fatal blow or finishing event

_____ e. coupon   (5) sudden, violent overthrow of government

_____ f. cope   (6) theatrical success

6. What does the word *nonsectarian* mean? _____

_____

O Ye Gods! Part One
WORDS FROM MYTH AND LEGEND

In Context. Before studying the definitions, try reasoning out the meaning of each word, using context as your guide.

1. Jan and I want to have a graduation party, but our folks are afraid it will be a wild *bacchanal* that will disturb the neighbors.

    Keys: Logic, synonym   **Bacchanal** means _____ .

2. Carrie's absorption in her growing bank account has caused Dad to tease her, accusing her of *cupidity*.

    Keys: Partial definition, logic   **Cupidity** means _____ .

3. "You'll be the *cynosure* of all eyes in that dress," Dad assured Jan as he admired her modeling of the latest style.

    Key: Logic   **Cynosure** means _____ .

4. Our new principal's relaxed style of governing is in marked contrast to the *draconian* methods of our former principal.

    Key: Contrasting phrase   **Draconian** means _____ .

5. Mom coached Carrie for her part in the play. "Remember to be delicate, a sort of spiritual and *ethereal* girl—someone just on loan to the earth."

    Key: Synonymous phrases   **Ethereal** means _____ .

6. My camp counselor Rob was the best *mentor* I could have had, and I've patterned myself after him in many ways.

    Keys: Synonym, logic   **Mentor** means _____ .

7. Changeable Charlie is a private name for my cousin Chuck, whose *mercurial* temperament makes us wonder what he'll do or say next.

    Keys: Synonym, logic   **Mercurial** means _____ .

8. The first *mnemonic* device I learned was "*M*ary's *v*iolet *e*yes *m*ake *J*ohn *s*it *u*p *n*ights, *p*eriod." Is that how everyone remembers the names and order of the planets?

    Keys: Logic, example   **Mnemonic** means _____ .

9. Our guidance counselor suggested that a "touch of *narcissism*" was probably normal for seniors who had to focus intensely on themselves and their immediate future throughout the year.

    Key: Partial definition   **Narcissism** means _____ .

10. The *nemesis* of our school is East High, as we rarely beat them in athletics and usually tie in scholastic awards.

    Key: Logic   **Nemesis** means _____ .

11. Our new basketball coach, unafraid of *Promethean* tasks, devised a brilliant offense that we think will outwit East High.

    Keys: Logic, example   **Promethean** means _____.

12. The *saga* of our first game against East High is a long and complex tale, ending in a narrow defeat for us.

    Key: Definition   **Saga** means _____.

13. After reading the mythology about Saturn, an often gloomy, authoritative figure, I began describing our grumpy neighbor as *saturnine*.

    Key: Synonyms   **Saturnine** means _____.

14. Dad would like to think he's a *solon*, a wise law-giver, but he admits that guiding four kids is trickier than he had imagined.

    Key: Definition   **Solon** means _____.

15. When our cat Marigold is sleeping and we vacuum nearby, she opens one *somnolent* eye to glare at the noisy, hateful machine.

    Keys: Near synonym, logic   **Somnolent** means _____.

16. Last Halloween was a night of *stygian* darkness, murky and forbidding enough to send the younger trick-or-treaters home earlier than usual.

    Key: Synonyms   **Stygian** means _____.

17. At eight, Andy is small, but he's a *titan* when we go camping. He sets up our camp almost single-handedly.

    Key: Antonym   **Titan** means _____.

Word Study

Greek and Roman mythology seem far away and not very important anymore, until we realize how many of those ancient gods, goddesses—and some real-life figures—have survived and come into our language as everyday words. Most of their names are now common nouns, uncapitalized, and no longer of epic proportions. Once they were important elements of a set of beliefs held by early people with limited scientific knowledge. Today, they are some of our most descriptive words, with amazing histories.

1. **bacchanal** (ˈbak-ən-ᵊl, ˌbak-ə-ˈnal) n.   A wild party, drunken carousal; a reveler or carouser (person)

   Plato once remarked that he had seen the entire population of Athens drunk at a *bacchanal* in honor of Bacchus.

   Relatives: *bacchant* (n.), *bacchanalia* (wild orgy)
   Synonym: *orgy*
   Derivation: Bacchus (Dionysus to the Greeks) was god of grapes and wine. Worshiping Bacchus involved gallons of wine, grapes on every table—and you can imagine the rest.

2. **cupidity** (kyù-ˈpid-ət-ē) n.   Excessive greed or desire, often for wealth
   When he refused to donate any of his vast fortune to the library's building fund, the businessman was accused of *cupidity*.

Synonyms: *avarice, greed, lust*

Derivation: Eros to the Greeks, the Roman Cupid originally symbolized only physical desire. Gradually he came to embody strong desire of all sorts, especially greed for money. Until his conversion, Scrooge was guilty of cupidity.

3. **cynosure** ('sī-nə-,shu̇[ə]r) n.   A center of attention or attraction, as the North Star in the constellation Cynosure. Ursa Minor (Little Bear) is Cynosure's other name.

Meadows trim, with daisies pied,
Shallow brooks, and rivers wide,
Towers and battlements it sees
Bosomed high in tufted trees,
Where perhaps some beauty lies,
The cynosure *of neighboring eyes.*
         —John Milton, "L'Allegro"

Derivation: Cynosura, a nymph of Mount Ida, was one of the nurses to Zeus, king of the Greek gods. When she died, Zeus transformed her into the constellation Cynosure, "Dog's Tail" (Gr., *kynos oura*), which we call the Little Dipper.

4. **draconian** (drā-'kō-nē-ən) adj.   Extremely severe or harsh (usually applied to laws, rules, methods)

Most of today's prison administrators realize that the *draconian* regulations of the past did not help to rehabilitate their inmates.

Relatives: *draconic, Draconism*
Synonyms: *rigorous, harsh, cruel, severe* (none exact)
Antonyms: *lax, weak, loose, slack*

Derivation: The Greek statesman of Athens who first codified their laws was Draco, a farsighted fellow who nonetheless imposed barbarously harsh laws and punishments. An orator of the time said that "Draco's code was written in human blood."

5. **ethereal** (i-'thir-ē-əl) adj.   Exceedingly delicate and lovely; heavenly, intangible as air itself

And all my days are trances,
    And all my nightly dreams
Are where thy grey eye glances,
    And where thy footstep gleams—
In what ethereal *dances,*
    By what eternal streams.
         —Edgar Allan Poe, "To One in Paradise"

Relatives: *ether* (the heavens); *ether* ($C_4H_{10}O$, the light, flammable liquid anesthetic/ solvent), *ethereally, etherealize, etherealness*
Synonyms: *celestial, unworldly, heavenly, spiritual*

Derivation: Daughter of the Greek Nox (Night) was Ether, who symbolized the soul of the universe.

6. **mentor** ('men-,tȯ[ə]r) n.   A respected guide and counselor, more than just a tutor or teacher

Each person struggling to make a career in the arts hopes to find a *mentor* who will be both friend and advice giver along the way.

Synonyms: *counselor, coach, tutor* (none exact)

Derivation: When the Greek Odysseus (Ulysses) left home to fight in the Trojan War, he appointed his most trusted friend Mentor as counselor to his son Telemachus.

7. **mercurial** ([ˌ]mər-ˈkyùr-ē-əl) adj.   Greatly variable or changeable, as mercury is in a thermometer (often used to describe personality)

Old belief said that the little finger was the *mercurial* finger; if square, it denoted sound judgment, and if pointed, it indicated eloquence.

Relatives: *mercurially, mercury* (the element)
Synonyms: *inconstant, variable*
Antonyms: *impassive, phlegmatic, saturnine, constant*
Derivation: Mercury (Hermes to the Greeks) was the original hyperactive kid, zipping blithely through the world. He was god of communication, conductor of souls to Hades, and god of business. His name remains in *commerce, merchant, mercer, merchandise,* and the planet *Mercury.*

8. **mnemonic** (ni-ˈmän-ik) adj.   Assisting memory; **mnemonics** is a technique to improve memory

"I'll never survive this art history class," Jan said, "if I don't create some *mnemonic* aids to remember the major works of art in their proper time periods."

Derivation: Mnemosyne was only one of Zeus's many wives. She was goddess of memory and parent with Zeus of the nine Muses: *Calliope* (eloquence), *Clio* (history), *Erato* (love poetry), *Euterpe* (music), *Melpomene* (tragedy), *Polyhymnia* (sacred lyrics), *Terpsichore* (dance), *Thalia* (comic and pastoral poetry), and *Urania* (astronomy). The noun *muse* can mean *the poet* or *the poet's inspiration*. As a verb, *muse* means *to ponder* or *think over slowly*.

9. **narcissism** (ˈnär-sə-ˌsiz-əm) n.   Extreme fondness of or absorption with oneself; self-centeredness

Sometimes an artist is unfairly accused of *narcissism* because he or she is so totally absorbed and solitary, but usually this absorption is with the work, not the self.

Relatives: *narcissist, narcissistic*
Synonyms: *egoism, egocentrism*
Antonyms: *selflessness, altruism*
Derivation: After the lovely nymph Echo faded into a faint sound because Narcissus failed to return her love, Nemesis punished him by causing him to fall in love with his own reflection in a fountain. Narcissus yearned for himself until he, too, died and was metamorphosed into the trumpet-shaped white and yellow flower we call by his name.

10. **nemesis** (ˈnem-ə-səs) n.   A relentless pursuer of evildoers; an opponent who usually wins

I did well in math until I reached advanced calculus, which may prove to be my *nemesis* this year.

Synonyms: *bane, jinx, hex* (none exact)
Derivation: Nemesis was the sister of Ether—both daughters of Nox (Night). As the goddess of fate, Nemesis made sure that criminals or those guilty of excess pride were found and punished.

11. **Promethean** (prə-ˈmē-thē-ən) adj.   Unusually creative and original; life giving (note that the capital letter remains)

From women's eyes this doctrine I derive:
They are the ground, the books, the academes,
From whence doth spring the true Promethean *fire.*
        —Shakespeare, *Love's Labour's Lost*

Derivation: Prometheus was the Titan who formed man from clay and stole fire from Mount Olympus for humankind's use, giving them the potential to rival the gods. As punishment, Zeus chained Prometheus to a rock and each day sent an eagle to eat his liver, which grew again at night while the eagle slept. (It was not smart to cross Zeus.)

12. **saga** ('säg-ə, 'sag-) n.   A lengthy prose story or account including all the details; from ON, *saga,* saw

Jan spent hours preparing an oral book report on *Kristin Lavransdatter,* which is the best *saga* ever written, as far as Jan's concerned.

Derivation: Saga was a Scandinavian goddess, who was a friend of Odin, king of the Norse deities. Her name, now in lowercase, refers to any long tale reminiscent of the old Icelandic sagas.

13. **saturnine** ('sat-ər-ˌnīn) adj.   Gloomy and heavy of temperament; steady in nature, slow to change

Is there in the world a climate more uncertain than our own? And, which is a natural consequence, is there any where a people more unsteady, more apt to discontent, more saturnine, *dark, and melancholic than our selves?*
    —William Congreve, *Amendments of Mr. Collier's False and Imperfect Citations*

Relative: *saturnalia* (orgy, bacchanal, bacchanalia)
Synonyms: *dour, dull, heavy, surly, gloomy*
Derivation: Saturn, Roman god of sowing, was generally regarded as a grim disciplinarian, yet festivals in his honor were wild and unrestrained bacchanals. A *saturnalia* began on December 17, close to the winter solstice on the twenty-second, and lasted for days and days.

14. **solon** ('sō-lən) n.   An extremely intelligent lawgiver; or a member of a legislative body

Many have suggested that the *solons* in our Congress would have more time to enact sensible legislation if they weren't always running for reelection.

Derivation: The original poet and statesman Solon lived in Athens in the sixth century B.C. and brought about wise legal reforms that allowed citizens to share in government.

15. **somnolent** ('säm-nə-lənt) adj.   Drowsy, sleepy; apt to bring on sleep, as *a lengthy, somnolent lecture*

When I asked Jan if she would watch David Letterman with me, she gave only a *somnolent* "Mmmhm," and I knew she'd be asleep before the end of Letterman's monologue.

Relative: *somnolence*
Synonyms: *sleepy, drowsy, lethargic*
Antonyms: *alert, wakeful* (and sometimes *wary*)
Derivation: Somnus was the Greek god of sleep, also called **Hypnos,** from which we get *hypnotism* and *hypnosis.* **Morpheus,** son of Somnus, gave his name to the addictive narcotic *morphine.*

16. **stygian** ('stij-[ē-]ən) adj.   Forbiddingly dark and gloomy, as was the river Styx

What *stygian* corners in the mind of an author can give rise to such ghoulish tales that we remember them years later and shiver?

Derivation: The route to Hades (the Greeks' underworld) was across the daunting river Styx. Charon ferried dead souls across for the price of a coin placed in each corpse's mouth prior to burial.

17. **titan** ('tīt-ᵊn) n.   Anyone huge in size, great in power, or both; an extraordinarily high achiever, as *a titan of industry*

Joseph Kennedy, a *titan* in the American business world, passed on his ambitious drive to a family of sons and grandchildren.

Relatives: *titanic* (colossal), *The Titanic* (ship), *titanism* (rebellion against conventions)
Derivation: Titans were the twelve giants (six male, six female) who ruled when the earth was new, until the gods of Olympus took over. Famous Titans include Prometheus, Mnemosyne, and Oceanus, who was in charge of the seas. Atlas was the son of the Titan Iapetus.

Root Study

Roots *arch, dei, div,* and *the* plus *somn* have an obvious connection to List 4. *Brev* is what these ancients proved not to be in history.

1. ARCH means rule, law, order, or ancient.
   monarch—one who is a sole ruler
   hierarchy—structure of elements ranked in order of importance
   anarchy—lack of law and order
   matriarch—female ruler; *patriarch*—male ruler
   archaeology—study of artifacts of ancient civilizations
   (Note: Remember that the prefix *arch-* means first, main, or chief.)

2. BREV means short or brief.
   brevity—briefness, shortness of duration or extent
   abbreviate—to make shorter or to curtail
   breviary—a small book of hymns, prayers, songs

3. DEI, DIV, and THE mean god.
   deity—a god or godlike figure
   deism—a religion based on reason, emphasizing morality
   divine—supremely good, perfect; of God or a god
   theology—a distinct system of religious beliefs
   pantheon—temple for all gods; the gods of a people; any group of illustrious persons
   atheist—one who denies the existence of God

4. SOMN means sleep.
   somnambulist—a sleepwalker
   somnambulism—sleepwalking
   insomnia—the inability to sleep

Using the Words

List 4 Review

bacchanal	mentor	nemesis	solon
cupidity	mercurial	Promethean	somnolent
cynosure	mnemonic	saga	stygian
draconian	narcissism	saturnine	titan
ethereal			

Exercise I. Fill-ins. Select the most appropriate word from List 4 and Roots, based on clues in context. The word form may change.

1. Dad said, "If I were a _____ of industry such as Mr. Iacocca, when

   would I ever have time to play golf?"

2. Marigold's lazy, _____ movements as she stretches after a nap mirror the motions of African lions, her far-off cousins.

3. "Has Rembrandt run to Venice?" was Jan's _____ device for remembering the seventeenth-century Dutch painters.

4. When I began running track, the fourth mile was my _____. I could never get past it without a short walking spell.

5. Mom says that E. B. White has been her literary _____, even though she's only studied his work and was never able to meet the author in person.

6. "Imagine," Mom says, "the humorous yet _____ beauty of Charlotte's web glistening with dew in the sunlight, and containing the words 'SOME PIG' above Wilbur's pen."

7. In the _____ of angels, Satan was once the archangel until he fell from grace. (Hint: Check out those roots.)

8. "Bob's _____ absorption with himself makes me burn," Jan fumed. "He never thinks of anybody else!"

9. Our neighbors had a party last weekend that was a real _____, and the whole street is still talking about it.

10. Almost any movie star appearing at her premiere hopes to be the _____ of the evening.

11. Marigold and her kittens, Poucette and Figment, dance about on their hind paws and swat delicately at the fireflies winking above the grass. "A feline _____ performance," Dad says laughingly. (Hint: Turn a Muse's name into an adjective.)

12. When our guide turned off the lights down in Kentucky's Mammoth Cave, Jan grabbed my arm and complained of the _____ darkness.

13. James Bond, the legendary 007, has need of _____ skills and a constantly ingenious mind to match as he reels from one adventure to the next.

14. Someone with a _____ temperament might find a desk job too confining and routine to suit his quicksilver nature.

15. Many stimulating late-night discussions in a college dorm revolve around _____, especially when classmates of several different religions expound their views. (Hint: Search among the roots.)

16. After he realized that he'd been guilty of _____, Scrooge's stingy and _____ personality altered radically, so that he became both generous and lighthearted.

17. One of the most beloved _____ of all time was the lawyer Abraham

Lincoln, who became our sixteenth president.

18. China's desperate attempt to control population by limiting each couple to one child seems

_____ on first hearing, yet an intelligent appraisal has convinced most

Chinese of the ultimate wisdom of this severe policy.

Exercise II. Analogies. Complete each analogy with the best pair possible, using words from List 4 and Roots. Now that analogies are more familiar to you, they will be offered with 5 answer choices, as on many standardized tests.

_____ 1. titan : weakling ::
  (a) infant : fledgling
  (b) mother : father
  (c) giant : midget
  (d) gnome : troll
  (e) dancer : artist

_____ 2. saturnine : dour ::
  (a) nightly : daily
  (b) harsh : strong
  (c) atheistic : devout
  (d) mercurial : inconstant
  (e) matriarchal : feminine

_____ 3. deity : Zeus ::
  (a) leader : assistant
  (b) dancer : Winston Churchill
  (c) nymph : Echo
  (d) goddess : Somnus
  (e) artist : Margaret Thatcher

_____ 4. miser : cupidity ::
  (a) mentor : leadership
  (b) enemy : fear
  (c) judge : bias
  (d) postman : letters
  (e) grocer : philanthropy

_____ 5. alert : somnolent ::
  (a) groggy : exhausted
  (b) stygian : dead
  (c) Promethean : inventive
  (d) divine : exalted
  (e) selfless : narcissistic

_____ 6. Cynosure : sky ::
  (a) pine : forest
  (b) house : property
  (c) Mount Olympus : myth
  (d) Styx : underworld
  (e) Oceanus : heaven

_____ 7. physician : medicine ::
  (a) waitress : tips
  (b) landlord : welfare
  (c) solon : law
  (d) patriarch : philosophy
  (e) archaeologist : construction

_____ 8. religion : Deism ::
  (a) college : university
  (b) Muse : Terpsichore
  (c) titan : giant
  (d) god : pantheon
  (e) science : Einstein

_____ 9. daringly inventive : Promethean ::
  (a) amazingly strong : saturnine
  (b) extremely cute : mercurial
  (c) unfailingly generous : ethereal
  (d) unusually complex : mnemonic
  (e) brutally harsh : draconian

—— 10. *The Mikado* : opera ::
    (a) *The Iliad* : saga
    (b) cartoon : "Peanuts"
    (c) *Gone with the Wind* : short story
    (d) "The Raven" : poem
    (e) *Julius Caesar* : lampoon

Exercise III. Antonyms. Find an antonym (or opposing phrase) for each word on the left. One lettered choice is used twice.

—— 1. **draconian**

—— 2. **mercurial**

—— 3. **anarchy**

—— 4. **abbreviate**

—— 5. **saturnalia**

—— 6. **stygian**

—— 7. **Promethean**

—— 8. **saturnine**

—— 9. **divine**

—— 10. **cupidity**

(a) funeral

(b) cheerful, pleasant, bright

(c) soft, lax, weak

(d) deadening

(e) hellish

(f) responsible government

(g) generosity

(h) steady, constant

(i) extend, lengthen

Exercise IV. Word Analysis

1. *Somnambulist* literally means sleepwalker because *ambul,* or *amb* means *walk* in Latin. With this knowledge, match the English derivatives with their meanings.

—— a. ambulatory

—— b. amble

—— c. ambulance

—— d. perambulate

—— e. preamble

—— f. perambulator, a "pram"

(1) vehicle for moving those who cannot walk

(2) baby carriage

(3) introductory remarks

(4) stroll idly, in a relaxed manner

(5) capable of walking, not bedridden

(6) walk on an inspection

2. Knowing just one fact about a mythological being can enable you to create the modern-day word in our dictionary. Have a go at the following:
  a. The old sea god Proteus could change form at will.
    Adjective meaning *imaginatively adaptable, diverse* = _ _ _ _ ean.
  b. Juno, queen of the gods, was a handsome, statuesque woman.
    Adjective referring to a *tall, attractive, impressive female* = _ _ _ _ esque.
  c. Urania, daughter of Mnemosyne, was the Muse of astronomy.
    Noun that is the *name of a planet* = _ _ _ _ us.
  d. Aeolus was god of the winds.
    Adjective *referring to the winds* = _ _ _ _ ian.
  e. Eros (Cupid) was god of passionate love.
    Adjective referring to *passionate or sexual love* = _ _ _ tic.
  f. Mars was god of war.
    Adjective meaning *warlike; suited for army or military life* = _ _ _ tial.
  g. Mount Olympus was the home of Zeus and his royal court.
    Adjective meaning *majestic, regal or commanding* = _ _ _ _ _ ian.

3. The prefix **pan-** used with *pantheon* and *pandemic* means all or entire. The following words, also prefixed by *pan-,* are useful to know. Can you make an intelligent guess at their meanings?

WORD	MEANING
a. panorama	_____
b. Pan-American	_____
c. pandemonium (literally, *all demons*)	_____
d. Panhellenic	_____
e. panhuman	_____
f. pantomime	_____
g. panacea (Hint: Panacea was daughter of the god of healing.)	_____

4. From memory, jot down an *antonym* or *opposing phrase* for the following words from List 4 and Roots:

a. saga _____

b. somnolent _____

c. saturnine _____

d. narcissism _____

e. mercurial _____

f. draconian _____

g. cupidity _____

5. The names of planets and the heavenly constellations derive mainly from classical mythology. With the exception of Earth, which is the oddball (forgive the pun), list the other classically named planets. How about the constellations? The signs of the zodiac?

_____

_____

_____

_____

Review

This lesson reviews the words and roots in Lists 1–4, giving you opportunities to use these words ONE MORE TIME. You should say each word aloud as you read through the following lists. You may be one of those people who learn best by *hearing*, not seeing.

LIST 1	LIST 2	LIST 3	LIST 4
atone	allegory	abut	bacchanal
burgeon	burlesque	aver	cupidity
coerce	comedy	cant	cynosure
defile	farce	coup	draconian
disparage	lampoon	crux	ethereal
entice	parody	dole	mentor
evince	satire	dupe	mercurial
exhort	travesty	fiat	mnemonic
feign	baroque	flay	narcissism
intimate	classic	gibe	nemesis
nurture	denouement	mire	Promethean
perpetrate	free verse	rank	saga
redress	genre	sect	saturnine
relinquish	Gothic	sham	solon
stigmatize	protagonist	wary	somnolent
truckle	rococo	whit	stygian
	thespian	wile	titan

ROOTS

AGON	BON/BENE	EV/AEV	SOMN
ANIMA	BREV	GEN	VER (truth)
ANTHROP	CRED	PHIL	VERS and VERT
ARCH	DEI, DIV, and THE	SEQU/SECUT	VINC and VICT

Using the Words

Exercise I. Fill-ins. Select the most appropriate word from the choices offered, based on clues in context.

atoned	satire	dole	cynosure
defile	classic	sect	mnemonic
feign	thespian	whit	titan
relinquished	coup	wiles	

1. a masterful _____ that seized control of the region

2. remembering long lists through use of _____ aids

3. _____ his claim to the property with regret

4. once a tiny _____, now a religion numbering millions

5. only necessary to _____ eagerness and we'll fool them

6. not even a _____ of interest in the subject

7. a veritable _____ where work is concerned

8. amused by the _____ of Thurber's perceptive story

9. having _____ for his error with repeated signs of goodwill

10. the simple, _____ lines of the fashion collection

11. awesome creation, the _____ of all eyes at its unveiling

12. the practiced _____ of the detective as he elicits information

13. no longer on the _____ and proudly independent

14. a role which calls for an experienced _____

15. impossible to _____ so fine a reputation overnight

Exercise II. Analogies. Complete each analogy with the best pair possible. Remember to clarify the given relationship first, *before* you begin hunting the answer.

_____ 1. genre : Gothic ::
    (a) bacchanal : saturnalia
    (b) theosophy : religion
    (c) disposition : mercurial
    (d) somnolence : drowsiness
    (e) sequence : order

_____ 2. nemesis : jinx ::
    (a) bane : travesty
    (b) animation : quiet
    (c) coercion : force
    (d) verity : falsehood
    (e) solon : ruler

_____ 3. dim : stygian ::
    (a) smelly : rank
    (b) rococo : elaborate
    (c) wary : cautious
    (d) primeval : primitive
    (e) weak : invincible

_____ 4. books : bibliophile ::
    (a) stamps : stampophile
    (b) Germany : Anglophile
    (c) cuisine : musician
    (d) philanthropist : business
    (e) French : Francophile

_____ 5. classic : rococo ::
    (a) comedic : farcical
    (b) complimentary : disparaging
    (c) divine : nice
    (d) nervous : tense
    (e) saturnine : dour

_____ 6. dupe : credulous ::
    (a) satirist : tragic
    (b) Prometheus : inventive
    (c) anthropologist : dull
    (d) Zeus : truckling
    (e) protagonist : pitiful

_____ 7. episode : saga ::
    (a) comedy : lampoon
    (b) cathedral : St. Patrick's
    (c) Gothic : novel
    (d) Norman Conquest : Dark Ages
    (e) World War I : Boer War

_____ 8. somnolence : yawn ::
    (a) burlesque : laughter
    (b) archetype : prototype
    (c) deception : wile
    (d) stigma : brand
    (e) exhortation : misery

_____ 9. satirist : words ::
  (a) leadership : mentor
  (b) diplomat : coercion
  (c) victor : credibility
  (d) professor : position
  (e) philosopher : wisdom

_____ 10. mire : entanglement ::
  (a) sham : verity
  (b) animus : motion
  (c) allegory : animal
  (d) lampoon : ridicule
  (e) redress : refinement

Exercise III. Find the Oddball. Select the one word in each group that does not fit with the others in meaning. (Note: Words in a group may not be synonyms but members of a larger category, e.g., architectural terms.)

_____ 1. (a) dour   (b) gloomy   (c) omnipresent   (d) saturnine   (e) heavy

_____ 2. (a) archenemy   (b) archrival   (c) archetype   (d) duplicity   (e) archangel

_____ 3. (a) deity   (b) divine   (c) theology   (d) pantheon   (e) heavenly

_____ 4. (a) dishonor   (b) laud   (c) brand   (d) stigmatize   (e) mark

_____ 5. (a) disclaim   (b) intimate   (c) hint   (d) suggest   (e) imply

_____ 6. (a) allegory   (b) parody   (c) travesty   (d) lampoon   (e) farce

_____ 7. (a) comedy   (b) protagonist   (c) tragedy   (d) baroque   (e) antagonist

_____ 8. (a) engender   (b) ingenuous   (c) genius   (d) gene   (e) germane

_____ 9. (a) flourish   (b) burgeon   (c) nursery   (d) sprout   (e) grow

_____ 10. (a) bacchanal   (b) solon   (c) mercurial   (d) cupidity   (e) Junoesque

_____ 11. (a) nemesis   (b) pretense   (c) sham   (d) deception   (e) feigning

_____ 12. (a) bonus   (b) beneficial   (c) benevolent   (d) bond   (e) bonhomie

_____ 13. (a) entice   (b) lure   (c) whim   (d) beguile   (e) tempt

_____ 14. (a) assert   (b) affirm   (c) assist   (d) declare   (e) aver

_____ 15. (a) verse   (b) vestments   (c) divert   (d) versatile   (e) diversify

Exercise IV. Antonyms. From the choices offered, select an antonym for each word or phrase.

coerce	denouement	wary	abutted
evince	verify	nurture	free verse
invincible	animated	narcissism	somnolence
gibe	brevity	cupidity	

_____ 1. to discourage or inhibit growth or progress

_____ 2. to hide or disguise

_____ 3. separated

_____ 4. compliment, praise

_____ 5. foolhardy, rash

_____ 6. generosity

_____ 7. to deny or refute

_____ 8. sluggish, dull

_____ 9. prologue

_____ 10. easily conquered

_____ 11. length

_____ 12. to encourage or request politely

_____ 13. insomnia

_____ 14. concern for others

_____ 15. metered rhyme

Exercise V. Fill-ins. Select the most appropriate word from the choices offered, based on clues in context. The word form may need changing.

exhort	redress	truckle	crux
perpetrate	baroque	cant	flay
fiat	ethereal	mentor	anthropomorphic

1. Some rooms are interestingly furnished with a few _____ pieces among furniture of simpler, plainer design.

2. Refusing to comply with an authoritarian decree, the rebellious mob ignored their dictator's _____.

3. The Siamese cat from across the street _____ to Marigold in the most subservient way, meowing pathetically as he approaches.

4. Hidden in the dark hold of the steamship, the stowaway listened to the _____ of the sailors but learned little from their jargon.

5. _____ by her harsh criticism, I went to the woods to think over her words.

6. When we counted the fish in our aquarium, we found that Marigold had most likely _____ another wily theft.

7. Some readers prefer that books be faithful records of real life, but Jan and I enjoy _____ characters like Hazel, Fiver, and Kehaar in *Watership Down*.

8. A respected _____ as well as a friend, my uncle Alan is a frequent, welcome visitor in our house.

9. Where I work this summer is not as important as my boss and my fellow employees are. They are the _____ of the situation for me.

10. A magnetic and dynamic speaker, Abraham Lincoln _____ his countrymen to _____ the wrongs of slavery with abolition as the first step.

11. Jan tried to capture the _____ beauty of sunrise over the lake but said that her skill with paint on canvas was inadequate.

The Incredible Hunk
PREFIXES THAT GIVE MEANING

This is the second time around for a few of these prefixes. Remember Unit I? We repeat, because the brief group of letters called a prefix really is an incredible hunk. A prefix may give positive or negative meaning to a word. It can indicate size, place in time or space, number— even specific information such as *orth-,* meaning *right or straight.* Knowledge of prefixes plus intelligent use of context often give you the meaning of a word you've never seen before.

Positive Prefixes

1. **Bene-** and **bon-**   **good, well**
   A *benediction* is a blessing, literally meaning *good speech.*
   A *bonbon* is a delicious chocolate- or fondant-coated candy.
      (Refer to roots, List 2.)

2. **Eu-**   **good, well**
   The *euphony* (sweet, pleasing sound) of her voice appeals to every listener.
   His eloquent funeral *eulogy* profoundly affected the audience.

3. **Pro-**   **for, in favor of, forward**
   His work with the *pro-liberal* cause gained wide recognition.
   Mike's *proclivity* for sweets led to cavities in his teeth.
   The modern world believes in *progress.*

Negative Prefixes

1. **A-**   **no, not**
   Twain's "mysterious stranger" was an *amoral* youth without a sense of right or wrong.
   An *atypical* high jump differs from the normal, expected jump.
   His *apathy* toward schoolwork is probably a form of "senioritis."

2. **Anti-, ant-**   **against, opposite**
   Her idea is the *antithesis* (direct opposite) of mine.
   You'll need an immediate *antidote* (remedy to counteract bad effects) for that poison.
   Helen's *antipathy* (hatred, strong dislike) toward snakes is obvious.
   Antarctic (region of the South Pole, opposite of the arctic, North Pole) wild life is a
      fascinating study.

3. **Counter-, contra-**   **against, opposing**
   A successful *counterattack* wiped out the enemy.
   Those statistics *contradict* commonly held beliefs.
   His *contrary* nature leads him into frequent arguments.

4. **Dif-, dis-**   **negative, not**
   Although twins, Jan and I *differ* with each other often.
   Jan was *distraught* when she thought she'd lost the car keys.
   Her *dismay* changed to joy when she found the keys.

5. **For-**   **against, away**
   Andy will *forgo* (renounce, give up) the egg hunt in favor of an Easter party.
   She *forbade* her son to swim alone.
   Naturally, athletes agree to *forsake* smoking in order to remain healthy.

6. **In-, il-, im-, ir-**   **not**

The *infidel* (unbeliever) knew better than to attack the shrine.
An *illiterate* person cannot read or write.
His *impassive* expression revealed nothing.
Whistling during a sermon would be *irreligious* behavior.

7. **Non-, un-**   **not**

Gandhi exhibited *nonviolent* resistance.
A *nonentity* is a nobody—someone seeming to lack personality.
Her *unfeigned* (genuine, not pretended) approval was shown by the magnificent prize she awarded to the winner.

8. **Ob-, of-, op-**   **against, opposing**

Sally announced her *objections* loudly.
The *offensive* (or *opposing*) team has impressive tackling skills.

9. **Mal-, mis-**   **bad, wrong**

A *malcontent* is always stirring up trouble.
Misbehavior comes naturally to Andy when he's tired.
Someone who dislikes mankind is a *misanthrope*.

Prefixes of Size or Amount

1. **Macro-**   **big, large**

Macroeconomics concerns economic systems, not one sector of the economy.
Universe is a synonym for *macrocosm*.

2. **Micro-, min-**   **small**

A *microcosm* is a tiny segment of the world representative of the larger whole.
Antique dollhouse *miniatures* appeal to modern collectors.

3. **Pan-, panto-, omni-**   **all, entire**

A *panacea* is a universal cure-all.
The Greek *pantheon* included dozens of different gods and goddesses.
The old Roman *pantomime* featured one dancer with a narrative chorus. (Now means *all mime*.)
Unlike most carnivorous cats, Marigold is *omnivorous;* she especially likes the blend of meat and vegetables in Mexican tacos.

Prefixes of Number

Number prefixes were covered in Unit I, "What You Already Know." They are briefly listed here as memory joggers.

half	hemi-, demi-, semi-, med-	**ten**	dec-, deca-
one	uni-, mono-, sol-	**twelve**	duodec-, dodeca-
one and a half	sesqui-	**hundred**	cent-, hect-, hecato-
two	di-, bi-, du-, duo-, diplo-	**thousand**	milli-, kilo-
three	tri-, ter-	**ten thousand**	myria-
four	quadr-, tetr-	**million**	meg-, mega-
five	quinque-, quint-, penta-	**first**	arch-, prim-, prin-, proto-
six	sex-, hexa-	**both**	ambi-, amphi-
seven	sept-, hepta-	**equal**	equi-, iso-, par-
eight	oct-, octa-, octo-	**few**	oligo-, pauci-
nine	nona-, novem-, ennea-	**many**	multi-, poly-, myria-

Remember also the number *suffixes,* **-teen** (and ten) and **-ty** (times ten).

Prefixes Indicating Time (Sometimes Place)

1. **Ante-, anti-**   **before**
   Those Roman artifacts *antedate* (go before in time) Julius Caesar.
   Anticipation is half the joy of birthdays or holidays.
   The intimate *anteroom* (small room leading to, or coming just before, a larger main room) was ornately decorated.
2. **Ex-**   **former**
   Often it is difficult for *ex-convicts* to find jobs.
   My aunt's *ex-husband* continues to visit us frequently.
3. **Fore-**   **before**
   The old proverb says, "*Forewarned* is *forearmed*."
   Can you *foresee* any difficulty?
4. **Pre-**   **before**
   We should *predetermine* the desired color before mixing our paint.
   Mozart was *predestined* by his genius for musical fame.
   The PSAT, or *preliminary* SAT exam, is composed of ex–SAT questions.
5. **Post-**   **after**
   Twain's novelette, "The Mysterious Stranger," was published *posthumously* (after his death).
   When I *postpone* homework, I begin to worry about it.
   Postpartum care refers to the care of a mother after child delivery.

Using the Prefixes (Part 1)

Review Words Using Prefixes (Part 1)

benediction	antipathy	illiterate	macroeconomics
bonbon	antarctic	impassive	macrocosm
euphony	counterattack	irreligious	microcosm
eulogy	contradict	nonviolent	miniatures
pro-liberal	contrary	nonentity	panacea
proclivity	differ	unfeigned	pantheon
progress	distraught	objection	pantomime
amoral	dismay	offensive	omnivorous
atypical	forgo	opposing	antedate
apathy	forbade	malcontent	anticipation
antithesis	forsake	misbehavior	anteroom
antidote	infidel	misanthropist	
	ex-convicts	predestined	
	ex-husband	predetermine	
	forewarned	preliminary	
	forearmed	posthumously	
	foresee	postpone	
		postpartum	

Exercise I. Antonyms. Clues on the left will point to the desired antonym on the right. Each dash indicates a missing letter. The first one is shown as an example.

CLUE	ANTONYM
1. do on time or ahead of time	post *pone*
2. following, coming after	pre _ _ m _ _ _ _ _

3. prenatal   post _ _ _ _ _ _

4. postdate   pre _ _ _ _ or

                     ante _ _ _ _

5. dread   anti _ _ p _ _ _

6. universe   micro _ _ _ _

7. many, a great number   pauci _ _

8. huge, extremely large   minia _ _ _ _

9. literate   il _ _ _ _ r _ _ _

10. defense   of _ _ _ _ _

Exercise II. Fill-ins. Add the missing items in the chart.

	PREFIX	WORD	DEFINITION
1.	mis-	_____	someone who dislikes or hates people
2.	_____	object (v.)	_____
3.	un-	_____	genuine, not pretended
4.	_____	impassive	
5.	fore	_____	to look into the future, expect
6.	_____	pantheon	_____
7.	_____	_____	equally skilled with both hands
8.	_____	forsake	_____
9.	non-	_____	someone without significance, a nobody
10.	_____	omniscient	_____

Exercise III. Definitions. Use your knowledge of roots and prefixes to define the words.

1. bonny (adj.) _____

2. discredit (v.) _____

3. invalidate (v.) _____

4. irrational (adj.) _____

5. atheism (n.) _____

6. eurythmic (adj.) _____

7. proclivity (n.) _____

8. antithesis (n.) _____

9. apolitical (adj.) _____

10. counteract (v.) _____

Exercise IV. Find the Oddball. In each word group, one word is *pretending* to have a number prefix, but it is an impostor. Select the oddball by writing its letter in the blank beside each number.

_____ 1. (a) pentagon   (b) pentathlon   (c) quinquereme   (d) quinine   (e) quintet

_____ 2. (a) semantic   (b) demitasse   (c) hemisphere   (d) semifinal   (e) demigod

_____ 3. (a) decalogue   (b) decant   (c) decathlon   (d) December   (e) decennial

_____ 4. (a) monotone   (b) unit   (c) monetary   (d) solitary   (e) unilateral

_____ 5. (a) octopus   (b) October   (c) octogenarian   (d) octave   (e) oculist

_____ 6. (a) triad   (b) trip   (c) tertiary   (d) trimester   (e) triple

_____ 7. (a) equestrian   (b) equal   (c) equitable   (d) inequity   (e) unequal

_____ 8. (a) principal   (b) primitive   (c) protozoa   (d) prim   (e) archetype

_____ 9. (a) centennial   (b) hecatomb   (c) hector   (d) hectometer   (e) century

_____ 10. (a) November   (b) novena   (c) ennead   (d) nonagon   (e) novel

_____ 11. (a) multitude   (b) polymath   (c) multiply   (d) myriad   (e) mulct

_____ 12. (a) septet   (b) heptavalent   (c) hepatoma   (d) September   (e) heptagon

_____ 13. (a) quadruped   (b) squadron   (c) quadrangle   (d) tetralogy   (e) tetrarchy

_____ 14. (a) sexton   (b) sextuplets   (c) hexagon   (d) hexameter   (e) sextet

_____ 15. (a) omnipresent   (b) pandemic   (c) pantomime   (d) ominous   (e) panacea

Exercise V. Missing Prefixes. English would be hilarious—but not very clear—without prefixes. In the following story, underline the thirty-two words that are missing their prefixes. Then write the correct words on the lines at the end of the tale.

"Oh, I am so cited!" Jan said, with a cipatory smile on her face. "I've been looking ward to this party for ages."

Sently, Dad strode to the room, a frown wrinkling his head. "Well, Jan, you have ritated me gain," he toned solemnly. "You knew I was posed to your driving downtown less you had a(n) perienced driver side you. There'll be no party for you tonight."

Comprehending, Jan blinked in fusion. "But I didn't!" she torted quickly, may written all over her features. "And I ject to being cused!"

"Then who stroyed the front fender?" Dad plied.

Traught, Jan shook her head and turned to look out the window at their mobile. Standing, plus a grin, placed the fusion as she cognized the car. "Dad," she said slowly, poning the moment of truth in her joyment, "that's not our car. It's actly like ours, but it longs to Aunt Dolly. You made a teensy take."

_____

_____

_____

_____

Prefixes Determining Place/Relationship

1. **Com-, co-, col-, con-, cor-** and
   syn-, syl-, sym-, sys-, sy-   **with, together**

   A *complex* process *compresses* many layers into a wafer-thin chip.

   Let's *coordinate* our jobs, *collaborating* on the work whenever possible.

   Our leaving on time is *contingent* upon your prompt arrival.

   His expert *synthesis* (*combination* into a *coherent* whole) combined the various parts of a *complex* speech into a set of simpler ideas we could understand.

   The *symmetrical* design of Greek temples appeals to those who like regularity and order.

2. **Amphi-, circum-, peri-**   around

They enjoyed the perfect acoustics in the ancient Greek *amphitheater* at Epidaurus.
   (Note: Remember that *amphi-* also means *both,* as in *amphibian.*)
Circumnavigating the globe in a small yacht sounds exciting, but risky, too.
Up went the submarine's *periscope* to inspect the neighboring seascape.

3. **Epi-, ecto-**   on, outer, outside

The *epidermis* (outer skin layer) of an elephant looks like heavy gray leather.
In the *epilogue,* the author explained the main events in her character's lives for the five-
   year period following the story.
Unlike the round endormorph, the slender *ectomorph* is a lightweight.

4. **Ab-, abs-** and **apo-, ap-**   from, away, out, down

A cat with many *aberrations* (actions straying from right or normal) in behavior,
   Marigold gobbles all her food quickly like a dog.
Absconding with (taking away illegally) company funds proved to be the accountant's
   downfall.
Although attributed to Charlemagne, many of "his" famous sayings may be *apocryphal*
   (of doubtful authorship).
Future historians will judge at which point twentieth-century life reached its *apogee*
   (highest point, culmination).

5. **E-, ex-, ec-, ef-**   out, away

The old steam engine *emitted* clouds of steam.
To *exhale* is the opposite of to inhale.
His *eccentric* (away from normal) behavior attracts much attention.
The new prison governor *effected* (brought about) many reforms.
Old designs in the stone had been *effaced* (worn away, erased) by weather and time.

6. **De-** and **cata-**   away, down, negative

Anne Boleyn, second wife of Henry VIII, was *decapitated* at age twenty-nine. (Maybe
   it's apocryphal, but she is supposed to have said, "My neck is very slender," as she
   placed her head upon the block.)
Deciduous trees shed their leaves each autumn.
Oscar Wilde's sensational London trial *defamed* him for the rest of his short life.
Catacombs, with their natural recesses for tombs, form many underground cemeteries.

7. **Se-**   away, apart

I always hunt a *secluded* place to study for exams.
At our vet's office, well animals are *segregated* from sick ones.

8. **A-, ad-, af-, ag-, al-, an-, ap-, as-, at-**
   and **ob-, oc-, of-, op-**   to, toward, against

Please *adhere* (stick) to school rules during all trips.
He was *alleged* (avowed to be) guilty even before the trial.
Annealed (toughened, strengthened) in the fire of war, the character of many Indian chiefs
   seemed hard as steel.
I was breathless after running the new *obstacle* course.
Offensive weapons such as claws, talons, and quills are part of nature's armor for certain
   animals.
Andy is *opposed* to the idea of homework.

9. **In-, il-, im-, ir-** and **endo-, en-, em-**   in, into, within

A tiny *incision* was made to remove the mole on her arm.
Twain's writings *illuminate* mid-American life in the nineteenth century.
The tumor was *irradiated* after its partial removal by surgery.
The thyroid and pituitary are two *endocrine* glands of the body.
Carrie can *empathize* with anyone who's lost something special, as she remembers how
   she felt when she lost her watch.

10. **Intro-, intra-**   **in, among, within**
   Introductory is often a synonym for preliminary.
   After her operation, Millie was put on an *intravenous* (entering the body by way of a vein)
      feeding system.
   Intramural (within the system, e.g., between class groups) games are normally scheduled
      after classes.

11. **Ana-, re-, retro-**   **back, over, again**
   Anastrophe is the inverted order of words in a phrase or sentence to achieve a special
      effect; e.g., going to the store for the first time he was—and excited about it, too.
   A *reversal* of word order is another way to explain anastrophe.
   Hal's behavior *retrogressed* (or *regressed*) after he was released from the asylum.

12. **Inter-**   **between**
   "Interrupt me during my speech," Jan warned the cast, "and I'll forget my lines!"
   She *interjected* her opinion before I had finished speaking.

13. **Tele-**   **far, distant**
   Telepathy (communication of thoughts without speech) between sympathetic individuals
      remains a mystery to science.
   Telecourse is the modern word for a study course taught by television.

14. **Sub-, suc-, suf-, sug-, sum-, sup-, sus-**
   and **hyp-, hypo-**   **beneath, under**
   Dolphins and whales *submerge* below water for long periods.
   A blush *suffused* her face with color as Jan stood up to speak.
   Witnesses are formally *summoned* to appear in court.
   A *hypodermic* needle is inserted under the skin.
   A victim of *hypochondria* focuses on ailments real and imagined.

15. **Over-, super-, ultra-, hyper-**   **over, beyond** (sometimes
                                                                  excessive, exceeding)
   Send any *overabundance* of chocolate chip cookies to my house.
   For a few years, my studying will have to *supersede* other things.
   Ultraconservative measures are needed to preserve endangered wildlife.
   A *hyperactive* student often has difficulty in school.

16. **Exter-, extra-, extro-**   **outside, beyond**
   External forces sometimes control our lives.
   Extramundane means outside the normal, material world.
   The shy introvert often longs to be the outgoing *extrovert*.

17. **Trans-, tra-**   **across**
   Modern, exciting fabrics are often created by *transferring* ancient designs to new
      materials.
   Astronomers understand the *trajectory* of Halley's comet well enough to predict its
      return. (Roughly every seventy-five years. It appeared in 1835 when Mark Twain was
      born, again in 1910 when he died, and most recently in 1985–86.)

18. **Dia-, di- and per-**   **through, between**
   Dialogue, diameter, and *diagonal* are just a few words sharing the same prefix.
   A *diaphanous* gown is ethereal in effect, floating delicately around the form of its wearer.
      (Note: Often, you can see through something diaphanous.)
   As Mom fixed spaghetti, the smell of garlic *permeated* the house.

More Specific Prefixes

1. **Alter-** and **hetero-**   **different, other**
   Plan B is our *alternative* strategy.
   A *heterodox* opinion differs from an orthodox, accepted opinion.

2. **Homo-** **same**
   Homogeneous grouping puts like individuals together.
   Homonyms sound alike and are spelled alike but have different meanings, e.g., *quail* (v.), to shrink in terror, and *quail* (n.), a species of bird.

3. **Meta-** **change, beyond**
   Andy's *metamorphosis* from grubby kid to scrubbed student amazed us all.
   One stage of meiosis and mitosis is *metaphase,* when the chromosomes change their arrangement.
   [Remember *prophase* (early stage) and *anaphase* (later)?]

4. **Para-, par-** **beside, variation**
   Any exceptionally clear pattern or archetype which may stand as a model for others is a *paradigm.*
   A *paradise* is any heavenly, perfect place.
   Paralegal and *paramedical* assistants aid the professionals.

5. **Orth-** **right, straight**
   The *orthodontist*'s goal is to straighten teeth and align them correctly in the mouth.
   The correction or prevention of skeletal deformities is called *orthopedics.*

6. **Wri-, wro-** **make, work, twist, wring**
   An OE and Ger. prefix, **wri-, wro-** begins many words basic to our language: *wring, wrench, wrist, wrinkle, writhe, wrong, wreath, wrath, wrought,* and *wry.* It is the root in *playwright, cartwright,* and *wheelwright,* which refer to people who make plays, carts, and wheels.
   Mom's *wrath* (extreme anger) was something to behold when she realized that Andy had lost her car keys.
   Carrie's *wry* (twisted out of shape) expression made us wonder if she liked the tart apple.
   The critic's *wry* (ironic, grimly humorous) remarks made the audience laugh.

Using the Prefixes (Part 2)

Review Words Using Prefixes (Part 2)

complex	exhale	empathize	hyperactive
compress	eccentric	introductory	external
coordinate	effect (v.)	intravenous	extramundane
collaborate	efface	intramural	extrovert
contingent	decapitate	anastrophe	transfer
synthesis	deciduous	reversal	trajectory
symmetrical	defame	retrogress	dialogue
combine	catacombs	regress (v.)	diameter
coherent	seclude	interrupt	diagonal
amphitheater	segregate	interject	diaphanous
circumnavigate	adhere	telepathy	permeate
periscope	allege	telecourse	alternative (adj.)
epidermis	anneal	submerge	heterodox
epilogue	obstacle	suffuse	homogeneous
ectomorph	offensive	summon	homonym
aberration	oppose	hypodermic	metamorphosis
abscond	incision	hypochondria	metaphase
apocryphal	illuminate	overabundance	paradigm
apogee	irradiate	supersede	paradise
emit	endocrine	ultraconservative	paralegal

paramedical	wrist	playwright	wrinkle
orthodontist	writhe	cartwright	wrong
orthopedics	wrath	wheelwright	wreath
wring	wry	wrench	wrought

Yes, a *big* list. You probably know over half of these words already, but don't stew over the strangers. Hitch each prefix to a word that you *do* know as a memory device. The "must" words are taught again in later lessons.

Exercise I. Fill-ins. Add the missing items to the following chart.

	PREFIX	ROOT	WORD	DEFINITION
1.	_____	fame	_____	to destroy someone's reputation
2.	_____	greg	_____	to set one group apart from another
3.	_____	_____	empathy	_____
4.	_____	mit	_____	to give out, give off
5.	homo	_____	_____	similar in type or kind
6.	_____	ge	_____	highest point, culmination
7.	_____	_____	adhere	_____
8.	trans	_____	_____	to move from one place to another
9.	_____	digm	_____	model, archetype
10.	_____	_____	anachronism	_____

Exercise II. Antonyms. Change the prefix, and voilà! an opposite word. Match these absurdly easy antonyms.

____ 1. **heterodox**

____ 2. **ectoderm**

____ 3. **submerge**

____ 4. **prologue**

____ 5. **exclude**

____ 6. **irrefutable**

____ 7. **mundane**

____ 8. **inject**

____ 9. **intramural**

____ 10. **symmetry**

____ 11. **thesis**

____ 12. **analysis**

(a) extramundane

(b) asymmetry

(c) reject

(d) emerge

(e) extramural

(f) orthodox

(g) include

(h) epilogue

(i) synthesis

(j) endoderm

(k) refutable

(l) antithesis

Exercise III. Analogies. Complete each analogy with the best pair possible.

_____ 1. disaster : catastrophe ::
    (a) malformation : limb   (d) heterodoxy : religion
    (b) prophase : anaphase   (e) introversion : reversion
    (c) permeation : seepage

_____ 2. submarine : periscope ::
    (a) car : sedan   (d) tank : turret
    (b) turtle : amphibian   (e) ship : deck
    (c) slide : microscope

_____ 3. interjection : between ::
    (a) prologue : middle   (d) monologue : throughout
    (b) prelude : above   (e) epilogue : end
    (c) rejection : prior

_____ 4. apocryphal : doubtful ::
    (a) eccentric : odd   (d) interdependent : aware
    (b) wry : straight   (e) maladroit : artful
    (c) orthodox : religious

_____ 5. orthopedist : skeleton ::
    (a) pharmacist : people   (d) orthodontist : teeth
    (b) astronomer : moon   (e) internist : physician
    (c) accountant : papers

Exercise IV. Add-a-Prefix. To the Latin root *jac, jact, ject* (meaning *to throw, cast,* or *hurl*), add the necessary prefix to create the word defined on each numbered line. (Some of these are tough. Don't hesitate to ask for help.)

	PREFIX +	ROOT	=	WORD	DEFINITION
1.	_____ +	ject	=	_____	to oppose firmly, disapprove
2.	_____ +	ject(ory)	=	_____	the path of an object
3.	_____ +	ject	=	_____	to refuse to accept
4.	_____ +	ject	=	_____	to throw or toss out, usually with some force
5.	_____ +	ject(ure)	=	_____	a guess or surmise
6.	_____ +	jac(ulation)	=	_____	an impromptu, heartfelt remark
7.	_____ +	ject	=	_____	to cast into the future, make a prediction
8.	_____ +	ject(ive)	=	_____	a describing or modifying word
9.	_____ +	ject(ed)	=	_____	depressed in spirit, downcast
10.	_____ +	ject	=	_____	downcast, sad, woeful

Exercise V. Fill-ins. Select the most appropriate word from the choices offered, based on clues in context. (This is a hard exercise again—but you can get help from a friend, parent, or teacher.)

contingent	effected	writhed	diaphanous
correlation	effaced	wrought	metamorphosis
aberration	alleged	suffused	annealing

1. The outcome of our game against East High is _____ upon our players' performance more than anything else.

2. The _____ perpetrator of the crime said that he was innocent.

3. Her normally pale complexion _____ with color, Shelley _____ on the floor as laughter overcame her.

4. The (n.)_____ (v.)_____ upon the nymph Daphne as she fled from Apollo's embrace caused her to change into a laurel tree.

5. After Mom locked him in his room, Andy _____ a rapid escape through his open window onto the porch roof.

6. Time has _____ many handsome murals on interior as well as exterior walls, leaving us to guess at their former beauty.

7. As a freshman, I discovered a direct _____ between the quality of my class notes and my score on quizzes.

8. The heating and cooling process called _____ serves to soften glass or steel, making it tougher as it cools and less brittle.

9. "A bit of a(n) _____ for me," Mom confessed as she stroked her new gown, a filmy, _____ creation resembling gossamer.

Note: Congratulate yourself if you survived this lesson. It is long—and difficult in spots—but you need this knowledge *early* in your vocabulary study. You will use it over and over in the subsequent lessons. Now, how about treating yourself to an ice-cream cone as a reward??

An Eldritch Cry
ADJECTIVES, THE DESCRIBING WORDS

In Context. Before studying the definitions, try reasoning out the meaning of each word, using context as your guide.

1. Jan says that her *astringent* lotion tightens facial skin and dries excess oil.

    Key: Synonyms   **Astringent** means _____.

2. Andy's new friend came into our kitchen, *"brazen* as you please," said Mom, "and announced that it was his birthday so I should bake him a cake."

    Key: Logic   **Brazen** means _____.

3. Mom usually explains things slowly and carefully, as she deplores a *brusque* approach.

    Key: Opposite phrase   **Brusque** means _____.

4. A woman of *catholic* tastes, Aunt Dolly rummages happily in hardware stores, spends hours in art museums, and enjoys hiking on weekends.

    Key: Logic   **Catholic** means _____.

5. "We haven't a *diffident* person in this family," Dad remarked. "No one lacks confidence around here, even when he's wrong!"

    Key: Definition   **Diffident** means _____.

6. "That's really creepy," Andy said, shivering as he listened to the *eldritch* moan of Gollum in the TV version of *The Hobbit*.

    Key: Synonym   **Eldritch** means _____.

7. Dad and I did errands in an *expedient* manner, as he wanted, but that allowed me no time to window-shop.

    Key: Logic   **Expedient** means _____.

8. In spite of repeated scolding and punishment, Marigold has proved *incorrigible*. She insists on fishing in our aquarium.

    Key: Logic   **Incorrigible** means _____.

9. As we divided chores for opening the lake cabin, Dad said that it was *incumbent* on Jan and me to clean windows and floors.

    Key: Logic   **Incumbent** means _____.

10. "Not exactly a *lithe*, quick devil, is he?" Jan said, grinning at the somnolent hippo in his pool at the zoo.

    Keys: Opposing idea, near synonym   **Lithe** means _____.

11. I've formed only one definite plan for college—to major in science. Which particular science is still *nebulous*.

        Keys: Antonym, logic   **Nebulous** means _____ .

12. Our parents like the *pastoral,* slow-paced life of summer at the lake, but Jan and I get restless after a month away from the city.

        Keys: Contrast, logic   **Pastoral** means _____ .

13. "That's a *plausible* theory," the chem teacher agreed when I explained my experiment, "but we'll need scientific proof of your beliefs."

        Key: Logic   **Plausible** means _____ .

14. Mom barred the door to the cabin. "Now that it's spotless, I hate to let anyone ruin the *pristine* appearance with actual living!"

        Keys: Synonym, logic   **Pristine** means _____ .

15. "Big guys are fine," the coach told our football team, "but the *requisite* skills for my teams happen to be determination and cooperation."

        Key: Logic   **Requisite** means _____ .

16. The most difficult part for my spitfire sister Carrie was playing the role of a *stolid* servant who spoke little and moved woodenly.

        Key: Contrasting idea,
           example   **Stolid** means _____ .

Word Study

Adjectives make sentences both specific and colorful. An *ancient car,* for instance, gives a more definite picture than just a *car.* A *dilapidated car* is even more specific, giving the reader or listener further information. While general statements are nearly always boring, specific ones are interesting. When you write, try to be precise. Rather than flooding your material with descriptive words, select carefully and let a *few* well-chosen adjectives carry the paragraph.

1. **astringent** (ə-'strin-jənt) adj.   Severe, drily austere, as *an astringent remark;* drawing together soft tissues, as a styptic pencil dries facial cuts; puckery, like a sour lemon; from L. *ad + stringere,* to bind fast (tightly)

The critic's *astringent* comments on the play were humorous but extremely negative.

Relatives: *astringent* (n.), *astringently*
Synonyms: *dry, tonic; puckery*

2. **brazen** ('brāz-ᵊn) adj.   Unduly bold, forward, or "pushy"; having the color or sound of brass; from OE *braes,* brass

Newscaster of the Trojan War, Stentor was described by the blind poet Homer in *The Iliad:* "Great-hearted Stentor with *brazen* voice, who could shout as loud as fifty other men."

Relatives: *brazen* (v.), as *to brazen it out* (be boldly defiant); *brazenly, brazenness*
Synonyms: *impudent, insolent*
Antonyms: *timid, timorous, diffident, shy*

3. **brusque** ('brəsk) adj.   Abruptly short and blunt of speech or manner (even rude); from L. *bruscus,* butcher's broom

We were put off at first by the manager's *brusque* manner, but we learned later that he was merely a man in a hurry.

Relatives: *brusquely, brusqueness*
Synonyms: *curt, bluff, terse*
Antonyms: *unctuous, bland, voluble*

4. **catholic** ('kath-[ə-]lik) adj.   All-encompassing, comprehensive (in interests or tastes), universal; referring to the old, undivided Christian church; when capitalized, means Roman Catholic; from Gr. *katholikos,* universal, general

Ben Franklin, a man of *catholic* interests, bent his mind to writing and printing, town and federal government, optometry, the nature of electricity, and international diplomacy.

Relatives: *catholically, catholicize, catholicity*
Synonyms: *comprehensive, broad, wide-ranging*
Antonyms: *narrow, limited, parochial, provincial*

5. **diffident** ('dif-ə-dent) adj.   Shy, withdrawn, and lacking confidence, hesitant; from L. *dis + fidere,* to trust

Determined to get the job, Bob masked his normal *diffident* personality with a firm handshake and an outwardly confident manner.

Relatives: *diffidence* (n.), *diffidently*
Synonyms: *shy, reserved, unassertive*
Antonyms: *confident, bold, brazen*

6. **eldritch** ('el-drich) adj.   Weird, unnatural, and eerie; possibly from OE *elfrice,* fairy realm

As one of the witches in *Macbeth,* Carrie mastered an *eldritch* cackle that made our hair stand on end.

Synonyms: *weird, eerie, unearthly*

7. **expedient** (ik-'spēd-ē-ənt) adj.   Suitable, practical; opportunistic or advisable (but not necessarily admirable); from L. *ex + ped, pes,* foot

We hurled our luggage from the burning hotel, which was *expedient* under the circumstances but hard on the luggage.

Relatives: *expediency* (n.), *expediential, expediently*
Synonyms: *advisable, politic*
Antonym: *inexpedient*

8. **incorrigible** (['ˈ]in-'kȯr-ə-jə-bəl) adj.   Uncontrollable or uncorrectable, not manageable; determined; depraved or not reformable; from L. *in + corrigere,* to correct

The *incorrigible* behavior of many criminals ensures their return to prison.

Relatives: *incorrigibility, incorrigible* (n., person), *incorrigibly*
Synonyms: *uncontrollable, depraved, delinquent* (none exact)
Antonyms: *docile, amenable, complaisant, compliant, submissive*

9. **incumbent** (in-'kəm-bənt) adj.   Referring to a duty or obligation, used with *on;* from L. *in + cumbere,* to lie down

When I have house guests, it is *incumbent* on me to see that they have clean bedding and towels, plus a place to hang their clothes.

Relatives: *incumbent* (n., holder of an office); *incumbency*
Synonym: *obligatory*

10. **lithe** ('līth) adj.   Gracefully and easily flexible; easily bent; from L. *lentus,* slow, through OE *lithe,* gentle

Jan works to achieve the *lithe*, supple movements necessary for any serious ballet student.
Relatives: *lithely, litheness, lithesome (lissom)*
Antonyms: *rigid, inflexible*

11. **nebulous** ('neb-yə-ləs) adj.   Vague, unclear, indistinct; from L. *nebulosus*, misty
Andy wanted to take the bus home, but his *nebulous* ideas of bus stop locations led him down several wrong streets.
Relatives: *nebulously, nebulousness, nebula (galaxy)*
Synonyms: *indistinct, cloudy, vague*
Antonyms: *distinct, clear*

12. **pastoral** ('pas-t[ə-]rəl) adj.   Referring to the countryside or rural areas; peaceful, with a suggestion of innocence and simplicity; of a minister's (pastor's) job or duties; from L. *pastor*, herdsman
Turner is noted for his idyllic *pastoral* scenes of the English countryside.
Relatives: *pastor (clergyman), pastorally*
Synonyms: *rural, bucolic, idyllic*
Antonyms: *urban, metropolitan*

13. **plausible** ('plȯ-zə-bəl) adj.   Believable; from L. *plausibilis*, worthy of applause
Dad said, "I'm afraid that your reasons for coming home late are neither *plausible* nor acceptable."
Relatives: *plausibility, plausibly*
Synonyms: *credible, believable*
Antonyms: *implausible, incredible, unbelievable*

14. **pristine** ('pris-ˌtēn) adj.   Fresh and clean, pure and uncorrupted; from L. *pristinus*, early
An early riser, Dad appreciates the *pristine* glories of dawn.
Relative: *pristinely*
Antonyms: *impure* or *imperfect, tainted* (none exact)

15. **requisite** ('rek-wə-zət) adj.   Necessary or essential; from L. *requirere*, to seek or ask
Carrie will take any part in any play in order to learn the *requisite* acting skills for her future.
Relatives: *requisite (n.), prerequisite, requisition (v.)*
Synonyms: *essential, necessary, vital*
Antonyms: *nonessential, unnecessary*

16. **stolid** ('stäl-əd) adj.   Revealing little (or no) emotion; from L. *stolidus*, dull, stupid
The typical *stolid* facial expression of the old cigar store Indian statue probably helped to create a stereotype.
Relatives: *stolidly, stolidity*
Synonyms: *impassive, phlegmatic, unemotional*
Antonyn: *sensitive*

Root Study

Two of these roots are found in List 6 adjectives (**fid** and **string, strict**). The other two have contributed many vital words to English—words that you depend upon.

1. AGOG means lead or leader.
   demagogue—a leader who says what people want to hear, who identifies with popular causes and prejudices
   synagogue—a Jewish house of worship
   pedagogue—instructor, teacher; originally, a Greek slave who led children to school

2. FID means faith or trust.
   fidelity—faithfulness
   infidel—one who does not share a set of particular beliefs, especially religious beliefs
   confidential—shared between friends or associates as a secret is shared; referring to any information given on trust

3. GREG means flock or herd.
   gregarious—enjoying the company of others; sociable, convivial, friendly
   congregate—to gather together or crowd together
   egregious—highly noticeable in a negative way, as *an egregious error;* outstandingly bad

4. STRING and STRICT mean to tie or bind fast.
   constrict—to draw together closely, even uncomfortably, as *throat muscles constrict with nervousness;* to contract or squeeze; to inhibit
   stringent—strict, rigorous, or rigid, as *stringent rules at the academy;* also referring to credit strictness when money is scarce, as *a stringent budget*
   strictures—restrictions, limitations

Using the Words

List 6 Review

astringent	diffident	incumbent	plausible
brazen	eldritch	lithe	pristine
brusque	expedient	nebulous	requisite
catholic	incorrigible	pastoral	stolid

Exercise I. Fill-ins. Select the most appropriate word from List 6, based on clues in context.

1. a(n) _____ character, never revealing his emotions

2. careful listing of the _____ items for the lab experiment

3. a strangely _____ figure, hovering vaguely out of reach

4. wanting _____, not ridiculous, reasons for action

5. the graceful, _____ motions of a leaping gazelle

6. realized that it was _____ on me to give clear directions

7. heard in the night the _____ cry of a hoot owl

8. aware that her _____, hesitant manner lacked impact

9. rubbed us the wrong way with his _____ approach

10. a sour apple, nearly as _____ as some lemons

Exercise II. Synonyms. Each word on the left has *two* synonyms in the right-hand column. Enter both synonyms on the appropriate lines.

1. **pastoral** _____

   _____

2. **pristine** _____

   _____

3. **expedient** _____

   _____

4. **incorrigible** _____

   _____

5. **catholic** _____

   _____

6. **diffident** _____

   _____

7. **eldritch** _____

   _____

8. **astringent** _____

   _____

9. **brusque** _____

   _____

10. **brazen** _____

   _____

Choice of Synonyms

advisable
bucolic
dry
weird
forward
fresh
politic
bluff
puckery
unassertive
uncontrollable
shy
comprehensive
curt
rural
uncorrupted
insolent
delinquent
eerie
wide-ranging

Exercise III. Analogies. Complete each analogy with the best pair possible.

_____ 1. rabbi : synagogue ::
   (a) minister : pastor
   (b) reverend : board
   (c) instructor : camp
   (d) pedagogue : school
   (e) demagogue : market

_____ 2. dog : fidelity ::
   (a) cat : claws
   (b) cheetah : speed
   (c) puma : diffidence
   (d) giraffe : spots
   (e) mouse : stolidity

_____ 3. diffident : gregarious ::
   (a) requisite : necessary
   (b) nebulous : cloudy
   (c) specious : suspect
   (d) stolid : impervious
   (e) timorous : brazen

_____ 4. catholic : parochial ::
   (a) expedient : suitable
   (b) gregarious : convivial
   (c) incredulous : questioning
   (d) plausible : reasonable
   (e) open : restricted

_____ 5. repeated offender: incorrigible ::
  (a) impassive judge : stolid
  (b) awkward dancer : lithe
  (c) legal incumbent : defensible
  (d) nebulous theory : precise
  (e) astringent remark : weak

Exercise IV. Fill-Ins. Select the most appropriate word from the choices offered. Hint: Read all sentences quickly first and fill in the most obvious answers. Then work by the process of elimination.

expedient	**demagogue**	**astringent**	**infidel**
pristine	**egregious**	**incorrigible**	**brazen**
incumbent	**nebulous**		

Deliver me from . . .

—a guide dog for the blind who is _____.
                                        1

—a family room that must maintain a(n) _____ appearance at all times.
                                          2

—_____ criticism when I need encouragement.
     3

—people who feel it _____ on them to point out my faults.
                         4

—_____ directions that merely suggest the location of your house.
     5

—making such a(n) _____ blunder that everyone will think I'm a dodo.
                      6

—any false leader, the _____ who says only what people want to hear.
                           7

—the _____ clanging of my alarm before I'm ready to get up.
         8

—the wild-eyed _____ who kills for the sake of his cause.
                    9

—people who say, "The end justifies the means," to excuse doing the

_____ thing instead of what is right.
     10

Exercise V. Antonyms. Write an antonym or opposing phrase for each word.

1. **plausible** _____

2. **incorrigible** _____

3. **catholic** _____

4. **diffident** _____

5. **lithe** _____

6. **pastoral** _____

7. **pristine** _____

8. **requisite** _____

9. **stolid** _____

10. **stringent** _____

Exercise VI. Word Analysis.

1. The word _catholic_ (small _c_) is often confused with the word _parochial_, yet they are opposites. Why (or how) could this confusion have arisen? _____

_____

2. Originally, a pastoral poem concerned shepherds (pastors). No wonder *bucolic* is still a synonym; *boukolos* is Greek for cowherd. But now a work dealing with idyllic rural life can be termed *pastoral* or *bucolic*. Shakespeare's *As You Like It* is a pastoral play. What poems, stories, or plays do you know that could be called *pastoral?*

_____

_____

3. Latinate (or Greek) words are nearly always longer than Anglo-Saxon words. Try to think of shorter or simpler words for the following:*

LATINATE (OR GREEK)	ANGLO-SAXON/OTHER
astringent	_____
diffident	_____
requisite	_____
stringent	_____
pedagogue	_____
congregate	_____
catholic	_____
confident	_____
synagogue	_____

*Notice that your answers are rarely perfect synonyms, even though their meanings may be close. *That* is why we have so many words in the English language—each word with its connotations, or shades of meaning.

4. What is the appropriate tone for the following dialogue?

    Editor: You infidel! You dared to split an infinitive!

    Journalist: I can't bear to write "significantly to increase" when I could write "to significantly increase," sir. I just can't bear it!

    Editor: Maybe you're right. Don't let it go to your head.

_____

Question: Why is *infidel* a good choice of word in this context?

_____

Parlez-Vous Français? Absolument!

FRENCH WORDS COMMONLY USED IN ENGLISH

In Context. Before studying the definitions, try reasoning out the meaning of each word, using context as your guide.

1. "No more following the crowd," Jan announced firmly as she added the final touches to her outfit. "*Avant-garde* from now on," she added, as we eyed her unusual getup with misgivings.

    Keys: Contrasting phrase, logic   **Avant-garde** means _____ .

2. "It's an American hotel," Dad told us, "but they've hired a *concierge*. Wonderful fellow! He helped me to hire a car, got tickets for a play, and made dinner reservations for our group."

    Keys: Logic, partial definition   **Concierge** means _____ .

3. Mom staggered in the door. "An utter *debacle*," she said, collapsing into a chair. "Three messy road accidents along the way, and none of us on the road went anywhere for two hours."

    Key: Logic   **Debacle** means _____ .

4. Apparently tired of fighting each other, Marigold and the neighboring calico cat have reached a temporary *détente*. They merely hiss when they pass in the yard.

    Key: Contrasting phrases   **Détente** means _____ .

5. If I think of my cumulative school record as my *dossier,* it sounds more impressive.

    Key: Definition   **Dossier** means _____ .

6. Newspapers feature stories about government figures in the top *echelon,* and we rarely learn about the thousands of federal workers on lower levels.

    Key: Synonym   **Echelon** means _____ .

7. Wearily Jan tapped one bored heel on the weathered planks of our boat dock. "I'm drowning in *ennui,*" she moaned. "Where are all the people in the world?"

    Keys: Synonyms, logic   **Ennui** means _____ .

8. "The typical *entrepreneur* is a real go-getter," Mom commented. "Anyone eager to start and maintain a business can't be afraid of work."

    Key: Definition   **Entrepreneur** means _____ .

9. Nonchalant, cap tilted at a rakish angle, Dad approached his sailing lessons with an *insouciance* that belied his serious desire to become a competent sailor.

    Keys: Synonym, logic   **Insouciance** means _____ .

10. Every spring, our entire *ménage* shifts to the lake on weekends as everyone in the family prepares the cabin for summer living.

> Keys: Definition, logic   **Ménage** means _____.

11. "Don't you think that's a bit *outré*," Mom said, viewing Jan's latest outfit before school. "Avant-garde I understand, but that costume is bizarre."

> Key: Synonym   **Outré** means _____.

12. *Piqued* by Mom's criticism, Jan tossed her head defiantly and went out the door without a word.

> Key: Logic   **Pique** means _____.

13. Our English teacher explained the *précis* as a concise summary. "I will mark you down for wordiness," she warned, "and failure to include all of the vital facts."

> Key: Definition   **Précis** means _____.

14. Jan and I don't agree on everything, but our *rapport* as twins is obvious to all who know us.

> Keys: Logic, near synonym   **Rapport** means _____.

15. With three years of French behind her, Jan likes to toss phrases around. *"Quel sangfroid,"* she said admiringly as Indiana Jones coolly survived one life-threatening adventure after another in two thrilling movies.

> Keys: Near synonym, logic   **Sangfroid** means _____.

16. "Just a *soupçon* of garlic salt," Jan reminded me as I seasoned the pizzas. "I've got a date, and I don't want to paralyze him when he comes in the door."

> Key: Logic   **Soupçon** means _____.

Word Study

Of course you know *ballet* and *bouquet* and *filet*—the last medium rare and the first performed by someone like Mikhail Baryshnikov. We cannot ignore the enormous influence that French (with its Latin roots) has had on English. For example, the word *boil* that means "an inflamed swelling" is Anglo-Saxon, but *boil* meaning "to bubble up" is French. I could go on for pages, but I'll spare you. Just trust me when I say that William the Conqueror and his Norman French made a whopping difference in our language, as many English words were booted out in favor of French words.

In Paris they simply stared when I spoke to them in French; I never did succeed in making those idiots understand their own language.
    —Mark Twain

1. **avant-garde** (ˌäv-ˌän[t]-ˈgärd)   n. Someone in the forefront with new developments, often in the arts.   adj. Referring to anything bold, new, or unusually innovative; F., *vanguard*.

   Once thought strangely *avant-garde*, Pablo Picasso is now acknowledged a master in the art world.

   Relatives: *avant-gardism, avant-gardist*

2. **concierge** (kōⁿ-ˈsyerzh) n.   A representative of the landlord who acts as building manager (especially in France); a hotel staff member who handles guests' needs (tours, luggage, reservations, etc.); pl., *concierges;* F. through L. *conservus,* fellow slave

We arranged for three Paris tours through our *concierge,* a multitalented man who spoke several languages.

3. **debacle** (di-'bäk-əl) n.   A rout or huge disaster, tremendous disruption; also, a total failure, fiasco, flop; from F. *debacler,* to unbar
Unfortunately for us, the second basketball game against East High was a *debacle,* because half our team was sick, the other half demoralized.
Synonyms: *rout, fiasco* (neither exact)
Antonyms: *success, victory*

4. **détente** (dā-täⁿ[n]t) n.   The lessening of ill feeling or tension, as between two countries; an easing of strain; from L. *des + tendere,* to stretch.
As long as I have been reading the newspaper, I have read about America's struggle for *détente* with Russia.
Opposed idea: escalation or heightening (of tension)
Derivation: The early *destente* mechanism of a crossbow released the bow's string. This literal slackening of the string's tension corresponds well to today's meaning of lessened strain in relations.

5. **dossier** ('dòs-,yā) n.   A file of information or group of papers with detailed reports of information; from F. *dossier,* bundle of documents labeled on the back, from L. *dorsum,* back.
Imagine how interesting it would be to read the *dossier* of James Bond, Ian Fleming's fictional master spy.

6. **echelon** ('esh-ə-,län) n.   One of a series of levels or ranks in an organization, as *top echelon;* a corps of people with a certain rank; from F., literally, *rung of a ladder*
"I'm still in the lower *echelon* of workers," Chet said, grinning. "I'm getting pretty good with a broom, though."
Relatives: *echelon* (v.t.), to arrange or line up a group in an echelon; (v.i.), to take your place in an echelon
Synonyms: *rank, level*

7. **ennui** ('än-'wē) n.   Boredom plus a feeling of tiredness and dissatisfaction; a ho-hum feeling; from OF *enuier,* to annoy
I think it's the *ennui* of a long summer that makes me ready to return to school, where something is always happening.
Synonym: *boredom* (not exact)

8. **entrepreneur** (,äⁿn-trə-p[r]ə-'nər) n.   One who develops a business (or enterprise) and bears its developmental risks; from OF *entreprendre,* to undertake
Dad said he'd rather be an *entrepreneur*—with all the risks involved—than work for a large company.
Relatives: *entrepreneurial, entrepreneurship*

9. **insouciance** (in-'sü-sē-ən[t]s) n.   Cheerful lack of concern or care; from F. *in + souciant,* care
Andy approached the dentist's chair with amazing *insouciance,* forgetting that he munches candy whenever he can.
Relatives: *insouciant, insouciantly*
Synonym: *nonchalance*

10. **ménage** (mā-'näzh) n.   A household, domestic setup; from OF *mesnage*, dwelling
Noël Coward's *Design for Living* concerns a humorous love triangle, a *ménage à trois*, with its modern counterpart in TV's "Three's Company."
Synonym: *household*

11. **outré** (ü-'trā) adj.   Bizarre, far-out; referring to something outside conventional standards; from F. *outrer*, to carry to excess
Summer boredom at the lake was relieved by our new neighbors, a couple whose *outré* clothing and possessions became the talk of our lake community.
Synonym: *bizarre* (weak)
Antonyms: *conventional, traditional, classic*

12. **pique** ('pēk)   v. To irritate, annoy, offend; to rouse curiosity, interest, or pride; to provoke into awareness, as by a challenge or intentional snub.   n. Resentment or slight feeling of injured pride, as *she stamped off in a fit of pique;* from F. *piquer*, to prick.
A brief stay in Vienna *piqued* my curiosity about Empress Elizabeth, the Bavarian princess who led a sad, lonely life.
Synonyms: (v.) *provoke*, (n.) *resentment* (neither exact)

13. **précis** (prā-'sē) n.   A brief summary of vital facts, points, and ideas; pl., *précis;* from F. *precise*
We concentrated on writing in that class, beginning with paragraphs and working toward mastery of the *précis*.

14. **rapport** (ra-'pō[ə]r) n.   A state of agreement, closeness of understanding, and harmony; from L. *ad* + *portare*, to bring, through F. *rapporter*, to bring back
The beloved operas of Gilbert and Sullivan are notable for the *rapport* between Gilbert's words and Sullivan's music.
Antonym: *discord*

15. **sangfroid** ('sä^n-'f[r]wä) n.   Coolness, calm, and imperturbability, even under stress; self-possession; from *sang* + *froid*, blood, cold
In a fashion show at school, Jan modeled with a *sangfroid* that Carrie openly envied. "Must be the ballet training," she concluded as she watched Jan's smooth, graceful movements.
Synonyms: *equanimity, composure, coolness*

16. **soupçon** (süp-'sō^n, 'süp-,sä^n) n.   A tiny bit, trace, or dash of something; from L. *suspicere*, to suspect, through F. *soupçon*, suspicion
"I wish I weren't so conventional," Ellen complained. "A *soupçon* of daring would be a healthy spice in my personality."
Synonyms: *trace, dash* (neither exact)

Root Study

You will recognize all of these as being roots of words in List 7.

1. DORS means *back* (of the body).
    dorsal—at the back or near the back of a major body part
    endorse—to sign (a document); to approve, as *I endorse his candidacy*

2. PORT means *to carry* or *bring*.
    portable—able to be carried, lifted, or moved from place to place
    report—anything carried back, such as information or sound, as *the report of a gun*

deport—to send legally out of a country

export—to send out of a country, typically products such as cars, clothing, etc.

import—to bring into a country, as *we import perfume from Paris*

3. TEND/TENS/TENT means *to stretch*.

tendency—an inclination, leaning toward something

tensile—usually refers to strength, and is the measure of how much lengthwise stress a substance will take before tearing apart

attention—observation or notice; applying the mind to a subject or object; consideration of others' needs or wants

Using the Words

List 7 Review

avant-garde	dossier	insouciance	précis
concierge	echelon	ménage	rapport
debacle	ennui	outré	sangfroid
détente	entrepreneur	pique	soupçon

Exercise I. Synonyms. Write the vocabulary word from List 7 on the line next to its synonym or definition.

1. coolness, composure _____

2. helpful hotel staffer _____

3. nonchalance _____

4. file of information _____

5. harmony, accord _____

6. developer of a business _____

7. concise summary _____

8. disruption, rout _____

9. vanguard _____

10. lessened tension _____

11. rung, rank, level _____

12. household _____

13. bizarre _____

14. a tiny bit _____

15. boredom _____

16. provoke _____

Exercise II. Antonyms. Select the letter of the best antonym or contrasting phrase for each word, and enter it on the line next to its opposite.

_____ 1. **sangfroid**   (a) musical   (b) exhausted   (c) tiny (d) agitation   (e) composure

_____ 2. **soupçon**   (a) trace   (b) dinner's ready   (c) large amount   (d) bit   (e) spice

_____ 3. **avant-gardist**   (a) civilian   (b) soldier   (c) leader
(d) oddball   (e) follower

_____ 4. **debacle**   (a) bangle   (b) rout   (c) success
(d) strike   (e) achievement

_____ 5. **détente**   (a) heightened tension   (b) grave difficulty
(c) increased length   (d) added awareness
(e) brighter vision

_____ 6. **outré**   (a) inside   (b) boring   (c) common
(d) bizarre   (e) within

_____ 7. **rapport**   (a) silence   (b) unwillingness   (c) clarity
(d) discord   (e) confusion

Exercise III. Fill-ins. Write the appropriate words from List 7 in the blank spaces in this Parisian dream.

You are renting un appartement à Paris. Your sink is stopped up, so you trot downstairs pour visiter with the _____. As the renter of this pleasant flat, you adopt two stray
                              1
pussycats and a homeless poodle. Your old college roommate moves in tout de suite. No longer alone, you now have a(n) _____. With a plugged sink, a pair of felines
                              2
jealous of ze poodle, and an amused roommate, you never suffer from

_____.
        3

But poverty is très nearby. Time to dig out the résumé, the college transcript, and tous les papiers needed for hunting ze job. _____ under your arm, you present
                              4
yourself with confidence, even _____. It will be only a matter of time until
                              5
someone snaps you up, oui?

Non!

The Parisian employers' interests are not _____ by your application. They
                              6
do not care a fig, not a(n) _____. "Votre français est terrible!" they cry.
                              7
Back in votre appartement, you take stock of yourself, noting your good qualities and knowledge—all the vital information in a brief _____ titled "ME." You
                              8
realize that you must give birth to une bonne idée. You know that you adore cooking.

Magnifique! Un restaurant américain, run by you! Confidently you present your bonne idée to the banque, which lends ze money to set up your business. You have just become a(n)

_____ _____.
        9

Exercise IV. French in Print. French phrases constantly pop up in books, newspapers, and magazines. It's frustrating not to know what these phrases mean. Scan the key below; then decode a few of the more common French expressions, matching them with the English. If stumped, ask a friend who's studying French.

coterie = clique, set   _fait_ = fact, act   _faire_ = to do or make
rigueur = strictness   _savoir_ = to know   _faux_ = false, bad
vis = beside, next to;   _vu_ = seen   _tête_ = head
      derives from _face_

_____ 1. **coterie**

_____ 2. **déjà vu**

_____ 3. **de rigueur**

_____ 4. **faux pas (or gaffe)**

_____ 5. **fait accompli**

_____ 6. **noblesse oblige**

_____ 7. **pièce de résistance**

_____ 8. **protégé**

_____ 9. **savoir faire**

_____ 10. **tête-à-tête**

_____ 11. **tour de force**

_____ 12. **vis-à-vis**

(a) feat of strength, skill, ingenuity

(b) the responsible obligations of those with rank, nobility, position

(c) savvy, know-how, social competence

(d) select group, set

(e) proper, what is required by society's rules of behavior

(f) related to, compared with

(g) unpleasantly familiar, known or seen before

(h) private conversation between two

(i) an accomplished fact, usually unchangeable

(j) special, favored pupil

(k) a social false step, a boo-boo

(l) outstanding item, the showpiece

Note: All of these phrases, and more, occur in standard, abridged *English* dictionaries. Many were favorites of Hawkeye on "M.A.S.H." and Mork of "Mork and Mindy."

Exercise V. Roots of Derived Words. Write the correct roots on the line beside their derived words. Roots: *dors, port, tend, tens, tent*. Also, underline the prefixes in the numbered words.

_____ 1. retention

_____ 2. support

_____ 3. détente

_____ 4. dossier

_____ 5. rapport

_____ 6. tension

_____ 7. comportment

_____ 8. extended

_____ 9. endorse

_____ 10. deportation

_____ 11. dorsal

_____ 12. export

_____ 13. attention

_____ 14. import

_____ 15. dorsispinal

Exercise VI. Word Analysis

1. In French, *souci* means *worry* or *care*. Why, then, is Sans Souci a good name for a seaside resort?

_____

_____

2. The Latin root *sang/sangui* meaning *blood* has given us several words. What is the difference between *sanguine* and *sanguinary*? Why do you hope not to *exsanguinate* until you're very old?

_____

_____

_____

3. Match these well-known French words with their definitions:

    _____ a. bourgeois   (1) meeting, usually secret

    _____ b. connoisseur   (2) trite remark

    _____ c. rendezvous   (3) young woman formally entering society

    _____ d. debutante   (4) middle-class, common

    _____ e. cliché   (5) an expert, specialist, or professional

4. How do you regard France and all things French if you are a *Francophile?* a *Francophobe?*

_____

_____

5. *Canard* means *duck* in French. One English use of this word might read as follows:

    Judge: You are accused of theft!
    Defendant: That, sir, is a base *canard*. I stole nothing.

Obviously, *canard* doesn't mean *duck* in English. What does *Webster's New Collegiate Dictionary* say about ye olde French duck and today's usage?

_____

_____

_____

6. Looking back over List 7, note how few of the words have clear-cut synonyms in English. Almost none. Likewise, few have good antonyms. *Why* have these words come into our language?

_____

_____

_____

Mrs. Malaprop Is Alive and Well

WORDS ABOUT LANGUAGE AND SPEECH

In Context. Before studying the definitions, try reasoning out the meaning of each word, using context as your guide.

1. Mom *alleged* that Andy was the most likely thief of the Oreo cookies, but Andy protested, saying that he'd been at a friend's house all afternoon.

    Key: Logic   **Allege** means _____ .

2. Our English teacher is a favorite with students because his amusing *anecdotes* offer personal glimpses into authors' lives.

    Key: Partial definition   **Anecdote** means _____ .

3. Being an *articulate* speaker is one of Dad's goals. He prepares his material carefully and practices each speech before making a presentation.

    Key: Logic   **Articulate** means _____ .

4. Skill at playful *badinage* in social situations is usually an advantage. Anyone who can entertain others with witty talk or who is known for humorous retorts never seems to lack invitations.

    Key: Definitions   **Badinage** means _____ .

5. "I hate to see that pie go to waste," Mom murmured, reaching for the last chocolaty wedge. Dad grinned. "Intentional *double entendre*," he teased, "or just a slip of the tongue?"

    Key: Logic (*Waste* and *waist*
    are homophones.)   **Double entendre** means _____ .

6. Mark Twain valued both wit and brevity. Perhaps that is why his *epigrams* are so often quoted today.

    Keys: Partial definition, logic   **Epigram** means _____ .

7. The *etymology* of "bonfire" tells us it derived from "bone fire," referring to the open burning of old bones saved for this purpose.

    Key: Example, logic   **Etymology** means _____ .

8. We labeled our cousin Gary *garrulous,* or "G-Squared," because he talks nonstop.

    Key: Definition   **Garrulous** means _____ .

9. In a recent TV western, we listened to the condemned man *gibber* insanely as he was led toward the hangman's noose.

    Key: Logic   **Gibber** means _____ .

10. A last-minute reprieve released the prisoner from both the gallows and his fear. His relief was visible and his *inflection* altered dramatically in tone and clarity as he gave moving thanks for his deliverance.

> Keys: Sentences 9 and 10,
> partial definition   **Inflection** means _____.

11. Comedian George Gobel loves *irony*. On a TV program he said, "The National Safety Council has predicted 407 accidents due to careless driving over the weekend . . . and so far only 209 have been reported. . . . Now, some of you folks just aren't trying."

> Key: Logic, example   **Irony** means _____.

12. My favorite *laconic* question and reply belong to Victor Hugo and his publisher. Shortly after publication of *Les Misérables*, author Hugo wrote: "?" The reply was, "!" Now that is being succinct.

> Keys: Logic, synonym   **Laconic** means _____.

13. When Aunt Dolly said she needed "an anecdote for pain," we roared with laughter at her *malapropism*—then handed her two aspirin.

> Key: Logic   **Malapropism** means _____.

14. My old friend Bill is a great *raconteur*, able to make all the family grin at his humorous accounts of our escapades at camp years ago.

> Keys: Partial definition, logic   **Raconteur** means _____.

15. Jan taunted me for days about my beet-red sunburn, but I was unable to come back with a *riposte* cutting enough to silence her.

> Key: Logic   **Riposte** means _____.

16. Asked to find examples of *tautology*, or redundancy, in the newspaper, I came up with: *visible to the eye, center around, close proximity, past history*, and *each and every one* on just the front page.

> Keys: Synonym, examples   **Tautology** means _____.

17. Much as we enjoy the anecdotes of our English teacher, we don't enjoy his red pencil as it ruthlessly circles every *trite* remark—every single cliché—on our papers.

> Key: Synonym   **Trite** means _____.

Word Study

Language is an ever-changing thing, with new words born daily. Gelett Burgess, an American humorist who loved to coin words, created *blurb*, which is now very common. We have a particularly large number of words to describe language itself, and speech. Many are French words—perhaps because the French so love speech and language. (Their own, of course.)

Speaking of languages, did you know that Urdu is Pakistan's official literary language? "I am referred to in that splendid language (Urdu) as, 'Fella belong Mrs. Queen,' " Prince Philip, Duke of Edinburgh, said once.

1. **allege** (ə-'lej) v.   To state as truth although not proved, or before proof; to give as a reason or excuse; from L. *ad + legare*, to depute, to legate

For some time, historians *alleged* that Richard III murdered his two nephews in the Tower of London, but now many English scholars believe Henry VII guilty of that crime.

Relatives: *alleged* (so-called, assumed), *allegation*
Synonyms: *claim, assert* (neither exact)
Antonyms: *contravene, traverse* (to deny at law), *contradict, deny*

2. **anecdote** ('an-ik-,dōt) n. A brief story that is humorous or unusually interesting, often biographical; from Gr. *anekdota,* unpublished items

A popular *anecdote* about Mark Twain quotes a cable that he sent from London to the Associated Press after his lengthy absence from the United States: "The reports of my death are greatly exaggerated."

Relatives: *anecdotal, anecdotist, anecdotically*

3. **articulate** (är-'tik-yə-,lāt) v. To pronounce clearly and distinctly; to state effectively; to arrange in a systematic whole, as *articulating a music program throughout a school.* adj. Understandable, intelligible, as, *an articulate speech*); speaking clearly, easily, and well (*the articulate speaker*); jointed, as the segments of an animal; plainly marked off, as *the articulated parts of a computer program;* from L. *articulus,* joint, division.

Still under anesthetic, the patient was unable to *articulate* his words, and we couldn't understand his slurred speech.

Relatives: *articulately, articulateness, articulative, articulator, articulation, articulatory*
Synonym: *jointed* (articulate animals)
Antonyms: *inarticulate, unintelligible, mute*

4. **badinage** (,bad-ᵊn-'äzh) n. Playful, light (often humorous) talk or banter; from F. *badin,* fool

Dating back to thirteenth-century French, *badinage* is an excellent synonym for repartee, another French word from the same era.

Synonyms: *repartee, banter, persiflage, raillery*

5. **double entendre** (,düb[-ə]-,läⁿ[n]-'täⁿ[n]drᵊ) n. Ambiguity arising from a word or phrase that may be interpreted two ways, one often risqué; F., literally, *double meaning;* pl., *double entendres*

Known for her wit, Dorothy Parker once telegraphed an intentional *double entendre* to her friend who had just had a baby: "Congratulations, we all knew you had it in you."

6. **epigram** ('ep-ə-,gram) n. A brief, typically witty saying that expresses much in few words; from L. *epi + gram,* to write

What is an epigram? *A dwarfish whole,*
Its body brevity, and wit its soul.
    —Samuel Taylor Coleridge

7. **etymology** (,et-ə-'mäl-ə-jē) n. The study of the earliest beginnings of words and idioms and their language histories; from Gr. *etymon,* earliest known true form of a word, + *-ology,* study of

Willard Espy's research in *etymology* is presented with irresistible wit and impeccable scholarship.

Relatives: *etymologist* (person), *etymological, etymologically*

8. **garrulous** ('gar-ə-ləs, 'gar-yə-ləs) adj. Talkative to an annoying degree, boringly loquacious; from L. *garrire,* to chatter

It was the best place to be, thought Wilbur, this warm delicious cellar, with the garrulous geese, the changing seasons, the heat of the sun. . . .
　　　　　—E. B. White, *Charlotte's Web*

Relatives:　*garrulity, garrulously, garrulousness*
Synonyms:　*talkative, loquacious, voluble, prolix, wordy, verbose, long-winded*
Antonyms:　*laconic, taciturn, reticent, silent, reserved*

9. **gibber** ('jib-ər) v.　　To speak with great speed, little thought, and almost zero clarity; to gabble, chatter; origin uncertain

The graves stood tenantless and the sheeted dead
Did squeak and gibber *in the Roman streets.*
　　　　　—Shakespeare, *Julius Caesar*

Relatives:　*gibberish* (incoherent speech)
Synonyms:　*gabble, chatter, jabber, babble* (Note all the *b*'s.)
Antonym:　*articulate*

10. **inflection** (in-'flek-shən) n.　　Difference in loudness or pitch of the voice; the spelling change of words to show plurality, possession, tense, gender, voice, case, or mood; from L. *in* + *flectere*, to bend

The pronoun is our part of speech with the most *inflections*, changing as it does from subject (*I*), to possessive (*my, mine*), to object (*me*), and into the plural as a different form altogether (*our, ours*).

Relatives:　*inflect, inflective, inflectional, inflectionally*

11. **irony** ('ī-rə-nē) n.　　The use of words to convey a meaning other than (often opposite to) the literal meaning; ironic expression that implies the opposite of what is said; an outcome or result just the opposite of what would be expected; from Gr. *eiron*, dissembler

The prophet Elijah gives us an example of direct *irony* when he jeers at the priests of Baal (heathen god) as they invoke their idols. Elijah taunts: "Cry louder! Baal is a god, but perhaps he is talking, or walking or traveling, or perhaps he is sleeping and must be awakened."

Relatives:　*ironic, ironically, ironist* (person)
Synonyms:　*sarcasm, wit* (weak)

12. **laconic** (lə-'kän-ik) adj.　　Using as few words as possible, concise almost to the point of rudeness; from Gr. *lakonikos*, spartan

One hopeful conqueror sent a message to Laconia: "If I come to Laconia, not one brick will stand on another." The *laconic* answer was "If."

Relatives:　*laconically, laconism*
Synonyms:　*terse, concise, pithy*
Antonyms:　*verbose, voluble, garrulous, wordy, talkative, loquacious, prolix*
Derivation: Laconia and Sparta (its capital city) are synonymous in connotation. The Laconians (Spartans) were physically oriented folk—proud of their skills in games and war, but sparing of speech and emotionally self-contained. Anything described as *Spartan* is simple to the point of self-denial, just as *laconic* speech or writing is pared to the bone.

13. **malapropism** ('mal-ə-,präp-,iz-əm) n.　　From Mrs. Malaprop, a character in Sheridan's *The Rivals;* a humorous misuse of words, putting a similar-sounding word in place of the correct one; from F. *mal à propos*, inopportune, unseasonable

Mrs. Malaprop's verbal fumbles include "as headstrong as an allegory on the Nile," "a progeny of learning," and "Illiterate him, I say, quite from your mind!" Each case of language misused in this way is termed a *malapropism.*

Relatives: *malaprop, malapropian, malapropos*

14. **raconteur** (ˌrak-ˌän-'tər) n.   One who tells stories or jokes with exceptional skill; from F. *raconter,* to tell

Oscar Wilde, noted *raconteur* and epigrammatist, said on his deathbed as he was offered a glass of champagne: "I am dying beyond my means."

Synonym: *storyteller* (not exact)

15. **riposte** (ri-'pōst) n.   A quick verbal retort; any retaliatory thrust, as the fencer's rapid return to a thrust following a parry; from L. *respondere* through It. *rispondere* and F. *riposter,* to respond.

Mistress of the cutting *riposte* was Dorothy Parker. When told that President Calvin Coolidge had died, she said, "How can they tell?"

Relative: *riposte* (v.i., to retort)
Synonyms: *retort, rejoinder* (neither exact)

16. **tautology** (tȯ-'täl-ə-jē) n.   The unnecessary repetition of words, ideas, statements, as *a young kitten* (kittens, by definition, are always young); from Gr. *tautologos,* to say

Trite writing cluttered by *tautology* sends readers to bed or to the television set.

Relatives: *tautological, tautologically, tautologous*
Synonym: *redundancy*

17. **trite** ('trīt) adj.   Overused to the point of staleness; lacking freshness and originality; from L. *tritus,* rubbed, worn away (past participle of *terere*)

"My personal opinion" and "first and foremost" are only two of the dozens of *trite* phrases that are also tautologous.

Relatives: *tritely, triteness*
Synonyms: *hackneyed, banal, common, ordinary, insipid, stale*
Antonyms: *novel, fresh, original*

Root Study

Roots referring to written and spoken language dominate this study group.

1. FLEX/FLECT means bend, turn, curve.
    flex—to move or bend, as muscles
    inflexible—unyielding, stubborn, unwilling to bend
    reflection—thought (bending the mind back in time or over material again); image reflected to the viewer, as by a pond or mirror
    deflect—to turn away or aside

2. GRAPH/GRAM means to write.
    biography—written record of a person's life
    graphic—something written, drawn, or transmitted; extremely vivid, clear, expressive, as a graphic description
    telegram—message sent rapidly to a distant location
    gramophone—(formerly capitalized) trademark meaning phonograph, record player

3. LEG means law, legal.
    legacy—anything left by a deceased or absent person to someone else (e.g., personality traits, possessions, privileges, money)

legality—established law
legislature—lawmaking body

4. ROG means to ask.
interrogate—to question, often repeatedly
prerogative—a special right, privilege, power
derogatory—belittling, disparaging, as a derogatory remark

Using the Words

List 8 Review

allege	epigram	inflection	raconteur
anecdote	etymology	irony	riposte
articulate	garrulous	laconic	tautology
badinage	gibber	malapropism	trite
double entendre			

Exercise I. Synonyms. Each word from List 8 has two synonyms in the group of lettered words. Enter the letters of these synonyms on the lines.

_____ 1. **trite**
    (a) ripe   (b) stale   (c) fresh
    (d) hackneyed   (e) used

_____ 2. **tautology**
    (a) redundancy   (b) science
    (c) originality   (d) repetition   (e) usefulness

_____ 3. **allege**
    (a) announce   (b) cite   (c) shelve
    (d) state   (e) set forth as possible

_____ 4. **articulate**
    (a) disjointed   (b) aware
    (c) understandable   (d) arranged
    (e) intelligible

_____ 5. **garrulous**
    (a) loquacious   (b) crotchety   (c) voluble
    (d) voluminous   (e) ancient

_____ 6. **laconic**
    (a) grim   (b) terse   (c) concise
    (d) wordy   (e) inner

_____ 7. **riposte**
    (a) remail   (b) redress   (c) redirect
    (d) retort   (e) rejoinder

_____ 8. **gibber**
    (a) chatter   (b) poker   (c) mince
    (d) affirm   (e) babble

_____ 9. **badinage**
    (a) plaster   (b) repartee   (c) ill humor
    (d) banter   (e) wordiness

_____ 10. **irony**
    (a) laundry   (b) confusion   (c) sarcasm
    (d) wit   (e) annoyance

Exercise II. Analogies. Complete each analogy with the best pair possible.

_____ 1. anecdote : book ::
    (a) novel : history
    (b) epigram : monologue
    (c) script : play
    (d) riposte : thrust
    (e) dialogue : address

_____ 2. laconic : garrulous ::
   (a) verbose : prolix
   (b) wordy : prolonged
   (c) terse : hackneyed
   (d) novel : trite
   (e) ironic : humorous

_____ 3. Oscar Wilde : raconteur ::
   (a) Benjamin Franklin : poet
   (b) William Wordsworth : mayor
   (c) Teddy Roosevelt : actor
   (d) Miles Standish : carpenter
   (e) Mark Twain : satirist

_____ 4. repetition : speech ::
   (a) tautology : writing
   (b) etymology : music
   (c) inflection : voice
   (d) badinage : raillery
   (e) dynamics : medicine

_____ 5. malapropism : words ::
   (a) sculpture : chisel
   (b) composition : music
   (c) extremism : art
   (d) gibbering : speech
   (e) defeatism : theory

Exercise III. Fill-ins. Write the French words (from List 8 *and its synonyms*) that fit their descriptions on the lines provided. The first letter is given for each answer.

1. trite expression .... c_____

2. light banter .... r_____

3. double interpretation possible for
   a word or expression .... d_____

4. storyteller .... r_____

5. quick rejoinder, retort .... r_____

6. humorous misuse of words .... m_____

7. hackneyed, stale .... b_____

8. light, witty talk .... p_____

9. playful talk, banter .... b_____

10. a clever remark, witticism .... b____ m_____

(This one is not given here, although it occurs in a previous lesson. Ask a friend who takes French, a parent, or a teacher.)

Exercise IV. Terms in Use. The following sentences are examples of general types of verbal expression taught in this lesson. Label each example with the word that describes its type. (Two quotes may be more fully described by *two* of the vocabulary words.)

_____ 1. One of the stories told about Elizabeth Taylor concerns her discovery by the film industry. When told she was too short to play the lead role in *National Velvet,* she replied, "I will grow." And grow she did. By the time filming began, she had added just enough height to qualify.

_____ 2. The boy said, "My aunt has bellicose veins, too, and may need an operation just like your mom."

_____ 3. Gazing from a hilltop down onto Washington, D.C., a woman observed, "Much needs doing down there, but I wish they'd begin by managing the traffic better."

"Capital improvement!" exclaimed her friend.
(Hint: Washington, D.C., is the U.S. capital, remember?)

_____ 4. "Experience is the name everyone gives to his mistakes," said Oscar Wilde.

_____ 5. **battology** (bætə-lədzi) needless repetition in writing or speech, from Battos, the stammering man in Herodotus' history of the Greco-Persian wars.

_____ 6. Report of an Indian after guiding a visiting Englishman on a hunting shoot: "Our guest shot beautifully, but heaven was very merciful to the birds."—Cited by L. Feinberg, *Introduction to Satire*.

_____ 7. After a long, boring evening, Dorothy Parker's somewhat stuffy escort remarked to her, "I can't bear fools."
"That's strange. Your mother could," Miss Parker rejoined.

_____ 8. The frisky young foal romped and gamboled in the pale green meadow fragrant with new spring grass.

Exercise V. Roots. Match the words (from the section on Roots) with their meanings in the lettered columns on the right.

____ 1. **derogatory**		(a) special right or privilege
____ 2. **legacy**		(b) story of a life
____ 3. **graphic**		(c) to turn aside or away
____ 4. **flex**		(d) to question
____ 5. **inflexible**		(e) study of handwriting
____ 6. **gramophone**		(f) extremely vivid and clear
____ 7. **prerogative**		(g) easily bent, yielding
____ 8. **reflection**		(h) to move or bend
____ 9. **biography**		(i) unyielding
____ 10. **deflect**		(j) thought or image
____ 11. **interrogate**		(k) disparaging
____ 12. **flexible**		(l) not lawful
____ 13. **graphology**		(m) inherited trait, possession, privilege
____ 14. **legislate**		(n) record player
____ 15. **illegal**		(o) to enact laws

Exercise VI. Word Analysis.

1. Give one or more *antonyms* for the following words:

_____ (a) alleged (assumed, so-called)

_____ (b) articulate (adj.)

_____ (c) garrulous

_____ (d) trite

_____ (e) laconic

2. Several words in List 8 (plus their synonyms) refer to conversation that would contain *bons mots* (literally, *good words*). How many of these words can you find and list?

_____

_____

3. Since *malapropism* refers to the inappropriate use of words, what does its root *apropos* mean?

_____

    Examples: a. Her outfit was *apropos* for the occasion.
                b. That speech was *apropos* of nothing significant that we could discover.

4. For a bit, think about inflection as it refers to voice. How does the inflection of a person's voice reflect fear? sorrow? joy? a need for secrecy? anger?

_____

_____

_____

    If your voice were incapable of inflection, could you cheer at a ball game? or whisper?

_____

    How much does inflection in the voice of a character influence your opinion? (Think of the Big Bad Wolf's voice versus those of the three little pigs, as in the Walt Disney cartoon.)

_____

_____

Exercise VII. Just for Fun. Ever played Stinky Pinkies? It's a word game that gives a definition and requests a two-word rhymed response that names the thing defined.
    Q. an Italian robber bug?
    A. mosquito bandito
Here's a Double Stinky Pinky, which is a tougher kind to dream up:
    Q. a fat cat?
    A. a flabby tabby
Try these if the conversation lags over dinner.

a. aviator?	f. rodent's home?
b. fast crowd?	g. childbirth at the North Pole?
c. cheerful father?	h. nervous/stupid fowl?
d. chicken purchaser?	i. one crazy about the theater?
e. rose-colored basin?	j. submerged friar?

Review

This lesson reviews the words and roots in Lists 5, 6, 7, and 8. As you read over these lists, remember to say each word or prefix aloud to help trigger your memory and plant both the meanings and the spellings in your mind.

List 5 (in order as taught)

bene-, bon-
eu-
pro-
a-
anti-, ant-
counter-, contra-
dif-, dis-
for-
in-, il-, im-, ir-
non-, un-
ob-, of-, op-
mal-, mis-
macro-
micro-, min-
pan-, panto-, omni-
ante-, anti-
ex-
fore-
pre-
post-
com-, co-, col-, con-, cor-
syn-, syl-, sym-, sys-, sy-
amphi-, circum-, peri-
epi-, ecto-
ab-, abs-, apo-, ap-

e-, ex-, ec-, ef-
de-, cata-
se-
a-, ad-, af-, ag-, al-, an-,
　　ap-, as-, at-
ob-, oc-, of-, op-
in-, il-, im-, ir-
endo-, en-, em-
intro-, intra-
ana-, re-, retro-
inter-
tele-
sub-, suc-, suf-, sug-,
　　sum-, sup-, sus-
hyp-, hypo-
over-, super-, ultra-,
　　hyper-
exter-, extra-, extro-
trans-, tra-
dia-, di-, per-
alter-, hetero-
homo-
meta-
para-, par-
orth-

wri-, wro-
hemi-, demi-, semi-, med-
uni-, mono-, sol-
sesqui-
di-, bi-, du-, duo-, diplo-
tri-, ter-
quadr-, tetr-
quinque-, quint-, penta-
sex-, hexa-
sept-, hepta-
oct-, octa-, octo-
nona-, novem-, ennea-
dec-, deca-
duodec-, dodeca-
cent-, hect-, hecato-
milli-, kilo-
myria-
meg-, mega-
arch-, prim-, prin-, proto-
ambi-, amphi-
equi-, iso-, par-
oligo-, pauci-
multi-, poly-, myria-

List 6
astringent
brazen
brusque
catholic
diffident
eldritch
expedient
incorrigible
incumbent
lithe
nebulous
pastoral
plausible

List 7
avant-garde
concierge
debacle
détente
dossier
echelon
ennui
entrepreneur
insouciance
ménage
outré
pique
précis

List 8
allege
anecdote
articulate
badinage
double entendre
epigram
etymology
garrulous
gibber
inflection
irony
laconic
malapropism

pristine	rapport	raconteur
requisite	sangfroid	riposte
stolid	soupçon	tautology
		trite

ROOTS

AGOG	FLEX/FLECT	LEG	STRING/STRICT
DORS	GRAPH/GRAM	ROG	TEND/TENS/TENT
FID	GREG	PORT	

Using the Words

Exercise I. Know Those Roots and Prefixes. Circle any prefixes in the following numbered words. Underline the roots. Then, write a synonym or brief definition on the line.

1. bonus _____

2. interrogate _____

3. rapport _____

4. malapropism _____

5. inflection _____

6. epigram _____

7. allege _____

8. détente _____

9. insouciance _____

10. expedient _____

Exercise II. Antonyms. Find the antonym or contrasting phrase for each word on the left and enter its letter on the correct line.

_____ 1. **microcosm**   (a) extra, superfluous

_____ 2. **brazen**   (b) ordinary

_____ 3. **catholic**   (c) gibber

_____ 4. **requisite**   (d) shy

_____ 5. **sangfroid**   (e) original

_____ 6. **outré**   (f) amenable

_____ 7. **debacle**   (g) macrocosm

_____ 8. **tautology**   (h) definite

_____ 9. **articulate** (v.)   (i) parochial

_____ 10. **trite**   (j) bold

_____ 11. **pastoral**   (k) agitation, nervousness

_____ 12. **nebulous**   (l) laconic

_____ 13. **incorrigible**   (m) concise thought

_____ 14. **diffident**   (n) success

_____ 15. **garrulous**   (o) urban

Exercise III. Fill-in Chart. Add the missing items in the chart.

	PREFIX	ROOT	WORD	DEFINITION
1.	_____	_____	restricted	_____
2.	dem-	agog	_____	popular leader
3.	_____	_____	infidel	_____
4.	_____	dors	_____	to sign; to give support
5.	_____	_____	deport	_____
6.	meta-	morph	_____	a noticeable change of form or personality
7.	_____	rog	_____	disparaging, downgrading
8.	epi-	_____	_____	short witty saying
9.	_____	_____	astringent	_____
10.	_____	greg	_____	to set apart

Exercise IV. Sentence Completion. Select the most appropriate word from the choices offered, based on clues in context. The word form may change.

brusque	dossier	irony	incumbent
eldritch	anecdote	raconteur	plausible
avant-garde	badinage	précis	pristine

1. As class treasurer, it was _____ on me to keep track of moneys in our account, sign checks, and make a monthly report.

2. Mom viewed Andy's filthy face and jeans, muddy shoes, and torn shirt. "Well," she said with heavy _____, "it'd be a shame to make you clean up and ruin your perfect boy-at-play image."

3. As Jan reeled off the likes, dislikes, and recent comments of the new, good-looking senior, I had to grin. "I didn't know girls kept a _____ like that on each guy's life," I teased.

4. Used to traditional music, Mom and Dad were startled by the _____ piano compositions at a recent recital.

5. The coin collector's album Carrie gave me keeps each new coin in

_____ condition in a separate, plastic pocket.

6. I sprinkled my speech about Teddy Roosevelt with amusing quotes and

_____ to keep everyone's interest high.

7. Mom confessed, "I was so annoyed with the checkout girl that I spoke quite

_____ to hurry her along. I hate to be rude, though," she added.

8. Stories can be told in a variety of ways, but the good _____ knows how to interest and hold an audience.

9. With a steely eye Jan glared at our cat Marigold. "I suppose you have a

_____ reason for sleeping next to the aquarium," she said, just as though Marigold would reply with a logical answer.

10. After the class read five different versions of life in wartime Britain, the history teacher assigned a _____ on the topic, warning us that four pages would be the maximum allowable length.

11. Nothing wakes our family quicker than the _____ nighttime howl of the neighboring Siamese as he woos Marigold.

12. Dad has a great sense of humor, but he's not much at small talk or casual

_____.

Exercise V. Analogies. Complete each analogy with the best pair possible.

_____ 1. dancer : lithe ::
    (a) singer : graceful
    (b) manager : brusque
    (c) columnist : incumbent
    (d) speaker : laconic
    (e) entrepreneur : resourceful

_____ 2. stolid : impassive ::
    (a) pristine : keen
    (b) expedient : unnecessary
    (c) naughty : incorrigible
    (d) ironic : sarcastic
    (e) insouciant : careful

_____ 3. enthusiasm : ennui ::
    (a) riposte : retort
    (b) plausibility : illogic
    (c) gibberish : confusion
    (d) stricture : tension
    (e) diffidence : provocation

_____ 4. repartee : riposte ::
    (a) détente : compromise
    (b) raconteur : tale
    (c) inflection : anticipation
    (d) rapport : requisition
    (e) echelon : rank

_____ 5. words : etymology ::
    (a) frogs : biology
    (b) mind : psychology
    (c) science : geology
    (d) books : bibliophile
    (e) music : conservatory

Exercise VI. Word Analysis.

1. How and why do words come into the English language? _____

_____

Cite some words adopted from France. Other countries? _____

2. How does the root meaning of *echelon* correspond to its present meaning and usage?

_____

3. Fill in as many prefixes as you can in the following chart:

Good, Well, Favoring	Bad, Negative, Not	Above, Over	Out/Away

Below, Under	With, Together	Indic. Time/Place	Size/Amount
	In, Into, Within		

4. Describe your *ménage* briefly. _____

_____

_____

5. What is the difference in these two usages of *pique?*
   (a) *Piqued* by her refusal, I strode away.
   (b) My curiosity *piqued* by the painting, I wanted to ask several questions of the artist.

_____

6. Students like phrases with a double interpretation because they're laughable. Can you recall a recent *double entendre?*

_____

_____

7. Would someone crazy about Mexican food like only a *soupçon* of chili powder? _____

A Hirsute Simian
WORDS FROM THE ANIMAL KINGDOM

In Context. Before studying the definitions, try reasoning out the meaning of each word, using context as your guide.

1. I could tell from his foolish grin and generally *asinine* look that Steve wasn't comprehending what I had said.

   Keys: Synonym, logic   **Asinine** means _____ .

2. A look of *bovine* contentment spread over Carrie's face as she chewed gum and watched her favorite video. Jan giggled. "You remind me of old Bossie chewing her cud," she said.

   Keys: Logic, colloquial synonym   **Bovine** means _____ .

3. A favorite family documentary titled "*Denizens* of the Deep" explores the lives and habits of sea creatures in the Pacific.

   Key: Logic   **Denizen** means _____ .

4. The noisy, demanding *fledglings* in our oak tree keep the parent birds frantically hunting food for them all day.

   Keys: Antonym, logic   **Fledgling** means _____ .

5. "I've fed enough *fodder* into this computer today. I ought to get quite a report," Jan said, her eyes glued to the screen.

   Key: Logic   **Fodder** means _____ .

6. The 1960s brought a great awareness of hair. People who'd never thought much about hair eyed the *hirsute*, bearded young men with amazement.

   Key: Synonym   **Hirsute** means _____ .

7. That part calls for a *leonine* actor—someone with a full head of hair and a beard—someone who exudes the power and vitality demanded by the role.

   Keys: Definition; look for the root. **Leonine** means _____ .

8. Several beloved *porcine* characters include the Three Little Pigs, Porky Pig, and Wilbur of *Charlotte's Webb*.

   Key: Synonym   **Porcine** means _____ .

9. The *prehensile* tail of a monkey is fascinating to watch as the monkey swings nimbly from branch to branch, grasping as well with his tail as with his hands and feet.

   Keys: Logic, example   **Prehensile** means _____ .

10. Carrie took one look at the cobra and shuddered. "They're just plain icky. *Reptilian* heads and slithery bodies, ugh!"

    Keys: Example; look for the root. **Reptilian** means _____ .

11. The faraway, thoughtful look in Jan's eyes told me that she was *ruminating* yet again on her college choices.

       Key: Synonymous phrase   **Ruminate** means _____ .

12. As a play title, Eugene O'Neill's *The Hairy Ape* sounds better than *The Hirsute Simian*.

       Key: Synonym   **Simian** means _____ .

13. Caught up in the movie, we followed the *spoor* of a wounded water buffalo with nearly the same intensity as the tracker, alert for any drops of blood, any patches of trampled grass.

       Keys: Examples, logic   **Spoor** means _____ .

14. When humane *vivisection* is responsibly practiced, when necessary laboratory experiments on animals lead to cures for humans, when understanding of the animals' physiology is required by veterinary science—only then will the antivivisectionists be quiet.

       Keys: Definition, logic   **Vivisection** means _____ .

15. The *vixen* is known for intelligence, cunning, and ferocity—especially when called upon to defend her fox cubs.

       Keys: Synonym, logic   **Vixen** means _____ .

16. Our Labrador retriever had nine *whelps* in her last litter, so we had to find nine homes.

       Key: Logic   **Whelp** means _____ .

Word Study

Human beings and animals have been interdependent since time began. Animals have fed us, clothed us, worked for us, amused us, and kept us company. They've been an irreplaceable source of medical and behavioral information. And think of the books: *Moby Dick, Watership Down, Black Beauty, A Cricket in Times Square, Charlotte's Web, Lassie Come Home, Born Free, The Incredible Journey*—just for openers. It's impossible to picture our planet without animals.

Man is the only animal that blushes.
Or needs to.
     —Mark Twain

1. **asinine** ('as-ᵊn-ˌīn) adj.   Remarkably stupid or ridiculous; lacking good sense or judgment; from L. *asinus,* ass

    Hoping for an intelligent answer, Hank was both dismayed and annoyed by Jim's *asinine* response.

    Relatives: *asininely, asininity*
    Synonyms: *inane, ridiculous, absurd; asslike, stubborn*
    Antonyms: *wise, judicious, sensible*

2. **bovine** ('bō-ˌvīn, 'bō-ˌvēn) adj.   Referring to cows (and oxen) or cowlike behavior; slow-moving, stolid, not terribly quick witted; from L. *bov, bos,* ox or cow

    Thelma waited with *bovine* patience—sitting placidly in her chair, knitting one row after another onto the shawl.

    Relatives: *bovine* (n., cow, ox); *bovinely, bovinity*

3. **denizen** ('den-ə-zən) n.   An inhabitant, either plant or animal; someone who habitually goes to or lives in one place, as *denizens of the shopping mall;* from L. *de* + *intus,* within (through F. *denz,* within)

Students of ecology refer to plants, and sometimes animals, that have adapted to a nonnative ecosystem as *denizens.*

Synonym: *inhabitant*
Antonym: *alien*

4. **fledgling** ('flej-liŋ) n.   A young bird growing flight feathers; one young or lacking experience, as the young bird is untried in flight; from OE *fleōgan,* to fly

In politics, young Henderson is a *fledgling,* but anyone with his power of oratory is bound to take off sooner than most.

Relative: *fledge* (v.)
Synonyms: *novice, tyro, beginner, neophyte*
Antonyms: *expert, ace, specialist, master*

5. **fodder** ('fäd-ər) n.   Food for domestic animals; anything used regularly like a food, as *fodder for the computer* (being the steady supply of data); from OE *fōdor,* food

O, it sets my heart a-clickin' like the tickin' of a clock,
When the frost is on the punkin and the fodder's *in the shock.*
        —James Whitcomb Riley, "When the Frost Is on the Punkin"

6. **hirsute** ('hər-ˌsüt, 'hi[ə]r-ˌsüt) adj.   Hairy, or bristly with hairs; from L. *hirsutus* and *horrere,* to bristle

Of baby gorillas, *hirsute* and charming, satirist Will Cuppy said, "Young gorillas are friendly but they soon learn."

Relatives: *hirsuteness, hirsutism* (excess hair), *hirsutulous* (very slightly hirsute)
Synonym: *hairy*
Antonym: *hairless*

7. **leonine** ('lē-ə-ˌnīn) adj.   Resembling a lion; like a lion in appearance (heavy mane of hair) or behavior; from L. *leonis,* lion

I can still picture my grandfather, his *leonine* head and beard rising above a powerful set of shoulders.

Relatives: *Leo* (constellation, fifth zodiacal sign); *Leonid* (one of the shooting stars); *lionize* (to treat as very important); *leopard* (*leo* + *pardos,* leopard)

8. **porcine** ('pȯr-ˌsīn) adj.   Referring to a pig, or swine; fat, obese; from L. *porcus,* pig

A disagreeable figure, Gouge bulked ominously in his chair, his *porcine* eyes fixed on the doorway.

Relatives: *pork, porker, porcupine* (*porcus* + *spina,* spine)
Synonyms: *fat, obese* (Careful. These don't always work.)

9. **prehensile** (prē-'hen[t]-səl) adj.   Able to grasp or seize quickly and naturally, as *a monkey's prehensile tail grasps a branch,* or *a prehensile mind grasps ideas well;* from L. *prehendere,* to grasp

Gifted with a *prehensile,* precocious mind, Mozart was composing music at an age when the rest of us are learning to tie our shoes.

Relatives: *prehensility, prehension* (mental understanding)

10. **reptilian** (rep-'til-ē-ən) adj.   Referring to snakes, reptiles; snakelike; groveling, sneaky, despicable; from L. *reptilis,* creeping

The lyric from *My Fair Lady* that goes "He oiled his way across the floor, / Oozing charm from every pore" refers to a *reptilian* character whom Professor Higgins despised.

Relative:　　*reptile*

11. **ruminate** ('rü-mə-,nāt) v.　　To ponder repeatedly, slowly, thoughtfully, the way a cud-chewing animal deals with its food; to chew again the swallowed food (the cud of a ruminant mammal); from L. *rumen*, gullet

When I hear of a mind like Einstein's, I wonder if he *ruminated* at length to solve knotty problems or if flashes of inspiration came to him like lightning.

Relatives:　　*rumen* (first compartment of a ruminant's stomach); *ruminant* (cud-chewing mammal); *ruminant* (adj.); *rumination, ruminative, ruminatively, ruminator*
Synonyms:　　*reflect, ponder, meditate*

12. **simian** ('sim-ē-ən) adj.　　Similar to apes or monkeys in character, behavior, or appearance; from L. *simia*, ape

The famous Scopes trial of 1925, known as the Monkey Trial, pitted lawyer Clarence Darrow against William Jennings Bryan, noted orator and religious fundamentalist. Darrow defended Scopes, an instructor who had taught Darwin's theory of evolution, or "*simian* science," as one reporter derided it. (Note: The movie *Inherit the Wind*, from the play of that name, is an excellent dramatization of the Scopes trial.)

Relative:　　*simian* (n., monkey, ape)

13. **spoor** ('spu̇[ə]r,, 'spō[ə]r) n.　　The trail, prints, or droppings of a wild animal; akin to OE *spor*, footprint, spoor

Hungry hunters soon learn to follow the *spoor* of animals if the hunters are serious about eating dinner.

Relative:　　*spoor* (v., to track by following a spoor)
Synonyms:　　*track, trail* (neither exact)

14. **vivisection** (,viv-ə-'sek-shən) n.　　An operation on a live animal, usually for medical or scientific reasons but sometimes for less legitimate experimental reasons (strong negative connotations); from L. *vivus*, life, + E. *section*, cutting into sections

The Plague Dogs, by Richard Adams, is one man's passionate outcry against irresponsible *vivisection*.

Relatives:　　*vivisect, vivisector, vivisectional, vivisectionally, vivisectionist*

15. **vixen** ('vik-sən) n.　　A female fox; a woman of nasty, shrewish temperament; from Middle E. *fixene*, female fox

She was a vixen *when she went to school:*
And though she be but little, she is fierce.
　　　—Shakespeare, *A Midsummer Night's Dream*

Relatives:　　*vixenish, vixenishly, vixenishness*
Synonyms:　　*shrew, termagant, scold, virago*

16. **whelp** ('hwelp, 'welp)　　n. Offspring of a carnivorous mammal, especially of a dog; youngster; an upstart or unrespected person.　　v. To give birth; from OE *hwelp*, whelp, to bring forth young.

And in that town a dog was found,
As many dogs there be,
Both mongrel, puppy, whelp, *and hound,*
And curs of low degree.
　　　—Oliver Goldsmith, "An Elegy on the Death of a Mad Dog"

Root Study

This group of roots relates to animals, the land, and life—basic roots for sure.

1. CARN means flesh, meat.
    carnivorous—meat-eating
    incarnate—given human nature and form
    carnage—massacre, a bloody slaughter
    reincarnation—a rebirth in a new body or form of life; the rebirth of a soul in a new body

2. MUT/MUTAT means change.
    mutation—a significant or basic change of genetic material
    transmute—to transform or change to a higher form
    immutable—unchangeable, unvariable
    commute—to change or alter, as a severe penalty may be *commuted* to a lesser one; also, to travel regularly between one place and another

3. TERR/TER means land, earth.
    terrestrial—of the earth or land
    terrier—a small breed of dog originally bred to hunt furred game, carrying the fight underground if needed; literally, *earth dog*
    terra firma—solid ground, dry land
    inter—to bury (in the ground); *disinter*, to dig up from underground
    terrace—to arrange land in levels as for planting; any paved or planted area near buildings

4. VITA and VIV mean life.
    vitality—vigor, liveliness, physical or mental strength
    vitamin—an organic substance needed for good nutrition
    vivid—extraordinarily clear and lifelike
    viviparous—bearing live young

Using the Words

List 9 Review

asinine	fodder	prehensile	spoor
bovine	hirsute	reptilian	vivisection
denizen	leonine	ruminate	vixen
fledgling	porcine	simian	whelp

Exercise I: Definitions. Review List 9, pronouncing the words out loud, skimming the definitions as a refresher. Then write each word beside its definition or synonym.

1. hairy, bristly   h_____

2. well-adapted for grasping   p_____

3. lacking sense or judgment   a_____

4. lionlike   l_____

5. to reflect, ponder   r_____

6. inhabitant   d_____

7. apelike   s_____

8. food   f_____

9. trail, track   s_____

10. fat, obese   p_____

11. cowlike   b_____

12. operation on a living animal   v_____

13. youngster   w_____

14. young, untried individual   f_____

15. shrewish female   v_____

16. snakelike   r_____

Exercise II. Adjectives. Some of our most descriptive words are adjectives borrowed from the animal kingdom. Besides the few in List 9, we have *lupine* from **lup,** wolf; *ovine* from **ovus,** sheep; *taurine* from **taurus,** bull; *ursine* from **ursa,** bear; and *piscine* from **pisces,** fish—plus several others that you already know or can guess.

From the choices offered, select the best adjective for each blank. Each word is used only once.

leonine	reptilian	piscatory	feline
lupine	asinine	elephantine	ovine
equine	ursine	simian	canine
taurine	porcine	bovine	

1. Someone familiar with the habits of trout and bass would be a great companion on a(n) _____ expedition.

2. Don't offer your _____ buddy another box of chocolates.

3. The old saying "A dog is man's best friend" refers to the _____ trait of faithfulness.

4. "Hey, Toro, Toro!" is the taunt in Madrid's _____ spectacle.

5. Big Bear and Little Bear are the _____ constellations.

6. Purring is the traditional sign of _____ contentment.

7. The _____ growl of the Big Bad Wolf didn't scare the Little Pig in the brick house.

8. With _____ agility the tightrope walker scaled the rope ladder and negotiated the high wire like a monkey.

9. An expression you don't want on your face is one of _____ stupidity.

10. The _____ slitherers of the desert often have deadly fangs.

11. A proud conqueror favors the _____ look of command.

12. The phrase "Tiny, angry eyes in a _____, fleshy face" describes someone we don't want to know.

13. Fleet _____ hooves flash across the finish line each May in the Kentucky Derby.

14. Placid, unemotional women may be described as _____ creatures, but that phrase isn't considered a compliment.

15. Following the crowd with _____, unquestioning loyalty should be the behavior only of sheep, not of people.

Exercise III. Antonyms. Match the words from List 9 and Roots with their antonyms or contrasting phrases.

_____ 1. **terrestrial**   (a) ace

_____ 2. **asinine**   (b) whelp

_____ 3. **denizen**   (c) variable

_____ 4. **adult**   (d) to dig up

_____ 5. **hairless**   (e) intelligent

_____ 6. **fledgling**   (f) nebulous

_____ 7. **immutable**   (g) stable

_____ 8. **vivid**   (h) celestial

_____ 9. **mutable**   (i) hirsute

_____ 10. **inter** (v.)   (j) alien

Exercise IV. Fill-ins. Select the most appropriate word from List 9 and Roots to complete each sentence.

1. A sharp-tongued, ill-tempered female is a _____ .

2. Lab experiments with white mice to determine genetic transference may be termed

_____ .

3. A sassy, impudent kid is a _____ .

4. Animals bearing live young—as opposed to those who lay eggs—are termed

_____ .

5. *Dis* + *inter* = _____, meaning to dig up.

6. Noun to mean bloody slaughter = _____ .

7. If carnivores eat meat (and they do), *omnivores* eat _____ .

8. *Termagant, virago,* and *shrew* are synonyms for a _____ .

9. Cud-chewing sheep, giraffe, deer, and camels are _____ .

10. *Planet of the Apes* depicted future life with the _____ in control.

Exercise V. Word Analysis.

1. What is the *piscatorial* art? _____

2. How do you suppose an astrologer would describe the personality of someone born under the sign of Leo (July 22–23 through August 23)? _____

_____

3. Match the young with their parents:

____ a. cygnet		(1) cow (bovine)
____ b. cub		(2) horse (equine)
____ c. whelp		(3) swan
____ d. foal		(4) kangaroo
____ e. calf		(5) fox
____ f. joey		(6) dog (canine)

4. *Aviator, aviatrix* (fem.), *aviary,* and *rara avis* come from the root *avi,* bird. What is an *aviary?* A *rara avis?* (Hint: Old Webster knows . . .) _____

_____

_____

5. When a French girl calls for *la poussiquette,* what animal will come? _____

6. Match the *-ologies* (studies of) with the subject studied.

____ a. etymology		(1) birds
____ b. ornithology		(2) mind and behavior
____ c. entomology		(3) mammals
____ d. psychology		(4) words
____ e. mammalogy		(5) insects

7. What is *educational fodder?* _____

8. Generations have repeated adages such as "Every dog has his day," "a bull in a china shop," and "a wolf in sheep's clothing." How many other sayings can you think of that delineate human behavior in animal terms? _____

_____

_____

"If man could be crossed with cat, it would improve man, but deteriorate the cat."
　　—Mark Twain.

LIST 10
Bigots and Bagatelles
NOUNS NICE TO KNOW

In Context. Before studying the definitions, try reasoning out the meaning of each word, using context as your guide.

1. "I prefer the *ambience* at the elementary school," Mom said. "The atmosphere there is charged with excitement about learning and exceptional warmth."

    Key: Synonym   **Ambience** means _____ .

2. We considered the *amenities* of each hotel in town before selecting one for the holiday dance. We chose Blake House because of its large dance floor, outstanding band, and reasonable food prices.

    Keys: Logic, examples   **Amenities** means _____ .

3. Carrie is the *anomaly* in our family, as she's the only one of us who doesn't love chocolate.

    Key: Partial definition   **Anomaly** means _____ .

4. The work force at Dad's office is reduced by *attrition*. As people resign, die, or retire, no one replaces them.

    Key: Partial definition   **Attrition** means _____ .

5. "If you and Jan want luggage for graduation," Dad said, "I need to start saving now. Sets of good luggage are not *bagatelles*, you know; they are a major purchase."

    Key: Opposing phrase   **Bagatelle** means _____ .

6. "He's such a chauvinist—such a *bigot!*" Jan fumed. "He's never hired a girls' lawn service. He told me only boys could have the job. How narrow-minded can you get?"

    Key: Synonyms   **Bigot** means _____ .

7. Seniors would be more tolerant of freshmen if their *demeanor* were more adult. Unfortunately, some freshmen behave like fifth-graders.

    Keys: Near synonym, logic   **Demeanor** means _____ .

8. "I can't stand *duplicity*," Mom said. "Please don't tell me this dress looks good on me if you think I look like a sack of potatoes. I'd rather hear the truth."

    Keys: Antonym, logic   **Duplicity** means _____ .

9. Our schools have regular fire drills so that we know how to evacuate the buildings rapidly in any *exigency*—whether it's fire or not.

    Key: Logic   **Exigency** means _____ .

10. "It's the *logistics* that get me," confessed the marching band director. "Transportation to the games, seating arrangements till we perform, getting on and off the field properly. . . . All those details wear me out!"

    Keys: Examples, logic   **Logistics** means _____ .

11. Jan's favorite era is the Middle Ages, when the humble simplicity and poverty of most lives formed a stark contrast to the *ostentation* and wealth of a privileged few.

    Key: Opposing phrase   **Ostentation** means _____.

12. Mom wants us to get a bulldog. "I grin every time I see one," she said, "and I admire their *pertinacity*. You know I've always respected determination."

    Key: Synonym   **Pertinacity** means _____.

13. "What a *quisling!*" Jan snorted. "Al promised to vote with us, then voted for the other side."

    Keys: Example, logic   **Quisling** means _____.

14. Aware of the *rancor* he'd incurred by being a turncoat, Al tried to win back the classmates he'd deserted, but we were too bitter to listen.

    Key: Near synonym   **Rancor** means _____.

15. As we prepared for the state marching band contest, our director was merciless, marching us up and down the field with no *respite* until he was satisfied.

    Key: Logic   **Respite** means _____.

16. "If Al has the *temerity* to think he can act nice for a while and we'll forget," Jan said, "then he's got more nerve than I thought!"

    Keys: Synonym, logic   **Temerity** means _____.

17. Leaving nothing to the *vagaries* of chance, our band director made us practice until we could execute each number perfectly.

    Key: Logic   **Vagaries** means _____.

Word Study

As a writer and speaker, you will always depend on two parts of speech: nouns and verbs to convey the center of your meaning. Select them carefully and you'll be an effective user of language. No quantity of adjectives and adverbs can compensate for weak nouns and verbs. The word *house,* for example, gives only a general picture. But if you specify what sort of house by calling it a *mansion,* a *shack,* or a *Cape Cod cottage,* then a more definite picture emerges—and a more interesting one.

Remember that general, overused words are dull. The specific is interesting. The nouns (and verbs) you use should paint a vivid picture in your reader's or listener's mind, because that is the secret to good communication.

1. **ambience** ('am-bē-ən[t]s) n.   The environment or feeling of a place or area, its atmosphere; from L. *ambi* + *ire,* to go around

   The excellent food, cheerful waiters, and overall mood of contentment create an *ambience* at Mama Luisa's restaurant that draws customers from a wide area.

   Synonyms: *atmosphere, environment* (neither exact)

2. **amenities** (ə-'men-ət-ēz) pl. n.   The qualities (of a place or of social interaction) that are desirable, pleasant, and agreeable; any qualities that add to the comfort, salability, or desirability of a property or place; sing., *amenity;* from L. *amoenus,* pleasant

   We chose our summer cottage site based on the local *amenities:* a nearby golf course plus an excellent lake for boating, fishing, and swimming.

3. **anomaly** (ə-'näm-ə-lē) n.   An irregularity or deviation from what is normal or expected; pl., *anomalies;* from Gr. *anomalos,* uneven

The "black sheep" in a family is the *anomaly*—the one who doesn't share the standards of the rest.

Relative: *anomalous*
Synonyms: *irregularity, paradox* (neither exact)

4. **attrition** (ə-'trish-ən) n.   Lowering in number (of people) by means of resignation, death, or retirement; annoyance or harassment by frequent attack to the point of exhaustion (derived from the meaning of friction or rubbing together, as stones are smoothed and worn down in water by *attrition*); from L. *ad* + *terere,* to rub

Large companies prefer to reduce employee numbers by *attrition,* because firing people or laying them off attracts undesirable publicity.

Relatives: *attritional, attrited* (worn down by attrition)
Opposing ideas: *expansion, addition, accretion*

5. **bagatelle** (ˌbag-ə-'tel) n.   A small, unimportant item, a trifle; also, a table game played with balls and a cue; from It. *bagattella,* trifling

The wealthy woman gestured casually at the bracelet on her wrist. "Only pearls," she murmured. "A mere *bagatelle,* I assure you."

Synonyms: *trifle, trinket*

6. **bigot** ('big-ət) n.   Someone stubbornly attached to or prejudiced by his own beliefs, sex, political party, church, etc.; a narrow-minded, opinionated person; from Middle F. *bigot,* a religious, overdevout hypocrite, a bigot

Sinclair Lewis's satiric novel *Babbitt* is the story of George F. Babbitt, a self-satisfied man of the middle class whose name is now synonymous with *bigot.*

Relatives: *bigoted, bigotry, bigotedly*
Synonym: *Babbitt, chauvinist*

7. **demeanor** (di-'mē-nər) n.   Manner, appearance, or bearing; behavior; from OF *demener,* to conduct

I am a courtier grave and serious,
Who is about to kiss your hand:
Try to combine a pose imperious
With a demeanor *nobly bland.*
        —W. S. Gilbert, *The Gondoliers*

Relative: *demean* (to behave; or, to degrade, debase)
Synonyms: *bearing, behavior, conduct*

8. **duplicity** (d[y]ù-'plis-ət-ē) n.   Crafty or underhanded double-dealing; deception by words or actions in order to hide the truth; from L. *duo* + *plex,* double fold

Not many of us are comfortable with *duplicity;* we expect others to be straightforward and honest.

Relatives: *duplicitous, duplicitously*
Synonyms: *double-dealing, hypocrisy*

9. **exigencies** ('ek-sə-jən-sēz, ig-'zij-ən-sēz) pl. n.   The needs or requirements of a given situation; in singular form, any occasion making urgent demands, as *a lifeguard must act quickly in any sudden exigency;* from L. *exigere,* to demand

The *exigencies* of World War II in England were such that citizens were rationed to three ounces of laundry soap and one egg per month.

Relative: *exigent* (demanding)
Synonyms: *needs, junctures* (neither exact)

10. **logistics** (lō-'jis-tiks, lə-'jis-tiks) pl. n.   The management of details in any operation or situation; in military life, the administration, management, and ordering of troops, supplies, and facilities; from Gr. *logos,* reason, + *logistikos,* calculation

Mandy wanted to plan a trip around the United States, but the *logistics* of her excursion seemed daunting.

Relatives: *logic, logistic, logistician*

11. **ostentation** (ˌäs-tən-'tā-shən) n.   Showy, extensive display of wealth, possessions, skills, etc.; from L. *ostentare,* to display excessively

Modest people deplore *ostentation* because they are genuinely embarrassed by any show of material wealth or special skills.

Relatives: *ostentatious, ostentatiously, ostentatiousness*
Synonyms: *pretentiousness, showiness*
Antonyms: *modesty, restraint, humility, reserve*

12. **pertinacity** (ˌpərt-ᵊn-'as-ət-ē) n.   The quality of obstinacy, persistence, and determination that makes someone hang on stubbornly, often in the face of great odds; from L. *per + tenere,* cling to

Anyone who has spent long hours scraping barnacles off a boat understands *pertinacity.*

Relatives: *pertinacious, pertinaciously*
Synonyms: *obstinance, stubbornness, tenacity, perseverance*

13. **quisling** ('kwiz-liŋ) n.   A traitor who works with invaders in his country, even to the extent of serving in their government (See "Derivation.")

Once a Norwegian surname, *quisling* has come into the language as a common noun meaning traitor, just as *mesmerize* and *odyssey* were transformed from names of people into common nouns.

Relative: *quislingism*
Synonym: *traitor*
Derivation: As an English word, *quisling* was "born" about 1945, and comes from the Norwegian politician Vidkun Quisling. During World War II he served the Germans who took over Norway and thus earned the scorn of the free world. At war's end he was tried for treason and executed.

14. **rancor** ('raŋ-kər) n.   Extreme ill will or bitter feeling, usually deep-rooted; from Late L. *rancor,* rankness

'Tis not my speeches that you do mislike,
But 'tis my presence that doth trouble ye.
Rancor *will out.*
    —Shakespeare, *King Henry the Sixth,* Part II

Relatives: *rancorous, rancour* (British)
Synonyms: *enmity, antagonism, hostility, animosity*
Antonyms: *accord, friendship* (neither exact)

15. **respite** ('res-pət) n.   A welcome rest or relief from anything difficult, tiring, or demanding; a reprieve or delay; from L. *respectus,* the act of looking back

I pray the gods some respite *from the weary task of this long year's watch that lying on the Atreidae's roof on bended arm, doglike, I have kept. . . .*
    —Aeschylus, *Agamemnon*

Synonyms: *pause, rest, lull*

16. **temerity** (tə-'mer-ət-ē) n.   Extreme, rash boldness beyond what is wise or acceptable; flagrant or foolhardy recklessness; from L. *temere*, randomly, rashly

    When young Oliver asked for "more" at the orphanage meal, he was guilty of *temerity* in the opinion of those who ran the orphanage. (Have you read *Oliver Twist* or seen the musical version? Great story.)

    Relatives: *temerarious, temerariously*
    Synonyms: *effrontery, audacity, chutzpah, rashness, recklessness, nerve, gall*
    Antonyms: *caution, circumspection*

17. **vagaries** ('va-gə-rēz) pl. n.   unpredictable, whimsical things, ideas, or actions, as *the vagaries of fate;* sing., *vagary;* from L. *vagari*, to wander

    Rather than risk the *vagaries* of a wandering, elderly Newfoundland, our neighbor fenced his yard to confine old Brutus.

    Relatives: *vagarious, vagariously*
    Synonyms: *caprices, whims*

Root Study

All these roots except **spec, spic, spect** have derived words in List 10. But what would we do without all of our words that refer to *looking?*

1. LOGOS means reason.
   logic—the science that deals with reasoning and explains a valid (reliable) inference compared with a faulty one
   illogical—not conforming to the principles of sound logic; unreasonable

2. PLEX, PLIC, and PLY mean to fold.
   complex—not simple; involved, complicated; literally, *with folds*
   explicit—precise, exact, clear, straightforward
   multiply—-to grow in number; literally, many fold (manifold)

3. SPEC, SPIC, and SPECT mean to look.
   spectator—one who looks on (not a participant)
   conspicuous—highly noticeable; outstanding
   inspector—an investigator, examiner who's supposed to notice everything significant
   specimen—sample or example of a kind or type
   perspicacious—keen, shrewd; wisely observant

4. TEN, TIN, TAIN, and TENT mean to hold.
   tenacious—holding on stubbornly, often against great odds; *pertinacious*
   abstinence—refraining from strong drink (or from food, as in a fast); restraint
   retain—to hold back or keep in one place
   contention—belief, opinion "held" in the mind

Using the Words

List 10 Review

ambience	bigot	logistics	rancor
amenities	demeanor	ostentation	respite
anomaly	duplicity	pertinacity	temerity
attrition	exigency	quisling	vagaries
bagatelle			

Exercise I. Synonyms. From the choices offered, select *two* synonyms for each word in bold type. Write the letters of the synonyms on the appropriate lines.

_____ 1. **vagaries**   (a) whims   (b) chances   (c) trials
(d) caprices   (e) opportunities

_____ 2. **rancor**   (a) level   (b) enmity   (c) animosity
(d) sergeant   (e) stench

_____ 3. **pertinacity**   (a) appropriateness   (b) vivacity   (c) lack of
appeal   (d) tenacity   (e) perseverance

_____ 4. **duplicity**   (a) multiplication   (b) confusion   (c) double-
dealing   (d) two-fold   (e) hypocrisy

_____ 5. **demeanor**   (a) behavior   (b) appearance   (c) lowering
(d) nastiness   (e) character

_____ 6. **bagatelle**   (a) tricycle   (b) satchel   (c) trifle
(d) trinket   (e) instrument

_____ 7. **perspicacious**   (a) keen   (b) thoughtless   (c) shrewd
(d) nervous   (e) uneasy

_____ 8. **explicit**   (a) indefinite   (b) precise   (c) lengthy
(d) clear   (e) involved

_____ 9. **tenacious**   (a) wary   (b) persistent   (c) timid
(d) aware   (e) determined

_____ 10. **ambience**   (a) atmosphere   (b) walkway   (c) thought
(d) environment   (e) desire

Exercise II. Antonyms. Give as many antonyms as you can for these words from List 10.

1. duplicity _____

2. temerity _____

3. rancor _____

4. ostentation _____

5. anomalous (adj.) _____

Exercise III. Fill-ins. Select the most appropriate word from the choices given, based on clues in context.

pertinacity	quisling	anomaly	exigency
bigot	ambience	demeanor	attrition
vagaries	respite		

1. the luxurious atmosphere of the Ritz, justifiably known for its _____

2. dismayed by Andy's _____ when he insisted on coming with Jan and me

3. walking with queenly _____ down the aisle

4. in need of _____ from exhausting toil

5. self-righteous, opinionated pronouncements of the neighborhood _____

6. loss of several staff members through _____

7. admirable person who can handle any _____ that arises

8. a(n) _____ who belied his promises

9. didn't want to gamble on the _____ of the spring weather

10. a(n) _____ in our happy midst, conspicuous because of his gloomy expression

Exercise IV. Analogies. Complete each analogy with the best pair possible.

_____ 1. amenities : desirable ::
    (a) exigencies : admirable
    (b) logistics : understandable
    (c) vagaries : unpredictable
    (d) anomalies : likable
    (e) measles : inevitable

_____ 2. attrition : reduction ::
    (a) ostentation : awareness
    (b) bearing : demeanor
    (c) rancor : station
    (d) quisling : contestant
    (e) spectator : participant

_____ 3. bigoted : tolerant ::
    (a) keen : perspicacious
    (b) duplicitous : two-faced
    (c) logical : plausible
    (d) ostentatious : modest
    (e) foolhardy : reckless

_____ 4. temerity : effrontery ::
    (a) expansion : attrition
    (b) exigency : superfluity
    (c) pertinacity : obstinacy
    (d) respite : continuity
    (e) vagary : rarity

_____ 5. annoyance : rancor ::
    (a) gall : nerve
    (b) logic : reason
    (c) bigotry : prejudice
    (d) amenity : quality
    (e) display : ostentation
(Be careful here. This is a fine distinction.)

Exercise V. In Your Own Words. Use the given words in sentences that illustrate their meanings. Be as specific as possible.

1. amenities _____

_____

2. anomaly _____

_____

3. logistics _____

_____

4. duplicity _____

_____

5. explicit _____

_____

6. conspicuous _____

_____

7. restrain _____

_____

8. respite _____

_____

Exercise VI. Word Analysis.

1. What *one noun* from List 10 can you use to express the following idea: management of the many details for the operation of a circus (for example, the deployment of circus personnel, the animals, all equipment; ordering of supplies and foodstuffs for the circus; plus scheduling of performances and transportation from one place to another).

_____

2. This lesson has stressed nouns and the amount of specific information they can convey. For the following common, overused nouns, suggest more specific alternatives.

    a. friend _____

    b. car _____

    c. smell _____

    d. shoes _____

    e. nervousness _____

3. Lesson 10 taught four nouns commonly used in plural form: *amenities, exigencies, logistics,* and *vagaries.* What other, better-known nouns can you think of that always appear in plural form? _____

_____

4. What is the difference between *vagariously* (rarely used) and *vicariously,* which is used a great deal?

_____

_____

5. Stones on the seashore or in a rock polisher rub against one another and are worn down, smoothed, and polished through *attrition.* How is this meaning of attrition related to the other meaning of annoyance or harassment?

_____

_____

    How is the current, popular usage of attrition (reduction of employee numbers) related to the above uses?

_____

_____

6. The roots **plex/plic/ply, spec/spic/spect,** and **ten/tin/tain/tent** are three of the ten special Latin and Greek roots from which we get over 2,500 English words. (Ta da!) How many words can you list that have derived from these three STAR ROOTS?

_____

_____

_____

LIST 11
See Spot Run
VERBS ONE MORE TIME

In Context. Before studying the definitions, try reasoning out the meaning of each word, using context as your guide.

1. Our family enjoys Chinese food, but we always ask the chef not to *adulterate* the fresh meat and vegetables with foreign substances like monosodium glutamate.

      Keys: Partial definition, logic   **Adulterate** means _____ .

2. When we *ascertain* which cats are raiding the nest of baby rabbits, we'll put bells on them, but we want to be absolutely certain before we bell any cat.

      Key: Definition   **Ascertain** means _____ .

3. We'd like to *conciliate* our neighbors about our cats' behavior, but the neighbors are fonder of birds and young rabbits than they are of cats, so we have little hope of placating them.

      Key: Synonym   **Conciliate** means _____ .

4. Andy *connived* with his friend Billy to make a batch of cookies when no adult was home. In spite of their careful, secret planning, we found out because they'd spilled flour everywhere.

      Key: Definition   **Connive** means _____ .

5. "I can't *discern* any difference in color between the repaired area and the hood," Dad said as he examined the repainted fender.

      Key: Logic   **Discern** means _____ .

6. Although Jan and I put bells on Marigold, Poucette, and Figment, we're afraid that we *exacerbated* the problem. Now they stalk their prey so warily that they're more successful hunters than before.

      Key: Logic   **Exacerbate** means _____ .

7. "You have only to recognize the nature of cats to be able to *extrapolate* what ours will do now and in the future," Mom said. "Cats are hunters and that's that."

      Key: Logic (Try substituting   a word you know.)   **Extrapolate** means _____ .

8. Fortunately for me, I can *improvise* a talk better than I can plan one if I have a week, so I'm not nervous about speaking impromptu.

      Keys: Antonym, synonymous   phrase   **Improvise** means _____ .

9. Mom *inferred* from Andy's cooking messes that he wanted to learn how to cook, and now she's teaching him to be a chef.

      Key: Logic   **Infer** means _____ .

10. Since Andy began cooking, we've been *inundated* with cookies, cakes, and pizza—all the foods he loves.

        Key: Logic   **Inundate** means _____ .

11. Whenever we see Andy reading, he is *perusing* a cookbook, examining it carefully to see which recipes turn him on.

        Key: Definition   **Peruse** means _____ .

12. Andy has discovered the joys of making candy, which *portends* no good for the waistlines and teeth of our family.

        Key: Logic   **Portend** means _____ .

13. Proud of his culinary successes, Andy is *promulgating* himself throughout the neighborhood as one of America's best chefs. We're afraid he'll announce that he's giving dinner parties, too.

        Keys: Synonym, logic   **Promulgate** means _____ .

14. A handsome ginger tomcat has been pursuing Marigold recently, but so far she has *spurned* all of his advances.

        Key: Logic   **Spurn** means _____ .

            (Note how the little word "but" influences the meaning of the sentence.)

15. Mindful of its promise to be a home for the homeless, America continues to *succor* the less fortunate, offering refuge and assistance to many in need.

        Key: Definition   **Succor** means _____ .

16. Marigold appears to have *succumbed* to the blandishments of the ginger tom. Instead of rejecting him, she now strolls with him in our back yard.

        Keys: Antonym, logic   **Succumb** means _____ .

17. Journalists who irresponsibly *vilify* citizens may find themselves sued for libel.

        Keys: Synonym, logic   **Vilify** means _____ .

Word Study

    Verbs again, because they are important. They breathe life into your sentences. Also, it is more fun to have a large verb vocabulary. Isn't it more interesting to say that Brent *pigged out* or *gorged* himself at the party than that he ate a lot?

    Each verb has shades of meaning all its own. True synonyms are rare. Dictionaries suggest that *traverse* or *perambulate* or *stroll* may substitute for *walk,* and sometimes they may—but certainly not in all sentences. Always remember to select the verb that most clearly expresses your meaning.

1. **adulterate** (ə-ˈdəl-tə-rāt) v.   To render a food or substance impure by adding an inferior or corrupting element to it; to lower or corrupt by the addition of foreign matter; to debase; from L. *ad* + *alter,* other, else

    Classes about drug abuse warn us that pushers often *adulterate* the drugs they sell with even more dangerous substances.

Relatives: *adulterator, adulteration*
Synonyms: *corrupt, debase*
Antonym: *purify*

2. **ascertain** (as-ər-'tān) v.   To discover or learn with absolute certainty; from L. *ad* +
   certus (from *cernere,* to sift, decide, discern)

   In order to include that quote, we must *ascertain* who said it so that we can credit it
   properly.
   Relatives: *ascertainable, ascertainment*
   Synonym: *discover* (not exact)

3. **conciliate** (kən-'sil-ē-āt) v.   To achieve smooth, pleasant relationships by agreeable
   behavior; to reconcile, appease; from L. *conciliare,* to win over, unite, procure,
   assemble

   Unable to *conciliate* their captors, the desperate hostages tried to devise a plan for escape.
   Relatives: *conciliation, conciliator, conciliatory, conciliative*
   Synonyms: *appease, pacify, propitiate, mollify, placate*
   Antonyms: *antagonize, oppose*

4. **connive** (kə-'nīv) v.   To conspire, plot, or intrigue secretly; to agree or plan privately;
   from L. *connivere,* to close the eyes, connive

   When Brutus *connived* with Cassius, the result was the assassination of Julius Caesar.
   Relatives: *connivance, conniver, connivery*
   Synonyms: *intrigue, conspire, collude*

5. **discern** (dis-'ərn) v.   To see, as *he discerned their campfire in the clearing;* to reason,
   conclude, or detect by more than sight alone, as *she discerned from his behavior that he
   was exhausted;* to separate one thing/trait/idea from another by careful discrimination,
   noting differences; from L. *dis,* apart, + *cernere,* to sift

   Through our own recovered innocence we discern *the innocence of our neighbors.*
      —Henry David Thoreau, *Walden*
   Relatives: *discernment, discerner, discernible, discernibly, discerning*
   Synonym: *discriminate*

6. **exacerbate** (ig-'zas-ər-bāt) v.   To worsen or increase in severity, as *a drought always
   exacerbates a farmer's woes;* from L. *ex* + *acer(bus),* harsh, bitter, sharp

   Trying to rub away the stain on my car's paint only *exacerbated* the problem, as I rubbed
   off some of the paint, too.
   Relative: *exacerbation*
   Synonyms: *aggravate, intensify, irritate*
   Antonyms: *alleviate, relieve, allay*

7. **extrapolate** (ik-'strap-ə-lāt) v.   To use previously gathered or known information to
   formulate new images or ideas, perhaps of the future or an unknown territory; to forecast
   by using past experience or facts; from L. *ex* + *-polate* (from *interpolate,* where *-polate*
   means polish)

   Based on their training, astronauts are expected to *extrapolate* how they will react
   physically, mentally, and emotionally to actual travel in space.
   Relatives: *extrapolation, extrapolative, extrapolator*
   Synonym: *deduce* (works sometimes, not always)

8. **improvise** (im-prə-'vīz) v.   To create or provide by use of whatever is on hand, as *we improvised a bed, using pine boughs and a quilt;* to receive or perform impromptu, without rehearsal; from L. *improvisus,* unforeseen

A tough opponent forced our football team to *improvise* different strategies based on what we learned during the game.

Relatives: *improvisation, improvisator, improvisatorial, improvisatory, improviser* (or *improvisor*)
Synonym: *extemporize* (perform impromptu)

9. **infer** (in-'fər) v.   To reach a conclusion or opinion based on facts, experiences, or conditions; to make a logical guess, as *I infer from your recent letter that you are contented;* to hint or suggest, as *a recent survey infers that more women will hold full-time jobs in the future;* from L. *in* + *ferre,* carry or bear

Actors playing the role of Shakespeare's Richard III usually adopt a crippled posture so that their audience *infers* that Richard was deformed.

(Note: Many historians refute this concept, as well as the notion that Richard murdered his two nephews in the Tower.)

Relatives: *inference, inferable, inferrer, inferential, inferentially*
Synonyms: *deduce, conclude, judge, gather, hint, suggest*

10. **inundate** ('in-[,]ən-,dāt) v.   To overflow or overwhelm, washing over in a flood; from L. *in* + *unda,* wave

The homework for six demanding subjects *inundated* Jerry, so that he vowed to schedule a lighter course load next semester.

Relatives: *inundation, inundator, inundatory*
Synonyms: *overwhelm, deluge*

11. **peruse** (pə-'rüz) v.   To study thoroughly or examine in a careful, detailed manner; to consider thoughtfully while reading; from L. *per-,* thoroughly, + Middle E. *usen,* to use

When I peruse *the conquered fame of heroes and the victories of mighty generals, I do not envy the generals.*
        —Walt Whitman, *Leaves of Grass*

Relatives: *perusal, peruser*
Synonyms: *study, examine, consider*

12. **portend** (por-'tend) v.   To indicate as a sign or omen of what is to come; to bode, as *those clouds portend rain;* from L. *por-,* forward, + *tendere,* to stretch

These late eclipses in the sun and moon portend *no good to us.*
        —Shakespeare, *King Lear*

Relatives: *portent* (omen), *portentous, portentously*
Synonyms: *foreshadow, bode, forebode, forewarn*

13. **promulgate** ('präm-əl-,gāt) v.   To announce or declare openly, to proclaim; to activate a rule or law; from L. *promulgare,* expose to public view

Modern teenage literature is realistic. It no longer *promulgates* the idea that ages twelve to eighteen are solely years of hilarity and youthful high jinks.

Relatives: *promulgation, promulgator*
Synonyms: *declare, proclaim, announce*

14. **spurn** ('spərn) v.   To reject or scorn with contempt; to refuse to accept; from Old High Ger. and OE *spurnan,* to kick

Fair sir, you spat on me on Wednesday last;
You spurn'd *me such a day; another time*
You called me dog; and for these courtesies
I'll lend you thus much moneys?
        —Shakespeare, *The Merchant of Venice*

Relative: *spurner*
Synonyms: *reject, decline, scorn*
Antonyms: *crave, embrace, hanker for, yearn for,* or *long for*

15. **succor** ('sək-ər) v.   To help in time of need or stress; to aid or relieve; from L. *sub +*
    currere, to run

    The city council decided that it was their duty to *succor* the struggling symphony orchestra
    through a financial crisis.

    Relatives: *succor* (n.), *succorer*
    Synonyms: *relieve, aid, help*

16. **succumb** (sə-'kəm) v.   To yield to a greater force or give in to a powerful desire or
    appeal; to give way (as in death) to something overwhelmingly destructive; from L. *sub*
    + cumbere, to lie down

    When I *succumb* to my yearning for a hot fudge sundae, I have an odd mixture of feelings:
    delight at the taste mixed with annoyance at my lack of will power.

    Synonym: *yield*
    Antonym: *resist*

17. **vilify** ('vil-ə-fī) v.   To defame or malign by strongly negative statements; to slander;
    from L. *vilis,* of little value, cheap, common

    It is easier to *vilify* an enemy than to create a solution which will ease the enmity.

    Relatives: *vilification, vilifier, vile* (base, contemptible), *vilely, vileness*
    Synonyms: *malign, defame, slander*
    Antonyms: *praise, eulogize*

Root Study

You will recognize three of these roots that have derived words in List 11. **Fer** belongs to the
Star Roots club (ones that have contributed the most words to English). **Cur** gives us many
verbs as well as other frequently used words.

1. AC/ACR means bitter, sharp, sour.
    acrid—deeply bitter; sharply pungent, as *acrid smoke*
    acute—penetrating, as *acute powers of observation;* sharp or severe, as *acute pain;*
        needing immediate attention
    acumen—keen mental perception; discernment, shrewdness
    acrimonious—very bitter or caustic in feeling, as *an acrimonious argument*

2. CUMB and CUB mean to lie down.
    incumbent—(n.) one holding an office; (adj.) referring to a duty or obligation (See List 6.)
    incubator—an apparatus in which environment is controlled
    recumbent—resting, leaning, lying down in a relaxed manner, prone
    incubate—to hatch (an egg or an idea); to ponder and develop a concept, answer, or idea

3. CUR, CURR, CURS, and COURSE mean to run.
    recur—to happen again, to *occur* another time
    current—of the present time; timely; (n.) the flow of water, as *a swiftly moving current*

cursory—hasty, lacking thoroughness
recourse—a looking to someone (or something) for assistance; or the source of help itself, as *the last recourse* (resort) *in our long search*

4. FER means to carry, bear.
defer—to postpone, delay; to yield to the wisdom, wishes, or superior position of another
deference—honor, esteem, or respect due to someone worthy or someone in a superior position
fertile—able to germinate crops or ideas profitably and well, as *a fertile garden* and *a fertile mind*
confer—to discuss with another; to consider with someone else

Using the Words

List 11 Review

adulterate	exacerbate	inundate	spurn
ascertain	extrapolate	peruse	succor
conciliate	improvise	portend	succumb
connive	infer	promulgate	vilify
discern			

Exercise I. Synonyms. The words at the left are synonyms of words taught in Lesson 11. Write the correct study words on the lines. Use the clue letter to jog your memory before looking back at definitions.

SYNONYM		STUDY WORD
1. conspire	c	_____
2. discriminate	d	_____
3. extemporize	i	_____
4. corrupt	a	_____
5. deduce	e	_____
	i	_____
6. examine	p	_____
7. proclaim	p	_____
8. yield	s	_____
9. aid	s	_____
10. discover	a	_____
11. overwhelm	i	_____
12. foreshadow	p	_____

Exercise II. Antonyms. The words at the left are antonyms or phrases in contrast to words in List 11. Write the correct study word on the lines.

ANTONYM/CONTRASTING PHRASE	STUDY WORD
1. crave	_____
2. purify	_____

3. alleviate _____

4. to plan openly _____

5. antagonize _____

6. to rehearse or practice repeatedly _____

7. to review the past _____

8. eulogize _____

9. to deny assistance or support _____

10. resist, stand firm _____

Exercise III. Switcheroo—*Verbs into Nouns*. Match the noun forms of Lesson 11 verbs with their meanings.

_____ 1. portent

_____ 2. adulteration

_____ 3. improvisation

_____ 4. inference

_____ 5. concilation

_____ 6. discernment

_____ 7. promulgation

_____ 8. succor

_____ 9. connivance

_____ 10. vilification

_____ 11. exacerbation

_____ 12. perusal

_____ 13. inundation

_____ 14. ascertainment

_____ 15. extrapolation

(a) appeasement

(b) declaration

(c) discrimination

(d) aggravation

(e) consent to wrongdoing

(f) discovering beyond doubt

(g) omen

(h) deduction

(i) flood

(j) prediction based on past knowledge or experience

(k) corruption

(l) relief, help

(m) abuse, defamation

(n) spontaneous creation

(o) examination

Exercise IV. Analogies. Complete each analogy with the best pair possible, using words from List 11.

_____ 1. criticism : vilification ::
   (a) discernment : sight
   (b) history : portent
   (c) acumen : perception
   (d) shower : inundation
   (e) succor : concealment

_____ 2. spurn : hanker for ::
   (a) infer : hint
   (b) peruse : study
   (c) alternate : traverse
   (d) promulgate : announce
   (e) exacerbate : relieve

_____ 3. improviser : ingenuity ::
   (a) conciliator : diplomacy
   (b) promulgator : secrecy
   (c) planner : deference
   (d) conniver : publicity
   (e) vilifier : sanity

_____ 4. ascertainment : conclusion ::
    (a) inference : suggestion   (d) exacerbation : cure
    (b) adulteration : invention   (e) perusal : knowledge
    (c) succor : decision

_____ 5. discern : differences ::
    (a) peruse : condiments   (d) extrapolate : concerns
    (b) infer : conclusions   (e) portend : worries
    (c) defer : positions

Exercise V. Fill-ins. Select the most appropriate word from the choices offered, based on clues in context.

deference	defer	acumen	recumbent
cursory	confer	recourse	acrimonious
acrid	incubate		

"I've put your problem into my mental computer," Dad assured me, "but it will have to _____ (1) awhile before I have a good answer." He stretched out in his customary _____ (2) position on the couch, and I assumed he was mulling over my latest worry.

Minutes later he sat up. "Did you _____ (3) with your teacher about your grade?"

"Well, sort of. Actually we had a(n) _____ (4) discussion that left both of us furious. I told him that he'd given my paper only a(n) _____ (5) reading, instead of reading it carefully. He told me that his mental _____ was sufficiently great for him not to have to study every word of a student's paper. Then he said that I must _____ (6) to his judgment, because he was the teacher."

Dad nodded. "Yes, _____ (7) is due to your instructor, certainly. But you didn't achieve anything with that sort of discussion. Instead, there's a bad aftertaste, like the _____ (8) smoke which lingers after a fire."

Glumly, I nodded agreement. "I guess I have no _____ (9) except talking to him again."

Dad smiled. "I think you just solved your own problem."

Exercise VI. Word Analysis.

1. The word *infer* is often misused because people confuse it with *imply*, *intimate*, or *impute*. Using a dictionary, sort out the meanings of these separate verbs and use each correctly in a sentence.

_____

_____

_____

_____

2. How does a *cursory inspection* of a book differ from *perusal?* _____

   _____

3. The Latin root *fer* is one of the Star Roots used to form so many English words. Aside from the ones already given, how many words can you list that derive from *fer?*

   _____

   _____

   _____

4. Substitute a few of your new verbs for the everyday words and expressions that follow:

   a. to find out _____

   b. make up something on the spot _____

   c. study carefully _____

   d. to plot secretly _____

   e. to overwhelm _____

   f. to reject _____

   g. to give in or up _____

   h. to talk with someone else _____

   i. to put off, postpone _____

   j. to ruin the purity of something
      by adding an inferior substance _____

5. A nearly perfect synonym for *exacerbate* is *aggravate,* because both share the meaning element of making an already-existing problem worse or increasing its severity. How have *you* heard the word *aggravate* used? Is it being correctly used in everyday speech?

   _____

   _____

6. How does the phrase *coursing with hounds* relate to the root meaning of the word *course?* Is coursing still a popular sport?

   _____

   _____

7. Using the original prefix and root meanings, can you deduce the current meanings of *defer, refer,* and *confer?* If so, explain.

   _____

   _____

Mind and Matter
PSYCHOLOGICAL AND MEDICAL TERMS

In Context. Before studying the definitions, try reasoning out the meaning of each word, using context as your guide.

1. "I made a super suggestion," Carrie told us, "but you wouldn't believe the *anemia* of their response. No excitement, no vitality, just blah. I don't get it!"

   Keys: Antonyms, colloquial
   synonym   **Anemia** means _____ .

2. The young collie that we were "puppy-sitting" for neighbors ate something mildly poisonous. We rushed him to the vet to see if an *antidote* was needed.

   Key: Logic   **Antidote** means _____ .

3. "Saccharin's supposed to cause cancer, and repeated suntans are asking for skin cancer. If those are *carcinogens,* how can I ever stay thin and look gorgeous?" Jan moaned.

   Key: Definitive phrases   **Carcinogen** means _____ .

4. Exhausted from putting in the boat dock, Dad and I flopped down on the beach. Andy danced around us, pretending we'd had heart attacks, and yelling, *"Cardiac* arrest! *Cardiac* arrest!"

   Key: Synonym   **Cardiac** means _____ .

5. When our old cat, Napoleon, had a terminal case of feline leukemia, we opted for *euthanasia,* reasoning that an easy death was kinder than a long illness.

   Key: Definition   **Euthanasia** means _____ .

6. Mom examined Andy's cut daily to be sure that it didn't ooze pus or become inflamed. "If it *festers,*" she told him, "we'll see the doctor."

   Key: Definition   **Fester** means _____ .

7. "I just have to smell a charcoal fire," Dad said with a grin, "and the *gastric* juices in my stomach churn in anticipation."

   Keys: Logic, synonym   **Gastric** means _____ .

8. "We'll keep an eye on that *lesion,*" Dad said. "A gash of that size in the bark could cause us to lose our favorite maple tree."

   Keys: Near synonym, logic   **Lesion** means _____ .

9. "The body's *lymph* system discharges its fluid into the blood through the thoracic duct," our biology teacher explained. "This lymphatic fluid is like blood plasma but normally contains only white blood cells. Lymph nodes trap bacteria to prevent their passage into the blood."

   Key: Definition   **Lymph** means _____ .

10. "Andy's concern about these cupcakes is almost *paranoia*," Mom told me. "He's convinced that we're going to eat them all before he's finished his dinner and can have one."

        Key: Logic   **Paranoia** means _____ .

11. We have sympathy for a neighbor whose *phobia* about heights prevents him from hiking the local mountains and skiing.

        Key: Logic   **Phobia** means _____ .

12. Knowledge of CPR, cardiopulmonary resuscitation, is necessary when you live by a lake. Last summer we had to *resuscitate* a visitor who nearly drowned.

        Key: Logic   **Resuscitate** means _____ .

13. "Nothing like a *salutary* swim to make you feel invigorated," Jan announced as she toweled her hair. "I always feel so strong and healthy after swimming across the lake and back."

        Key: Logic   **Salutary** means _____ .

14. Aunt Dolly came home from the hospital with a list of *therapeutic* exercises, which she did faithfully to restore muscle tone.

        Keys: Logic, example   **Therapeutic** means _____ .

15. In art class Jan studied Greek and Roman sculptured *torsos*, concentrating on the proportions of the body's trunk without the distraction of head, arms, and legs.

        Key: Definition   **Torso** means _____ .

16. All of the *toxic* substances in our house have been labeled "Poison" to prevent any disastrous errors.

        Key: Synonym   **Toxic** means _____ .

17. The *vascular* system of higher plants is comparable to the human blood vessel system in that both conduct vital body fluids through a series of channels.

        Keys: Definition, example   **Vascular** means _____ .

Word Study

Medical science seems to interest more people than any other science. Naturally, we are concerned with our health. Medical programs like "Quincy" and "M.A.S.H." abound, as do books. *Arrowsmith,* by Sinclair Lewis, *Dear and Glorious Physician,* by Taylor Caldwell, and the more recent Robin Cook novels, *Coma* and *Brain,* are only a few of the hundreds of popular titles. Stephen King has capitalized on our fascination with the powers of the mind in books like *Firestarter*. Medical movies and psychological thrillers draw millions.

Obviously, we need to learn the lingo—not only for the TV programs, books, and movies, but to communicate intelligently with our own physicians.

1. **anemia** (ə-ˈnē-mē-ə) n.   A condition resulting from insufficient red blood cells or reduction of hemoglobin content in these cells; a lack of sparkle, verve, or liveliness; from Gr. *anaimia,* bloodlessness

    Anemia may result from iron deficiency, loss of blood, excessive destruction of red corpuscles, or a malfunction of the liver or bone marrow.

Relatives: *anemic, anemically*
Synonyms: *dullness, apathy* (second meaning)
Antonyms: *sparkle, verve, vitality, liveliness* (second meaning)

2. **antidote** (ˈant-i-ˌdōt) n.   A counteracting remedy that minimizes or eliminates a poison's effects; anything that behaves as a counteracting force, as *an antidote to the materialism of our time;* from Gr. *anti* + *didonai,* to give against, to give as a counteragent

Macbeth asked his doctor:

Canst thou not minister to a mind diseased,
Pluck from the memory a rooted sorrow,
Raze out the written troubles of the brain,
And with some sweet oblivious antidote
Cleanse the stuffed bosom of that perilous stuff
Which weighs upon the heart?
     —Shakespeare

Relatives: *antidotal, antidotally*

3. **carcinogen** (kär-ˈsin-ə-jən, ˈkärs-ᵊn-ə-ˌjən) n.   Anything that causes cancer (a malignant tumorous disease); from Gr. *karkinos,* cancer, + *gen,* kind, type, cause

One *carcinogen* currently under heavy attack by doctors and laymen alike is smoking tobacco.

Relatives: *carcinogenic, carcinogenesis, carcinoid* (usually benign tumor), *carcinoma* (malignant tumor), *carcinomatosis* (multiple tumors developing simultaneously)

4. **cardiac** (ˈkärd-ē-ˌak) adj.   Referring to the heart or its bodily region, or to heart disease; from Gr. *kardia,* heart

Known as an EKG or ECG, an electrocardiogram is the paper tracing that shows changes of electrical potential during the heartbeat; thus, it is useful for diagnosing *cardiac* abnormalities.

Relatives: *cardiology, cardiogram, cardiograph, cardiopulmonary* (referring to heart and lungs), *-cardium* (suffix = heart), *cardialgia* (heartburn)

5. **euthanasia** (ˌyü-thə-ˈnā-zh[ē-]ə) n.   The killing or allowing to die, for merciful reasons, of a person or animal ill or injured beyond hope of recovery; from Gr. *eu,* good or easy, + *thanatos,* death

Determined not to linger through a hopeless illness, many people have signed living wills, which authorize their *euthanasia* when the doctor agrees that death is preferable to living.

Relatives: *euthanasic*

6. **fester** (ˈfes-tər) v.   To form pus or to make inflamed, as *a wound that festers is not healing;* to rankle, irritate, or worry, as *his insult festered in my mind;* from Middle F. *festre* and L. *fistula,* pipe, fistulous ulcer

Her cruel remark still *festers* in my brain, infecting it with an anger I dare not release.

Relatives: *fester* (n.), an oozing sore
Synonyms: *rankle, inflame*
Antonyms: *soothe, alleviate*

7. **gastric** (ˈgas-trik) adj.   Referring to the stomach; from Gr. *gastr-,* belly

A man whose *gastric* juices probably did double duty was actor Orson Welles, who confessed, "Gluttony is not a secret vice."

Relatives: *gastrectomy, gastral, gastrin, gastritis, gastronome* (epicure, gourmet), *gastronomy* (study of fine eating or cooking customs)

8. **lesion** ('lē-zhən) n.　　A change (for the worse) in bodily tissue due to injury or disease, especially one clearly defined area of injury like a cut; from L. *laedere,* to injure

While the dolphin was suspended in a canvas sling, the veterinarian treated two separate *lesions* in the heavy, glistening skin.

9. **lymph** ('lim[p]f) n.　　The nearly colorless bodily fluid that bathes tissues, has its own system of channels and ducts, and passes into the blood; from L. *lympha,* water goddess, water

One indication of infection is enlargement of the *lymph* nodes, as in Hodgkin's disease, which typically progresses to severe anemia.

Relatives:　*lymphatic, lymphocyte, lymphoma* (tumor of lymphoid tissue)

10. **paranoia** (ˌpar-ə-'nȯi-ə) n.　　An illogical, persistent feeling of distrust or suspicion of others, the "everybody's out to get me" syndrome; the mental state characterized by delusions of being picked on *or* of being greater than everyone else; from Gr. *paranous,* demented

A modern song lyric rhymes "may destroy you" with *paranoia,* which certainly is a self-destructive mind set.

Relatives:　*paranoid, paranoiac*

11. **phobia** ('fō-bē-ə) n.　　An extreme fear, usually illogical and inexplicable; from Gr. *phobos,* fear, flight

Some of the more common *phobias* include *claustrophobia* (fear of enclosed spaces), *acrophobia* (fear of heights), and *agoraphobia* (fear of open, limitless spaces).

Relatives:　*phobic* plus the names of all recognized phobias, as above

12. **resuscitate** (ri-'səs-ə-ˌtāt) v.　　To revive or bring back to life (from near death or unconsciousness); to give new life or revitalize; from L. *resuscitare,* to stir up again

For three years, out of key with his time,
He strove to resuscitate *the dead art*
Of poetry; to maintain "the sublime":
In the old sense.
　　　—Ezra Pound, *Hugh Selwyn Mauberley*

Relatives:　*resuscitation, resuscitative, resuscitator*
Synonyms:　*revive, revitalize*

13. **salutary** ('sal-yə-ˌter-ē) adj.　　Having a good effect on health; curative or remedial; from L. *salut,* health

Taking the dog for a brisk walk is a *salutary* exercise for both human and animal.

Relatives:　*salutarily, salutariness*
Synonym:　*healthful*

14. **therapeutic** (ˌther-ə-'pyüt-ik) adj.　　Beneficial to recovery from an ailment, disease, or problem, as *hospitals prescribe therapeutic diets for patients with special ailments;* medicinal, curative; from Gr. *therapeuein,* to attend or treat

"After studying all week, I find a weekend of friends and fun is positively *therapeutic*," Jan announced.

Relatives:　*therapy, therapist*

15. **torso** ('tȯr-[ˌ]sō) n.　　The human trunk or main body portion, as in a statue whose head, arms, and legs have been broken off; anything that is minus parts, or unfinished, as *the torso of a manuscript;* pl., *torsos* or *torsi;* from L. *thyrsus,* stalk

Michelangelo's *David,* a larger-than-life sculpture, depicts the *torso* of an ideal man, with head, arms, and legs of equal perfection.

Synonym: *trunk*

16. **toxic** ('täk-sik) adj.   Poisonous; influenced by a poison or toxin; from L. *toxicum,*
    poison

    A skull and crossbones label *toxic* substances to warn of their danger.

    Relatives: *toxin, antitoxin, toxicity, toxicant, toxicogenic, toxicological, toxicology,*
                  toxicosis, toxemia

    Synonym: *poisonous*

17. **vascular** ('vas-kyə-lər) adj.   Referring to a channel system conveying fluids: the blood
    of animals and people, or the sap of plants; composed of these channels, as *a vascular*
    area; from L. *vasculum,* small vessel

    Vascular surgery to relieve the problem of varicose veins has become increasingly
    sophisticated, to the joy of many.

    Relatives: *vascularity, vascularization, vasculature*

Root Study

Ail of these roots fit tidily into a lesson about physical and mental health.

1. CIDE and CIS mean to cut or to kill.
     incision—a cut, usually made in surgery
     incise—to cut, engrave, or carve
     incisive—clear-cut, biting, crisp, as *an incisive remark*
     homicide—the killing of another person

2. DERM means skin.
     dermatitis—irritation or disease of the skin
     dermatologist—physician specializing in skin and its diseases
     epidermis—the outer skin layer
     pachyderm—an elephant, rhinoceros, or pig; literally, *thick-skinned*

3. MANIA means craving or insanity.
     maniac—a deranged, demented person; or someone wildly enthusiastic about something
     pyromaniac—someone who feels compelled to start fires
     manic-depressive—describing a mental state that varies from wild enthusiasm to deep
         depression
     megalomania—mental illness characterized by delusions of grandeur and a conviction of
         great personal power

4. PATH means feeling, suffering, disease.
     pathology—study of the nature of disease
     sympathy—a feeling of pity or concern for another
     empathy—an identical, shared feeling when you know exactly how another feels
     apathy—lack of feeling, indifference

5. VIRUS means poison.
     virus—the cause of an infectious disease
     virulent—malignant; unusually strong, rapid, or destructive
     viricide—a substance that kills viruses
     virology—scientific study of viruses

Using the Words

List 12 Review

anemia	fester	paranoia	therapeutic
antidote	gastric	phobia	torso
carcinogen	lesion	resuscitate	toxic
cardiac	lymph	salutary	vascular
euthanasia			

Exercise I. Substitution. Cross out the words in italics and substitute the correct terms from List 12.

1. We had to make a tracing of the human *blood* system for advanced biology class.

2. Has your lifesaving class learned the CPR method of *reviving* an accident victim?

3. Bobbie has a noticeable *fear* of cats; she won't even go near a kitten.

4. I have excellent salve for this *wounded area* on my arm.

5. Tobacco has been implicated as a *cancer-causing agent* in several organs of the body.

6. Physicians are understandably wary, but veterinarians have long practiced *a good death* for hopelessly ill or suffering animals.

7. *Stomach* ulcers tend to flare up in times of stress.

8. Jack's *feeling of persecution* overwhelms him at times, and he sounds quite deranged.

9. We've given up sugar, caffeine, and animal fats. How's that for a *healthful* diet?

10. The day our neighbor collapsed he was rushed to the hospital for care by a team of *heart* specialists.

Exercise II. Matching. From the choices listed below, select the specialist who could best treat or diagnose the symptoms you have. (Note: *Neur* means nerve; *ophthalm* means eye.) These are not the simplest decisions. Ask a friend, teacher, or parent if you need help.

oculist/ophthalmologist	obstetrician	toxicologist
pediatrician	physical therapist	pathologist
internist	neurologist	vascular specialist
psychiatrist	orthodontist	podiatrist/chiropodist
dermatologist	cardiologist	

1. Your baby's on the way. _____

2. You have pains around your heart. _____

3. You drank something out of a bottle decorated with a skull and crossbones. _____

4. You're continually depressed. _____

5. You are unable to see distant objects. _____

6. You have a weird rash on your legs. _____

7. Mysterious symptoms need diagnosis. _____

8. You need a vein transplant. _____

9. Your ingrown toenails are "killing" you. _____

10. You don't want to be with people anymore.   _____

11. You have recurrent gastric pain.   _____

12. Now that the baby's born, it's colicky.   _____

13. Your muscles are weak from disuse.   _____

14. You suffer from flat feet and aching ankles.   _____

15. Your teeth are crooked.   _____

16. You've had two seizures and fear a brain tumor.   _____

Exercise III. Chart Fill-in. Add the missing items in the following chart.

	PREFIX	ROOT	WORD	DEFINITION
1.	_____	_____	incision	_____
2.	_____	path	_____	knowing exactly how someone else feels
3.	hypo-	_____	_____	injection under the skin
4.	_____	didonai	_____	counteracting remedy
5.	_____	_____	fratricide	_____
6.	xx	virus	_____	unusually strong, rapid, or destructive
7.	mega-	_____	_____	delusions of power
8.	_____	_____	euthanasia	_____
9.	re-	_____	_____	to revive, revitalize
10.	_____	toxicum	_____	remedy to counteract a poison

Exercise IV. Antonyms. Select two antonyms for each word in bold type and write their letters on the appropriate lines.

_____ 1. **indecisive**   (a) incisive   (b) vague   (c) shallow
                            (d) marginal   (e) clear-cut

_____ 2. **salutary**   (a) worthy   (b) toxic   (c) farewell
                            (d) harmful   (e) greeting

_____ 3. **fester**   (a) bother   (b) soothe   (c) rankle
                            (d) slower   (e) alleviate

_____ 4. **anemic**   (a) lackluster   (b) profound   (c) vivacious
                            (d) sparkling   (e) acidic

_____ 5. **maniacal**   (a) sane   (b) wild   (c) composed
                            (d) unruly   (e) disturbed

Exercise V. Definitions. Some words don't have synonyms or antonyms but require explanation instead. If you had to explain the following words to a younger person, what would you say?

1. Anemia _____

_____

2. Lymph _____

_____

3. Paranoia _____

_____

4. Torso _____

_____

5. Therapeutic _____

_____

Exercise VI. Word Analysis.

1. What is a *carcinoma?* _____

2. *Homeopathy,* derived from the root *path,* is an alternative to traditional medical practice. Check your dictionary for a brief explanation of homeopathy. Why might patients abandon the customary medical treatment and seek an alternative? _____

_____

3. Statistics say that the average man has 2.21 phobias. The average woman is reputed to have 3.55. See how many of the more common phobias you can match correctly.

    ____ a. acrophobia   (1) dreadful fear of thunder

    ____ b. pyrophobia   (2) dreadful fear of confined places

    ____ c. aquaphobia   (3) dreadful fear of lightning

    ____ d. agoraphobia   (4) dreadful fear of fire

    ____ e. claustrophobia   (5) dreadful fear of heights

    ____ f. keraunophobia   (6) dreadful fear of wide open spaces

    ____ g. astraphobia   (7) dreadful fear of water

4. What is a *salutation?* Does that word have the same root as *salutary?* _____

_____

_____

5. Pretend that you're the surgeon who will perform the operations listed below. In each case, tell what organ or part of the body you are removing or operating on. (**Tomy** = *to cut.*)

    a. Tonsillectomy _____

    b. Lobotomy _____

    c. Appendectomy _____

    d. Hysterectomy _____

    e. Gastrectomy _____

    f. Mastectomy _____

6. Remember the root *sang* from List 7? What word is used to mean death through excessive loss of blood?

   _____

7. What is the subject of William Cullen Bryant's famous poem titled "Thanatopsis"? (Check that root against words in this list.)

   _____

8. Match the words at the left with their synonyms or definitions. Remember to use the process of elimination. Do the ones you know first.

   _____ a. incision   (1) optimistic, cheerful

   _____ b. epidermis   (2) cause of infectious disease

   _____ c. kleptomania   (3) division into two parts

   _____ d. apathy   (4) science of the nervous system

   _____ e. virus   (5) surgical cut

   _____ f. dermatitis   (6) lack of feeling or interest

   _____ g. virology   (7) compulsion to steal

   _____ h. sanguine   (8) irritation or disease of the skin

   _____ i. neurology   (9) outer skin layer

   _____ j. dichotomy   (10) scientific study of viruses

Review

This lesson reviews the words and roots in Lists 9 through 12, with the hope of planting each one in your mind for all time. As you read over the lists, please pronounce each word out loud. The sound of a word is often an excellent memory aid.

List 9	List 10	List 11	List 12
asinine	ambience	adulterate	anemia
bovine	amenities	ascertain	antidote
denizen	anomaly	conciliate	carcinogen
fledgling	attrition	connive	cardiac
fodder	bagatelle	discern	euthanasia
hirsute	bigot	exacerbate	fester
leonine	demeanor	extrapolate	gastric
porcine	duplicity	improvise	lesion
prehensile	exigency	infer	lymph
reptilian	logistics	inundate	paranoia
ruminate	ostentation	peruse	phobia
simian	pertinacity	portend	resuscitate
spoor	quisling	promulgate	salutary
vivisection	rancor	spurn	therapeutic
vixen	respite	succor	torso
whelp	temerity	succumb	toxic
	vagaries	vilify	vascular

ROOTS

AC/ACR	DERM	PATH	TEN/TIN/
CARN	FER	PLEX/PLIC/PLY	TAIN/TENT
CIDE/CIS	LOGOS	SPEC/SPIC/	VIRUS
CUMB/CUB	MANIA	SPECT	VITA/VIV
CUR/CURR/	MUT/MUTAT	TERR/TER	
CURS/COURSE			

Using the Words

Exercise I. Antonyms. Find an antonym for each word on the left. Write its letter in the space provided.

_____ 1. **asinine**

_____ 2. **duplicity**

_____ 3. **adulterate**

_____ 4. **exacerbate**

_____ 5. **spurn**

_____ 6. **whelp**

_____ 7. **hirsute**

_____ 8. **denizen**

(a) to welcome

(b) variable

(c) honesty

(d) hairless

(e) to mollify, appease

(f) alien

(g) judicious

(h) parent

_____ 9. **immutable**　　　　　　　(i) to antagonize

_____ 10. **conciliate**　　　　　　(j) to purify

Exercise II. Analogies. Complete each analogy with the best pair possible. Remember to clarify the given relationship first, before you begin hunting the answer.

_____ 1. rumination : idea ::
- (a) exigency : need
- (b) mutation : anomaly
- (c) lesion : wound
- (d) amenities : niceties
- (e) thought : result

_____ 2. whims : vagaries ::
- (a) trinket : bagatelle
- (b) patriot : quisling
- (c) resuscitate : depress
- (d) inundation : waters
- (e) concepts : conclusions

_____ 3. bovine : herbivorous ::
- (a) simian : monkey
- (b) porcine : multifarious
- (c) ovine : omnivorous
- (d) leonine : carnivorous
- (e) masculine : portentous

_____ 4. dismay : phobia ::
- (a) antidote : poison
- (b) exercise : therapy
- (c) anger : conciliation
- (d) behavior : demeanor
- (e) glance : perusal

_____ 5. spoor : pawprint ::
- (a) fledgling : adult
- (b) adder : cobra
- (c) temerity : backtalk
- (d) inference : deduction
- (e) terrier : animal

_____ 6. grain : fodder ::
- (a) nutrition : food
- (b) anemia : illness
- (c) poison : toxin
- (d) vixen : mare
- (e) life : vitality

_____ 7. duplicity : truth ::
- (a) confusion : logic
- (b) succumbing : yielding
- (c) attrition : reduction
- (d) decision : action
- (e) discernment : understanding

Exercise III. Definitions. Write each word beside its synonym or definition. The first letter is given as a hint.

1. able to grasp well and quickly　　　p _____

2. operations on live animals for medical or scientific reasons　　　v _____

3. referring to the blood channel system　　　v _____

4. the trunk of the body　　　t _____

5. beneficial to recovery　　　t _____

6. persistent feeling of distrust or suspicion of others　　　p _____

7. the bodily fluid that bathes
   tissues   l _____

8. referring to the heart   c _____

9. the environment of a place   a _____

10. management of details; strategies   l _____

11. to discover with certainty   a _____

12. project into the future using
    past experience or facts   e _____

13. extemporize, perform impromptu   i _____

14. referring to the stomach   g _____

15. merciful death to relieve
    incurable pain in hopeless cases   e _____

Exercise IV. Fill-ins. Select the most appropriate word from the choices offered, based on clues in context. The word form may need changing.

salutary	lesion	antidote	discern
resuscitate	fester	succor	connive
carcinogen	vilify	promulgate	attrition
succumb	portend	infer	

1. "Red sun at night, sailor's delight," is a well-known adage that _____ a fair day on the morrow.

2. Vidkun Quisling _____ with the Germans in their takeover of Norway during World War II, but his treachery earned him a traitor's death.

3. Hoping to provide _____ for the starving in Ethiopia, an impressive group of musicians staged "LIVE-AID" simultaneously in London and Philadelphia in the summer of 1985.

4. Last summer, as a(n) _____ to boredom, we tried teaching Andy and his friends to water-ski, but that created problems worse than the boredom.

5. "I _____ from all the arguments," Dad commented dryly, "that the water-skiing lessons aren't going too well."

6. Mom said, "Water sports are supposed to be so _____, but our version is not contributing to my mental health."

7. _____ to parental pleading, Jan and I gladly deferred lessons on the water skis until another time.

8. I am always more suspicious of the politician who _____ an opponent than I am of the individual under attack.

9. To please Mom, Carrie tried to _____ a childhood interest in sewing, but her effort was only halfhearted.

10. The larger the company, the more employees it loses through _____, as men and women leave for other jobs, die, or retire.

11. _____ of extreme or weird ideas is one way to gain attention, but it may not be the sort of attention you want.

12. Substances suspect as _____ are under heavy scrutiny in scientific labs, because we would like to eliminate as many cancer-causing agents as possible from our lives.

13. Examining the _____ on Andy's leg, Mom said that she could

    _____ no alarming redness or other sign of infection that would prompt a trip to the doctor's office.

14. "If the wound begins to _____ or fails to heal," Mom assured Andy, "we'll certainly see the doctor."

Exercise V. Remembering Roots.

1. The common root in *speculate*, *despicable*, and *inspector* is _____,

   meaning _____.

2. *Explicit, complicated*, and *Plexiglas* share the root _____, meaning

   _____.

3. The shared root in *incisive, incision, homicidal*, and *genocide* is _____,

   meaning _____.

4. *Occurrence, cursive, cursory, course*, and *current* share the root _____,

   meaning _____.

5. The common root in *tenacity, abstinence, retain*, and *retention* is

   _____, meaning _____.

Circle the roots in the following words and write the root meanings on the lines provided.

6. acrid   acrimonious   acumen   _____

7. transfer   defer   confer   _____

8. terrace   terrier   extraterrestrial   _____

9. vitality   vivacious   vivid   _____

10. apathy   pathology   empathy   _____

Exercise VI. Find the Oddball. In each numbered group of words, select the **one** unrelated word or phrase. Cross out the oddball.

1. pachyderm   skin   hypodermic   needle   dermatitis

2. recumbent   incubate   cumbrous   incumbent   idea

3. maniac   insanity   paranoia   megalomania   thought

4. poison   viricide   virulent   health   toxin

5. mask   opinionated   bigot   Babbitt   hypocrite

6. bearing   taste   demeanor   manner   conduct

7. display   ostentation   showiness   indigence   pretentiousness

8. timorousness   obstinacy   determination   pertinacity   perseverance

9. relief   alteration   rest   respite   pause

10. ill will   enmity   accord   rancor   bitterness

Accentuate the Positive
WORDS WITH A POSITIVE CONNOTATION

In Context. Before studying the definitions, try reasoning out the meaning of each word, using context as your guide.

1. The hearty applause of the audience and the congratulations of her classmates are the sort of *adulation* Carrie enjoys each time she performs in a play.

    Keys: Logic, examples   **Adulation** means _____.

2. Our play director is exceptionally *astute* at casting and is known for making the wisest choice possible for each role in the production.

    Key: Definitive phrase   **Astute** means _____.

3. "Everyone's on time, the stage and lighting crews look alert, and the props are in place—an *auspicious* beginning for our first full rehearsal!" exulted the director.

    Key: Logic   **Auspicious** means _____.

4. Carrie shed her customary *blithe* personality and became Marguerite instead, a glum character of woeful countenance.

    Key: Antonyms   **Blithe** means _____.

5. The director cautioned Carrie to remember that she was no longer a *congenial* girl. "As Marguerite, you distrust people and don't like them at all," he said.

    Keys: Opposing idea, logic   **Congenial** means _____.

6. Carrie is anticipating the *exhilaration* she will feel at the end of their first performance. "It's a real high in emotion—like nothing else," she says.

    Key: Definitive phrase   **Exhilaration** means _____.

7. A play critic hopes that his summation of a play will be a *felicitous* remark—the most fitting or apt comment that could have been made about the play.

    Keys: Synonyms, definition   **Felicitous** means _____.

8. As she left for school on the night of dress rehearsal, we could hear Carrie muttering *fervent* prayers to a host of unseen beings, beseeching their help with her performance.

    Key: Logic   **Fervent** means _____.

9. Mom grinned at Carrie's retreating back. "If I didn't know better, I'd swear she pays *homage* to a group of ancient goddesses."

    Keys: Previous sentence, logic   **Homage** means _____.

10. As an actress, Carrie is extremely particular about her costume and makeup. She works until her appearance is *impeccable*.

    Key: Logic   **Impeccable** means _____.

11. *The Unsinkable Molly Brown* is a musical about an *indomitable* woman whose innate intelligence and good humor made her truly "unsinkable."

      Key: Synonym   **Indomitable** means _____ .

12. A favorite character in the movie *Mary Poppins* is *jocular* Uncle Albert, whose love of laughter and jokes often causes him to float to the ceiling in high spirits.

      Keys: Definition, logic   **Jocular** means _____ .

13. It's a good thing that Dad is *placid* by nature. A nervous or irritable father would go crazy in our house with all the commotion.

      Key: Antonyms   **Placid** means _____ .

14. In spite of commotion and occasional flare-ups, Dad remains *sanguine*—ever optimistic about the future of his family.

      Key: Definition   **Sanguine** means _____ .

15. Balding now, Dad assures us that he was once a *suave* lady-killer, a debonair man-about-town whom Mother was delighted to capture.

      Keys: Synonym, logic   **Suave** means _____ .

16. "As for your mother," Dad says, "she was a *zany,* unpredictable character, who fascinated me the first time I met her. Crazy girl, but just right for me."

      Keys: Synonyms, logic   **Zany** means _____ .

Word Study

This list is only a tiny sample of the words we use to describe life when everything is going just right. You know many positive words such as *hilarious, ecstasy,* and *joyful.* Others you can deduce from the context or from knowing roots. If someone has made a *magnanimous* gesture that met with approval, you can guess that it was "a good, big gesture," and you'll be correct. You can also suppose that *euphoria* is an "absolutely wonderful feeling" by examining the context and by knowing that the prefix **eu-** means "good."

Some words are trickier to puzzle out and may not appear as often as the ones you know well. Instead of using the same old vocabulary, try adding these to your repertoire.

1. **adulation** (ˌaj-ə-'lā-shən) n.   Extreme admiration or flattery, sometimes amounting to adoration; from L. *adulari,* to flatter

   People of a shy, retiring nature do not seek the *adulation* of a crowd, but prefer to live quiet lives.

   Relatives: *adulate, adulator, adulatory*
   Synonyms: *idolatry, veneration, worship* (none exact)
   Antonyms: *revulsion, repugnance, loathing, abhorrence*

2. **astute** (ə-'st[y]üt) adj.   Wise, perceptive, and shrewd to an acute degree; from L. *astus,* craft, cunning

   Known for his *astute* observations on human nature, Mark Twain is as alive for American readers today as when he began writing in the early 1860s.

   Relatives: *astuteness, astutely*
   Synonyms: *shrewd, discerning, cagey, canny*
   Antonyms: *gullible, credulous, naive*

3. **auspicious** (ȯ-'spish-əs) adj.　　Promising good, favorable in outlook, boding success, as *an auspicious beginning;* from L. *auspic-*, diviner by birds (See "Derivation.")

Being born a turkey is not an *auspicious* start in life, as most turkeys end up on holiday platters.

Relatives:　*auspice* (favorable prophetic sign), *auspiciously, auspiciousness, inauspicious*
Synonyms:　*favorable, promising, propitious*
Antonyms:　*inauspicious, ill-omened*
Derivation: Auspicious derives literally from the Latin *avis* (bird) and *specere* (look at). The ancients depended upon an *auspex* or *augur* to divine the future by careful examination of birds in flight or birds feeding. Nearly everything of importance depended on the augur's report. If the *auspices* were bad, elections could be declared invalid. Likewise, auspices were read before a commander set forth in battle and before any important ceremony, such as marriage.

4. **blithe** ('blīth or 'blīth) adj.　　Joyous and lighthearted; casual or careless, as *with blithe disregard;* from OE *blithe*, joyous

Hail to thee, blithe *spirit!*
Bird thou never wert,
That from heaven or near it,
Pourest thy full heart
In profuse strains of unpremeditated art.
　　—Percy Bysshe Shelley, "To a Skylark"

Relatives:　*blithely, blithesome, bliss* (n., state of joy)
Synonyms:　*merry, cheerful, joyful*
Antonyms:　*morose, downcast, glum, sulky, sullen*

5. **congenial** (kən-'jēn-yəl) adj.　　Sharing like tastes, kindred; pleasant, sociable, harmoniously agreeable; from L. *con-* + *genius*, inclination

To me more dear, congenial *to my heart,*
One native charm, than all the gloss of art.
　　—Oliver Goldsmith, *The Deserted Village*

Relatives:　*congeniality, congenially*
Synonyms:　*consonant, kindred; genial, sociable*
Antonyms:　*uncongenial* (of persons), *abhorrent* (of jobs or required duties)

6. **exhilaration** (ig-ˌzil-ə-'rā-shən)) n.　　The feeling of being cheerful, stimulated, and exceedingly positive in outlook; from L. *ex* + *hilarare*, to gladden

As we went ahead of our traditional football rival, the wild *exhilaration* in the stands was audible for several blocks around the school.

Relatives:　*exhilarate, exhilarating, exhilarative, exhilaratingly, hilarious, hilarity*
Synonym:　*invigoration*
Antonyms:　*dullness, deadness, stupefaction*

7. **felicitous** (fi-'lis-ət-əs) adj.　　Aptly expressed, fitting or well chosen (of remarks); pleasant; from L. *felicitare*, to make happy

Sometimes, when we're most eager to make a *felicitous* remark, we suffer from the "foot-in-mouth" disease that plagues all of us at times.

Relatives:　*felicitate, felicitation, felicitator, felicitously, felicitousness, felicity*
Synonyms:　*apt, fit, appropriate, delightful, pleasant*
Antonyms:　*infelicitous, inappropriate*

8. **fervent** ('fər-vənt) adj.　　Showing sincere and heartfelt emotion, impassioned; from L. *fervere*, to boil, glow

The effectual fervent *prayer of a righteous man availeth much.*
> —The Holy Bible, James 5:16

Relatives: *fervor, fervently, fervency, fervid, fervidly, fervidness*
Synonym: *impassioned*
Antonyms: *apathetic, emotionless*

9. **homage** ('[h]äm-ij) n.   Respectful deference as tribute to someone or something deemed worthy; any act of respectful admiration; from L. *homin,* man

The idea of paying *homage* dates back to feudal days when a man swore allegiance to his lord, and was then bound to his service by sacred honor.

Relative: *homager* (vassal)
Synonym: *honor*

10. **impeccable** (⁽¹⁾im-'pek-ə-bəl) adj.   Without fault or blame; free from error or sin; from L. *in + peccare,* to sin

Confident that he spoke *impeccable* English, Jason moved to London, only to discover that American English was somewhat different from English as spoken in England.

Relatives: *impeccability, impeccably, peccadillo* (Sp. *pecadillo,* a small sin, slight offense)
Synonyms: *flawless, faultless*
Antonyms: *flawed, faulty, imperfect*

11. **indomitable** (in-'däm-ət-ə-bəl) adj.   Unconquerable, dauntless, incapable of being overcome; from L. *in + domitare,* to tame or daunt

I love Vermont because of her hills and valleys, her scenery and invigorating climate, but most of all because of her indomitable *people.*
> —Calvin Coolidge, 1928

Relatives: *indomitability, indomitableness, indomitably*
Synonyms: *unconquerable, dauntless*

12. **jocular** ('jäk-yə-lər) adj.   Normally happy, witty, and merry, fond of jesting and joke making; from L. *jocus,* joke

Len once wanted to be a comedian, but his nature became more serious than *jocular* as he aged.

Relatives: *jocularity, jocularly, jocose, jocund*
Synonym: *witty*
Antonym: *humorless*

13. **placid** ('plas-əd) adj.   Of a peaceful nature, serene, calm, and quiet; from L. *placere,* to please

I think I could turn and live with the animals,
*   they are so* placid *and self-contained . . .*
They do not sweat and whine about their condition . . .
Not one is dissatisfied, not one is demented
*   with the mania of owning things.*
> —Walt Whitman, *Leaves of Grass*

Relatives: *placidity, placidly, placidness, placate*
Synonyms: *calm, unruffled, serene, quiet*
Antonyms: *ruffled, choleric, jittery*

14. **sanguine** ('saŋ-gwən) adj.   Optimistic, positive, and confident in outlook; cheerful; from L. *sanguin,* blood

Around the fourteenth century, four main humors of the body were believed to determine personality: blood, phlegm, choler, and melancholy. In *sanguine* folk, the healthy red blood predominated, giving them their positive, confident outlook on life.

Relatives: *sanguineness, sanguinely, sanguinity, sangfroid* (equanimity), *sanguinary* (bloodthirsty), *exsanguinate*

Synonyms: *confident, optimistic*

Antonyms: *pessimistic, melancholic*

15. **suave** ('swäv) adj.   Smoothly sophisticated and polite in social situations, socially polished or finished (said of men); from L. *suavis*, sweet

Macavity, Macavity, there's no one like Macavity,
There never was a Cat of such deceitfulness and suavity.
      —T. S. Eliot, *Old Possum's Book of Practical Cats*

Relatives: *suavity, suavely, suaveness*

Synonyms: *urbane, smooth, bland, politic, diplomatic*

Antonyms: *bluff, boorish, ill-mannered, unrefined*

16. **zany** ('zā-nē) adj.   Wildly, usually humorously, silly or funny; crazy, but likeable; from It. *zanni*, traditional masked clown

Always a highlight at circuses, the clowns with their *zany* antics amuse both young and old.

Relatives: *zany* (n., clown or buffoon), *zanily, zaniness*

Synonyms: *crazy, nonsensical, absurd* (none exact)

Antonyms: *sensible, sober, practical, logical*

Root Study

Only one of these roots occurs in List 13. The others are still worth knowing, though. One of them may earn you a correct answer on a test someday. (Remember—not all tests occur in schoolrooms.)

1. BELL means beautiful.
     belle—a girl popular because of looks and charm
     embellish—to adorn, to decorate
     belles lettres—sophisticated, entertaining literature

2. BELL means war.
     bellicose—inclined to fight or dispute
     belligerence—an aggressive attitude, prone to argument
     rebellious—hard to manage or discipline, refractory
     postbellum—usually referring to the period following the U.S. Civil War; literally, *after war*

3. DOC/DOCT means to teach.
     docile—easily taught, managed, or led
     doctrine—teaching or belief
     doctor—originally, one who taught
     document—to furnish with documents or proof (v.); informative writing, official paper (n.)

4. HOM means man, human being.
     Homo sapiens—the species name of human beings; literally, *wise man*
     homicide—the killing of a human being
     hombre—Eng., fellow, guy; Sp., *man*
     homburg—man's hat with a firm, curled brim and a high crown with a lengthwise crease

5. LEV means to raise and light in weight.
   levity—humor, lightness of approach (to a subject)
   levitate—to float in air, seemingly defying gravity
   alleviate—to relieve the severity of a condition, as pain or sorrow; to lessen in severity
   elevator—a mechanism that lifts or raises something

Using the Words

List 13 Review

adulation	congenial	homage	placid
astute	exhilaration	impeccable	sanguine
auspicious	felicitous	indomitable	suave
blithe	fervent	jocular	zany

Exercise I. Antonyms. Select the word or phrase most nearly opposite in meaning to the word in bold type in each question.

_____ 1. **zany**   (a) insane   (b) sober   (c) dull   (d) wild
                          (e) sleepy

_____ 2. **impeccable**   (a) external   (b) normal   (c) rich
                          (d) mistaken   (e) flawed

_____ 3. **blithe**   (a) morose   (b) lengthy   (c) down
                          (d) casual   (e) uncaring

_____ 4. **adulation**   (a) reduction   (b) revulsion   (c) praise
                          (d) confusion   (e) subtraction

_____ 5. **suave**   (a) cool   (b) uncomfortable   (c) cultured
                          (d) boorish   (e) aged

_____ 6. **jocular**   (a) dull   (b) quiet   (c) humorless   (d) dry
                          (e) unathletic

_____ 7. **fervent**   (a) apathetic   (b) disorganized   (c) eager
                          (d) distraught   (e) peaceable

_____ 8. **felicitous**   (a) well-spoken   (b) ill-timed   (c) ill-bred
                          (d) well-endowed   (e) ill-fitting

_____ 9. **astute**   (a) careful   (b) reluctant   (c) eager
                          (d) credulous   (e) native

_____ 10. **auspicious**   (a) unimportant   (b) discouraging
                          (c) vital   (d) ill-omened   (e) bad

Exercise II. Analogies. Complete each analogy with the best pair possible, using words from List 13 and Roots.

_____ 1. friend : congenial ::
         (a) doctor : medicinal   (d) Carol Burnett: placid
         (b) Daffy Duck : zany   (e) parent : professional
         (c) hombre: prompt

_____ 2. temperament : sanguine ::
         (a) water : vital   (d) writing : belles lettres
         (b) gaiety : blithe   (e) chemistry : studious
         (c) document : belligerent

_____ 3. happiness : exhilaration ::
   (a) depression : worry
   (b) conviction : determination
   (c) panic : fear
   (d) naughtiness : rebellion
   (e) humor : levity

_____ 4. homage : respectful deference ::
   (a) sanguinity : pessimism
   (b) calmness : placidity
   (c) fervency : lack of passion
   (d) levity : noted seriousness
   (e) alleviation : exacerbation

_____ 5. fortress : indomitable ::
   (a) warrior : bellicose
   (b) classroom : cozy
   (c) cottage : accessible
   (d) guard dog : timorous
   (e) office : embellished

Exercise III. The Right Word. From List 13 and Roots select the word that most aptly illustrates the following. The word form may need changing.

1. the girl everyone wants to be with at the ball _____

2. the well-mannered, well-behaved, _____ kid who always sits in the front row in class

3. a Georgia mansion built after the Civil War _____

4. the human species of today _____

5. what your teacher *won't* appreciate in the middle of an angry lecture about late homework

   _____

6. what laughter causes Uncle Albert to do in the film *Mary Poppins* _____

7. the best attitude to have before a test _____

8. the way you want your room to look before a parental inspection tour _____

9. what you look for in a close friend _____

10. what many rock stars seem to crave _____

11. one word you'd love to have applied to your solution of a tough math problem

    _____

12. the feeling you want when you see your test score _____

13. the adjective describing a particularly apt comment _____

14. the honor and respect we give our country _____

15. a _____ plea to be allowed one more hour of sleep on weekend mornings

Exercise IV. Switcheroo. The words in this lesson appear in several forms, not just as taught. Match the words at the left with their correct synonyms or definitions.

_____ 1. **inauspicious**   (a) teach with a definite opinion/point of view

_____ 2. **bliss**   (b) merry, jolly

_____ 3. **exhilarate**   (c) boding ill

_____ 4. **indomitably**   (d) adorned, decorated

_____ 5. **jocund**   (e) state of delight

——— 6. **placidly**

——— 7. **suavely**

——— 8. **alleviation**

——— 9. **indoctrinate**

——— 10. **embellished**

(f) relief

(g) enliven, excite, refresh

(h) unconquerably

(i) in a polished manner

(j) serenely

Exercise V. Truth or Fiction. Mark the statements below (**T**) for truth, and (**F**) for fiction.

——— 1. A homburg is best kept in the refrigerator.

——— 2. *Homicide* can refer to killing a woman.

——— 3. With the proper leverage you can lift more than you would think possible.

——— 4. Euphonious music is apt to give you a headache.

——— 5. A sanguine person would be bloodthirsty in battle.

——— 6. When "the roll is called up yonder," you hope to be found impeccable . . . or nearly so.

——— 7. Blithe is an appropriate name for a shy, rather solemn girl.

——— 8. Misplacing the wedding ring prior to the ceremony will get the day off to an auspicious start.

——— 9. At the funeral of your little brother's gerbil, noticeable levity on your part will be comforting.

——— 10. *Truculence* is a synonym for *belligerence,* and neither is recommended in polite society.

Exercise VI. Word Analysis.

1. Both *bell* (beautiful) and *bell* (war) are spelled the same. How can you distinguish the separate meanings when you are trying to figure out a strange word?

   _____

   _____

2. (a) Words ending in *-or* and *-er* are often persons, or at least live beings. Think of *idolator, adulator, professor, performer, dancer,* and so on. How many others can you remember?

   _____

   _____

   (b) In what way can this knowledge of a suffix help you on a verbal test such as the PSAT, SAT, or ACT?

   _____

   _____

3. (a) *Repugnance* (strong distaste, abhorrence) is the opposite of *adulation* or *admiration.* What does the root in question—**pug, pugn**—mean? (See Webster's handy book.) What or who is a *pugilist?* Is he *pugnacious?* Can *pugnacious* be a synonym for *belligerent* and *truculent?*

   _____

_____

_____

(b) And did the *pug dog* get his name from this root? _____

4. Girls' names have changed considerably over time. To what personalities would you give the names Blithe, Felicity, Faith, Patience, Prudence, and Charity?

_____

_____

_____

_____

_____

5. (a) When you *placate* someone, what are you doing? _____

_____

6. Just for the heck of it, consider the roots **stupere** and -**fy**. Together they make *stupefy,* which literally means *to make senseless, benumbed, or astonished.* What other words come from **stup,** according to Webster?

_____

_____

Eliminate the Negative
WORDS WITH A NEGATIVE CONNOTATION

In Context. Before studying the definitions, try reasoning out the meaning of each word, using context as your guide.

1. Our family enjoys scary novels; the more grisly the theme or horrifying the outcome, the better we like it, as long as all of the *atrocious* details are pure fiction.

   Keys: Synonyms, logic   **Atrocious** means _____.

2. We don't enjoy the *captious* critic who writes book reviews for our newspaper because he delights in finding fault with every book that's published.

   Key: Definition   **Captious** means _____.

3. The *choleric* nature of this book critic permeates his work, making us wonder if he's irascible in real life, too, venting his spleen on anyone within range.

   Keys: Synonym, definition   **Choleric** means _____.

4. Dad agreed with the critic on one book, however, saying that it was an *execrable* piece of work, with the most wretched philosophy of any he'd read in a long time.

   Key: Synonym   **Execrable means** _____.

5. "I hope I wasn't seen returning that book to the library," Dad said. "I slipped it into the return slot in a *furtive* manner, and got out of there fast."

   Key: Logic   **Furtive** means _____.

6. Jan took her cue from Dad. "I've had it with *heinous* crimes and ghoulish ideas," she confessed. "Time to read something uplifting and admirable for a change."

   Key: Antonyms   **Heinous** means _____.

7. "I'm with Jan," Mom said. "All that gore is *inimical* to my nature. It's beginning to rub me the wrong way."

   Key: Logic   **Inimical** means _____.

8. The more proficient equestrians laughed at Jan and me, awkwardly astride our horses for the first time. "We must look pretty *ludicrous* to people who've ridden all their lives," I whispered to Jan.

   Key: Logic   **Ludicrous** means _____.

9. I listed all the gruesome things that could happen to us if our mounts bolted, but Jan begged me to spare her the *lurid* details.

   Key: Synonym   **Lurid** means _____.

10. I laughed when Jan accused me of being a *macabre* person who liked to contemplate the most gruesome possibilities.

        Key: Definition   **Macabre** means _____ .

11. Pressed to defend myself, I reminded Jan that I really wasn't the *morbid* sort, who brooded about death or gloomy things, but that I believed in being prepared for the worst, especially when riding a horse.

        Key: Partial definition   **Morbid** means _____ .

12. "You have a point," Jan admitted. "I'm sure my horse has a *nefarious* plan to scrape me off under a low-hanging branch—or some equally evil idea."

        Key: Synonym   **Nefarious** means _____ .

13. As we set off down the horse trail, I could hear Jan's *plaintive* cries behind me as she pleaded with her horse to stay on the path.

        Key: Logic   **Plaintive** means _____ .

14. Fortunately, our trail guide wasn't a *pompous* sort, impressed by his own experience or importance, and he gave us a great deal of friendly, useful advice.

        Key: Partial definition   **Pompous** means _____ .

15. An intriguing sidelight to our ride was the flood of *scurrilous* talk that poured from the mouth of one of the riders, who apparently knew every obscenity in the book and used them all on his horse.

        Keys: Logic, synonym   **Scurrilous** means _____ .

16. Jan gestured at the loudmouth and whispered to me. "There goes one of life's more *sordid* characters. He must be the meanest mouth in these here parts, eh, podner?"

        Keys: Logic, synonym   **Sordid** means _____ .

17. It is probably *specious* logic to think that everyone who seeks the company of animals will become basically good and innocent like the animals. That idea seems plausible on the surface but lacks proof in real life.

        Keys: Definition, example   **Specious** means _____ .

Word Study

The popular 1940s song by Johnny Mercer and Harold Arlen goes, "You've got to accentuate the positive, eliminate the negative, latch on to the affirmative, and don't mess with Mister In-Between." Besides being tuneful, the song expresses an admirable philosophy: we'd all like to eliminate what is negative or depressing from our lives.

But an ever-happy state is elusive, and so our vocabulary abounds with negative words. Some, like *defunct* and *putrid,* give themselves away by sounding utterly negative. Others, like **dis**consolate, **ig**noble, and **in**famous, tell us what they mean with a negative prefix, plus context to point the way to meaning. If someone shows us a picture of a starving child, asking that we note "the pitiful emaciation of the figure," we can deduce that *emaciated* means *physically wasted away.*

The problem is what to do when no context points the way—as in antonym questions on the PSAT or SAT—or when context gives no clue. The answer is a line you've heard before— *learn more words.*

1. **atrocious** (ə-'trō-shəs) adj.   Absolutely revolting, appalling, or wicked; of extremely low or bad quality, as *atrocious cooking;* from L. *atroc-,* gloomy, atrocious
One of my brother Andy's most *atrocious* habits is listening in on other people's phone conversations.
Relatives: *atrocity, atrociously, atrociousness*
Synonyms: *outrageous, barbaric, appalling, revolting, horrifying, abominable*
Antonym: *admirable*

2. **captious** ('kap-shəs) adj.   Excessively critical, inclined to object or point out faults; designed to embroil in argument or dispute; from L. *captio,* the act of taking or deceiving
Snow White could never please her *captious* stepmother, who delighted in finding fault with her.
Relatives: *captiously, captiousness*
Synonyms: *critical, faultfinding*
Antonym: *appreciative*

3. **choleric** ('käl-ə-rik or kə-'ler-ik) adj.   Easily irritated, annoyed, or made angry; hot-tempered, irate; from L. *cholera,* bilious disease
A reader seldom peruses a book with pleasure until he knows whether the writer of it be . . . of a mild or choleric *disposition, married or a bachelor.*
    —Joseph Addison, *The Spectator,* No. 1
Relatives: *choler, cholera* (the disease)
Synonyms: *irascible, splenetic*
Antonyms: *placid, imperturbable*

4. **execrable** ('ek-si-krə-bəl) adj.   Detestable, evil, thoroughly reprehensible; extremely bad or wretched, as *execrable handwriting;* from L. *ex + sacr-,* sacred
That execrable *sum of all villanies, commonly called the Slave Trade.*
    —John Wesley, *Journal,* 1772
Relatives: *execrate, execrableness, execrably, execrator*
Synonyms: *detestable, evil; wretched, foul* (second meaning)
Antonyms: *noble, admirable, praiseworthy*

5. **furtive** ('fərt-iv) adj.   Stealthy or sly in manner, hoping not to be discovered, surreptitious; also, stolen, as *furtive goods;* from L. *fur,* thief
Some nocturnal blackness, mothy and warm,
When the hedgehog travels furtively *over the lawn.*
    —Thomas Hardy, *Afterwards*
Relatives: *furtively, furtiveness*
Synonyms: *secret, stealthy, surreptitious; stolen* (second meaning)
Antonyms: *forthright, brazen, straightforward*

6. **heinous** ('hā-nəs) adj.   Outrageously evil or appalling, shocking in the extreme; from Middle F., *haineus,* hateful
A famous rhyme about a double murder (murderer still unknown) accuses the murder victims' own daughter, Lizzie Borden, of a *heinous* crime:
Lizzie Borden took an axe,
And gave her mother forty whacks;
When she saw what she had done,
She gave her father forty-one.
    —Author unknown

Relatives: *heinously, heinousness*
Synonyms: *outrageous, abominable, odious, villainous*
Antonyms: *admirable, praiseworthy*

7. **inimical** (in-ˈim-i-kəl) adj.   Hostile, as an enemy would be, distinctly unfriendly and uncongenial; adverse or contrary to, as an enemy; from L. *inimicus,* enemy

The *inimical* relationship between neighboring nations like Israel and the Arab countries, or England and Ireland, creates tension worldwide.
Relative: *inimically*
Synonyms: *hostile; adverse*
Antonyms: *friendly, congenial; favorable*

8. **ludicrous** (ˈlüd-ə-krəs) adj.   Laughable because of oddness, ineptitude, foolishness, or absurdity; deserving of scornful laughter for the same reasons; from L. *ludus,* play or sport

Andy's early attempts at cooking were so *ludicrous* that I'm amazed we didn't discourage him altogether with our laughter.
Relatives: *ludicrously, ludicrousness*
Synonyms: *ridiculous, laughable, comical*

9. **lurid** (ˈlùr-əd) adj.   Arousing horror or undue sensation by being gruesome or revolting; formerly, exceedingly pale in appearance; from L. *luridus,* sallow or pale yellow

Seen in the light of a Council fire, the warpaint of avenging Indians must have appeared *lurid* and foreboding.
Relatives: *luridly, luridness*
Synonyms: *gruesome, sensational*

10. **macabre** (mə-ˈkäb(-rə) or mə-ˈkäb-ər) adj.   Dwelling on death; gruesome or extremely horrible in aspect; from F. *danse macabre,* dance of death

The logical literary predecessor of Stephen King was Edgar Allan Poe, who penned *macabre* short stories.
Derivation: The danse macabre (or macaber) was supposed to be danced by all those who were dead and was presided over by Death himself. This allegory on the mortality of mankind was a favorite subject of medieval artists and poets.
"What are these paintings on the wall
around us? The danse macaber."
    —H. W. Longfellow, *The Golden Legend*

11. **morbid** (ˈmȯr-bəd) adj.   Preoccupied with unwholesome, gloomy, or macabre feelings; referring to or typical of disease; causing disease; from L. *morbus,* disease

Not everyone is drawn by *morbid* curiosity to scenes of fire, accident, or disaster.
Relatives: *morbidity, morbidly, morbidness*
Synonyms: *grisly, gruesome* (neither exact); *diseased*
Antonym: *wholesome*

12. **nefarious** (ni-ˈfar-ē-əs) adj.   Noticeably evil, wicked, or impious; from L. *nefas,* crime

What Hitler tried to disguise with rhetoric was actually a *nefarious* plan to exterminate the Jewish people.
Relatives: *nefariously, nefariousness*
Synonyms: *vicious, wicked, evil, sinful*
Antonyms: *benevolent, pious, kind, charitable* (none exact)

13. **plaintive** ('plānt-iv) adj.   Revealing misery, woe, or suffering; melancholy or dismal; from L. *plangere,* to beat one's breast or lament

Jan had to sing a brief solo for the holiday concert, and although she began in a *plaintive* treble, she gained true soprano tone and confidence as she sang.

Relatives: *plaint* (wail, lamentation), *plaintively, plaintiveness, complain, complaint*
Synonyms: *woeful, melancholy, lugubrious* (none exact)
Antonyms: *cheerful, merry, buoyant*

14. **pompous** ('päm-pəs) adj.   Full of self-importance, often arrogant in manner; high-flown or ornate, as *pompous speech or writing;* from L. *pompa,* procession, pomp

I am no lover of pompous *title, but only desire that my name may be recorded in a line or two, which shall briefly express my name, my virginity, the years of my reign, the reformation of religion under it, and my preservation of peace.*
        —Elizabeth I, discussing her epitaph with her ladies

Relatives: *pomp, pomposity, pompously, pompousness*
Synonyms: *self-important, pretentious*
Antonyms: *self-effacing, unpretentious, modest*

15. **scurrilous** ('skər-ə-ləs) adj.   Abusive, coarse, or vulgar, as *scurrilous language;* base and evil, as *scurrilous liars;* from L. *scurra,* buffoon

It takes a pretty gullible person to believe the often-*scurrilous* innuendo in the weekly pulp newspapers.

Relatives: *scurrility, scurrilously, scurrilousness*
Synonyms: *blasphemous, obscene* (neither exact)

16. **sordid** ('sȯrd-əd) adj.   Base, gross, or vile, mean and dishonorable in intent; marked by squalor or wretchedness, as *the sordid village huts;* from L. *sordes,* dirt

The world is too much with us; late and soon,
Getting and spending, we lay waste our powers:
Little we see in Nature that is ours;
We have given our hearts away, a sordid *boon!*
        —William Wordsworth, "The World Is Too Much with Us"

Relatives: *sordidly, sordidness*
Synonym: *mean* (meaning low, base, vile)
Antonyms: *honorable, noble*

17. **specious** ('spē-shəs) adj.   Appearing truthful or genuine on the surface, plausible but false; from L. *speciosus,* beautiful, plausible

To murder thousands takes a specious *name,*
War's glorious art, and gives immortal fame.
        —Edward Young, *Love of Fame* (satire)

Relatives: *speciosity, speciously, speciousness*
Synonym: *plausible*

Root Study

Three of these roots have representatives in List 14. The fourth (**dur**) has not only contributed many words to English but also lived up to its promise by being *durable* and *lasting.*

1. CAP, CAPT, CEIVE, CEPT, and CIP mean to take.
    captivate—to influence or attract by means of special charm or appeal
    intercept—to take, stop, or interrupt in progress or prior to arrival

deceive—to give a false appearance, mislead, delude
anticipate—to foresee or act ahead of time; to expect

2. DUR means hard, lasting.
   endurance—the capability of lasting a long time, even under stress
   obdurate—firm-minded, stubborn
   duration—the time which something lasts or exists
   duress—restraint through force; threat for the purpose of gaining a desired end

3. MOR/MORT means death.
   moribund—nearly dead
   mortician—the professional who prepares the dead for burial
   mortal—human *(our mortal failings)*; awful or dreadful *(a mortal shame)*; fatal *(a mortal wound)*; conceivable *(every mortal day)*; trying to the spirit or long-lasting *(four mortal hours)*
   mortify—to embarrass severely

4. SACR and SACER mean sacred.
   sacrilege—a serious lack of reverence toward a sacred place, person, or thing; profanation
   desecrate—to profane or defile a holy place, person, memory, or thing
   consecrate—to affirm as sacred, holy; to dedicate to a purpose solemnly

Using the Words

List 14 Review

atrocious	heinous	macabre	pompous
captious	inimical	morbid	scurrilous
choleric	ludicrous	nefarious	sordid
execrable	lurid	plaintive	specious
furtive			

Exercise I. Definitions. Please review List 14, pronouncing the words out loud, skimming the definitions as a refresher. Then write each word beside its definition or synonym.

1. overly concerned with gloomy thoughts or grisly details; diseased

   m _____

2. self-important, arrogant

   p _____

3. base, low, vile

   s _____

4. plausible on the surface

   s _____

5. noticeably evil, shocking, appalling

   h _____

6. hostile, uncongenial; adverse

   i _____

7. surreptitious, secretive

   f _____

8. irascible, splenetic

   c _____

9. overly critical, fault-finding

   c _____

10. wretched, exceedingly bad

    a _____

    e _____

11. laughable, ridiculous

    l _____

12. woeful, melancholy

    p _____

Exercise II. Fill-ins. Select the most appropriate word from the choices offered for each sentence. Write your choice on the line in each sentence.

1. Revolted by the inclusion of so many _____ details about the crime, I turned off the TV set.
   (a) heinous   (b) pompous   (c) inimical   (d) lurid

2. I read about the spy's _____ plan to infiltrate our foreign service and sell secrets to our enemies.
   (a) captious   (b) atrocious   (c) nefarious   (d) morbid

3. The _____ conditions in many prisons have been the subject of several TV documentaries.
   (a) sordid   (b) scurrilous   (c) macabre   (d) inimical

4. "The Masque of the Red Death" by Edgar Allan Poe has the appropriate setting of a masked ball, to which a particularly _____ figure comes disguised as the Red Death.
   (a) morbid   (b) macabre   (c) ludicrous   (d) choleric

5. With luck you can _____ the phone call, so that you hear the information before anyone else does.
   (a) interrupt   (b) intercept   (c) interview   (d) execrate

6. "I've been worried every _____ moment all evening long," she explained. (Refer to Root Study.)
   (a) morbid   (b) putrid   (c) mortal   (d) mortifying

7. He would never admit that, unless he were under extreme _____.
   (a) durability   (b) infamy   (c) morbidity   (d) duress

8. She can _____ any boy with her personality, but when you add those homemade chocolate chip cookies—wow!
   (a) endure   (b) consecrate   (c) captivate   (d) anticipate

9. If he weren't so _____, he'd have given in a long time ago.
   (a) obdurate   (b) durable   (c) scurrilous   (d) inimical

10. When the coach promised that strenuous exercise would prevent all colds and illnesses, I suspected that that was an example of _____ reasoning.
    (a) ignoble   (b) specious   (c) sacrilegious   (d) mortal

Exercise III. Antonyms. Select the word or phrase most nearly opposite to the word in bold type. Circle each antonym you select.

_____ 1. **choleric**   (a) placid   (b) irritable   (c) quiet   (d) healthy   (e) heated

_____ 2. **execrable**   (a) wretched   (b) admirable   (c) well   (d) sanguine   (e) interior

_____ 3. **disconsolate**   (a) emaciated   (b) plaintive   (c) buoyant   (d) introspective   (e) euphonious

_____ 4. **mortal**   (a) unready   (b) untried   (c) not in time   (d) not fatal   (e) inseparable

_____ 5. **specious**   (a) suspect   (b) flawed   (c) positive   (d) uplifting   (e) genuine

_____ 6. **pompous**   (a) direct   (b) pretentious   (c) self-effacing   (d) self-rewarding   (e) optimistic

_____ 7. **plaintive**   (a) whiny   (b) cheerful   (c) unbraided   (d) healthful   (e) forewarned

_____ 8. **furtive**   (a) self-starting   (b) forward-looking   (c) sly   (d) aboveboard   (e) external

_____ 9. **inimical**   (a) congenial   (b) warm   (c) sanguine   (d) fake   (e) comical

_____ 10. **captious**   (a) accepting   (b) creditable   (c) not taken   (d) intercepted   (e) free

Exercise IV. Analogies. From List 14 and Roots enter the word that best completes the analogy. The first letter of each answer is given as a clue.

1. pollute : waterway :: d_____ : temple

2. slander : scurrilous :: enemy : i_____

3. sacrilege : heinous :: squalor : s_____

4. deed : n_____ :: motion : furtive

5. moribund : slightly sick :: a_____ : misdeed

Exercise V. Matching. Match each sentence to the noun it best represents. Write the correct letter on each line.

_____ 1. **endurance**   (a) I did it in stealth.

_____ 2. **mortification**   (b) I solemnly dedicated myself.

_____ 3. **furtiveness**   (c) I rarely find anything I like.

_____ 4. **morbidity**   (d) He looked so silly I roared with laughter.

_____ 5. **consecration**   (e) You can't do anything for me.

_____ 6. **ludicrousness**   (f) I reveled in every gruesome detail.

_____ 7. **captiousness**   (g) I can withstand anything.

_____ 8. **pomposity**   (h) We gasped as he destroyed the icon.

_____ 9. **luridness**   (i) I nearly died of embarrassment.

_____ 10. **sacrilege**   (j) I'm fascinated by accidents.

Exercise VI. Word Analysis.

1. Can the theft of someone's pencil be considered a *heinous crime?* Explain. _____

_____

2. Laughter comes in many forms. What element is present in *derisive* laughter (e.g., at something ludicrous) that is missing when we laugh at our favorite comedians?

_____

_____

3. Your knowledge of negative words is probably greater than you think. Match these frequently used negatives with their definitions. If in doubt, shout for assistance.

_____ a. destitute

_____ b. dissolute

_____ c. disconsolate

_____ d. infamous

_____ e. ignominy

_____ f. defunct

_____ g. putrid

_____ h. ignoble

(1) utter shame or disgrace

(2) base, low, contemptible

(3) lacking necessary possessions or resources

(4) worn out, useless, dead

(5) morally loose, unrestrained

(6) unable to be consoled, downcast

(7) foul, rotten, malodorous

(8) notorious

4. What is the difference between a crime and an *atrocity?* _____
_____

5. What connotation has the word *furtive* that the word *wary* lacks? _____
_____

Test Tubes and Dinosaurs

TERMS FROM SCIENCE

In Context. Before studying the definitions, try reasoning out the meaning of each word, using context as your guide.

1. We're always nervous when Aunt Dolly comes to stay because her ideas about teenagers are *antediluvian*. Only Noah and other parents from the time before the flood share her opinions.

   Keys: Logic, partial
   definition   **Antediluvian** means _____ .

2. "Let's face it," Jan said glumly. "We always think just the opposite of Aunt Dolly. We love her, but our viewpoints are like the North and South poles—absolute *antipodes*."

   Keys: Logic, example   **Antipodes** means _____ .

3. Carrie said that we should form an *axis*—like that of Germany, Italy, and Japan during World War II—as a united front against our aunt. Scornfully Andy replied, "An *axis* is what the earth rotates around!"

   Keys: Examples, logic   **Axis** means _____ .

4. The cars on one ride at our amusement park whirl rapidly, pressing the riders in the cars back against their seats by *centrifugal* force. I tried to lean into the center of the car, but the force was stronger than I was.

   Keys: Logic, example,
   prefix clue   **Centrifugal** means _____ .

5. Jan made an oval silver pendant in jewelry class with a slightly *concave* surface. In the hollow, or concavity, she inscribed her initials.

   Key: Synonym   **Concave** means _____ .

6. "I don't want you kids in the *doldrums*," Mom said briskly as she prepared to leave on her trip. "You know Aunt Dolly loves cheerfulness, not the blues."

   Keys: Antonym, synonym   **Doldrums** means _____ .

7. Someone once advised me to throw out life's *dross* and concentrate instead on what was purely good and true.

   Key: Antonyms   **Dross** means _____ .

8. Nuclear *fission*, the splitting of an atomic nucleus that results in the release of large amounts of energy, is not unlike Andy in action.

   Key: Definition   **Fission** means _____ .

9. The *fusion* of a tiny silver clasp to the chain Jan made to hold her pendant took only seconds. She dripped a liquid called the "fixer" onto the silver, added a bit of solder, and

melted them together in the heat of a bluish flame.

Keys: Logic, example   **Fusion** means _____ .

10. On our trip West, we collected samples of *igneous* rock left by the volcanic eruption of Mount Saint Helens.

Key: Logic   **Igneous** means _____ .

11. After a cross-country race, I succumb to *inertia,* and I refuse to do anything for a few hours.

Keys: Logic, partial definition   **Inertia** means _____ .

12. Once an acronym meaning "**l**ight **a**mplification by **s**timulated **e**mission of **r**adiation," *laser* is now accepted as a word, like the acronyms "sonar" and "bacitracin."

Key: Definition   **Laser** means _____ .

13. Until astronomers understood *refraction,* the bending of light rays as they pass through the atmosphere, they must have had difficulty placing celestial bodies correctly in space.

Key: Definition   **Refraction** means _____ .

14. At an archaeological dig, Jan and I were shown how each artifact, each tiny *shard* of pottery, is meticulously numbered and located within the site.

Key: Logic   **Shard** means _____ .

15. Under the lab's high-power microscope, we were able to examine plant *spores* responsible for reproduction.

Key: Logic   **Spore** means _____ .

16. "The *velocity* of change in my department makes me wonder if I can keep up," Dad said. "Things are moving fast."

Key: Logic   **Velocity** means _____ .

Word Study

Aristotle could have avoided the mistake of thinking that women have fewer teeth by the simple device of asking Mrs. Aristotle to open her mouth.
　　—Bertrand Russell

Science has come a long way since the days of Aristotle. A time traveler from a past century would be agog at what science has created—and what it threatens to destroy if we are not vigilant. Only a few decades ago, science was a comparatively minor subject in America's schools. Today, everyone needs a strong, working vocabulary in several sciences in order to understand what is happening around us.

1. **antediluvian** (ˌant-i-də-ˈlü-vē-ən) adj.　　Referring to the time prior to the biblical flood; antiquated or out of date; from L. *ante* + *diluvium,* deluge

There was silence supreme! Not a shriek, not a scream,
Scarcely even a howl or groan,
As the man they called "Ho!" told his story of woe,
In an antediluvian *tone.*
　　—Lewis Carroll, *The Hunting of the Snark*

Relative:　　*antediluvian* (n.)

Synonym: *antiquated*
Antonym: *modern, up-to-date*

2. **antipodes** (an-ˈtip-ə-ˌdēz) pl. n. Parts of the earth exactly opposite one another; any exact opposites; from Gr. *antipod,* with feet opposite

Common sense is the very antipodes *of science.*
  —E. B. Titchener, *Systematic Psychology: Prolegomena*
Relatives: *antipodal, antipodean*

3. **axis** (ˈak-səs) n. The straight line about which a body such as the earth revolves or is symmetrically arranged; the pivotal neck vertebra; a plant stem; alliance, union, or partnership; (pl., *axes*) from L. *axis,* axle

The axis *of the earth sticks out visibly through the center of each and every town or city.*
  —Oliver Wendell Holmes, *The Autocrat of the Breakfast Table*
Relatives: *axial, axially, axillary, axile*
Synonyms: *partnership, alliance* (last meaning)

4. **centrifugal** (sen-ˈtrif-yə-gəl) adj. Directed away from an axis or center; employing this force, as *a centrifugal machine;* moving away from centralization, as *a centrifugal culture;* from L. *centr-* + *fugere,* to flee (from the center)

The centrifuge employs *centrifugal* force to separate substances of different densities, to simulate the effects of gravity, and sometimes, as in a washing machine, to remove moisture.
Relatives: *centrifuge, centrifugally, centrifugation*
Synonym: *separatist* (last meaning)

5. **concave** (kän-ˈkāv, ˈkän-kāv) adj. Resembling the inside of a bowl by being rounded inward, arched or curving inward; from L. *com* + *cavus,* hollow, cave

Have you not made a universal shout,
That Tiber trembled underneath her banks,
To hear the replication of your sounds
Made in her concave *shores?*
  —Shakespeare, *Julius Caesar*
Relatives: *concave* (n.), *concavity*
Antonym: *convex* (bulging or rounded outward)

6. **doldrums** (ˈdōl-drəmz, ˈdäl-drəmz) pl. n. The blues; also a state of inactivity, listlessness, or collapse; the area near the equator known for its variable winds and squalls alternating with total calm; perhaps from OE *dol,* foolish

Sailors aboard old-time vessels dreaded the *doldrums,* where a ship could be tossed by squalls or becalmed for days without wind.
Synonyms: *blues, slump*
Antonyms: *euphoria, sanguinity, cheerfulness* (none exact)

7. **dross** (ˈdräs, ˈdrȯs) n. The scummy waste occurring on the surface of molten metal; an impurity, a waste product, or foreign matter, like the dregs in the bottom of a bottle of wine; from OE *dros,* dregs

What men call treasure and the gods call dross.
  —James Russell Lowell, ode recited at Harvard Commemoration, 1865
Relative: *drossy*
Synonyms: *dregs, impurity*

8. **fission** ('fish-ən, 'fizh-ən) n.   Separation into parts, usually by splitting; the splitting of an atomic nucleus to release large amounts of energy; from L. *findere,* to split

Although we have recently joined the word nuclear to *fission,* the older meaning of *fission*—the spontaneous splitting of a body into two or more parts, each capable of growing into a complete organism—has been recognized by scientists for years.
Relatives: *fissile, fissionable, fissionability, fission* (v.), *fission bomb* (atom bomb)

9. **fusion** ('fyü-zhən) n.   A merging or partnership, a coalition; a joining or union by heat, as in melting; the union of certain atomic nuclei, resulting in the release of vast amounts of energy; from L. *fusus,* poured, melted
Space scientist Merton E. Davies predicts that by the year 2050, advances in nuclear *fusion* power plants will facilitate inexpensive travel through space in reasonably priced rockets.
Relatives: *fusionist, fusible, fusion bomb* (hydrogen bomb)
Synonym: *coalition* (first meaning)
Antonym: *dissolution* (first meaning)

10. **igneous** ('ig-nē-əs) adj.   Like fire, fiery; referring to a substance formed in great heat, as the magma from volcanoes is *igneous* rock; from L. *ignis,* fire
In fifth grade science class we studied the three major types of rock: *igneous,* metamorphic, and sedimentary.
Relatives: *ignite, ignition, ignitron, ignescent*
Synonym: *fiery*

11. **inertia** (in-'ər-shə) n.   The tendency of a thing not to change but to remain in the state it is in, as of a body to remain in motion or at rest, until acted upon by an external force; inertness; from L. *inert-,* unskilled, idle
Science has given us the knowledge needed to save our wildlife and our environment, but we must still combat mankind's old enemy: *inertia.*
Relatives: *inert, inertly, inertness, inertial, inertially*

12. **laser** ('lā-zər) n.   The acronym of **l**ight **a**mplification by **s**timulated **e**mission of **r**adiation; a device that generates electromagnetic radiation in the visible, infrared, or ultraviolet areas of the spectrum
For *The People's Almanac* in the late seventies, a theoretical physicist named Freeman J. Dyson predicted that we would be able to send vehicles into space on *laser* highways in just a few decades.
Relative: *lase* (v., back formation from laser)

13. **refraction** (ri-'frak-shən) n.   The supposed "bending" of light that we observe when light or energy waves pass from one medium (such as air) into another (such as water); the correction we must apply to the location of a body (e.g., a planet) because of this deflection from a straight path; from L. *re* + *frangere,* to break
Because the lake by our cabin is crystal clear, we often dive for quarters as a game. I can spot the coin from the surface; but *refraction* is confusing, and, once I am underwater, that quarter is never exactly where I thought it would be.
Relatives: *refract, refractive, refractively, refractiveness, refractivity, refractometer*

14. **shard** ('shärd), also **sherd** n.   A fragment or piece of pottery or (sometimes) shell, as a remnant of a pottery-making civilization; from OE *sceard,* cut, notch
For heathen heart that puts her trust
In reeking tube and iron shard,
All valiant dust that builds on dust,

And, guarding, calls not Thee to guard,
For frantic boast and foolish word—
Thy mercy on Thy People, Lord!
        —Rudyard Kipling, "Recessional"
Synonym: *potsherd*

15. **spore** ('spō[ə]r) n.   A normally one-celled reproductive or resistant body in plants and
        some invertebrates capable of developing into a new organism; from L. *spora,* seed,
        spore

    Organisms that produce reproductive *spores* may also reproduce by fission or by budding,
    whereas the nonreproductive, resistant *spore* is in a resting-cell stage and typically found in
    bacteria.
    Relatives: *spore* (v.), *sporicide, sporiferous, sporulation*

16. **velocity** (və-'läs-ət-ē) n.   Speed or rapidity of motion; the rate of occurrence, especially
        when rapid, as *the velocity of architectural change;* also the rate of turnover; from L.
        veloc-, quick

    "I don't think Andy needs a bike," Mom observed. "He has a natural *velocity* of his own
    that hurtles him from place to place."
    Relatives: *velocimeter, velocipede, velodrome*
    Synonyms: *speed, rapidity*

Root Study

This is a brief collection of roots often used in scientific contexts.

1. BIO means life.
    biology—the science that studies living organisms and life processes
    biophysics—the study of physical principles as they may be applied to biological
        problems
    biomedicine—the branch of medicine concerned with human survival in stressful
        environments
    antibiotic—substance capable of killing or inhibiting a microorganism (used in weak
        solution so as to preserve the host being)

2. FRAG and FRACT mean to break.
    fragile—something easily broken
    fragmentation—separation into smaller parts
    refractory—unmanageable, unruly, stubborn
    infraction—a violation or breaking of a law or rule

3. IGN and PYR mean fire.
    ignition—kindling, setting alight
    ignis fatuus—a misleading goal or hope; literally, *foolish fire*
    pyre—any pile to be burned, usually *a funeral pyre*
    pyrite—often called "fool's gold," actually FeS_2, iron disulfide
    pyretic—referring to fever

4. LAV and LU mean to wash.
    lave—to wash, as *he laved his body with the soap*
    lavatory—a place for washing, bathroom
    deluge—a flood; anything washing over someone in excessive amount, such as *a deluge*
        of work
    alluvial—referring to sand, silt, gravel, or similar substances deposited by running water

5. -LOGY/-OLOGY means study, discourse.
   anthropology—the study of humankind's development, origin, and civilizations
   criminology—the study of criminal behavior and motives
   paleontology—the study of fossil remains to learn about life in past geological periods
   petrology—the study of rocks and absolutely everything about them

Using the Words

List 15 Review

antediluvian	concave	fusion	refraction
antipodes	doldrums	igneous	shard
axis	dross	inertia	spore
centrifugal	fission	laser	velocity

Exercise I. Synonyms. Write a synonym or brief definition for each word.

1. velocity _____

2. shard _____

3. antediluvian _____

7. concave _____

5. doldrums _____

6. inertia _____

7. dross _____

8. igneous _____

9. fusion _____

10. fission _____

Exercise II. Substitution. Substitute words learned in List 15 for the words or phrases in italics. Cross out the italics and write the study word above.

1. The *unicellular reproductive bodies* of that mushroom are particularly interesting to examine with a microscope.

2. Leaders of different countries often epitomize *diametric opposites:* one may be informal and congenial, the other, formal and cold in manner.

3. Because of *bending of light,* I know that the North Star is not where it appears to be when seen from Earth.

4. In certain phases of World War II, the *alliance* formed a redoubtable adversary to England and her allies.

5. Our ear, nose, and throat doctor, who calls himself an otolaryngologist, is studying the latest techniques in *electromagnetic radiation* surgery.

6. Although my brain knows that The Mad Spinner at our amusement park will plaster me against its carpeted walls by an irresistible *away-from-the-center* force, my emotions suffer when the floor drops away in the whirling canister.

7. Jan and I totally lost our cool at the archaeological dig when we uncovered a layer of brightly colored *bits of broken pottery*.

8. Because of its *natural tendency to remain motionless,* Bill and I had to push with all our strength to get the stalled car rolling toward the curb.

9. The expression "separating the wheat from the chaff" reminds us to sort out what is worthwhile and to leave the *impurities* behind.

10. We were all amazed by the *coalition* of those three different officers into a cohesive unit for class leadership.

Exercise III. Analogies. Complete each analogy by selecting the best pair possible.

_____ 1. washing machine : centrifuge ::
    (a) doldrums : dregs
    (b) physics : biomedicine
    (c) plant stem : axis
    (d) velocity : change
    (e) cable : twine

_____ 2. biology : life systems ::
    (a) science : facts
    (b) petrology : transportation
    (c) anthropology : humankind's development
    (d) paleontology : brontosaurus
    (e) graphology : law

_____ 3. wine : dregs ::
    (a) metal : dross
    (b) food : cabbage
    (c) liquid : water
    (d) automobile : cart
    (e) orange : fruit

_____ 4. Dark Ages : unenlightened ::
    (a) period : medieval
    (b) time : fleeting
    (c) era : Mesozoic
    (d) tyrannosaurus : antediluvian
    (e) fossil : prehistoric

_____ 5. concave : convex ::
    (a) inner : within
    (b) invigorated : inert
    (c) porcine : obese
    (d) terrestrial : earthly
    (e) refracted : bent

_____ 6. axis : periphery ::
    (a) junction : highway
    (b) animal : fur
    (c) bicycle : transportation
    (d) cell : spore
    (e) tree heart : twig

_____ 7. shower : deluge ::
    (a) velocity : speed
    (b) pause : doldrums
    (c) trickle : drop
    (d) dew : moisture
    (e) linkage : fission

_____ 8. medicine : antibiotic ::
    (a) alluvium : sedimentary
    (b) lavatory : building
    (c) laser : beam
    (d) rock : igneous
    (e) biology : ecology

Exercise IV. Matching. Match each word on the left with its best synonym or definition.

_____ 1. **infraction**   (a) resistant single cell

_____ 2. **antipodal**   (b) hollow, depression

_____ 3. **fission**   (c) violation

_____ 4. **refraction**   (d) opposite

_____ 5. **spore**   (e) unruly

_____ 6. **petrology**   (f) bending of light

_____ 7. **ignition**   (g) separatist

_____ 8. **refractory**   (h) rapidity

_____ 9. **lave**   (i) splitting into parts

_____ 10. **velocity**   (j) the study of rocks

_____ 11. **concavity**   (k) kindling

_____ 12. **centrifugal**   (l) to wash

Exercise V. Completion. Select the best word from List 15 and Roots to complete the sentences. (See Root Study for 1–4.)

1. The medical science studying human survival and adaptation in stressful environments is _____.

2. A good adjective to apply to the detritus left in the streambed of a dried-up creek is _____.

3. The man next door who studies fossils, who told you all about the pterodactyl, is probably a _____.

4. The large ceremonial pile which Rajiv Gandhi solemnly lit with a torch was his mother's funeral _____.

5. Not to be confused with metamorphic rocks, which have undergone change over time, rocks formed by volcanoes are termed _____.

6. Unlike fission, which involves the splitting of atoms, _____ is the union of atomic nuclei to make heavier nuclei, resulting in the creation of huge amounts of energy when certain elements are joined.

7. The vertebra in your neck on which your head pivots is called the _____.

8. That period in August when the sun is too hot and there's no beach in sight, when everyone you enjoy is on vacation and you're home alone, can be called the _____.

9. Attending a party that turns into a brawl is usually the very _____ of what you had hoped for.

10. In the movie *Goldfinger,* James Bond lies strapped to a table, perspiring with fear as he watches a beam of light advancing to dissect him. We in the audience assume that that beam is a _____.

Exercise VI. Word Analysis.

1. What is a *velocipede?* A *velodrome?* _____

2. Do you agree with E. B. Titchener that "commonsense is the very antipodes of science"? _____ George Santayana says, "Science is nothing but developed perception, integrated intent, common sense rounded out and minutely articulated." With which comment are you more comfortable and why?

   _____

   _____

   _____

3. One of the newer *-ologies* is *ecology.* What does this science study?

   _____

   _____

4. Match some of the better-known *-ologies* with their definitions. Ask someone for help if you run aground, but remember to use elimination as your ally, as well as prefixes.

   _____ a. geology   (1) the study of birds

   _____ b. criminology   (2) the study of mammals

   _____ c. archaeology   (3) the study of the nature and cause of diseases

   _____ d. bacteriology   (4) the study of civilizations' artifacts or remains

   _____ e. pathology   (5) the study of Earth's history, makeup, etc.

   _____ f. virology   (6) the study of crime and criminal behavior

   _____ g. mammalogy   (7) the study of the origin and history of words

   _____ h. entomology   (8) the study of insects

   _____ i. ornithology   (9) the study of viruses

   _____ j. etymology   (10) the study of bacteria

The universe is full of magical things patiently waiting for our wits to grow sharper.
   —Eden Phillpots

Presto, A Bonanza!
WORDS FROM ITALY AND SPAIN

In Context. Before studying the definitions, try reasoning out the meaning of each word, using context as your guide.

1. When tired of winter, our family gathers for an indoor picnic by the fireplace, but we prefer to eat *alfresco* with the birds and bugs.

   Keys: Logic, antonym   **Alfresco** means _____ .

2. Our high school's art show drew not only parents and students but also the local *cognoscenti,* eager to share their expert knowledge with any willing listener.

   Key: Partial definition   **Cognoscenti** means _____ .

3. Mom said the art show drew its share of *dilettantes,* too, and she was particularly amused by one of our local dabblers in the arts who repeatedly misused artistic terms.

   Key: Definition   **Dilettante** means _____ .

4. Our most outspoken local art critic got into a regular *imbroglio* with a member of the press. They had a complicated and heated dispute that attracted quite a crowd.

   Keys: Logic, partial definition **Imbroglio** means _____ .

5. One of our classmates has spent the last three years adding to his art *portfolio,* which is required for admission to a nearby school of design.

   Key: Logic   **Portfolio** means _____ .

6. When the band fails to keep up the tempo of a piece, the whole school can hear our director shouting, *"Presto, presto!* Move it along, for heaven's sake!"

   Key: Logic   **Presto** means _____ .

7. After a recent band concert, we were overjoyed at the *salvos* of praise fired our way by the two town newspapers.

   Key: Logic (note the verb)   **Salvo** means _____ .

8. "Tone it down," whispered the band director. "This part is like a lullaby and we want it pianissimo, *sotto voce*.

   Key: Synonym   **Sotto voce** means _____ .

9. Twain's satire on feuding in the American South featured two families and their bitter *vendetta,* which Huckleberry Finn witnessed to his horror.

   Key: Synonym   **Vendetta** means _____ .

10. *Aficionados* of bullfights might not appreciate the fictional bull Ferdinand, who preferred to sit quietly and smell the flowers under his cork tree.

    Key: Logic   **Aficionado** means _____ .

11. We heard Carrie muttering, "*Bonanza* Steak House—a box office *bonanza*—a regular *bonanza* of gold," and we decided that she was learning the word for a vocabulary test.

     Key: Examples   **Bonanza** means _____ .

12. When we first bought our run-down lake property, Mom had visions of a beach *cabana* for guests' use down by the lakeshore. That's pretty funny because the cabin itself is only 40 feet from the lake.

     Key: Logic   **Cabana** means _____ .

13. A visiting student from Spain told us that her mother had never been allowed to go on dates alone with her father; a *duenna* had always been their chaperone, according to custom.

     Key: Synonym   **Duenna** means _____ .

14. Our Spanish guest referred to a recent upheaval in South America by a group of political plotters that she termed the worst *junta* yet.

     Key: Definition   **Junta** means _____ .

15. We asked Dad when we could have some kids over for a party, and he jokingly began humming an old song, "*Mañana, mañana, mañana* is soon enough for me." He broke off to ask, "How do you feel about sometime in the 1990s?"

     Keys: Logic, example   **Mañana** means _____ .

16. Sometimes Jan's *quixotic* nature is at real odds with my down-to-earth realism and practicality, but at least she's never boring to be around.

     Key: Antonyms   **Quixotic** means _____ .

17. Probably influenced by our Spanish-speaking neighbors in the Southwest, we named our saw-toothed western mountains the *Sierras*.

     Key: Synonym   **Sierra** means _____ .

18. Heat makes us drowsy, but the first two seasons we owned the lake property we had no time for a pleasant afternoon *siesta*.

     Key: Logic   **Siesta** means _____ .

Word Study

One of the reasons English is considered to be a rich language is its willingness to adopt words from other languages. Usually we do so because there is no precise English equivalent. Lovers of words love precision. We want to say exactly what we mean. We are particularly happy with an adopted word when it expresses a concept that would take many English words to encompass, like *quixotic* or *salvo*.

Without the healthy, interesting additions from Italian and Spanish cuisine like pasta, spaghetti, pizza, tacos, and enchiladas, we would be lonely and bored at the table. (When you're hungry for pizza or a taco, nothing else will do!) Also, most of our musical terms have come from Italy, home of song. And where did Italian and Spanish come from? *Latin, a major source of our language.*

1. **alfresco** (al-ˈfres-(ˌ)kō) adj., adv.   Outdoors, in the open air; from It. *al fresco*
   Hiking and mountain climbing take place in the great out-of-doors, but an outdoor picnic or musical entertainment with buildings adjacent is said to be held *alfresco*.

Synonym: *outdoors*
Antonym: *indoors*

2. **cognoscenti** (ˌkän-(y)-ə-'shent-ē) pl. n.   Experts or connoisseurs, especially in fashion or the arts; sing., *cognoscente;* from It.

Mom, who pays little attention to clothing, had to sit through a fashion show surrounded by *cognoscenti*, all keenly interested in the latest feminine attire.
Synonyms: *connoisseurs, experts*
Antonyms: *amateurs, tyros, dilettantes, dabblers*

3. **dilettante** ('dil-ə-ˌtänt) n.   Someone who dabbles in the arts (or another field of knowledge) and has a little information but lacks serious commitment; pl., *dilettantes* or *dilettanti;* from It.

In this strange, terrible world war there is a place for everyone, man and woman, old and young, hale and halt; service in a thousand forms is open. There is no room now for the dilettante, *the weakling, for the shirker, or the sluggard.*
        —Winston Churchill, speech in Canada, December 30, 1941
Synonyms: *amateur, dabbler, tyro*
Antonyms: *connoisseur, expert, professional*

4. **imbroglio** (im-'brōl-[ˌ]yō) n.   A complex, often bitter argument or dispute; a complicated situation or entanglement as in a play or book; pl., *imbroglios;* from It.

Watching Abbott and Costello or Laurel and Hardy weave their dexterous way through a hilarious *imbroglio* always sends me into gales of laughter.
Synonym: *embroilment* (off the mark)

5. **portfolio** (pōrt-'fō-lē-ˌō) n.   A loosely fastened case for carrying pictures, papers, artwork, etc.; the duties of a cabinet member or state official; securities, as *his stock portfolio* (meaning his investments in stocks or bonds); from It.

Dad gave Andy five shares of stock in a growing company as an encouragement to begin saving. He had no idea that Andy would mention his stock *portfolio* whenever the opportunity arose.

6. **presto** ('pres(ˌ)tō) adv., adj.   Right away, quickly; in music, at a rapid tempo; from It.
To the Duchess of Shrewsbury, a foreigner to the English language, the satirist Jonathan Swift was *Presto,* which meant the same thing as far as she was concerned.
Relatives: *prestissimo* (music, faster than presto), *presto* (n., musical passage, movement)
Synonyms: *quick(ly), rapid(ly)*
Antonyms: *slow(ly);* (music) *lento, andante*

7. **salvo** ('sal-[ˌ]vō) n.   The shooting of guns, either in fighting or as a salute; the firing of a number of pieces (weapons) in rapid succession; any salute in tribute to an achievement, as *they welcomed the salvo of praise from the* Daily Tribune; a spontaneous and sudden burst, as *surprised by the salvos of the excited fans;* from It.

Unnerved by repeated *salvos* from the enemy's bunker, the new recruit perspired heavily.
Relatives: *salvo* (v.), *salve!* (hail!)

8. **sotto voce** (ˌsät-ō-'vō-chē) adv., adj.   Whispered or in a soft undertone, usually in a private way; in music, very softly, pianissimo; literally, *under the voice;* from It.

Andy asked me *sotto voce* if Mom had said anything about his little before-dinner snack that had polished off the last of the brownies.
Antonyms: (music) *forte* (loud), *fortissimo* (very loud)

9. **vendetta** (ven-'det-ə) n.   A lengthy blood feud, typically marked by revenge; from It., *revenge*

The idea behind a *vendetta* is that the nearest kin of a murdered man is obligated to kill the murderer—a self-perpetuating vicious circle prevailing in Sicilian, Corsican, Druse, and Arab societies.

Synonym: *blood feud*

10. **aficionado** (ə-,fish-[ē]-ə'näd-[,]ō) n.   Fan, anyone keenly devoted to something, as *an aficionado of wrestling;* from Sp.

No one in our family is more eager to get a video cassette recorder than Carrie, a true movie *aficionada*.

Relative: *aficionada* (feminine)
Synonym: *devotee*

11. **bonanza** (bə-'nan-zə) n.   A great amount, as *a bonanza of attention;* something financially rewarding or valuable, as *a show-biz bonanza;* an unusually large vein of gold or silver ore; literally, *fair weather;* from Sp.

America's fondness for the chocolate chip cookie has been a *bonanza* for cookie-baking entrepreneurs.

Synonym: *goldmine* (colloquial)

12. **cabana** (kə-'ban-[y]-ə) n.   A small shelter by a pool, lake, or sea, with one open side usually facing the water; or, a rather tiny, not too substantial, live-in cabin; literally, *hut;* from Sp.

Movie scenes of the 1920s depict girls clothed in voluminous swim costumes emerging shyly and self-consciously from beach *cabanas*.

Relative: *cabin*

13. **duenna** (d[y]ü-'en-ə) n.   An older female chaperone, companion or governess for younger women in Spanish and Portuguese families; chaperone (or chaperon); from Sp. *dueña*

There is no duenna *so rigidly prudent and inexorably decorous as a superannuated coquette.*
    —Washington Irving, "Spectre Bridegroom"

14. **junta** ('hùn-tə, 'jənt-ə) n.   A political faction or group of plotters (pl., juntas); from Sp.

One historically famous *junta* consisting of Russell, Somers, Montagu, and others exercised enormous influence over the English nation during the reign of William III.

Relative: *junto* (group with a common purpose)

15. **mañana** (mən-'yän-ə) n., adv.   Some unspecified time in the future; literally, *tomorrow;* from Sp.

My friend Juan Carlos replies, "Oh, *mañana,*" if I ask him when he will finish a job, but this casualness is only a mask for his serious attitude about work.

16. **quixotic** (kwik-'sät-ik) adj.   Idealistic, lacking practicality; noble or lofty in motive, yet unrealistic; from Sp. literature

Cervantes's novel, *Don Quixote,* a satire on the chivalric romances of the Middle Ages, gave us the word *quixotic* from its hero and marked the end of knight-errantry.

Relatives: *quixotically, Quixote* (n.), *quixotical, quixotism*
Derivation: In the Cervantes novel, Don Quixote was a lovable, idealistic, impractical, rather ridiculous older man who imagined himself a knight. Sancho Panza was his faithful companion and Dulcinea was his sweetheart. *Man of La Mancha* is the musical

based on this book, and both works contrast idealism with reality. A quixotic scheme is noble in purpose but impossible to realize.

17. **sierra** (sē-'er-ə) n.   A range of saw-toothed or jagged mountains; the area near a sierra; literally, *saw;* from Sp.

I should be judged as a captain who went from Spain to the Indies to conquer a people numerous and warlike, whose manners and religion are very different from ours, who live in sierras *and mountains, without fixed settlements. . . .*
　　　—Christopher Columbus, letter, 1500

Relatives:　*Sierra* (code word for letter S), *sierran*

18. **siesta** (sē-'es-tə) n.   A rest or nap in the afternoon; literally, *sixth hour;* from Sp.

Mad dogs and Englishmen go out in the mid-day sun;
The Japanese don't care to, the Chinese wouldn't dare to;
Hindus and Argentines sleep firmly from twelve to one,
But Englishmen detest a siesta.
　　　—Noël Coward, *Mad Dogs and Englishmen*

Root Study

　　This tiny group of roots has contributed hundreds of words to our language. (**Duc** and **fac** are two of the Star Roots mentioned earlier.)

1. CAPIT means head.
   capital—punishable by death, as *a capital crime*
   　　—uppercase (refers to letter of alphabet)
   　　—of major importance or influence
   　　—excellent, fine, as *a capital idea*
   　　—major city or site, the seat of government of a state or country
   　　—money stake or accumulated goods
   recapitulate—to summarize, repeat the main points
   decapitate—to cut off the head

2. COGN means to know.
   recognize—to realize as known
   　　—to acknowledge, as *he was recognized for his part in the play with a special award*
   cognition—known through awareness and judgment
   cognizant—aware, informed
   incognito—with identity concealed
   connoisseur—expert, cognoscente

3. DUC/DUCT means to lead.
   ductile—malleable, easily molded or led
   inductive—leading on, referring to logical induction, as in *inductive reasoning*
   traduce—to betray or violate by lying or deliberate misrepresentation; also, to malign, defame
   abduct—to take or lead away, usually by force

4. FAC, FECT, FIC, FICT, and -FY mean to do, make, create.
   factitious—produced by special effort or artificial means, as *a factitious demand for the product created by advertising,* sham
   affect—to make a difference, influence

artificial—not genuine; false or imitative
factotum—servant with diverse duties, skills
fiction—something created, as a story
magnify—to make larger, increase in size

Using the Words

List 16 Review

alfresco	presto	bonanza	mañana
cognoscenti	salvo	cabana	quixotic
dilettante	sotto voce	duenna	sierra
imbroglio	vendetta	junta	siesta
portfolio	aficionado		

Exercise I. Fill-ins. Select the best word for each phrase from the choices given.

cabana	salvo	siesta	portfolio
imbroglio	sotto voce	presto	bonanza
quixotic	mañana	vendetta	sierra

1. a beach _____ complete with shower and dressing rooms

2. caterwauling that interrupted my afternoon _____

3. ". . . on the double, I mean _____!" hollered Dad

4. papers bulging out the sides of her dilapidated _____

5. various utopias, each a _____ yearning for perfection

6. Hatfields—9, McCoys—10: score in a famous _____

7. *Peter Rabbit*, a _____ for author Beatrix Potter

8. don't want to be involved in an embarrassing _____

9. in _____ country, where the peaks cast long shadows

10. might mention that _____, but certainly not now

11. the resounding _____ fired over the hero's casket

12. hinted, _____, that we keep quiet about it

Exercise II. Synonyms and Definitions. Choose the two lettered answers that best define or clarify each word in bold type.

_____ 1. **alfresco**   (a) wall mural   (b) outdoors   (c) in the open air   (d) under the trees   (e) new soft drink

_____ 2. **junta**   (a) coalition with a definite purpose
(b) administrative body   (c) plotters
(d) casual get-together   (e) political party

_____ 3. **dilettante**   (a) loser   (b) idler   (c) dabbler   (d) one lacking commitment   (e) a devotee

_____ 4. **aficionado**   (a) friend   (b) fan   (c) swain
(d) devotee   (e) partner

_____ 5. **duenna** (a) wife   (b) relative   (c) chaperone   (d) companion   (e) buddy

_____ 6. **cognoscenti** (a) experts   (b) persons learning an art   (c) critics   (d) connoisseurs   (e) persons versed in diplomacy

_____ 7. **capital** (a) okay   (b) outstanding   (c) of major importance   (d) building   (e) insignificant

_____ 8. **ductile** (a) referring to pipes   (b) easily molded   (c) referring to reason   (d) concerning water   (e) malleable

_____ 9. **factitious** (a) sham   (b) genuine   (c) artificial   (d) hypocritical   (e) handmade

_____10. **imbroglio** (a) Italian umbrella   (b) pasta dish   (c) embroilment   (d) broiling instructions   (e) hostile, confusing argument

Exercise III. Logic. Enter the word from List 16 that fits best with each of the following comments.

_____ 1. "There'll be no stolen kisses while *I'm* around."

_____ 2. "I'm gonna get him. He wasted my brudder!"

_____ 3. "I just love art, don't you? I mean, being around artists is so thrilling. They're such interesting people, and I feel so interesting myself when I hang out with them."

_____ 4. "I've seen every Paul Newman film ever made. Did you know he has an apartment in New York and a house in Westport? I have the labels from his marinara sauce and his salad dressing on my bulletin board."

_____ 5. "I think that if we all decided to be really nice to each other, no matter what, all our problems would go away."

Exercise IV. Contrasting Ideas. Match the antonyms or contrasting ideas. Take your time. Fill in answers by remembering what a word does *not* represent as well as what it does.

_____ 1. **alfresco**   (a) meager amount

_____ 2. **cognoscenti**   (b) yesterday

_____ 3. **sotto voce**   (c) mansion

_____ 4. **presto**   (d) reduce

_____ 5. **bonanza**   (e) desert

_____ 6. **cabana**   (f) tyros

_____ 7. **junta**   (g) single shot

_____ 8. **manana**   (h) fortissimo

_____ 9. **sierra**   (i) indoors

_____ 10. **cognizant**   (j) introduce

_____ 11. **recapitulate**   (k) fact

_____ 12. **traduce**   (l) andante

_____ 13. **fiction**   (m) entire political party

_____ 14. **magnify**   (n) honor, praise

_____ 15. **salvo**   (o) unaware

Exercise V. Logic. Answer the questions using common sense and logic. Your answers may differ from your neighbor's.

1. For whom would a leather portfolio be a handsome present? _____

   _____

2. Why might a Latin-American require a siesta while Noël Coward's Englishmen "detest a

   siesta"? _____

   _____

3. Why are the words *mountain* and *sierra* not exactly interchangeable? _____

   _____

4. What sort of person is the antithesis of a quixotic soul? _____

   _____

5. What major change in social attitudes spelled the doom of the formal duenna? _____

   _____

6. Where, and in what form, does our society continue to endorse the "duenna concept"? ___

   _____

7. Why is a vendetta appropriately described as a vicious circle? _____

   _____

8. How does the altercation termed an *imbroglio* differ from an ordinary argument? _____

   _____

9. What old Christian ethic, still highly respected, does the dilettante flout? _____

   _____

10. Why might your father or mother say, "Without the general office factotum, our business

    would fall apart"? _____

    _____

Exercise VI. Word Analysis.

1. With the help of a dictionary, explain the difference between *junto* and *junta*.

   _____

   _____

   _____

2. The Spanish word *pecadillo*, respelled as *peccadillo*, has full acceptance in the English language and appears in our dictionaries just as the other words in this lesson. Do you remember (from a few lessons back) what it means?

_____

3. We have only to read a quote from a "classic" author like Washington Irving to notice the wealth of vocabulary he had and expected his readers to have. Rephrase Irving's quote (under no. 13, *duenna*), in current language.

_____

_____

4. *Deductive reasoning* is somewhat different from *inductive reasoning*. Try to explain both (with the aid of dictionary definitions) so that you see the difference between them.

_____

_____

_____

_____

_____

Review

This lesson reviews the words and roots in Lists 13–16. As you read over each word, try to remember a synonym or definition. Forgotten any? Recheck, fixing each in your mind before you begin the review exercises.

LIST 13	LIST 14	LIST 15	LIST 16
adulation	atrocious	antediluvian	alfresco
astute	captious	antipodes	cognoscenti
auspicious	choleric	axis	dilettante
blithe	execrable	centrifugal	imbroglio
congenial	furtive	concave	portfolio
exhilaration	heinous	doldrums	presto
felicitous	inimical	dross	salvo
fervent	ludicrous	fission	sotto voce
homage	lurid	fusion	vendetta
impeccable	macabre	igneous	aficionado
indomitable	morbid	inertia	bonanza
jocular	nefarious	laser	cabana
placid	plaintive	refraction	duenna
sanguine	pompous	shard	junta
suave	scurrilous	spore	mañana
zany	sordid	velocity	quixotic
	specious		sierra
			siesta

ROOTS

BELL	DUC/DUCT	LAV, LU
BIO	DUR	LEV
CAP, CAPT, CEIVE, CEPT, CIP	FAC, FECT, FIC, FICT, -FY	-LOGY/-OLOGY MOR/MORT
CAPIT	FRAG/FRACT	PYR
COGN	HOM	SACR/SACER
DOC/DOCT	IGN	

Using the Words

Exercise I. Analogies. Complete each analogy with the best pair possible.

_____ 1. connoisseur : dilettante ::
(a) neighbors : antipodes
(b) fight : imbroglio
(c) splitting : fission
(d) blues : doldrums
(e) impeccable : neat

_____ 2. sanguine : exhilarated ::
(a) discerning : astute
(b) choleric : testy
(c) satisfied : pompous
(d) adulation : scorn
(e) silent : furtive

_____ 3. sluggish : inert ::
    (a) axis : pivot
    (b) alfresco : indoors
    (c) fission : fusion
    (d) bad : heinous
    (e) goldmine : bonanza

_____ 4. presto : music ::
    (a) unusual : salvo
    (b) indomitable : spirit
    (c) zany : star
    (d) congenial : friendship
    (e) rushing : current

_____ 5. saleswoman : portfolio ::
    (a) professional : code
    (b) lawyer : client
    (c) desperado : crime
    (d) writer : instrument
    (e) aficionado : scrapbook

_____ 6. plaintive : sentence ::
    (a) nefarious : ideal
    (b) morbid : outlook
    (c) disinterested : homage
    (d) auspicious : value
    (e) lurid : menu

_____ 7. shard : pottery ::
    (a) ethic : doctrine
    (b) metal : dross
    (c) concavity : hollow
    (d) fragment : portion
    (e) atrocity : disease

_____ 8. sophistication : suavity ::
    (a) chaperone : duenna
    (b) beam : sight
    (c) peace : captiousness
    (d) junto : party
    (e) naiveté : knowledge

_____ 9. stance : ludicrous ::
    (a) action : delicious
    (b) attitude : inimical
    (c) velocity : repetitive
    (d) behavior : sotto voce
    (e) belief : blithe

_____ 10. cognoscente : respect ::
    (a) doctor : understanding
    (b) amateur : admiration
    (c) professor : felicitations
    (d) murderer : execration
    (e) expert : compassion

Exercise II. Fill-in Chart. Add the missing items in the chart. If you get stuck, refer to the Root Study sections for Lists 13–16.

	PREFIX	ROOT	WORD	MEANING
1.	_____	bell	_____	to adorn, decorate
2.	_____	_____	rebellious	_____
3.	in-	doc	_____	to teach beliefs
4.	_____	lev	_____	to relieve, lessen
5.	_____	cip	_____	to foresee, expect
6.	_____	_____	obdurate	_____
7.	im-	_____	_____	living forever

	PREFIX	ROOT	WORD	MEANING
8.	de-	sacr	_____	to profane, defile
9.	_____	bio	_____	medication to kill or inhibit microorganisms
10.	re-	fract	_____	stubborn, unruly
11.	_____	_____	reignite	_____
12.	petr-	-ology	_____	_____
13.	_____	lu	_____	a flood
14.	_____	_____	recapitulate	_____
15.	tra-	_____	_____	to betray or malign

Exercise III. Affect and Effect. Although both *affect* and *effect* come from the same root, their meanings are quite different. Because these words are often confused or misused, they are worth some time and thought.

Remember that **affect** means *to influence, to make a difference to,* or *to assume as a pretense*. **Effect** means *to cause to happen, to bring about*—or *the result,* when used as a noun. Using the correct form of *affect* or *effect,* fill in the blanks in the following sentences.

1. Rainy weather _____ my temperament, and I may become moody and quiet.

2. The prisoner _____ his escape from jail by disguising himself in order to slip past the guards.

3. We know some of the _____ of acid rain, and we may be doomed to learn others.

4. For her part in the play, Carrie _____ the halting gait of a deranged old woman.

5. Mom hopes that Carrie can use her dramatic talents to good _____ in college drama productions.

6. _____ to be exhausted from homework, Jan pulled a pillow over her head and hoped no one would ask her to do anything around the house.

7. One _____ of the chemistry experiment was the creation of a new compound.

8. Having _____ a cure for the animal's disease, the veterinarian sent his detailed results to a scientific journal.

Exercise IV. Antonyms. Select the lettered word or phrase most nearly opposite in meaning to the word in bold type.

_____ 1. **induce**   (a) return   (b) distress   (c) recite
(d) discourage   (e) uphold

_____ 2. **quixotic**   (a) stable   (b) practical   (c) thoughtful
(d) kind   (e) unrealistic

_____ 3. **vendetta**

(a) disbelief (b) acceptance
(c) incorporation (d) imbroglio (e) accord

_____ 4. **antediluvian**

(a) postwar (b) predated (c) foresight
(d) antisocial (e) current

_____ 5. **furtive**

(a) open (b) inner (c) noteworthy
(d) frequent (e) loud

_____ 6. **macabre**

(a) morose and downcast (b) religious and
uplifting (c) cheerful and jocular (d) zany
and ludicrous (e) regular and accepted

_____ 7. **scurrilous**

(a) fair (b) noble (c) caring
(d) acceptable (e) valuable

_____ 8. **honorable**

(a) lurid (b) inimical (c) sordid
(d) choleric (e) captious

_____ 9. **specious**

(a) above suspicion (b) under the table
(c) beneath contempt (d) from the heart
(e) beside the point

_____ 10. **apathetic**

(a) lazy (b) fervent (c) blissful
(d) placid (e) astute

_____ 11. **centrifugal**

(a) in opposite directions (b) toward
separation (c) with little motion (d) toward
a center (e) tending to disperse

_____ 12. **agitated**

(a) withdrawn (b) involved
(c) auspicious (d) placid (e) congenial

Exercise V. Story Fill-in. Select the best word for each blank in the following story. The word
form may need changing.

auspicious	nefarious	shard	pompous
impeccable	velocity	sanguine	felicitous
choleric	fusion	inimical	placid

A Cat Tale

Marigold's entrance into our household had a most _____ beginning. As a
_____1_____

young cat, she touched our hearts with her pathetic "meow." Cats know that a judicious meow

is as effective for a feline as any _____ remark for a human. We were too
_____2_____

naive as pet owners to suspect Marigold of any _____ motives. At first, her
_____3_____

behavior was _____, absolutely above reproach, and our viewpoint on pets
_____4_____

in general became _____ in the extreme. "I cannot believe that other people
_____5_____

have so much trouble with their pets," Dad would declare rather _____, as if
_____6_____

no more need be said on the subject.

Marigold thrived under our care, gaining weight at a rapid pace. This weight transformed

itself into six kittens overnight, or so it seemed. On that same night, Dad developed an

_____ attitude toward pet owning and eyed Marigold askance. Moreover,
_____7_____

our cat's once-_____ temperament became _____, and
                    8   9
she nipped us testily if we tried to inspect her litter.

   Still, the rest of us banded together—a familial type of _____—to defend
                                                                    10
poor Marigold and her babies. As the kittens grew, they needed our defense, for they rocketed

through the house with remarkable _____ and agility. One day we saw Mom
                                              11
sadly picking up the _____ of her favorite pot, knocked off the counter in an
                            12
exuberant kitten spree. Of the kittens, we kept Poucette and Figment, who have taught us more

about pets than we needed to know.

Exercise VI. Substitution. Replace each italicized phrase with the most appropriate word from the following list. Write your selections above the italicized phrases.

cabana	spore	captious	ludicrous
fission	siesta	homage	zany
execrable	salvo	mañana	exhilarating
indomitable	plaintive	dilettante	fusion

1. I am always disturbed by the *woeful, unhappy* sounds of animals in the Rescue League
   shelter.

2. One of the best weekends of my life was spent in a run-down *hut by the beach* in Florida,
   where two guys and I camped out.

3. We asked one boy if we could borrow his surfboard. He waved, hollered, "Sure, *in a little
   while*," and began paddling out to sea again, which made us think that we'd never see that
   surfboard.

4. None of us had ever surfed, so I suppose we looked *pretty silly* the first time we tried; but
   we didn't care what people thought.

5. Bob made breakfast the first morning on the beach, but his food was the most *wretched and
   disgusting* stuff I'd ever seen or eaten.

6. A good cook, I decided, deserves all the *respectful deference* in the world from those who
   gather at the table.

7. Our mom's no *dabbler* in the art of cuisine; she often spends hours trying out new recipes
   or bettering old ones.

8. Unfortunately, Andy's hard to please, and Mom often gets annoyed by his *nitpicky,
   negative* criticism at mealtime.

9. One night when it was Jan's turn to cook dinner, she served a *crazy, off-the-wall* meal
   composed of foods that everybody liked but which didn't blend well together.

10. Dad didn't criticize Jan's meal but rubbed his stomach in an odd manner and said, "I think
    I'll just lie down for a *little nap*."

11. Jan got Dad's subtle message, but with her customary *dauntless* spirit, she quoted old Ben Franklin: "Experience keeps a dear school, but fools will learn in no other." She grinned. "I guess I was the fool, but it certainly was *exciting for the mind and spirit* fixing that meal!"

12. Carrie's earth science class held a formal three-way debate on energy sources, one team favoring development of *the splitting of atomic nuclei,* one championing *the union of certain atomic nuclei,* and one promoting the use of fossil fuels.

13. My cousin, a botany major in his sophomore year, told me that he had spent a long time isolating one group of *reproductive cells* in order to make an acceptable slide.

14. Each cry of "¡Olé!" from the crowd, each *salute in tribute* of admiration, must be music to the ears of a matador.

Pardon the Pun
MORE WORDS ABOUT LANGUAGE AND SPEECH

In Context. Before studying the definitions, try reasoning out the meaning of each word, using context as your guide.

1. Ben Franklin was a natural with *aphorisms*. He sprinkled the pages of *Poor Richard's Almanac* with many adages, such as *Three may keep a secret, if two of them are dead.*

   Keys: Synonym, example   **Aphorism** means _____ .

2. One of Dad's former bosses, despised for his *bombast,* has taken his pompous, inflated style to another company.

   Key: Definition   **Bombast** means _____ .

3. Eyeing the essay face down on my desk, the teacher pointed to it and asked, "Should I *construe* that as a finished piece of work?"

   Key: Logic   **Construe** means _____ .

4. "All ayes and no nays?" the principal asked our committee. "Good. Since no one wishes to *dissent* on this issue, we can present a united front."

   Keys: Contrasting phrase, logic   **Dissent** means _____ .

5. "Her answer was a trifle *glib* to suit me," Mom explained. "I don't think she had thought about the matter at all. I've always distrusted a slick response like that."

   Key: Definition   **Glib** means _____ .

6. The wild exaggeration of comedians like Phyllis Diller or Eddie Murphy may be dismissed as *hyperbole,* but their humor often comes closer to truth than we care to admit.

   Key: Synonym   **Hyperbole** means _____ .

7. "She insinuated that I was out to get her boyfriend," Jan fumed. "You wouldn't have believed the *innuendo!* One nasty hint right after the other, so I just left."

   Keys: Definition, logic   **Innuendo** means _____ .

8. Jan and I had great hopes for the lecture on Mark Twain, but the speaker *prated* on at such length, chattering about whatever came to mind, that we left after half an hour.

   Key: Synonym   **Prate** means _____ .

9. Once I asked Granddad, who's addicted to *puns,* to explain what wise meant. He said, "It means a kid's question—like 'Wise the night dark?' 'Wise the moon white?' "

   Key: Example   **Pun** means _____ .

10. Aunt Dolly, never one to be *reticent,* talked at great length about her newest discovery.

    Key: Contrasting phrase   **Reticent** means _____ .

11. "Just so much empty *rhetoric,*" Dad said disgustedly as he tossed the paper on the floor. "You can't disguise lack of knowledge with a bunch of fancy words."

    Key: Logic   **Rhetoric** means _____.

12. Although Huck Finn's speech is filled with *solecisms,* such as "I seen him" or "he knowed what was comin'," I enjoy what he has to say and how he says it.

    Key: Examples   **Solecism** means _____.

13. Carrie practiced so long on her *soliloquy* for the play—giving that lengthy, reflective speech a dozen different interpretations—that we weren't sure we ever wanted to hear it again.

    Key: Definition   **Soliloquy** means _____.

14. The sideshow barkers at a circus have developed such compelling *spiels* that I am lured in by their extravagant promises in spite of myself.

    Key: Logic   **Spiel** means _____.

15. Just once, instead of her usual garrulousness, I would like to get a *terse* reply from Aunt Dolly.

    Key: Contrasting phrase   **Terse** means _____.

16. It's impossible to ignore Marigold, Poucette, and Figment at dinner time when their *vociferous* meows can be heard throughout the house.

    Key: Logic   **Vociferous** means _____.

Word Study

Language is the light of the mind.
          —John Stuart Mill

You know the old adage *The pen is mightier than the sword.* In other words, language has tremendous power. Nearly everything you do is influenced by your use of language or someone else's. According to the experts, about 90 percent (or more) of college study depends on reading comprehension. Many jobs are similarly dependent on reading and writing skills. Ideally, your proficient use of words will someday win you the career you want. Ask any person now in midcareer about the importance of language and accurate communication, and you're apt to hear an impassioned speech.

Even if it is extremely difficult for you, you need to master English grammar and as much vocabulary as possible. Your language will shape your life.

1. **aphorism** ('af-ə-ˌriz-əm) n.   A pithy saying that expresses an acknowledged truth or shared feeling; from Gr. *aphorismos,* definition, aphorism

   An aphorism *is never exactly truthful. It is either a half-truth or a truth and a half.*
        —Karl Kraus, *Aphorisms and More Aphorisms*

   Relatives: *aphorist, aphoristic, aphoristically, aphorize*
   Synonyms: *adage, saying*

2. **bombast** ('bäm-ˌbast) n.   Pompous, high-flown, pretentious writing or speech; from L. *bombac-,* cotton, especially cotton-wool used for padding

. . . He [Shakespeare] is many times flat, insipid; his comic wit degenerating into clenches, his serious swelling into bombast. *But he is always great, when some occasion is presented to him.*
　　　　—John Dryden, *Essay of Dramatic Poesy*

Relatives:　*bombastic, bombaster, bombastically*
Synonyms:　*pomposity, grandiloquence, lucubration, fustian*

3. **construe** (kən-'strü) v.　　To interpret or understand the intention of, as *he construed my attitude as favorable;* to analyze the construction of a sentence, especially when translating; from L. *construere,* to construct

I take the official oath to-day with no mental reservations, and with no purpose to construe *the Constitution or laws by any hypercritical rules.*
　　　　—Abraham Lincoln, First Inaugural Address

Relative:　*construe* (n., piecemeal translation)
Synonyms:　*interpret, understand, infer*

4. **dissent** (dis-'ent)　　v. To hold a different opinion, to differ, disagree.
　　n. A difference of opinion; from L. *dis* + *sentire,* to feel.

We must learn to welcome and not to fear the voices of dissent. *We must dare to think about "unthinkable things" because when things become unthinkable, thinking stops and action becomes mindless.*
　　　　—James W. Fulbright, speech in the Senate, 1964

Relatives:　*dissenter, dissension, dissentient*
Synonyms:　v., *differ, disagree*
　　　　　　n., *disagreement, difference*
Antonyms:　v., *assent, accord, agree*
　　　　　　n., *agreement, accordance*

5. **glib** ('glib) adj.　　Easily fluent in speech or writing, often slick and superficial; revealing lack of serious thought, as *a glib reply to my important question;* probably from Low Ger., *glibberig,* slippery

I want that glib *and oily art,*
To speak and purpose not.
　　　　—Shakespeare, *King Lear*

Relatives:　*glibly, glibness*
Synonyms:　*slick, superficial*
Antonyms:　*thoughtful, considered* (of responses, opinions)

6. **hyperbole** (hī-'pər-bə-[ˌ]lē) n.　　Extremely exaggerated speech or writing; from Gr. *hyper* + *ballein,* to throw

Although the word *hyperbole* may have predated the person, a man named Hyperbolus (far-throwing) lived in Athens around the fourth century B.C. and was known for his colorfully exaggerated figures of speech.

Relatives:　*hyperbolist, hyperbolic, hyperbolically*
Antonym:　*understatement*

7. **innuendo** (ˌin-yə-'wen-[ˌ]dō) n.　　An indirect hint or unpleasant insinuation about someone's reputation or character; a veiled, unflattering comment; in law, the person nodded at or indirectly referred to; pl., innuendos or innuendoes; from L. *in* + *nuere,* to nod

Political campaign speeches can feature obvious mud-slinging or the subtler *innuendo,* both designed to put an opponent on the defensive.

Synonym:　*insinuation*

8. **prate** ('prāt) v.   To chatter, usually at length and to little purpose; from Middle Du., *praten,* to prate, akin to prattle

> . . . *Thou sure and firm-set earth,*
> *Hear not my steps, which way they walk, for fear*
> *The very stones* prate *of my whereabout.* . . .
> —Shakespeare, *Macbeth*

Relatives: *prate* (n.), *prater, pratingly, prattle*
Synonyms: *chatter, babble, prattle*

9. **pun** ('pən) n.   The humorous or unusual use of a word or words to suggest a new/different meaning; from It. *puntiglio,* fine point, quibble

Some of my favorite *puns* use names of animals, as "He otter go fishing," "There's pandamonium in the bears' den," and "Ostrich in time saves nine."

Relative: *pun* (v.)

10. **reticent** ('ret-ə-sənt) adj.   Reserved in speech, tending to be silent; restrained in appearance or manner, as *the hall has an aspect of reticent grandeur;* from L. *re + tacere,* to be silent

When asked what a minister preaching on sin had said, the *reticent* Calvin Coolidge replied, "He said he was against it."

Relatives: *reticence, reticency, reticently*
Synonyms: *silent, reserved, restrained, taciturn, uncommunicative, close-mouthed*
Antonyms: *garrulous, talkative, voluble, loquacious*

11. **rhetoric** ('ret-ə-rik) n.   Insincere or high-flown writing or speech; originally, the study of effective communication or written composition; from Gr. *rhetorike,* art of oratory

In his book *On Language,* William Safire reminds us that *rhetoric* once meant "the science of persuasion." Safire regrets the degeneration of this word to its current meaning of empty talk.

Relatives: *rhetorical, rhetorically, rhetoricalness, rhetorician*
Synonyms: *grandiloquence, bombast*

12. **solecism** ('säl-ə-ˌsiz-əm) n.   An ungrammatical combination or use of words; also an impropriety in etiquette, decorum; from Gr. *soloikos,* an inhabitant of Soloi

A writer who is concerned about accuracy will write many a *solecism* as his characters move through the narrative; each character's speech must be distinctive and realistic rather than grammatically perfect.

Relative: *solecistic*
Derivation: Soloi was a city in ancient Cilicia (near present-day Syria) inhabited by colonists from Athens. The Athenian Greeks considered the colonists' speech to be corrupt and beneath them. Thus, *solecism* came to refer to an error in grammar or usage.

13. **soliloquy** (sə-'lil-ə-kwē) n.   A typically lengthy speech intended as someone's thoughts or reflections (usually in a play); from L. *solus,* alone + *loqui,* to speak

Written in the form of a *soliloquy,* Robert Browning's poem "Soliloquy of the Spanish Cloister" gives the thoughts of a spiteful monk jealous of a fellow monk, whom he tries to lead into sin.

Relatives: *soliloquist, soliloquize*

14. **spiel** ('spē[ə]l) n.   A loquacious, well-rehearsed line of talk, as a salesman's pitch; from Ger., *spielen,* to play

I wanted to buy something from a door-to-door salesman once, but his *spiel* was so long and so obviously full of hyperbole that I turned him away in anger.

Relatives: *spiel* (v.), *spieler*
Synonym: *pitch*

15. **terse** ('tərs) adj.   Succinct, pithy, concise, brief (of speech or writing); from L. *tersus*, clean, neat

Former President Harry Truman could be nicely *terse* at times, willing us at least two pithy sayings worth remembering: *If you can't stand the heat, get out of the kitchen* and *The buck stops here* (sign on his desk).

Relatives: *tersely, terseness*
Synonyms: *concise, succinct, pithy*
Antonyms: *verbose, wordy, prolix*

16. **vociferous** (vō-'sif-[ə-]rəs) adj.   Loudly and clamorously insistent; literally, *carrying the voice,* from L. *voc, vox,* voice + *ferre,* to carry or bear

It is nearly impossible to ignore the *vociferous* cries of a baby determined to be fed.

Relatives: *vociferate* (v., to shout), *vociferously, vociferant, vociferation, vociferousness*
Synonyms: *clamorous, strident*

Root Study

All of the following roots have contributed mightily to our vocabulary. Notice how many of the derived words refer to language and speech.

1. LUC and LUX mean light.
   lucid—sane, intelligible, as *a lucid argument*
   elucidate—to make clear through explanation
   translucent—allowing light through; genuine and open, as *her translucent charity and goodness*
   lucubration—a pompous expression in writing or speech, often purposely so; also, meditation
   Lucifer—the morning star, Venus; the fallen archangel known as the devil

2. PON and POS mean to place or put.
   posit—to postulate, assume that something exists
   postpone—to delay, put off until another time
   interpose—to insert or place in between; to toss in between parts of a conversation; to intervene
   propose—to set forth an idea

3. SENS and SENT mean to feel.
   sensation—a feeling; sometimes a great amount of feeling, as *her costume created a sensation at the ball*
   sentient—keenly aware/sensitive in feelings or perceptions
   sentiment—an emotion, usually deeply felt
   presentiment—a premonition that something will happen

4. VOC and VOKE mean voice and to call.
   vocal—referring to the voice
   vocation—career, job; literally, *one's calling*
   revoke—to call back, annul, rescind

> *irrevocable*—beyond the point of being called back; unchangeable, irremediable, irreversible
>
> *invoke*—to call upon for aid; to solicit or to cause

Using the Words

List 17 Review

aphorism	glib	pun	soliloquy
bombast	hyperbole	reticent	spiel
construe	innuendo	rhetoric	terse
dissent	prate	solecism	vociferous

Exercise I. Identification. Identify the following examples by writing the most appropriate term from List 17 on each of the lines.

_____ 1. "I seed where he was jittery, so I jest set back and waited."

_____ 2. "What's the opposite of wealth?" "Illth."

_____ 3. "I'm so exhausted I could sleep for a year."

_____ 4. "Children begin by loving their parents. After a time they judge them. Rarely, if ever, do they forgive them."—Oscar Wilde.

_____ 5. "That stranger's been eyeing the jewelry on the counter. Do you think he's contemplating something, perhaps?"

Exercise II. Definitions. Write the correct word from List 17 beside its definition or synonym.

_____ 1. pompous language

_____ 2. empty talk; literally, *the art of oratory*

_____ 3. loud and clamorous

_____ 4. a pitch or well-rehearsed flow of words

_____ 5. to interpret, understand

_____ 6. succinct, laconic, pithy

_____ 7. to chatter

_____ 8. long, reflective speech

_____ 9. to differ in opinion

_____ 10. silent, withdrawn, uncommunicative

_____ 11. suspiciously fluent

Exercise III. Aphorisms. You know the following aphorisms, but they have been elaborated upon by someone with *bombastic* tendencies or pretensions to impressive *rhetoric*. How many can you return to their original, uncluttered state by writing the real adage on the lines?

1. Members of an avian species possessing identical plumage congregate. _____

_____

2. Pulchritude possesses solely epidermal profundity. _____

_____

3. The stylus possesses more potency than the cutlass. _____

_____

4. Neophyte's serendipity. _____

_____

5. Individuals who domicile in vitreous abodes ought to refrain from catapulting petrous

missiles. _____

_____

6. Ligneous and petrous projectiles can potentially fracture my osseous structure, but

pejorative appellations will forever remain innocuous. _____

_____

7. It is bootless to indoctrinate a superannuated member of the canine species with innovative

artifices. _____

8. Male cadavers refrain from elucidation. _____

_____

9. A plethora of persons inclined toward culinary excellence vitiate the potable concoction

created by simmering certain comestibles. _____

_____

10. A revolving sample of petrous material accumulates no aggregation of bryophytes. _____

_____

Exercise IV. Antonyms. Match words from List 17 and Roots with their antonyms or
contrasting phrases.

_____ 1. **assent/consent**   (a) accusation

_____ 2. **glib**   (b) vociferous

_____ 3. **understatement**   (c) reticent

_____ 4. **innuendo**   (d) establish

_____ 5. **garrulous**   (e) unintelligible

_____ 6. **terse**   (f) dull, insensitive

_____ 7. **soft, quiet**   (g) dissent

_____ 8. **lucid**   (h) wordy, verbose

_____ 9. **sentient**   (i) hyperbole

_____ 10. **revoke**   (j) lacking fluency

Exercise V. Analogies. Complete each analogy with the pair that expresses the same relationship as the beginning pair. Remember to clarify the relationship of the first pair *before* hunting its mate.

_____ 1. construe : gesture ::
    (a) designate : building   (d) reverse : law
    (b) repeat : pattern   (e) insist : obedience
    (c) interpret : language

_____ 2. prate : speak haltingly ::
    (a) eat : hurriedly   (d) gibber : distractedly
    (b) run : stumble   (e) talk : with inflection
    (c) ask : with confusion

_____ 3. play on words : pun ::
    (a) satire : tragedy   (d) playful badinage : discussion
    (b) anecdote : speech   (e) grammatical error : solecism
    (c) raconteur : guest

_____ 4. demagogue : rhetoric ::
    (a) politician : analysis   (d) manager : products
    (b) door-to-door salesperson : spiel (e) minister : parsonage
    (c) lawyer : client

_____ 5. bombast : lucubration ::
    (a) innuendo : insinuation   (d) posit : inundation
    (b) sentiment : warning   (e) problem : elucidation
    (c) voice : vociferation

_____ 6. compassion : Lucifer ::
    (a) understanding : parent   (d) leniency: judge
    (b) comfort : hotel   (e) affability : host
    (c) mortality : deity

_____ 7. presentiment : future ::
    (a) hope : dream   (d) measurement : time
    (b) precursor : harbinger   (e) review : past
    (c) absent : present

_____ 8. thespian : soliloquy ::
    (a) director : sales   (d) mother : recreation
    (b) clerk : records   (e) artist : proposition
    (c) minister : invocation

Exercise VI. Word Analysis.

1. Your vocation is your career or job. What is your *avocation?* _____

2. When we say that an author's book is *marred by sentimentality,* what do we mean? (Puzzled? Ask any librarian or knowledgeable friend.) _____
_____

3. The nurse tiptoes out of a patient's room and informs the police that they cannot interview the injured person. "He's not *lucid,*" she says. What does she mean? _____
_____

4. A flood of words derive from the root **pon/pos.** How many can you list? _____

   _____

   _____

   _____

5. What is a *rhetorical question?* _____

   _____

6. Create your own high-flown aphorisms from the following: a. Silence is golden. (Hint: Use a word in List 17's definitions to begin this one.) _____

   _____

   b. Talk is cheap. (Guess what? You can begin this one with a word from List 17, too.) ____

   _____

   c. Never put off until tomorrow what you can do today. _____

   _____

7. Far from being the lowest form of humor, a well-made pun is a form that is highly respected. One of the best is biblical, in Matthew 16:18: *Thou art Peter* (Greek form, **Petros**), *and upon this rock* (Greek, **petra**) *I will build my church.*

   Shakespeare loved puns, even at strange times in a drama. After the murder of Duncan, Lady Macbeth says to Macbeth, "Give me the daggers. . . . If he do bleed, I'll *gild* the faces of the grooms withal, For it must seem their *guilt* [gilt]."

   The fancy name for puns is *paronomasia.* Check the dictionary definition of this term (especially its derivation) and write that definition here.

   _____

   _____

Latina Vivit
COMMON LATIN WORDS AND PHRASES

In Context. Before studying the definitions, try reasoning out the meaning of each word, using context as your guide.

1. When our senior adviser said we needed an *ad hoc* committee for graduation, we weren't sure what he meant until he explained that this would be a special committee to handle graduation details and arrangements.

       Key: Definition   **Ad hoc** means _____ .

2. Because I'd expected him to be just the opposite of me, I was astonished when my cousin Brad, who's lived half his life abroad, turned out to be my *alter ego*.

       Key: Contrasting phrase   **Alter ego** means _____ .

3. One little difference between Brad and me is his brain; the guy's a *bona fide* genius compared with me.

       Key: Logic   **Bona fide** means _____ .

4. "*Caveat emptor*," Dad commented regretfully as he examined a newly purchased tool that had broken on first use. "Some stores sell shoddy merchandise, and today's consumer had better beware."

       Key: Synonymous phrase   **Caveat emptor** means _____ .

5. "If we consider the *corpus delicti* in this case," Mom said, grimly viewing the mess around our aquarium, "we'll see that the evidence points to one mama pussycat with two feline accomplices."

       Key: Synonym   **Corpus delicti** means _____ .

6. "We should never have allowed those cats in the same room as the aquarium," Dad said, "but to forbid them now is *ex post facto*, just like locking the barn door after the horse has been stolen."

       Key: Logic   **Ex post facto** means _____ .

7. The new speech and drama teacher expects students to be able to speak *extempore* whenever called upon, as she believes that most of life's speeches are impromptu rather than planned.

       Keys: Synonym, antonym   **Extempore** means _____ .

8. "Can you issue a writ of *habeas corpus* on a pussycat?" Dad asked, trying not to grin. "I'd like to have that individual here right now to face our family court."

       Key: Definition   **Habeas corpus** means _____ .

9. On cleaning up the aquarium disaster, we found one tetra *in extremis* behind the tank, and although we put him back in the water, he failed to survive.

       Key: Logic   **In extremis** means _____ .

10. Andy got a little carried away with *Charlotte's Web*. After reading about that spider and her egg sac, Andy began claiming that his every accomplishment or good deed was his *magnum opus,* too.

> Keys: Example, logic   **Magnum opus** means _____ .

11. Noted for her hilarious *non sequiturs,* Aunt Dolly often has us laughing at comments that appear totally irrelevant to what we've been discussing.

> Key: Definition   **Non sequitur** means _____ .

12. Like unwelcome diplomats or students with too many demerits, Marigold, Poucette, and Figment were *persona non grata* for a while after their raid on the aquarium.

> Keys: Synonym, examples   **Persona non grata** means _____ .

13. Jan and I have a *quid pro quo* arrangement about tapes; I lend mine to her, and she does the same for me.

> Key: Example   **Quid pro quo** means _____ .

14. After Dad restocked the aquarium with tropical fish, he shut the door to the family room. "That closed door is vital," he announced. "It is the *sine qua non.* Otherwise, we'll lose this batch just as we lost the last ones."

> Keys: Synonym, logic   **Sine qua non** means _____ .

15. So far, with the door shut, we have preserved the *status quo* in the fish tank. We have every single fish that was put in there two weeks ago.

> Key: Logic   **Status quo** means _____ .

16. When the family-room door was left open by mistake, Dad joked about issuing *subpoenas* for every member of the family, to make us appear before him to give testimony.

> Key: Definition   **Subpoena** means _____ .

Word Study

Want to see an adult cry? Just tell a Latin teacher that Latin is a dead language. The instructor who doesn't cry may offer to duel. Others will list the ways in which Latin still lives, and you'll end by biting your tongue for starting the discussion.

Although Latin **per se** (as such) is not spoken, its roots form 60–70 percent of the English language and are the base of all the Romance languages—those modern languages going back to Latin through uninterrupted oral tradition: Portuguese, Spanish, Catalan, Provençal, French, Rhaeto-Romanic, Italian, Sardinian, and Rumanian.

Latin is especially lively in medicine and law, ensuring your acquaintance with it sooner or later. You refer to your old school as your **alma mater,** literally "fostering mother" for education. One female graduate or former student is an **alumna,** and all the girls, **alumnae.** A male is an **alumnus,** and all the boys, **alumni.** You read the list of the **dramatis personae** in your play program to see who's in the cast. New words like **computerist, space station,** and **biomedicine** are coined from ageless Latin roots. In altered form perhaps but . . ., *Latina definitely vivit.*

1. **ad hoc** ([']ad-'häk or [']äd-'hōk) adv., adj.   For a specific, particular purpose; literally, *for this*

The Student Council created an *ad hoc* judiciary board to deal with student misbehavior after school hours.

2. **alter ego** (ȯl-tə-ˈrē[ˌ]gō) n. phrase   The person most like you in temperament and tastes; literally, *another I*

The business tycoon had hoped for an *alter ego* in his brother, but he was disappointed by the younger man's involvement with the arts.

Synonymous phrase: *kindred soul*

3. **bona fide** (ˈbō-nə-ˌfīd) adj.   Sincere; genuine or authentic; literally, *in good faith*

Jan's attraction to good jewelry was intensified when Aunt Dolly gave her a pendant watch that was a *bona fide* antique over 150 years old.

Relative: *bona fides* (n., lack of fraud or deceit)
Synonyms: *genuine, authentic*
Antonyms: *bogus, counterfeit, fraudulent*

4. **caveat emptor** (ˈkav-ē-ˌät-ˈem[p]-tər)   In marketing, the buyer must assume the risk of anything purchased without a guarantee or warranty of quality; literally, *let the buyer beware*

Familiar Latin phrases include *Cave canem* (Beware of the dog), *Errare humanum est* (To err is human), and *Caveat emptor*.

Relative: *caveat* (n., any warning or prohibition; also an explanation necessary to prevent misunderstanding)

5. **corpus delicti** (ˈkȯr-pəs-di-ˈlik-ˌtī) n.   The basic, essential fact or facts necessary to prove a crime; or the body of a murder victim; literally, the *body of the crime;* pl., *corpora delicti*

Snatching the dead mouse from Marigold, Jan said to the cat, "I'm putting the *corpus delicti* in the trash, if you don't mind."

Relative: *corporeal* (referring to the physical or material elements in life, not the spiritual)

6. **ex post facto** (ˌek-ˌspōst-ˈfak-[ˌ]tō) adj., adv.   After the fact, as *an ex post facto law;* literally, *from a thing done afterward;* adv., retroactively

Not always popular, but sometimes necessary, the *ex post facto* law is one enacted after a crime to ensure justice.

7. **extempore** (ik-ˈstem-pə[ˌ]rē) adv.   On the spur of the moment, impromptu; literally, *of or at the time*

Addressing a group *extempore* becomes quite normal for any celebrity besieged by reporters.

Relatives: *extemporize, extemporaneous, extemporaneously*
Synonyms: *impromptu, extemporaneously*

8. **habeas corpus** (ˌhā-bē-ə-ˈskȯr-pas) n.   A legal writ or paper ordering someone before a judge or into court; literally, *you should have the body* (words beginning the legal writ); also your citizen's right to get a writ of *habeas corpus* to prevent illegal imprisonment

One of our most protective judicial devices is the writ of *habeas corpus,* which dates back to the English Magna Carta (1215).

9. **in extremis** (ˌin-ik-ˈstrē-məs) adv.   The last stages of life, near death; literally, *at the extremity*

Far from being *in extremis,* the butterfly struggled free of the net and fluttered away.

10. **magnum opus** (ˌmag-nə-'mō-pəs) n.   The chief or most significant work of a writer (or artist in any field); literally, *great work*

    I believe that *The Adventures of Huckleberry Finn* was Twain's *magnum opus,* but I often wonder what Twain thought was his greatest work.

11. **non sequitur** ([']nän-'sek-wat-ər) n.   A response that fails to follow the logic or sense of what has just been said and therefore seems ludicrous or inappropriate; literally, *it does not follow*

    One of our school newspaper's humorous *non sequiturs* concerned a new teacher. "Tall, of hefty build and smiling face, Mr. Smith has introduced some exciting lab skills to the chemistry department."
    (What, you may well ask, do Mr. Smith's height and appearance have to do with his lab skills in the chem department??)

12. **persona non grata** (pər-ˌsō-nə-ˌnän-grät-ə) adj.   Unacceptable or unwelcome; literally, *person not acceptable*

    Andy's early attempts at cooking were so messy that Mother considered him *persona non grata* in her kitchen until he learned to clean up after himself.
    Synonymous ideas: *outcast, pariah*
    Antonym: *persona grata* (personally welcome)

13. **quid pro quo** (ˌkwid-ˌprō-'kwō) n.   Like trade or barter, one thing given in exchange for something else; literally, *this for that* or *something for something*

    To those of us on the outside, high-level disarmament talks seem to be merely *quid pro quo,* a tense form of international barter.
    Synonymous idea: *tit for tat*

14. **sine qua non** (ˌsin-i-ˌkwä-'nōn) n.   An essential, vital thing considered to be indispensable; literally, *without which not*

    At the cooking school, Mom, Jan, and Andy asked the famous chef what had flavored the soup. "Ah," he replied quickly, "the spices. They are the *sine qua non* for this recipe."

15. **status quo** (ˌstāt-ə-'skwō or ˌstat-ə-'skwō) n.   The state of things as they now exist; literally, *the state in which*

    Eager to preserve the *status quo,* our town passed strict zoning laws to prohibit inappropriate or dangerous developments within town limits.
    Relative: *status* (condition, position, rank)

16. **subpoena** (sə-'pē-nə)   n. A formal writ ordering the person named to appear in court or face penalty; literally, *under penalty.*   v. To serve the writ of subpoena.

    Subpoenaed to appear in court, Mother calmed herself by writing down every detail of the accident she had witnessed so that she was sure about her evidence.

Root Study

In keeping with a Latinate lesson, here are four Latin roots that have contributed a vast number of words to English. Can you find the one *Greek* root, the oddball?

1. CEDE, CEED, and CESS mean to go or to yield.
    precede—to go before or ahead in time or place
    succeed—to follow in time or place

secession—withdrawal, retirement, as *the secession of the South at Civil War time*
intercede—to go between parties with the goal of reconciling differences; to interpose

2. LOC means place.
location—a distinct place or area
dislocate—to place or put out of position, as *a dislocated bone*
locomotion—movement from place to place

3. MORPH means form, shape.
morpheme—a meaningful language unit, e.g., *pin, bit,* that cannot be divided into smaller units containing meaning
amorphous—lacking definite shape, unformed
metamorphosis—a change of form, style, personality
morphology—the biological study of the form and structure of animals and plants

4. PEN (from *poena*) means punishment.
penalize—to punish
penance—an act or feeling of sorrow for a wrong
penitentiary—a state or federal prison
penitent—regretful or sorrowful, *repentant* of some sin or wrong, contrite

5. TEMPOR means time.
temporary—not permanent, for the time being
temporize—to compromise; to delay, thereby drawing out a discussion or negotiation to gain time
contemporary—of the current time, modern; of the same period in time, as *a contemporary of mine*
temporal—earthly (as opposed to heavenly or spiritual concerns); chronological

(Did you guess that the Greek root was **morph?** A common Greek letter combination is *ph-.*)

Using the Words

List 18 Review

ad hoc	corpus delicti	in extremis	quid pro quo
alter ego	ex post facto	magnum opus	sine qua non
bona fide	extempore	non sequitur	status quo
caveat emptor	habeas corpus	persona non grata	subpoena

Exercise I. Definitions. Write the Latin phrase from List 18 next to its definition or synonym. The first letter is a gift.

1. order to appear in court or face a penalty   s _____

2. for a particular purpose   a _____

3. near to death   i _____

4. supreme achievement   m _____

5. essential thing   s _____

6. other self, one's double   a _____

7. illogical response   n _____

8. tit for tat   q _____

9. buyer beware   c _____

10. retroactive(ly)   e _____

11. impromptu, unrehearsed   e _____

12. authentic   b _____

Exercise II. Fill-ins. Select the most appropriate word from List 18, based on clues in context.

1. A fair trade or barter arrangement is _____.

2. Learning to buckle your seat belt after having been pitched out of the car in a nasty collision is learning _____.

3. A commission was established _____ to investigate compliance with government safety regulations.

4. As long as no new kids join our class, we'll keep the same old _____.

5. Our band director, who finished the march he's been composing for four years, refers to it as his _____.

6. The way Andy carried on about writing his first book report, you'd have thought he was _____ and in need of an ambulance and stretcher.

7. Our motto for the garage sale had to be _____, as most of the sale items were pretty dilapidated.

8. Those who have seen Yul Brynner in *The King and I* believe that his inspired performance was the _____; he will be difficult, if not impossible, to replace.

9. It looks as though little Poucette will be Marigold's _____, and we will have two pets of equally strong personality in the house.

10. Fearful that he would be accused of a crime he had not committed, the nervous citizen obtained a writ of _____.

11. In front of all our friends at the lake, Dad began to declaim _____ on the joys of living far away from noisy traffic and hectic schedules.

12. Dad's business lawyer _____ employees to appear in court to testify to the sorry condition in which the latest merchandise had arrived. (Hint: Use the verb form.)

13. Agatha Christie's detective named Miss Marple is skilled at unearthing the _____, which convicts the guilty party.

14. "I doubt that this is a _____ gemstone," Aunt Dolly said, peering at the old ring Jan and I had found. She added, "It's an excellent counterfeit, however."

15. Jan was rhapsodizing about her new boyfriend when Dad broke in and asked if she'd completed her homework. In Jan's mind, Dad's question was a total _____.

16. Dad was serious about the homework, of course, and told Jan that the new boyfriend was

_____ at our house unless her schoolwork was up to date.

Exercise III. Logic. Using information from this lesson, answer the questions as completely as possible.

1. When might you be served a writ of habeas corpus? _____

_____

2. When would you want to secure a writ of habeas corpus as protection? _____

_____

3. Who in our government (general types/groups) would be considered *persona grata?* _____

_____

4. How do corporeal beings differ from spiritual beings? _____

_____

5. In what way is progress the enemy of the status quo? _____

_____

Exercise IV. Matching. Match the words learned in Roots with their meanings.

_____ 1. **precede**	(a) change of form, type
_____ 2. **intercede**	(b) withdrawal
_____ 3. **penance**	(c) earthly
_____ 4. **amorphous**	(d) language unit
_____ 5. **temporize**	(e) movement
_____ 6. **contemporary**	(f) contrite
_____ 7. **metamorphosis**	(g) to interpose
_____ 8. **temporal**	(h) to play for time
_____ 9. **secession**	(i) to go before
_____ 10. **morpheme**	(j) current
_____ 11. **penitent**	(k) an act of repentance
_____ 12. **locomotion**	(l) unformed, vague, shapeless

Exercise V. Useful Latin Bits.

1. Little bits of Latin pop up everywhere, and some of the most useful are abbreviations. Remember these?

e.g. = *exemplia gratia* = for example
(Introduces an example or several examples.)

et al. = *et alia* = and other
(Used, like *etcetera* or *etc.*, to eliminate a longer list of items.)

ibid. = *ibidem* = the same
(Used to avoid repetition of a reference, as in footnotes or in a reference volume.)

i.e. = *id est* = that is
     (Introduces a statement to clarify what has just been said.)
N.B. = *nota bene* = mark well
     (Calls attention to an important point.)

Enter the appropriate Latin abbreviation required by the following situations.

_____ a. Footnote 3 in your term paper or report refers to a quote from the book cited in footnote 2.

_____ b. You have written a fine general statement in an essay, but you wish to clarify with a more specific statement that will help to make your point.

_____ c. After a major Latin root, you want to list several examples of words derived from it.

_____ d. At the end of a paragraph on the English language, you want readers to remember one significant point.

_____ e. You have compiled a book list and listed one or two titles by your favorite authors, but you haven't room for more. How will you indicate that these authors have written other titles?

2. Using *per annum* (each year), *per capita* (each head or person), *per diem* (each day), and *per se* (as such), complete the story.

    In sixteen years, I have had only sixteen incredibly wonderful boxes of cookies, one box _____. And while chocolate chip cookies _____ are not worth anything, still everyone loves me when I share them. I have ten friends and 200 cookies, so I can lavish 20 cookies _____ on my friends. But then they will be all gone. If I give each friend only 5 cookies _____, they will last four days.

3. Match the words or phrases that directly *contrast* with one another.

    ____ a. bona fide   (1) rehearsed, planned

    ____ b. in advance   (2) ex post facto

    ____ c. extemporaneous   (3) welcome

    ____ d. persona non grata   (4) sine qua non

    ____ e. nonessential thing   (5) bogus

4. You have heard of people graduating *cum laude,* with honor or distinction. Might you rather graduate *magna cum laude,* _____, or perhaps *summa cum laude,* _____? (Write the English meanings in place.)

Exercise VI. Word Analysis.

1. We speak of someone who is chairman *pro tem* and understand that the position is held only temporarily. For what Latin phrase is *pro tem* the abbreviation?

_____

(The word you need is part of a word in List 18.)

2. Deduce the meaning of the Latin phrases in italics in the following sentences and write it in.

   a. We are acting *in loco parentis* for the orphan until adoptive parents can be found.

   _____

   b. We discovered fourteen major kinds of insects *in toto,* just in our backyard.

   _____

   c. And, *mirabile dictu,* among the insects was a pair of praying mantises.

   _____

   (N.B. Think of *miracle* and *dictate* to lead you to correct roots here.)

   d. Arms raised, the priest said, "*Pax vobiscum,*" at the end of mass.

   _____

   (N.B. *Pacifist* and *pacific* come from *pax*.)

   e. The entire plot was conducted *sub rosa* to ensure total secrecy.

   _____

   f. "*Tempus fugit,*" the teacher warned, eyeing the clock. _____
   (N.B. You know *tempus* from *tempore*. What does a *fugitive* from the law have to do?)

   g. Our captured insects seemed delighted to set their many feet on *terra firma* again after having been imprisoned in a jar for hours.

   _____

3. In *The Rime of the Ancient Mariner,* Samuel Taylor Coleridge writes, "The man hath penance done, And penance more will do." How would you explain this line to someone who had no idea of the word *penance?*

   _____

   _____

4. The Bible refers often to "a contrite heart." What word from Roots means *contrite?*

   _____

5. Latinate words tend to be longer—sometimes much longer—than Anglo-Saxon words. What reasons can you give for this?

   _____

   _____

   _____

Call My Lawyer!
LEGAL TERMS

In Context. Before studying the definitions, try reasoning out the meaning of each word, using context as your guide.

1. Our new principal announced that he plans to *abrogate* some of the school rules and institute others, which has us all wondering what will be abolished and what established.

    Key: Synonym   **Abrogate** means _____ .

2. When a sad-eyed holstein cow was discovered in school the morning after Halloween, certain sophomores were accused, then later *acquitted* when the guilty juniors confessed.

    Keys: Logic, antonym   **Acquit** means _____ .

3. The principal encouraged our student Disciplinary Review Board to *adjudicate* the Holstein Affair and later told us how pleased he was with our judicial process.

    Key: Near definition   **Adjudicate** means _____ .

4. The *advocate* for the sophomores' defense was the biology teacher, who'd hosted a party for the sophomores at his house on Halloween.

    Key: Logic   **Advocate** means _____ .

5. After hearing our sentence for the juniors, their advocate asked that we *commute* it to only one week of floor scrubbing instead of two, because the guilty ones had come forth voluntarily—and had returned the cow intact.

    Keys: Logic, example   **Commute** means _____ .

6. One of the messiest cases our Disciplinary Review Board had to settle concerned upperclass students who were *extorting* exam questions and answers from two frightened freshmen who worked part-time in the school office.

    Key: Logic   **Extort** means _____ .

7. Students from other schools who are found misbehaving on our school property are *extradited* to their own schools for disciplinary action.

    Keys: Logic, example   **Extradite** means _____ .

8. Our student court would never deal with a crime as serious as a *felony*.

    Key: Logic   **Felony** means _____ .

9. We had always known that our biology teacher was a skilled debater, but we were especially impressed with his *forensic* skills when he defended the sophomores.

    Key: Logic   **Forensic** means _____ .

10. The innocent sophomores in the Holstein Affair realized that their own reputations had *indicted* them before trial. Since their acquittal, they have all been model students.

    Key: Logic   **Indict** means _____ .

11. The juniors were relieved that the owner of the holstein did not charge them with *larceny*. As his cow was worth several hundred dollars, their theft would have been considered grand larceny had the animal died or disappeared.

        Key: Synonym   **Larceny** means _____ .

12. We were able to assign fair punishment for the offenders in the Holstein Affair within the confines of our school, whereas formal *litigation* in court would have embarrassed everyone.

        Keys: Logic, contrast   **Litigation** means _____ .

13. Our local mayor had been suspected of wrongdoing for several months, so it was actually a relief to the town when he was brought to court on a charge of *malfeasance*.

        Keys: Synonym, example   **Malfeasance** means _____ .

14. Not wishing to be convicted of malfeasance, the mayor lied under oath, but he was caught at that as well, and *perjury* was added to his list of offenses.

        Key: Definition   **Perjury** means _____ .

15. The *sanction* attached to smoking on our school grounds is a three-day suspension, which, as Dad said, "Certainly puts teeth into that rule."

        Keys: Near definition, example   **Sanction** means _____ .

16. In government class we discussed the law of *torts,* which came to us from England with the colonists. A tort is a legal wrong committed on the person or property of another independent of contract—such as trespass, nuisance, and defamation of character.

        Keys: Definition, examples   **Tort** means _____ .

17. Unlike New York City—vast, impersonal home of the bag ladies—our town is so small that a *vagrant* is immediately noticed and cared for.

        Keys: Logic, example   **Vagrant** means _____ .

Word Study

After a Latin lesson, you are in fine etymological shape for learning legal terms. Like *habeas corpus* and *corpus delicti,* many have come *verbatim* from Latin into the English language. Not long ago, a list of law terms would rarely have appeared in a text like this. Now, the number of legal suits has greatly increased, along with our awareness of human rights, so that everyone needs to understand legal terminology. A television series titled "The Paper Chase" and set in a law school clarified many legal terms for viewers in the early 1980s, but many missed that series, and so List 19 should prove helpful.

A state is better governed which has but few laws,
and those laws strictly observed.
    —René Descartes (1596–1650)

1. **abrogate** ('ab-rə-ˌgāt) v.   To annul, abolish or legally do away with; from L. *ab* + *rogare*, to ask, propose a law

    The word *abrogate* comes directly from the old Roman senate that asked the people *abrogare legem* (to speak, or solicit, against the law) when they wished to repeal a law.

    Relative: *abrogation*
    Synonyms: *annul, nullify*
    Antonym: *establish*

2. **acquit** (ə-'kwit) v.   To free of blame or obligation entirely; to behave well or acceptably, as *the novice class acquitted itself with distinction at the tournament;* from L. *ad + quite,* free of

We had blamed Marigold for attracting a stray black cat, but she was *acquitted* when we realized that the stray was wooing young Poucette.

Relatives: *acquittal, acquittance* (legal document/receipt)
Synonyms: *exonerate, exculpate; behave* (second meaning)
Antonyms: *accuse, inculpate*

3. **adjudicate** (ə-'jüd-i-,kāt) v.   To settle by legal process as a judge does, or to act as judge; from L. *ad + judicare,* to judge

Newly elected members to the Disciplinary Review Board think they will be able to *adjudicate* students' problems with ease, but they learn otherwise.

Relatives: *adjudicator, adjudge, adjudicative, adjudication, adjudicatory*

4. **advocate** ('ad-və-kət, 'ad-və-,kāt)   n. One who pleads a case or represents the accused, as a lawyer; anyone who defends or acts as champion for a cause or proposal.   v. To speak or write in favor of, as *his essay advocates fewer elections for longer terms of office;* from L. *ad + vocare,* to call, summon.

At the famous Scopes trial in 1925, the respected advocate for the defense, Clarence Darrow, said, "I do not pretend to know where many ignorant men are sure—that is all that agnosticism means."

Relatives: *advocator, advocation, advocative*
Synonyms: n., *lawyer, solicitor* (Brit.)
            v., *support*
Antonym: v., *decry*

5. **commute** (kə-'myüt) v.   To reduce or change a penalty or punishment to something less demanding; in law, to commutate; also to go back and forth with regularity, as *he commutes from New Jersey to New York every day;* from L. *commutare,* to exchange

The felon's sentence was *commuted* to twenty years when his rehabilitation became obvious to everyone.

Relatives: *commutation, commutate, commutable, commuter, commute* (n., the trip)

6. **extort** (ik-'stȯ[ə]rt) v.   To get something from another by force, power, intimidation, wits, etc.; to wring, as *he extorted a confession from the accused man;* from L. *ex + torquere,* to twist, wring

When more of the people's sustenance is exacted through the form of taxation than is necessary . . . such exaction becomes ruthless extortion *and a violation of the fundamental principles of a free government.*
        —Grover Cleveland, 2nd annual message, 1886

Relatives: *extortion* (gross overcharge, usually of money), *extorter, extortive, extortioner, extortionate, extortionately*
Synonyms: *educe, extract; elicit* (second meaning)

7. **extradite** ('ek-strə-,dīt) v.   To hand over an accused person to the authority with proper jurisdiction to try the case; from L. *ex- + tradition-, traditio,* act of handing over

International criminals are often *extradited* to their home countries, but exceptions have occurred when a victimized country refuses to *extradite* terrorists.

Relatives: *extradition, extraditable*

8. **felony** ('fel-ə-nē) n.   A crime serious enough to be legally declared a felony, usually incurring a severe penalty such as imprisonment for longer than a year or death; from L. *fellon-, fello,* villain, evildoer

*There shall be in England seven halfpenny loaves sold for a penny; the three-hooped pot
shall have ten hoops; and I will make it* felony *to drink small beer.*
        —Shakespeare, *King Henry VI, Part II*

(Note: Said by rebel Jack Cade. The normal three-hooped drinking mug held a quart, so a
ten-hooper would hold more than 3 quarts. Small beer was weak beer.)

Relatives: *felon* (criminal), *feloniously, felonry* (the convict population)

9. **forensic** (fə-'ren[t]-sik) adj.   Referring to or used in law courts or discussion and
    debate; argumentative or rhetorical; from L. *forensis,* public, from *forum*

The aim of forensic *oratory is to teach, to delight, to move.*
        —Cicero, *De Optimo Genere Oratorum*

Relatives: *forensic* (n., an exercise in argument), *forensically*

10. **indict** (in-'dīt) v.   To accuse or charge with a wrong; to charge with a crime by due
    process of law; possibly from L. *in + dicere,* to pronounce, utter

Injustice is difficult to bear, and we remember times when we were unfairly *indicted.*

Relatives: *indictment, indicter (-or), indictable*
Synonyms: *accuse, inculpate*
Antonyms: *absolve, exculpate*

11. **larceny** ('lärs-ᵊn-ē) n.   Theft; any offense by which property is gotten illegally; from L.
    latrocinium, robbery

"You're a mouse studying to be a rat," Wilson Mizner said, just as we might say that *petit
larceny* differs from *grand larceny* only in size.

Relatives: *larcenist, larcenous, larcenously*
Synonym: *theft*

12. **litigation** (ˌlit-ə-'gā-shən) n.   A legal suit in a court of law, a lawsuit; from L. *lit-, lis,*
    lawsuit *+ agere,* to drive

Large, wealthy corporations must employ numerous lawyers for *litigation,* some of which
is justifiable and some surely reprehensible for its waste of court time and everyone's
money.

Relatives: *litigant* (n., one party to a lawsuit), *litigant* (adj.), *litigate, litigable, litigious*
Synonym: *lawsuit*

13. **malfeasance** (['])mal-'fēz-ᵊn[t]s) n.   Official misconduct or wrongdoing, usually by
    someone in charge of public affairs; from AN, *malfaisance,* doing evil

The governor's shady dealings in the awarding of public contracts came to light and
resulted in his trial and eventual conviction of *malfeasance.*

14. **perjury** ('pərj-[ə-]rē) n.   Lying under oath, either by saying something untrue or by
    failing to do what was promised in the oath; from L. *per + jurare,* to swear

An oath, an oath, I have an oath in heaven:
Shall I lay perjury *upon my soul?*
No, not for Venice.
        —Shakespeare, *The Merchant of Venice*

Relatives: *perjure* (v.), *perjurer, perjurious, perjuriously*

15. **sanction** ('saŋ[k]-shən)   v. To confirm or authorize; to endorse, approve, or support.
        n. Authorization, support, or approval; that which gives force to a law, such as the
    penalty for breaking that law or the reward for upholding it or enforcing it; used in pl.:
    forceful, coercive measures to ensure compliance with law (usually international
    sanctions); from L. *sancire,* to make sacred.

I cannot *sanction* your attendance at a street gathering that is apt to become dangerous.

It will take the pressure of international *sanctions* to preserve many sea creatures from extinction.

Relatives: *sanctioner, sanctionable*
Synonyms: v., *authorize, endorse, approve*
  n., *authorization, support, approval*
Antonyms: v., *disapprove, interdict*
  n., *disapproval*

16. **tort** ('tȯ(ə)rt) n. With the exception of breach of contract, a wrongful act against another that results in injury or damage and for which satisfaction can legally be obtained; from L. *torquere,* to twist

Our U.S. law of *torts,* developed to protect a wide range of human interests against wrong, has its roots in the Norman Conquest of England in 1066, when the English common law was born.

17. **vagrant** ('vā-grənt) n. Someone lacking a definite home who wanders from place to place; a wanderer, rover; someone whose behavior is socially unacceptable, e.g., a drunkard, who can legally be classified a vagrant. adj. Roving, wandering, or fleeting, with no set course, as *a vagrant thought;* random; from AN, *vagaraunt,* vagrant.

Gifted actress-comedienne Lucille Ball no doubt enjoyed her challenging role as a New York *vagrant* in the television play "Stone Pillow."

Relatives: *vagrancy, vagrantly*
Synonyms: n., *wanderer, rover, vagabond, tramp*
  adj., *random, roving, wandering, errant*

Root Study

This collection of roots deals mainly with people and the law.

1. DEM and PLEB mean people.
   democracy—system of government wherein the people rule directly or through their elected representatives; literally, *rule by the people*
   endemic—confined within a specific, local area; native, as opposed to *epidemic,* which refers to something affecting many people at the same time, or *pandemic,* referring to anything occurring throughout a large area and affecting a high proportion of the population
   demagogue—a false leader of people who says what the people want to hear
   plebiscite—a vote by all people in a country/district
   plebeian—rude, common, low, coarse or crude, as *plebeian tasks;* literally, *of the common people*

2. DIC/DICT means to speak, say.
   verdict—the official ruling of a court or authority
   interdict—n., a prohibition, a formal decree that forbids something
     v., to forbid with authority, refuse to sanction
   malediction—a curse, execration
   dictator—one whose word is law, who exercises total control and authority
   jurisdiction—the power and authority to apply/interpret law; literally, *speaking in judgment*

3. JUD, JUR, and JUS mean judge.
   judicial—referring to a judge; in a considerate, deliberate, and thoughtful manner
   jurisprudence—the body of law with its working system; science/philosophy of law
   justice—a person, as *a chief justice* (judge); the acknowledged fair result, fairness
   abjure—to reject, renounce, or forswear, as *People on diets abjure desserts*. (Sigh.)
   adjure—to charge or command solemnly, to order, as *I adjure you to ignore that chocolate cake*.

4. JUNCT, JUG, and JOIN mean to join, to marry, mating.
   junction—a place of meeting or joining
   injunction—a court order requiring you to do or to refrain from doing something; an order or admonition
   conjugal—referring to marriage, matrimonial
   joint—adj., combined, united, as *joint effort*
       n., a skeletal point of contact, as *the elbow or knee joint;* large piece of roasting meat; anywhere two things or parts are joined

(Note: The root LEG, meaning law, was in List 8. Remember *legislate, legal, illegal, legacy?* A *paralegal* employee is one who works with the law but lacks a degree in law.)

Using the Words

List 19 Review

abrogate	extort	indict	perjury
acquit	extradite	larceny	sanction
adjudicate	felony	litigation	tort
advocate	forensic	malfeasance	vagrant
commute			

Exercise I. Definitions. Feeling comfortable with this list of words requires practice. Writing is a superb memory aid. Write a brief definition or synonym for words from List 19 and Roots.

1. **vagrant** _____

2. **acquit** _____

3. **tort** _____

4. **abrogate** _____

5. **sanction** _____

6. **adjudicate** _____

7. **perjury** _____

8. **malfeasance** _____

9. **advocate** (v.) _____

10. **litigation** _____

11. **commute** _____

12. **larceny** _____

13. **extort** _____

14. **indict** _____

15. **extradite** _____

16. **forensic** _____

17. **felony** _____

18. **annul** _____

19. **verdict** _____

20. **injunction** _____

Exercise II. You're the Lawyer. Using *all* of the information in List 19 and Roots, complete the following with the correct expressions or words on the lines.

1. A model prisoner hopes that his five-year sentence may be _____ to only two or three years.

2. I trespassed on your property in such a disorderly, noisy manner that your flock of turkeys panicked and several died in the crush. Under what law may you take me to court?

   _____

3. On the witness stand, I failed to mention that the accused had been at the scene of the crime on the fatal night. When this critical omission was discovered, I was charged with

   _____.

4. The final pronouncement of innocence or guilt is known as the _____.

5. The marriage of King Henry VIII and Anne of Cleves was not consummated, and Henry had their marriage abrogated by court order. This is commonly called

   _____.

6. The noise of my building crew exceeded that allowed by local ordinance, and I was prohibited from further building by a court _____ until the situation could be rectified.

7. I didn't have enough money to pay for the gas put in my tank. I took money from the gas station's cash box and was caught red-handed with the stolen five-dollar bill. The station owner prosecuted, charging me with _____.

8. On a dare, I dressed in rags, pretended to be sozzled, and loitered conspicuously around the bus station. Luckily, the policeman who questioned me believed my story and didn't haul me to the station as a _____.

9. Having watched lots of cops and robbers on television, I know that when taken to the police station I have the right to call my _____, who will act as _____ for my defense.

10. At an international meeting, members voted on _____ prohibiting excessive fishing of dolphins and whales, and establishing mileage limits within which the creatures would be safe from all fishing.

11. Although jaywalking and speeding may be classified as _____, homicide is definitely a major crime, a _____. (Hint: See sentence 8 of "In Context.")

12. I am a famous person—a household name, in fact—when my daughter is kidnapped and held for an enormous ransom. This particularly ugly form of _____ is legally a felony with severe penalties. (Clue: Check out word 6.)

13. The kidnapper of my daughter will need a lawyer with awesome _____ skills if he hopes to be imprisoned the minimum number of years required by law.

14. As elected treasurer of the Latin Club, I deposited the dues in my personal bank account so that I could collect the interest. The dues were spent over the year but I kept the interest and am guilty of _____.

15. My car rammed your car, which I maintain was crossing illegally in front of me. Neither of us will admit blame. We've hired lawyers and are now embroiled in _____.

16. Pity the judge who _____ the foregoing disputes. He must have some long days.

17. Everyone in our community is talking and reading about a much-publicized local murder. In order to ensure a fair trial, the governor of our state has agreed to _____ the alleged murderer to his home state to stand trial in a less emotionally charged atmosphere.

18. In his home state the alleged murderer was _____ by a grand jury on a charge of homicide.

19. Months later we heard that our alleged murderer was just that: alleged. He was innocent of the crime and _____ by a jury of his peers.

20. The Head Resident of our dorm explained that what went on in the dorm was under her _____. She said that she was required to enforce the college rules. (Hint: Hunt through Root Study.)

Exercise III. Antonyms. Find an antonym (or opposing phrase) for each word on the left.

____ 1. **interdict**	(a) to indulge in
____ 2. **establish**	(b) to absolve, acquit
____ 3. **advocate** (v.)	(c) to sanction
____ 4. **abjure**	(d) stable, fixed
____ 5. **indict**	(e) dictatorship
____ 6. **sanction** (v.)	(f) to abrogate
____ 7. **vagrant**	(g) separation

_____ 8. **democracy**   (h) to disapprove of

_____ 9. **adjure**   (i) to discourage, go against

_____ 10. **junction**   (j) to beg, plead with

Exercise IV. Analogies. Complete each analogy with the best pair possible.

_____ 1. felony : indictment ::
    (a) misdemeanor : wrong   (d) slander : libel
    (b) democracy : rule   (e) acquittal : accusation
    (c) libel : litigation

_____ 2. death : legacy ::
    (a) advocate : lawyer   (d) jurisdiction : territory
    (b) trial : verdict   (e) law : tort
    (c) commute : trip

_____ 3. noble : plebeian ::
    (a) fixed : vagrant   (d) joint : shared
    (b) illicit : illegal   (e) larcenous : timid
    (c) civil : polite

_____ 4. curse : malediction ::
    (a) sanction : disapproval   (d) prisoner : extradition
    (b) epidemic : health   (e) interdict : prohibition
    (c) abrogation : establishment

_____ 5. oath : perjury ::
    (a) tort : nuisance   (d) public office : malfeasance
    (b) junction : corner   (e) theft : larceny
    (c) adjudication : justice

Exercise V. The Root of It All. Answer the questions as fully as possible. If the dictionary cannot assist you, ask a helpful soul.

1. *Extort* and *tort* come from *torquere*, to twist or wring. What other words can you think of that derive from **tor-**? _____

2. DIC/DICT has many derivatives. How many can you list? _____
_____

3. Why is a first-year student called a *plebe* at the U.S. Military Academy, West Point?
_____

4. Why is the part of speech termed a *conjunction* well named? (Famous, beloved conjunctions include *and, but, or, nor, although, as, because, unless,* and *than.*)
_____

5. Distinguish between *pandemic* and *epidemic*. _____
_____

Exercise VI. Word Analysis.

1. What is the difference between a civil lawsuit and a criminal one? _____

_____

_____

2. Do you agree or disagree with René Descartes's assertion about the government of a state? Why? (See "Word Study," p. 226.)

_____

_____

3. The television program "Quincy" was about a medical doctor in the police department whose specialty was forensic medicine. Briefly, what is forensic medicine?

_____

_____

4. *Vagabond, rover, vagrant, wanderer,* and *tramp* can, at times, be synonymous, but their connotations are quite different. Which ones are positive or neutral in meaning, and which negative?

_____

_____

Which one(s) suggest(s) a carefree, independent person? _____

_____

Of the five words, which one could you accept as a description of yourself? _____

5. What is a *larcenous* thought? _____

And last, some "laws" to make you smile.

Calvin Coolidge: "A lost article invariably shows up after you replace it."

Sam Levenson: "Insanity is hereditary—you can get it from your children."

Joan Carris: The day you're proudest of your homework is the day the teacher decides not to collect it.

Jane and Spot Grow Up
VERBS YET ANOTHER TIME

In Context. Before studying the definitions, try reasoning out the meaning of each word, using context as your guide.

1. "This spring vacation," asserted Carrie, "I'm *abstaining* from everything that's good for me. Instead, I'm going to indulge myself: sleep late, avoid work, and eat goodies."

   Key: Contrasting phrase   **Abstain** means _____ .

2. "But Carrie, you'll wipe out all you accomplished by dieting and exercise!" Jan exploded. "You just couldn't *annihilate* all those great results, could you?"

   Key: Definitive phrase   **Annihilate** means _____ .

3. Often, Carrie won't *condescend* to reply when Jan explodes; she just stalks out of the room. But this time she unbent enough to snort, "Rubbish!"

   Key: Synonym   **Condescend** means _____ .

4. "I hate to *divulge* anyone's secrets," Mom said with a big grin, "but Carrie has told me she's running away from home if we serve so much as one more lettuce salad."

   Key: Logic   **Divulge** means _____ .

5. Carrie added, "I think that all recipes using lettuce should be *expurgated* from every cookbook in the world so that people on diets could eat something else for a change!"

   Key: Logic   **Expurgate** means _____ .

6. Hoping to *extricate* herself from the discussion, Mom said she was going for a walk, but Jan and Carrie tagged after her, so that Mom was still entangled in their argument.

   Key: Contrasting phrase   **Extricate** means _____ .

7. "I haven't *imbibed* a thing worth swallowing for weeks," Carrie continued. "Just tea and water and diet soda, ugh!"

   Key: Logic   **Imbibe** means _____ .

8. "You've *imputed* much of your hatred of dieting to the foods," Mom told Carrie. "Instead of attributing your dislike to the same old foods, you might consider trying new recipes."

   Key: Synonym   **Impute** means _____ .

9. "I didn't mean to provoke you, Carrie," Jan volunteered at last, "and I didn't want to *instigate* an argument, so let's drop it, okay?"

   Keys: Synonym, logic   **Instigate** means _____ .

10. "I'm not arguing!" Carrie *remonstrated*. "I said I'm going to do what I want now, and I'm not ever eating another bite of lettuce, and then you two got all excited."

    Key: Logic   **Remonstrate** means _____ .

11. "You should eat something you really love," Mom conceded, "and I don't mean one bite. Just *sate* yourself with a forbidden treat, and then you can forget about it."

        Key: Contrasting phrase   **Sate** means _____ .

12. Jan nodded. "That usually *suffices*. After a gooey hot fudge sundae I can be a noble dieter for weeks."

        Key: Logic   **Suffice** means _____ .

13. Carrie's face *suffused* with color as she poked Jan and Mom in the ribs. "Hush up about dieting. Don't you see those two cute guys walking right ahead of us?"

        Key: Logic   **Suffuse** means _____ .

14. Immediately, a discussion of the weather *supplanted* that of diets, and Carrie hissed, "Now we sound just plain stupid!"

        Keys: Logic, previous sentence   **Supplant** means _____ .

15. Mom sighed. "Carrie, I know that parents are supposed to *temper* their love with wisdom, discipline, and patience, but my patience with you today is wearing thin."

        Key: Logic   **Temper** means _____ .

16. I've always thought that Jan and Carrie needed a live-in referee to give the rest of us peace. I felt *vindicated* in this opinion when Mom reported their talk to me.

        Key: Logic   **Vindicate** means _____ .

Word Study

The verb is the sine qua non—the heartbeat—of every sentence. Choose the verb carefully, and your reader or listener will know exactly what you have in mind. Pick any old verb, and you will fail to communicate accurately.

Many of your best adjectives are past participles of verbs: *stooped, exhausted,* and *withered,* for example. Other descriptive adjectives are present participles like *whirring, stomping,* and *truckling.* Each of these adjectives gives a vivid picture because of the action feeling that the verb buried within it confers on the adjective. Likewise, great nouns are born from verbs: *condescension, instigation,* and *satiety,* to name just three from this lesson.

Author E. B. White—creator of Charlotte, Wilbur, Louis the trumpeter swan, Stuart Little, and several volumes for adults—is the final word on the subject of language. In *The Elements of Style,* he and the original author, William Strunk, remind us to "Write with nouns and verbs."

1. **abstain** (əb-'stān) v.   To refrain from an action or indulgence by exerting willpower; to refrain from voting; literally, *to hold back;* from L. *ab + tenere,* to hold

    Part of the Hippocratic oath taken by all physicians reads: "I will keep pure and holy both my life and my art. . . . In whatsoever houses I enter, I will enter to help the sick, and I will *abstain* from intentional wrongdoing and harm. . . ."

    Relatives: *abstainer, abstention, abstentious, abstinence, abstinent, abstinently*
    Synonym: *refrain*
    Antonym: *indulge*

2. **annihilate** (ə-'nī-ə-,lāt) v.   To wipe out, destroy, or vanquish completely; to rout, as *we annihilated the opposition;* to abolish; from L. *ad + nihil,* nothing

    Hoping not to *annihilate* ourselves, we still develop weapons capable of doing just that.

Relatives: *annihilation, annihilative, annihilator, annihilatory*
Synonyms: *nullify, destroy, vanquish, rout*
Antonym: *create*

3. **condescend** (ˌkän-di-ˈsend) v.   To bend or stoop to a less formal or exalted level; to put on a superior air, as *she condescended to grant me an interview;* from L. *com + descendere,* to descend

'Tis an old maxim in the schools,
That flattery's the food of fools;
Yet now and then your men of wit
Will condescend *to take a bit.*
      —Jonathan Swift, *Cadenus and Vanessa*

Relatives: *condescension, condescendence*
Synonyms: *stoop, unbend*

4. **divulge** (də-ˈvəlj, dī-ˈvəlj) v.   To reveal something held in confidence or secret; literally *to make known;* from L. *dis + vulgare,* make known

Further in the Hippocratic oath, the physician swears, "And whatsoever I shall see or hear in the course of my profession in my intercourse with men, if it be what should not be published abroad, I will never *divulge,* holding such things to be holy secrets."

Relative: *divulgence*
Synonym: *reveal*
Antonym: *conceal*

5. **expurgate** (ˈek-spər-ˌgāt) v.   To clean or purge of something objectionable, wrong, or harmful, as *the offensive lines in the play were expurgated before production;* from L. *ex + purgare,* to purge

A Shakespearean play may be *expurgated* not because its material is offensive but because the original is deemed too lengthy for modern audiences.

Relatives: *expurgation, expurgator, expurgatory*
Synonym: *purge*

6. **extricate** (ˈek-strə-ˌkāt) v.   To free from an entanglement or awkward situation; from L. *ex + tricae,* trifles, perplexities

The ancient "tricae" were hairs or strings tied round the feet of birds as fetters to prevent their wandering; a wily bird who escaped his fetters had quite literally *extricated* himself.

Relatives: *extrication, extricable*
Synonyms: *disentangle, untangle, disencumber*
Antonyms: *entangle, encumber, enmesh*

7. **imbibe** (im-ˈbīb) v.   To drink; to take in or soak up, as *our new bath towels imbibe moisture;* from L. *in + bibere,* to drink

Jason *imbibed* philosophical principles as though he were dying of thirst; his entire education, he felt, had been preparing him for the study of philosophy.

Relatives: *imbiber, imbibition, imbibitional*
Synonym: *absorb*
Antonyms: *exude, ooze*

8. **impute** (im-ˈpyüt) v.   To attribute or credit, as *their success has been imputed to their determination;* to charge or blame, often unfairly; from L. *in + putare,* to consider (Note: *Impute* is used with *to.*)

Andy *imputed* his failure at soccer to hatred of the game, but we told him that his muscle coordination would improve with age, and then he'd have more success even if he still disliked the game.

Relatives: *imputation* (n., insinuation), *imputable, imputability*
Synonyms: *ascribe, attribute, charge*

9. **instigate** ('in[t]-stə-ˌgāt) v.   To egg on or urge forward; to goad or provoke; from L. *instigare*, to incite

Huck Finn decided to "light out for the territory," unsure of what had *instigated* his departure, knowing only that he needed to escape civilization for a time.

Relatives: *instigator, instigation, instigative*
Synonyms: *incite, provoke, goad*
Antonyms: *deter, inhibit*

10. **remonstrate** (ri-'män-ˌstrāt, 'rem-ən-ˌstrāt) v.   To raise objections or argue in protest; to plead pro or con, as *she remonstrated gently, reminding her son of his manners;* from L. *re + monstrare*, to show

In the manner of a cat, Figment *remonstrated* with me vigorously as I fastened his new and detested collar. He stalked off when I finished, leaving his *remonstrances* behind in the form of several scratches on my hands and wrists.

Relatives: *remonstrance, remonstrant, remonstration, remonstrator, remonstrative, remonstratively*
Synonyms: *object, expostulate*

11. **sate** ('sāt) v.   To stuff or glut yourself to a point beyond satisfaction; or to indulge to the point of satisfaction; probably an alternative form of *satiate*, from L. *satis*, enough

When she had *sated* herself with sleep, Jan said she was finally ready to write her term paper.

Relatives: *satiate* (adj.), *satiable, insatiable, satiation, satiety*
Synonyms: *satiate* (v.), *surfeit, glut, gorge*
Antonym: *starve*

12. **suffice** (sə-'fĭs) v.   To be enough or sufficient for a need; from L. *sub + facere*, make or do

I think I know enough of hate
To say that for destruction ice
Is also great
And would suffice.
        —Robert Frost, *Fire and Ice*

Relatives: *sufficer, sufficiency, sufficient, sufficiently, insufficient*

13. **suffuse** (sə-'fyüz) v.   To spread throughout, as liquid or light spreads; to blush, flush; from L. *sub + fundere*, to pour (under)

Edgar Allan Poe's writing was *suffused* with gloom and foreboding, sadly befitting an author who expected to die both tubercular and insane.

Relatives: *suffusion, suffusive*
Synonym: *infuse* (off the mark)

14. **supplant** (se-'plant) v.   To take the place of or replace because of superiority, or by force or treachery; to erase and offer a substitute for, as *their attempts to supplant local slang met with no success;* from L. *sub + planta*, sole of the foot

In a coup d'état, one ruler or government *supplants* another.

Relatives: *supplanter, supplantation*
Synonym: *replace*

15. **temper** ('tem-pər) v.   To moderate or adjust as conditions require, as *she tempered discipline with love;* to strengthen through hardship, as *a ballet corps tempered by a*

worldwide tour; to soften steel or cast iron, or to toughen steel by definite heating/ cooling processes; from L. *temperare,* to moderate, mix, temper

Let the word go forth from this time and place, to friend and foe alike, that the torch has been passed to a new generation of Americans, born in this century, tempered *by war, disciplined by a hard and bitter peace, proud of our ancient heritage. . . .*
    —John F. Kennedy, Inaugural Address

Relatives: *temper* (n.), *temperament, temperamental, temperance, temperate, temperature*
Synonyms: *moderate, toughen*

16. **vindicate** ('vin-də-ˌkāt) v.   To confirm or justify, as *my confidence in them was vindicated by their performance;* to free from blame, absolve, as *he was vindicated by the tribunal;* to avenge, as *only by his death will I be vindicated;* from L. *vindicare,* to lay claim to, avenge

An old Roman method of settling a serious argument was to give each litigant a rod. The two crossed rods as if to fight. The person *vindicated* by the judge then broke his opponent's rod, called a *vindiciae,* from which we get the meaning *to justify* for vindicate.

Relatives: *vindicator, vindicable, vindication, vindicatory*
Synonyms: *justify, substantiate, confirm* (first meaning); *absolve, exonerate, exculpate, acquit* (second meaning); *avenge* (third meaning)

Root Study

From these four roots come dozens of English words, all strongly influenced by the verbs from which they sprang.

1. FLU, FLUCT, and FLUX mean to flow.
   fluctuate—to move one way, then another, at random
   effluent—outflowing material, e.g., the branch of a waterway or pollutants as waste
   influx—a flowing in, as *the influx of holiday crowds*
   mellifluous—richly smooth and flowing (of voice)

2. GRAD and GRESS mean to step.
   graduate—to move to another level or step within a process, like education; n., *graduate,* a person who has completed one level or step in a process.
   gradual—step by step in measured progression
   regress—to move backward, or to a former level
   egress—an exit; the act of going or coming out

3. MONI means advise, remind, warn.
   monitor—one who advises, warns, reminds, oversees others
   admonish—to warn or advise; to urge to good behavior through warning or advice; n., *admonition*
   premonition—a foreboding of ill; literally, *prewarning*

4. PEL and PULS mean to push.
   compel—to force compliance or urge in an irresistible way, as *the author felt compelled to write;* n., *compulsion;* adj., *compulsive*
   repel—to arouse strong dislike; to push backward or drive away or apart, *repulse*
   pulsate—to beat, throb; n., *pulsation*
   impulse—a sudden push or incentive; inspiration; whim or caprice

Using the Words

List 20 Review

abstain	expurgate	instigate	suffuse
annihilate	extricate	remonstrate	supplant
condescend	imbibe	sate	temper
divulge	impute	suffice	vindicate

Exercise I. Substitution. Substitute the best word from List 20 for the phrase or word in italics in each question. Write the word above its italicized counterpart.

1. her face *filled* with color at his compliment

2. glad to see my evaluation *justified* by her exam score

3. won't *purge* any of the beautiful, poetic lines

4. afraid that will have to *do* for today

5. strange that she had *ascribed* all the movie's flaws to one cause when there'd been many

6. no need to *object* so forcibly

7. steel being *strengthened* by the annealing process

8. better if you didn't *incite* ill will within the class

9. a way to *disentangle* Poucette from this ball of yarn

10. can't *soak up* any knowledge in all this commotion

Exercise II. Fill-ins. Select the most appropriate word from List 20 and Roots based on clues in context.

1. Dad _____ Jan and me about drinking as soon as we passed our driver's tests, warning us that unless we _____ from alcohol we would never be allowed to use the family car.

2. Carrie took Mom's advice and _____ herself on a rich chocolate cake, eating so much of it that she had a _____ she would be sick before very long.

3. Carrie's foreboding became grim truth. Although she never _____ how much cake she had gobbled, she did _____ to admit that she'd really overdone it.

4. When our archrival is scheduled for a basketball game, we dream of absolutely _____ them. We know that a narrow win gives less satisfaction than a rout.

5. The _____ of people from neighboring islands or oppressive regimes has _____ some natives of Florida, who have chosen to move to less populous states. (Hint: Check out Roots to fill the first blank.)

Exercise III. Switcheroo. Although List 20 consists of verbs, most can be *adjectives* as well. Match these adjectives with their correct *antonyms* or *contrasting phrases*.

_____ 1. **abstemious**

_____ 2. **condescending**

_____ 3. **divulged**

_____ 4. **sufficient**

_____ 5. **imbibed**

_____ 6. **insatiable**

_____ 7. **suffused**

_____ 8. **tempered**

_____ 9. **remonstrative**

_____ 10. **vindicated**

(a) exuded

(b) drained

(c) fulfilled or satisfied

(d) unaffected, natural, not superior in manner

(e) agreeable

(f) unavenged

(g) concealed

(h) self-indulgent

(i) weakened

(j) lacking

Exercise IV. Rhyme Completion. Complete the following verses with the appropriate *noun form* of words taught in this lesson. This is a bit tough. You really should review all the Relatives for List 20 words before beginning your career in poesy.

1. Her diet revolting, she yearned for variety;

   Offered some fudge, she succumbed to _____.

2. My cohort in writing is Reverend Kemper,

   A fellow who's loved for agreeable _____.

3. Tim flouted the rules about drink; thus, detention.

   He wrote fifty times, "I believe in _____."

4. Bowdler's been scorned for notorious translation.

   The classics sure suffered from his _____.
   (Note: Early in the 1800s, Dr. Thomas Bowdler decided to "clean up" the classics. *Bowdlerize* means *to rewrite to the detriment of the original.*)

5. How motley a group was that team's delegation!

   They quickly departed at our _____.

6. A spider's web's a dainty fabrication,

   But not to flies concerned with _____.

7. The notion of jogging fills Jan with revulsion,

   Yet her exercise is one form of _____.
   (Clue: Look among the Roots.)

8. There's just one trait I'd like to mention:

   I can't abide your _____.

9. On nuclear weapons he has reservations;

   To him they threaten mass _____.

10. My friend esteems his witty reputation.

    He'd choke at any other _____.

Exercise V. Find the Oddball. In each numbered group, select and cross out the one *unrelated* word or phrase.

1. exchange   supplant   imbed   replace   oust
2. object   defy   argue   remonstrate   expostulate
3. maintain   bowdlerize   expurgate   cleanse   purge
4. reveal   disclose   tell   discuss   divulge
5. expel   avenge   justify   vindicate   absolve
6. spread   suffuse   suffice   flush   infuse
7. incite   foment   instigate   annoy   egg on
8. imputation   innuendo   hint   suggestion   remonstrance
9. go back   regress   retreat   revile   relapse
10. beat   throb   palpitate   precipitate   pulsate
11. free   extricate   tricae   trickle   disentangle
12. dispute   toughen   moderate   soften   temper

Exercise VI. Word Analysis.

1. Within *annihilation* is the root *nihil* meaning *nothing*. What sort of doctrine is *nihilism*? (You know which book will help you if you're stuck.) _____

   _____

   If you are a believer in nihilism, what might be your viewpoint of war? _____

   _____

2. What is the *confluence* of rivers? _____
   What word derived from JUNCT, JUG, JOIN is a synonym for confluence? _____

3. How is a *vindictive* remark different from a *vindicatory* statement? (Same root, but note the difference.) _____

   _____

   _____

4. How does *precognition* differ from *premonition*? _____

   _____

5. Knowing the root TRICAE, can you explain the meaning of *intricate*? _____

   _____

6. AMAZING THING! Each word in this lesson comes from Latin, many almost *verbatim*, which happens to be a Latin word unchanged in 2,000 + years. (All but three in List 20 have Latin prefixes.) That's not so amazing, but . . . we have hundreds of everyday words that are spelled exactly as they were when Caesar and Antony walked the earth. How many can you think of? Take a peek at List 18, "Latina Vivit," for starters.

   _____

   _____

Review

This lesson reviews the words and roots in Lists 17–20. Read over all the words and roots, one by one, to see how many you remember. Forgotten a couple? Recheck, fixing each in your mind before you begin the review exercises.

LIST 17	LIST 18	LIST 19	LIST 20
aphorism	ad hoc	abrogate	abstain
bombast	alter ego	acquit	annihilate
construe	bona fide	adjudicate	condescend
dissent	caveat emptor	advocate	divulge
glib	corpus delicti	commute	expurgate
hyperbole	ex post facto	extort	extricate
innuendo	extempore	extradite	imbibe
prate	habeas corpus	felony	impute
pun	in extremis	forensic	instigate
reticent	magnum opus	indict	remonstrate
rhetoric	non sequitur	larceny	sate
solecism	persona non	litigation	suffice
soliloquy	grata	malfeasance	suffuse
spiel	quid pro quo	perjury	supplant
terse	sine qua non	sanction	temper
vociferous	status quo	tort	vindicate
	subpoena	vagrant	

ROOTS

CEDE, CEED, CESS	JUNCT, JUG, JOIN	PEN
DEM	LEG	PLEB
DICT	LOC	PON, POS
FLU, FLUCT, FLUX	LUC, LUX	SENS, SENT
GRAD, GRESS	MONI	TEMPOR
JUD, JUR, JUS	MORPH	VOC, VOKE
	PEL, PULS	

Using the Words

Exercise I. Antonyms. Select the word or phrase most nearly opposite to the word or phrase in bold type.

_____ 1. **terse**
  (a) short (b) vivacious (c) loquacious
  (d) patient (e) hasty

_____ 2. **abrogate**
  (a) establish (b) deny (c) ascertain
  (d) acquit (e) adjudicate

_____ 3. **sanction**
  (a) legalize (b) disapprove (c) end
  (d) disturb (e) equate

_____ 4. **bona fide**
  (a) honest (b) spurious (c) nauseous
  (d) similar (e) unpleasant

_____ 5. **innuendo**   (a) slur   (b) interrogation   (c) private comment   (d) open statement   (e) vindication

_____ 6. **bombast**   (a) regeneration   (b) peace   (c) reticence   (d) sympathy   (e) secession

_____ 7. **glib remark**   (a) hasty retort   (b) anxious question   (c) indecisive comment   (d) witty saying   (e) judicious statement

_____ 8. **fluctuation**   (a) ex post facto   (b) extrication   (c) status quo   (d) infiltration   (e) mirabile dictu

_____ 9. **abstain**   (a) release   (b) adjure   (c) divulge   (d) indulge   (e) misinterpret

_____ 10. **dissent**   (a) concur   (b) advise   (c) implicate   (d) egress   (e) instigate

Exercise II. Truth or Fiction. Mark **T** for statements that express truth and **F** for those that are fiction.

_____ 1. Your advocate in court will present the case for the county, city, or state.

_____ 2. Zack's term in prison may be commuted for good behavior.

_____ 3. Fearing illegal imprisonment, you may ask your lawyer to obtain a writ of habeas corpus to prevent such an unfortunate circumstance.

_____ 4. If you have a pressing engagement, you may ignore a subpoena.

_____ 5. Each carefully written, well-thought-out piece of creative writing can be thought of as your magnum opus.

_____ 6. A humorous non sequitur will help your listener to grasp the point you are trying to make.

_____ 7. If you deliberately omit something from your testimony in a trial, you have perjured yourself.

_____ 8. *Corpus delicti* can refer either to the victim of a murder or to the vital facts that prove the crime.

_____ 9. The term *rhetoric,* which historically refers to the art of writing and speech, is an example of a word whose meaning has degenerated.

_____ 10. *Either the players or the coach calls time out* is an example of a solecism.

Exercise III. Chart Fill-in. Add the missing items to the chart.

	PREFIX	ROOT	WORD	DEFINITION
1.	voc-	fer	_____	clamorously insistent
2.	_____	_____	extemporaneous	_____
3.	mal-	_____	_____	illegal use of public office
4.	_____	purg-	_____	to purge offensive matter
5.	pre-	_____	_____	foreboding, fear of what is to come

	PREFIX	ROOT	WORD	DEFINITION
6.	_____	_____	amorphous	_____
7.	_____	tricae	_____	to disentangle
8.	sol-	_____	_____	long, reflective speech
9.	in-	satis	_____	incapable of being satisfied or fulfilled
10.	_____	_____	endemic	_____

Exercise IV. Analogies. Complete each analogy with the best pair possible.

_____ 1. rootless : vagrant ::
  (a) regrettable : annihilation
  (b) fortunate : junction
  (c) likely : alter ego
  (d) handy : impulse
  (e) glib : spiel

_____ 2. felon : persona non grata ::
  (a) imbiber : satiated
  (b) adjudicator : impartial
  (c) president : reticent
  (d) punster : pathetic
  (e) extortionist : lithe

_____ 3. fondness : sentimentality ::
  (a) talk : prating
  (b) larceny : theft
  (c) understatement : hyperbole
  (d) felony : crime
  (e) hint : suggestion

_____ 4. legal code : law of torts ::
  (a) building : construction
  (b) medicine : profession
  (c) barter : quid pro quo
  (d) judgment : verdict
  (e) trees : maple

_____ 5. condescend : stoop ::
  (a) impose : put down
  (b) dictate : plead
  (c) secede : join
  (d) ascribe : impute
  (e) supplant : begin anew

_____ 6. progress : regress ::
  (a) instigate : discourage
  (b) acquit : exonerate
  (c) imbibe : inhale
  (d) extort : pressure
  (e) advocate : sponsor

_____ 7. suffice : sate ::
  (a) prate : chatter
  (b) abstain : refrain
  (c) suggest : dictate
  (d) indict : accuse
  (e) plead : remonstrate

_____ 8. sine qua non : essential ::
  (a) caveat emptor : trivial
  (b) in extremis : early
  (c) non sequitur : vital
  (d) extortion : intimidating
  (e) extradition : illegal

Exercise V. Fill-ins. Select the most appropriate word from the choices offered, based on clues in context.

construed	annihilate	in extremis	larceny
aphorism	ad hoc	pun	divulging
hyperbole	reticent	forensic	litigation
alter ego	caveat emptor	remonstrated	vindicated

Double Trouble

Horace and Maurice were identical twins, that is, identical in appearance, but one was certainly not the _____ of the other in personality. As someone who enjoyed creating an effect, Horace was given to _____; he loathed understatement. By contrast, Maurice was the strong, silent type, _____ in the extreme, rarely _____ even his name. Horace would say or do anything, which involved the two in constant _____. Poor Maurice was forever being dragged into court for something Horace had said or done.

Horace raised and sold turkeys with little regard for either his turkeys or his customers. _____ was his motto, and many an unwary customer had purchased a turkey _____ who died en route to its new home. When neighbors teased Maurice, telling him he had "double trouble," their _____ was painfully true.

Maurice decided that he needed a lawyer with powerful _____ skills to defend him in court, since he seemed doomed to spend much of his time there. A perceptive fellow, Maurice's lawyer sized up the twins' situation and accurately _____ it as one of constant tension. Vowing to _____ Horace in court at the first opportunity, the lawyer advised his distraught client to have patience and repeated his favorite _____: "Experience keeps a dear school, but fools will learn in no other."

"We'll nail the fool the next time," the lawyer promised. The lawyer created a(n) _____ team of teenagers to keep an eye on Horace and told another group of kids to keep Maurice company. Thus, he'd have witnesses to the actions of both men. Maurice's lawyer _____ with both of his investigative teams, urging them to behave professionally.

Maurice's worst fears were realized when he was accused of the theft of forty turkey hens, a(n) _____ he would never even have contemplated. Horace had stolen the turkeys, of course, but this time Maurice was _____ in court by his resourceful attorney, who had witnesses to both men's actions.

Exercise VI. Matching. Match the words on the left with the best possible synonym or definition on the right.

_____ 1. **ex post facto**   (a) take the place of

_____ 2. **acquit**   (b) repentant, contrite

_____ 3. **extradite**		(c)	low or common
_____ 4. **imbibe**		(d)	withdraw, go back
_____ 5. **suffuse**		(e)	continued flow, movement
_____ 6. **supplant**		(f)	postulate
_____ 7. **temper**		(g)	clear, sane
_____ 8. **recede**		(h)	urge forward
_____ 9. **flux**		(i)	exonerate, free
_____ 10. **conjugal**		(j)	absorb, take in
_____ 11. **lucid**		(k)	surrender to another authority
_____ 12. **posit**		(l)	retroactively, after the fact
_____ 13. **penitent**		(m)	marital
_____ 14. **plebeian**		(n)	flush, fill, infuse
_____ 15. **impel**		(o)	moderate

Here's to You, Simon and Garfunkel
TERMS FROM MUSIC AND THE ARTS

In Context. Before studying the definitions, try reasoning out the meaning of each word, using context as your guide. By now you should be good at finding key words, so no more hints.

1. When the full-length opera *Porgy and Bess* was produced in New York, Clamma Dale as Bess sang one memorable *aria* after another, to the delight of her audiences.

   Aria means _____ .

2. The execution of many *bravuras,* those always-difficult musical passages, requires the skill of someone like Segovia if the Spanish guitar is to sound its best.

   Bravura means _____ .

3. After their art appreciation course, Mom and Jan enjoyed using words like *chiaroscuro* to describe an artist's technique of depicting light and shade.

   Chiaroscuro means _____ .

4. Our school's music director explained that the *concerto* we'd be performing was typical: a lengthy orchestral composition with one or more instrumental solos.

   Concerto means _____ .

5. The caricature of a Wagnerian opera *diva* is a familiar cartoon figure. She is shown as a statuesque prima donna with a magnificent chest (presumed necessary to house her powerful voice).

   Diva means _____ .

6. Although we'd learned the concerto's notes, we had trouble mastering the *dynamics*. Instead of varying the force and loudness of contrasting passages, we played them much the same.

   Dynamics means _____ .

7. I adopted a *falsetto* voice in my attempt to be a soprano for the track team's skit. While the high-pitched singing was funny, it was a strain on my normally baritone voice.

   Falsetto means _____ .

8. After Jan had studied remnants of some old Roman *frescoes* in a museum, she was able to explain the technique of painting on moist, fresh plaster with water-based paints.

   Fresco means _____ .

9. Jan copied the design in a richly ornamented band of sculpture for a bracelet she made in art class. Her bracelet was displayed under the title "Grecian *Frieze.*"

   Frieze means _____ .

10. Our family's favorite librettist is William Gilbert, who wrote the *librettos* for the well-known Gilbert and Sullivan operas, like *The Pirates of Penzance* and *H.M.S. Pinafore*. Sullivan's music is made twice as memorable by its marriage with Gilbert's words.

   Libretto means _____.

11. We think of the Statue of Liberty as being green, but her color is the natural *patina* that forms on copper and bronze after long exposure, just as long wear and many polishings impart a satiny silver *patina* to sterling.

   Patina means _____.

12. Gershwin's *Rhapsody in Blue* stands for all that is glorious about the *rhapsody*—a highly melodic composition that appeals to our emotions.

   Rhapsody means _____.

13. Beethoven's *Moonlight Sonata* (No. 14 in C-sharp minor) is typical of the *sonata* form: it has three distinct movements, each one different in style.

   Sonata means _____.

14. One of the band's more difficult pieces had many *staccato* sections with short, sharp breaks between the notes, which forced each instrumentalist to pay close attention.

   Staccato means _____.

15. During Book Week, each English class wrote brief skits based on the class's favorite titles. These *vignettes* were then combined for an all-school assembly.

   Vignette means _____.

16. The violin *virtuoso* for the movie of *Fiddler on the Roof* was Isaac Stern, a Russian-born musician supremely skilled and perfectly appropriate for a musical set in Russia.

   Virtuoso means _____.

Word Study

If you are in high school or your early college years, familiarity with classical music and the arts may not seem important. But people change as they grow, and their minds reach out for new knowledge, often in the arts. If you were once dragged protesting through museums, you will find yourself seeking them out as an adult. Later, clutching another reluctant young hand, you will take your child to see the wonders of the past. Some day you may prefer classical music to the modern, popular tunes.

No doubt you know what an *opera* is, what *lyrics* are, and when the *overture* is played. You can tell the difference between a picture painted in *oil* and one done in *pastels* or *charcoal*. But you'll enjoy knowing even more about the arts. For instance, one student taking a recent SAT would love to have known the meaning of *diva* to earn herself 10 points (roughly) for a correct answer. These words most definitely appear on standardized tests.

1. **aria** ('är-ē-ə) n.   A melody, usually somewhat elaborate, sung by one person with musical accompaniment; an operatic solo; from It. *aria*, atmospheric air
   Dad said that he preferred the *aria* of a bird, accompanied by the great outdoors, to any operatic performance he had ever heard.

2. **bravura** (brə-'v[y]ùr-ə) n.   A musical passage requiring skill to execute well; a display of bravery, brilliance, or daring; from It. *bravura,* bravery

For the Dinkey-Bird's bravuras,
And staccatos are so sweet—
His roulades, appoggiaturas,
And robustos so complete,
That the youth of every nation—,
Be they near or far away—
Have especial delectation,
In that gladsome roundelay.
                    —Eugene Field, "The Dinkey-Bird" (children's poem)

3. **chiaroscuro** (kē-,är-ə-'sk[y]ù[ə]r-[,]ō) n.   The treatment of light and dark in a work of art; a picture rendered as light and shade, not in actual colors; a woodcut print using different tones of one color; from It. *chiaro,* clear, light, + *oscuro,* dark, obscure

Often called "black and white," *chiaroscuro* was conceived by Leonardo da Vinci to create the illusion of space by turning a two-dimensional canvas into something appearing to have three dimensions.

4. **concerto** (kən-'chert-[,]ō) n.   A musical piece with three different movements performed by an orchestra and featuring one or more soloists; from It. *concerto,* concert

A very famous *concerto* is Richard Addinsell's *Warsaw Concerto,* written during World War II for the British film *Dangerous Moonlight* and featuring the piano as solo instrument.

Relatives: *concert, concertina, concertize*

5. **diva** ('dē-və) n.   The lead female singer or prima donna (first lady); from It. *diva,* goddess

Literally *goddess* in Italian, *diva* is akin to many words in other languages, all referring to a deity with only four letters: *dieu* in French, *dios* in Spanish, *deus* in Latin, and *diva* again in Sanskrit.

6. **dynamics** (dī-'nam-iks) n. pl.   The variation in loudness or force (music); the forces operating in any matter subject to change or variation, as *the dynamics of the marketplace* or *the dynamics of personality;* that branch of physics concerned with matter in motion; from Gr. *dynamis,* power

When we say that a pianist can produce tremendous volume and variety of tone, we are commenting on the artist's mastery of *dynamics.*

Relatives: *dyne* (unit of force), *dynamic, dynamism, dynamite, dynamo*

7. **falsetto** (fòl-'set-[,]ō)   n. The artificially high voice, mainly above normal range. adv. In an artificially high voice, as *he sang amusingly falsetto;* from It. *falso,* false.

Many male comedians have used their voices to good effect, adopting the *falsetto* to indicate sudden terror or nervousness, as Richard Pryor did in the film, *Silver Streak.*

8. **fresco** ('fres-[,]kō) n.   Painting with water-based paints on fresh, moist plaster; a painting done by this technique; pl., frescoes, frescos; from It. *fresco,* fresh

At Fontainebleau in France, sixty different *frescoes* depict the travels of Ulysses.

Relative: *fresco* (v.)

9. **frieze** ('frēz) n.   The decorative band on a building, often sculptured to have three dimensions; the same ornamented band around the walls of a room; from L. *frisium*, embroidered cloth

   On ancient buildings in Europe, as well as some from the last century, the eye is drawn up the columns of a structure to the richly ornamented *frieze* depicting gods, battles, or memorable heroes.

10. **libretto** (lə-'bret-[,]ō) n.   The words (text) that go with a piece of music, such as an opera or operetta (light opera); from L. *liber,* book

    Stephen Sondheim, a famous modern musician, wrote the *libretto* for Leonard Bernstein's classic, *West Side Story*.

    Relative: *librettist* (the writer of a libretto)

11. **patina** (pə-'tē-nə, 'pat-ə-nə) n.   The much-admired look that time / weather / acids give to metals, usually a turquoise green on copper and bronze and a dulled satiny finish on sterling; from L. *patina,* shallow dish

    My young aunt used her sterling daily and polished it weekly until its *patina* satisfied her.

    Relative: *patine* (v., to cover with a patina)

12. **rhapsody** ('rap-səd-ē) n.   A musical composition without definite form, improvisational in type, usually expressing strong feeling; something said, written, or sung with fervent emotion, as *the dawn rhapsody of a bird;* from Gr. *rhapsoidia,* a recitation of epic poetry selections, rhapsody

    The well-loved Hungarian Rhapsody No. 2 by Liszt is based on Gypsy sources and is only one of his nineteen Hungarian *rhapsodies* originally written for a solo piano.

    Relatives: *rhapsodist, rhapsodize, rhapsodic, rhapsodical, rhapsodically*

    Derivation: Rhapsody literally means *songs strung together,* as the base roots **rhaptein** (to sew, stitch together) and **aidein** (to sing) tell us. The term rhapsody originally referred to the books of the *Iliad* and the *Odyssey,* which were in fragments until bards collected and sung them as long stories, the way we know them now. Red-robed bards sang the *Iliad;* those in blue robes sang the *Odyssey*.

13. **sonata** (sə-'nä-tə) n.   A fairly lengthy musical piece, usually with several distinct movements that contrast in key and style; from It. and L. *sonare,* to sound

    Three of Beethoven's most famous *sonatas* are known by the names *Moonlight, Pathétique,* and *Appassionata*.

    Relative: *sonatina* (shorter or simpler sonata)

14. **staccato** (stə-'kät-(,)ō) adj.   Abrupt, clear-cut, short, distinctly separate, as *staccato notes* in music; disjointed, disconnected; from It. *staccare,* to detach

    The sharp, *staccato* manner in which she delivered her orders revealed that she had lost her patience.

    Relatives: *staccato* (n.), *staccato* (adv.), *staccato mark* (the dot or pointed vertical stroke over a musical note to be played staccato)

15. **vignette** (vin-'yet) n.   A succinct verbal or literary sketch; a small segment representative of the whole, i.e., one scene of a play, book, or movie, usually selected for its excellence; from F. *vignette* (little vines, tendrils), diminutive of *vigne,* vine

    Originally a *vignette* was a portrait or small likeness of someone, bordered with vine leaves. (See the root.)

    Relatives: *vignettist* (n.), *vignette* (v., to describe briefly)

16. **virtuoso, virtuosa** (vər-chə-'wō-(ˌ)sō and vər-chə-'wō-(ˌ)sə) n.   One supremely skilled and knowledgeable in an art; from It. *virtuoso,* virtuous, skilled

The concertmaster of an orchestra (first violinist) is the *virtuoso* (or *virtuosa*) of the group and the assistant to the conductor.

Relatives: *virtuoso* (adj.), *virtuosity*
Antonyms: *beginner, neophyte, tyro, novice*

Root Study

This is a rather motley assortment of roots, but all are big contributors to our language and worth knowing.

1. DYN/DYNAM means power.
    dynasty—a hereditary line of rulers, owners, etc.
    dynamo—usually a small generator for electric current; also, someone with astonishing energy or drive
    dynamite—anything that sets off a powerful reaction, as nitroglycerine does in the explosive
    thermodynamics—branch of physics dealing with heat and related energy forms

2. HAL and SPIR mean breathe, breath, life.
    inhale—to breathe in; *exhale*—to breathe out
    inhalator or *respirator*—machines to aid breathing as means of artificial *respiration*
    expire—to breathe one's last, to die; to reach an end
    aspire—to seek, to hope or long for, as *she aspired to a career in music*

3. LEG, LIG, and LECT mean to choose, gather, read.
    legible—clear enough to be read; antonym, *illegible*
    eligible—capable of being selected because of skills, knowledge, availability, etc.
    select—to choose or pick out of a group
    legumes—peas or beans, which typically have to be chosen for ripeness, then gathered

4. NOC/NOX means night.
    nocturne—a dreamy musical composition, usually restful
    nocturnal—referring to night, as *nocturnal animals*
    equinox—a time when day and night are equally long; *autumnal equinox* = September 22, *vernal equinox* = March 21

5. NOC/NOX means harm, injury.
    innocent—free from blame, not guilty; unaware, unsophisticated, childlike
    nocuous and *noxious*—harmful, injurious, unpleasant
    innocuous—harmless

Using the Words

List 21 Review

aria	diva	frieze	sonata
bravura	dynamics	libretto	staccato
chiaroscuro	falsetto	patina	vignette
concerto	fresco	rhapsody	virtuoso/a

Exercise I. Definitions. Write the correct word from List 21 on the line following its definition.

1. short, abrupt, disconnected _____

2. aged/weathered film or appearance _____

3. richly ornamented band _____

4. watercolor painting on damp plaster _____

5. the lead female singer, prima donna _____

6. art technique using light and shade to give the illusion of depth _____

7. tricky musical passage or a show of brilliance, bravery, or daring _____

8. brief literary sketch _____

9. skilled, knowledgeable performer _____

10. demanding musical solo for voice _____

11. musical piece for a solo instrument, consisting of separate movements contrasting in key and style _____

12. the text for a musical drama _____

13. emotional piece of music with no set form, tending to be improvisational _____

14. variation in force or loudness of music _____

15. an unnaturally high voice _____

16. lengthy musical composition featuring one or more solo instruments, usually with three contrasting movements _____

Exercise II. Fill-ins. Words from List 21 are used every day, not solely with reference to the arts. From the choices offered, select the most appropriate word for each sentence.

bravura	rhapsodize	chiaroscuro	Diva
frieze	staccato	vignette	patina
aria	dynamics	virtuosa	

1. Because population _____ strongly affect our economy, modern professionals study various trends as people age, relocate, and change habits or attitudes.

2. Breaking up an angry fight between Andy and Carrie, Mom said, "We've witnessed this _____ of family life many times before. Both of you go to your rooms!"

3. Although young, Figment is notable for _____. Not a leaf stirs or a butterfly flutters without an arched back and a warning hiss from our "attack kitten."

4. "You don't need to _____ quite so often about the new guy in your class," Jan told Carrie. "We got the message sometime last week."

5. Mom's an authentic _____ with her food processor, creating delicious foods whose recipes are not in cookbooks.

6. My alarm clock is my dad's morning _____ in the shower as he tortures yet another operatic classic.

7. Andy must have told his entire school about Marigold's new kittens, because a _____ of kids wound its way up our sidewalk and around the house all one afternoon.

8. Although our house was new a few years ago, active living and energetic family members have given it that lived-in look, a _____ of age all its own.

9. In the very early hours on the lake, a dawn _____ etches a picture that needs no sharp coloration to be memorable.

10. Our neighbor's canary would be aptly named _____, because she spends hours trilling melodious solos.

11. The _____ beat of Jan's high heels as she marched up the sidewalk told us that she was in a hurry.

Exercise III. Logic. Based on the information given so far in this lesson, answer the following questions.

1. Which type of music might help a baby drift off to sleep? (Hint: Search among Roots.)

_____

2. Is a rabid dog *innocuous?* _____

3. When applied to people, does the word *dynamo* have positive or negative connotations?

_____

4. What are *aspirations?* _____

5. What word derived from LEG/LIG/LECT can describe the handwriting of many doctors and four-year-olds?

_____

6. What do the words *libretto* and *library* have in common?

_____

7. The soft drink *Fresca* was not named by accident. What good connotations does its name suggest?

_____

8. When people act *in concert* with one another, how are they behaving?

_____

What is a *concerted effort?* _____

9. Dynamics in music concerns degrees of loudness. Can you arrange the following musical terms in order of increasing loudness? *forte, pianissimo, fortissimo, piano*

_____

10. How is the word *falsetto* related to *false?*

_____

_____

Exercise IV. Analogies. Complete each analogy with the best pair possible, using words from List 21 and Roots.

_____ 1. wall : fresco ::
    (a) sidewalk : art
    (b) museum : exhibition
    (c) canvas : oil painting
    (d) newspaper : advertising
    (e) corridor : frieze

_____ 2. Beethoven : sonatas ::
    (a) Simon and Garfunkel : operas
    (b) Gilbert and Sullivan : operas
    (c) Walt Disney : horror films
    (d) Vienna Boys' Choir : rock and roll
    (e) symphonies : Boston Pops Orchestra

_____ 3.* mountain climbing : bravura ::
    (a) Windsor family : dynasty
    (b) legumes : soybean
    (c) lyrics : libretto
    (d) orchestra : concerto
    (e) politics : Kennedy family

*Keep calm on this one. Remember to *decide what kind of analogy it is* before examining answers. Eliminate the impossible answers, one by one.

_____ 4. physics : thermodynamics ::
    (a) concerto : rhapsody
    (b) song : aria
    (c) inhalator : respirator
    (d) architecture : designer
    (e) play : vignette

_____ 5. overture : finale ::
    (a) tempo : time
    (b) desires : aspirations
    (c) drama : scene
    (d) onset : expiration
    (e) selection : eligibility

Exercise V. Antonyms. Find an antonym or contrasting phrase for each word on the left.

_____ 1. **timidity**
_____ 2. **chiaroscuro**
_____ 3. **falsetto**
_____ 4. **inspire**
_____ 5. **dynamo**
_____ 6. **noxious**
_____ 7. **eligible**
_____ 8. **nocturnal**
_____ 9. **staccato**
_____ 10. **rhapsodic**

(a) dampen, discourage
(b) sloth
(c) harmless
(d) bravura
(e) flowing, connected
(f) diurnal (in the daytime)
(g) lacking emotion
(h) full color spectrum
(i) unsuitable
(j) bass

Exercise VI. Word Analysis.

1. *Vignette* (root meaning little vines or tendrils) is an example of many words with the suffix -ette or -etta. You are familiar with *novelette, cigarette, operetta, rosette,* and *sermonette,* to name a few. How does this suffix alter the meaning of the root words in these examples?

   _____

   _____

2. Each person's voice is unique, just like his or her fingerprints. But we have grouped singing voices into categories. Beginning with the word for the lowest (or deepest) singing voice, arrange the voices in order, ending with the highest. *baritone, soprano, contralto* (or *alto*), *tenor, basso, mezzo soprano*

   _____

3. The musical term to describe a *smooth and connected technique* is *legato*. What word in List 21 is its antonym?

   _____

4. A *crescendo* gradually increases in force or loudness. Add a prefix to *crescendo* to change the meaning to a gradual *decrease* in force or loudness.

   _____

5. If you describe an older person as "exhibiting the patina of age," what physical description do your words suggest?

   _____

   _____

6. What would be some differences between a funeral *dirge* and a *rhapsody?*

   _____

   _____

O Ye Gods! Part Two
MORE WORDS FROM MYTH AND LEGEND

In Context. Before studying the definitions, try reasoning out the meaning of each word, using context as your guide.

1. After the basketball game Carrie moaned, "That team had nothing but *amazons,* who kept dunking the ball. The girl I guarded ran me all over the floor, and my eyes were about level with her waistband!"

    Amazon means _____ .

2. Jan's art class studied *Attic* style before attempting to design a modern building along those Greek lines noted for refined simplicity.

    Attic means _____ .

3. Jan and I have ridden horseback several times, but we have little hope of emulating the *centaur* who leads our trail rides and who seems totally at one with his horse.

    Centaur means _____ .

4. When instruction on personal *hygiene* entered a school's curriculum long ago, it stressed cleanliness of the body and hair. Today's teaching includes moral issues.

    Hygiene means _____ .

5. Whenever we can get to an ocean beach, our family walks with eyes down, searching for mussels and oysters with their beautiful, *iridescent* shell linings.

    Iridescent means _____ .

6. Although the new principal is a strict disciplinarian, we have learned that he's basically a *jovial* person who would rather laugh than frown.

    Jovial means _____ .

7. One kid in our school is feared, not only because he is tough but because he has an ever-present gang of followers, *myrmidons* dumb enough to do whatever he tells them.

    Myrmidon means _____ .

8. "The human race would probably pay a fortune if a *panacea* could be discovered for all the cold viruses," Dad said as he reached for a tissue.

    Panacea means _____ .

9. The principal decreed that those of us with driver's licenses and parental consent could drive to school, even though he knew he was opening *Pandora's box,* and problems with cars would then plague his administration.

    Pandora's box means _____ .

10. In response to our persistent begging, Dad bought an old car that Jan and I could drive. He dubbed the car *Phaeton,* saying it was a rickety jalopy at best but heavy enough to protect us in case of an accident.

    Phaeton means _____ .

11. When he visited us at the cottage, Dad's business associate arrived in a small plane with *pontoons,* instead of wheels, for landing on water.

    Pontoon means _____ .

12. "Insistence upon conformity no-matter-what is not my style," the principal said. "We won't have *procrustean* discipline in this school. But we will have dress standards that reflect a professional attitude toward our work."

    Procrustean means _____ .

13. For a small girl, Carrie has a *stentorian* bellow. "I don't care if you were cheering for the team," Mom told her once. "No lady ever sounds like that!"

    Stentorian means _____ .

14. Poets revel in the wealth of words that English offers, but I prefer the poet who writes "wooded glen" to the one who pens *"sylvan* glen."

    Sylvan means _____ .

15. Andy was so bored over Easter vacation that he spent hours *tantalizing* the cats, holding catnip mice just out of reach and dangling balls of yarn above their heads.

    Tantalize means _____ .

16. "An absolute horde of *Valkyries,"* Mom gasped as she burst out the door of the department store. "I've never seen women so ferocious at a sale. Now I know how Carrie felt about the basketball amazons."

    Valkyrie means _____ .

17. "No spring *zephyr,* that's for sure," Dad observed as we gathered at the window to watch the trees bent nearly double in a windstorm.

    Zephyr means _____ .

Word Study

The words in this list were once proper nouns, and all have come to us from ancient times and legends. So many have survived that you can see what a giant sponge our language is. We refer to *martial arts,* the planet *Mars,* and the month of *March* without ever thinking of the Roman god **Mars** who fathered all these words. But it's interesting to know where words come from, and a word is always easier to remember if you know its etymology. All these words have a story to tell.

1. **amazon** ('am-ə-ˌzän) n.   A woman taller and stronger than average; literally, *without breast;* from Gr. *amazon,* female warrior

   Predecessor of today's tall, strong women whom we call *amazons* was Hippolyta, daughter of Ares (Greek god of war) and queen of the mythical race of Amazons.

   Relatives: *amazonian, Amazon* (the river)

   Derivation: According to Greek mythology, the Amazons were a ferocious race of African warrior-women. Men were not part of their nation; a baby boy was either killed at birth or sent to his father in a neighboring state. All girls had their right breast cut or burned off so that they could better draw a bow in battle. Near the end of the Trojan War, they came to help Priam, king of Troy.

2. **Attic** ('at-ik) adj.   Referring to Greece or Athens; noted for Grecian refinement and purity, as *an Attic architectural style;* from Gr. *attike,* Attica or Greece

   As a small, topmost story of a home, the attic gets its name from classical *Attic* architecture, which featured a small order (design form) placed above a much larger order.

   Relatives: *Attic salt* (delicate, elegantly refined wit); *Attic faith* (unassailable, sacred faith)

3. **centaur** ('sen-ˌtȯ[ə]r) n.   A member of a legendary race—half man, half horse—that lived in the part of ancient Greece known as Thessaly; a rider so attuned to his horse that they seem one; from Gr. *Kentauros,* centaur

   Why don't they knead two virtuous souls for life
   Into that moral centaur, *man and wife?*
           —Lord Byron, *Don Juan,* c. III

   Relative: *Centaurus* (southern constellation)

4. **hygiene** ('hī-ˌjēn) n.   Habits or conditions that promote good health, such as cleanliness; from Gr. *Hygeia,* goddess of health

   After many of us got plantar warts on our feet, we became extremely conscious of *hygiene* and everyone wore thongs into the showers in the boys' locker room.

   Relatives: *hygienist, hygienic, hygienically*

   Derivation: Health goddess Hygeia was the daughter of Asclepius, the Greek god of healing and son of Apollo. Hygeia's symbol was a serpent drinking from a cup in her hand. Her sister was Panacea, meaning "all-heal." Today's physicians still take the oath of Hippocrates, a famous Greek doctor, which begins: "I swear by Apollo, the Asklepios, and Hygeia and Panacea and all the gods and goddesses. . . ."

5. **iridescent** (ˌir-ə-'des-ᵊnt) adj.   Having the colors of the rainbow or a play of these colors when position is changed, as with a glass prism or a soap bubble; glittering, brilliant, as *a memorable and iridescent performance in a demanding role;* from L. *irid-,* iris, and *Iris,* goddess of the rainbow

   The purification of politics is an iridescent *dream. Government is force.*
           —John James Ingalls, newspaper article, 1890

   Relatives: *iridescence, iridescently, iridium* (the element)
   Synonyms: *glittering, brilliant, shining* (none exact)

   Derivation: Iris, goddess of the rainbow, carried messages for Zeus and Hera, rulers of the Greek gods. She has left her name to a part of the eye and a flower, and as a synonym for rainbow. In later Greek poetry, Iris is the wife of Zephyrus and the mother of Eros.

6. **jovial** ('jō-vē-əl) adj.   Merry and good-humored, jolly and convivial; from L. *Jovem,* Jove or Jupiter

   It's of three jovial *huntsmen, and a-hunting they did go;*
   And they hunted and they holloed, and they blew their horns also . . .
           —"The Three Jovial Huntsmen," Old English ballad

   Relatives: *joviality, jovially, Jovian* (of Jove, or Jupiter)
   Synonyms: *mirthful, merry, jolly, convivial*
   Antonyms: *dour, choleric, testy, gloomy, irritable*

   Derivation: The Roman (Latin) name of Zeus was Jove, or Jupiter, generally a merrier sort than Zeus. From the ancient root (**Ju** = **Ze**) we get the words *Tuesday, diva, deity, adieu, Diana, journey, adjourn, sojourn,* and *July.* It is said that Sagittarians born under Jupiter's sign are jolly folk.

7. **myrmidon** ('mər-mə-ˌdän) n.   Faithful follower, especially one who executes any order, no matter how distasteful, issued by his leader; from Gr. *Myrmidon,* a member of a Thessalian people

In *West Side Story,* both gang leaders have a band of *myrmidons* who will "rumble" when their leaders name the time and place.

Derivation: The Thessalian Myrmidons went with their king Achilles to the Trojan War. Although they did not figure prominently in mythology, their name lives on. Once, *myrmidon* meant loyal follower, but the word has degenerated in meaning.

8. **panacea** (ˌpan-ə-'sē-ə) n.   A universal cure-all or absolute remedy; from Gr. *pan,* all, + *akos,* remedy, and Panacea, "all-heal"

Those who know it consider the English traffic circle, while not a *panacea,* to be a far better method of regulating traffic flow than the ubiquitous American stoplight.

Relative: *panacean*
Synonym: *cure-all*
Derivation: See No. 4, *hygiene.*

9. **Pandora's box** (pan-ˌdōr-əz-'bäks) n.   A seemingly endless source of problems and difficulties; from Gr. *pan* + *dora,* all-gifted, plus the myth

Motivated by security reasons and/or idealism, the United States has taken several struggling countries under its wing—perhaps a modern version of *Pandora's box,* with the expected accompanying problems.

Derivation: Prometheus stole fire from the gods to benefit the human race, which made Zeus (Jupiter) furious. In retaliation, he ordered Hephaestus (Vulcan) to make the first mortal woman—Pandora—an exquisite creature to whom Zeus gave a box containing all the ills of the world with which he planned to punish human beings. When the box was opened—some say by Pandora, others by her husband, Epimetheus—the evils were let loose, but so was Hope, the last to fly out of the box.

10. **phaeton** ('fā-ət-ᵊn) n.   Either a lightweight, rather unstable carriage drawn by horses or a touring car; from Gr. *Phaëthon*

We yelled with excitement as the *phaetons* raced round the last curve and each driver flicked his whip at his horse's flanks.

Derivation: When a young man, Phaeton (Phaëthon) begged to be allowed to drive his father's chariot of the sun. Tired of listening to him, Apollo (Helios) finally gave in, but poor Phaeton was unable to keep the magnificent chariot and powerful horses in their usual track. He reduced Libya to barren sands and scorched most of Africa, turning its inhabitants black and nearly ruining its vegetation. Zeus was forced to thunderbolt him from the sky, and the boy plunged into a river.
(Note: One major purpose of a myth is to explain things. This one explains why your parents are reluctant to hand over the car keys.)

11. **pontoon** (pän-'tün) n.   A float used to support an airplane, raft, boat, or similar structure on water; from L. *pont,* bridge

At our lake cottage we have a dock supported by *pontoons* as well as a swimming raft with oil barrels as *pontoons* underneath its wooden planks.

Relatives: *ponton* (pontoon), *pontonier* (one who builds a pontoon bridge)
Synonym: *float* (n.)
Derivation: Pontus was the ancient name for sea, and Uranus meant the sky. Pontus has left his name in many words referring to bridges, as the Greeks viewed the sea as a bridge from one land to another. A *pontiff* was once a high Roman priest in charge of bridge construction, although a modern pontiff is a bishop or pope.

12. **procrustean** (p[r]ə-'krəs-tē-ən) adj.   Marked by insistence upon conformity no matter what, with total disregard for extenuating circumstances; from Gr. *Procrustes*

The anger and questions aroused by the Vietnam War forced America to reevaluate the military draft, that *procrustean bed* which conscripted youth regardless of temperamental fitness.

Relative: *procrustean bed* (pattern into which one is thrust arbitrarily)

Derivation: Procrustes was a giant Greek robber who redesigned wayfarers to fit his iron bed. He either stretched the victim to fit, or lopped off any excess length of leg. His nickname was "The Stretcher," and he was eventually killed by the hero Theseus.

13. **stentorian** (sten-'tōr-ē-ən) adj.   Exceedingly loud; from Gr. *Stentor*

Seven hundred years B.C. the poet Homer wrote of the *stentorian* sound of "Great-hearted Stentor with brazen voice, who could shout as loud as fifty other men."

Relatives: *stentor* (one with a loud voice; also a protozoan with a trumpet-shaped body), *stentorophonic* (extremely loud)

Synonyms: *booming, thunderous, bellowing* (none exact)

Derivation: Stentor was a Greek herald, known in the time of the Trojan War for his incredibly loud voice.

14. **sylvan** ('sil-vən) adj.   Referring to the woods or forest, wooded; from L. *sylva*, wood

Thou still unravished bride of quietness,
Thou foster-child of silence and slow time,
Sylvan *historian, who canst thus express*
A flowery tale more sweetly than our rhyme:
What leaf-fringed legend haunts about thy shape?
          —John Keats, "Ode on a Grecian Urn"

Relative: *sylvan* (n., one who hangs out in the woods)

Synonym: *wooded*

Derivation: Silvanus was a good-natured god who lived mostly in the woods and left his name behind to the joy of poets, who find the Latin *sylvan* infinitely more melodious than the Old English *wooded*.

15. **tantalize** ('tant-ᵊl-ˌīz) v.   To bedevil or tease by pretending to offer something, yet keeping the offering beyond reach; from Gr. *Tantalus*

The smell of our neighborhood pizza parlor *tantalizes* us with a nearly irresistible fragrance each time we go by.

Relatives: *tantalizing, tantalizingly, tantalus* (a glass cabinet displaying wine decanters unobtainable without a key)

Derivation: A wealthy king and son of Zeus, Tantalus did a sinful thing by serving up his own son Pelops as a dinner for the gods. His punishment in Hades put him in the middle of a lake. As thirst consumed him he bent to drink but the water always receded, while over his head hung luscious fruits, forever beyond his reach.

16. **Valkyrie** (val-'kir-ē, 'val-kə-rē) n.   A woman even tougher than an amazon; literally, *chooser of the slain;* from ON *valkyrja*

One of the most stirring pieces of orchestral music is the *Ride of the Valkyries,* a wild and soaring composition by Richard Wagner.

Derivation: Odin was king of the Norse gods, and the Valkyries were his beautiful-but-awful nymphs in Valhalla, heavenly home of warriors killed in battle. When a battle raged on earth, the Valkyries rode swift horses through the fray and chose the men destined to die. Back home in Valhalla, these nymphs served the heroes tasty drinks in the evenings and let them play at war all day long.

17. **zephyr** ('zef-ər) n.   A soft, gentle breeze, often westerly; from Gr. *Zephyros,* god of the west wind

   Fair laughs the morn, and soft the zephyr *blows,*
   While proudly riding o'er the azure realm
   In gallant trim the gilded vessel goes;
      —Thomas Gray, *The Bard*

   Opposing Idea: *boreal* (adj.) (from Boreus, god of the north wind; used to describe something chillingly cold)

   Derivation: Zephyrus, god of the west wind, led a more interesting life than most. With the Harpy named Podarge, he fathered Achilles' favorite horses, Xanthus and Balius. Meanwhile, he was married to Chloris, with whom he had a son, and somehow he was also married to Iris, and thereby the father of Eros—not Cupid, but another Eros. (Doesn't this sound like an ancient soap opera?)

Root Study

These four roots are the parents of dozens of our most common and useful English words.

1. GNOS and GNOM mean to know.
   prognosis—a prospect or forecast, as *the prognosis in severe cases of the disease is poor*
   agnostic—one who doubts or says he cannot know for sure, usually regarding the existence of God
   gnome—a sometimes-deformed dwarf of folklore who lives underground and guards treasure

2. MANU means hand.
   manuscript—originally something written by hand
   manacle—handcuff, shackle, or similar restraint for the hands or wrists
   manage—to handle, supervise, oversee, conduct

3. PEND and PENS mean to hang, to weigh, or to pay.
   pendant—an ornament that hangs or is *suspended,* as on a chain
   compensation—payment or remuneration, emolument; a thing that makes up for something else or takes its place satisfactorily
   suspense—anxiety or pleasurable excitement

4. TANG, TING, TACT, and TIG mean to touch.
   tangible—concrete, substantial, as opposed to *intangible,* not definite or concrete
   contingent—adj., dependent upon; n., group, as *the contingent from the office*
   tactile—referring to the sense of touch
   contiguous—adjacent, touching along a boundary

Using the Words

List 22 Review

amazon	jovial	phaeton	sylvan
Attic	myrmidon	pontoon	tantalize
centaur	panacea	procrustean	Valkyrie
hygiene	Pandora's box	stentorian	zephyr
iridescent			

Exercise I. Multiple Choice. In the blank for each word on the left, write the letter of the best definition or synonym.

_____ 1. **Valkyrie**   (a) shopper   (b) ferocious female   (c) fighter

_____ 2. **stentorian**   (a) unpleasant   (b) rigorous   (c) booming

_____ 3. **panacea**   (a) goddess   (b) cure-all   (c) answer

_____ 4. **jovial**   (a) merry   (b) pleasant   (c) shy

_____ 5. **Attic**   (a) Grecian   (b) ancient   (c) upper story

_____ 6. **zephyr**   (a) wind   (b) gust   (c) gentle breeze

_____ 7. **procrustean**   (a) irritable   (b) of arbitrary uniformity
(c) of serious trouble

_____ 8. **phaeton**   (a) carriage   (b) wagon   (c) vehicle

_____ 9. **centaur**   (a) beast   (b) warrior   (c) skilled rider

_____ 10. **amazon**   (a) African   (b) tall, strong woman
(c) basketball player

_____ 11. **tantalize**   (a) tease   (b) torture   (c) tenderize

_____ 12. **pontoon**   (a) rope   (b) float   (c) wheel

_____ 13. **Pandora's box** (a) source of trouble   (b) answer to
problems   (c) origin of questions

_____ 14. **myrmidon**   (a) subordinate   (b) leader
(c) unquestioning follower

_____ 15. **iridescent**   (a) roseate   (b) glassy   (c) glittering

_____ 16. **hygienic**   (a) healthful   (b) dental   (c) hopeful

_____ 17. **sylvan**   (a) outdoor   (b) wooded   (c) grassy

Exercise II. Who Said That? Using information from Word Study, write the name of the probable speaker for each of the following comments.

1. "He's uncommonly brave. He deserves to live in
Valhalla."   _____

2. "What harm could one little peek do—just to see what's
inside? We could close the lid if we had to."   _____

3. "Whatever you say, Chief, whatever you say."   _____

4. "All I want is one sip, just one itsy-bitsy sip!" _____

5. "No sweat, Dad, just watch me. See you at sundown." _____

6. "I can ride anything, anywhere."   _____

7. "Give me the shade of the woods anytime."   _____

8. "CAN EVERYBODY HEAR ME?"   _____

9. "I can cure anything."   _____

10. "Hmm, a trifle short. You'll have to stretch."   _____

11. "Ho, ho, ho!"   _____

12. "Black is for funerals. I love color."   _____

13. "I am the bridge."   _____

14. "No hurricanes or gusts for me."   _____

15. "Remember to brush your teeth and wash your face."   _____

16. "What's that man doing here? Show him the way to
go home."   _____

Exercise III. Analogies. Complete each analogy with the best pair possible, using words from List 22 and Roots.

_____ 1. Attic salt : wit ::
- (a) Stentor : leader
- (b) pontoon : plane
- (c) compensation : emolument
- (d) Procrustes : lord
- (e) hygiene : body

_____ 2. suspense : denouement ::
- (a) research : panacea
- (b) zephyr : gale
- (c) health : hygiene
- (d) tangent : angle
- (e) phaeton : race

_____ 3. pleasant : jovial ::
- (a) unruly : manageable
- (b) agnostic : doubting
- (c) tangible : accessible
- (d) bright : iridescent
- (e) appended : attached

_____ 4. amazon : gnome ::
- (a) Valkyrie : nymph
- (b) stentor : whisperer
- (c) hygienist : aide
- (d) giant : titan
- (e) listener : recorder

_____ 5. manage : conduct ::
- (a) prognosticate : inspect
- (b) contact : repel
- (c) abide : adhere
- (d) diagnose : reveal
- (e) tantalize : bedevil

Exercise IV. Fill-ins. Select the most appropriate word from the choices offered, based on clues in context.

Attic	sylvan	myrmidon	manacled
centaur	pontoons	pending	hygienic
zephyr	Pandora's box	intangible	agnostic

1. stepped out of the police car, _____ and defiant

2. real can of worms, a classic _____

3. keep that decision _____ until we know more

4. _____ habits instilled by medical training

5. typical Mafia _____ who does what he's told

6. classically elegant _____ prose style

7. the secret _____ silence of the forest

8. _____, yet definite; unthinkable, but true

9. his webbed feet gliding briefly on the surface of the water like intelligent

_____

10. her sigh, a gentle _____ in my ear

11. unspoken desire of the _____ to know for sure

12. a veritable _____, at home in the saddle

Exercise V. Word Analysis.

1. What parallels do you see between the story of Pandora and the story about Adam and Eve?

_____

_____

2. In the Ingalls quote illustrating *iridescent* in Word Study, what word might be substituted for *iridescent?* Is this substitution fully satisfactory? _____

_____

3. The words in List 22 are extremely old. Can you think of one overriding reason for their continued, useful existence? _____

4. Why does the term *Valkyrie* have a more negative impact than the word *amazon?*

_____

5. Valhalla was the Norse home for slain warriors. Where did the American Indian warriors go after death in battle? _____

And does anyone know where the women of these two societies went after death?

_____

The Greeks went to the Elysian fields or the Isles of the Blessed after death.

What is the Christian equivalent? _____

6. If you knew only mythology, and not the words themselves, what could you say about the aurora borealis? (Hint: Check the dictionary for *aurora* only, and take it from there.)

_____

_____

Torrid vs. Hot
ADJECTIVES, THE DESCRIBING WORDS

In Context. Before studying the definitions, try reasoning out the meaning of each word, using its context as your guide.

1. Looking at Jan and me in our formal prom clothes, Dad said slowly, "Toddlers one minute, adults the next." Mom nodded. "Childhood is all too brief, an *evanescent* thing . . . at least to parents."

   Evanescent means _____.

2. "Your kittenhood is an *extenuating* circumstance," Dad told Poucette and Figment. "But that excuse works for only a short time, you know."

   Extenuating means _____.

3. "Down to fifty cents," Jan moaned as she peered into her purse. "I wish I were the *frugal* sort, not someone who loved to spend money."

   Frugal means _____.

4. My English term paper earned a good grade, even though I added material that wasn't exactly *germane* to the topic.

   Germane _____.

5. Marigold stares out the window with an *inscrutable* expression on her face that none of us can interpret.

   Inscrutable means _____.

6. Are all cats *intransigent* creatures? Ours refuse to compromise on the subject of an evening stalk . . . or any other subject, for that matter.

   Intransigent means _____.

7. The upper regions of our sloping yard are carefully tended, but we let the *nether* regions turn to meadow because they're out of sight.

   Nether means _____.

8. At an early age, Poucette displayed a *palpable* interest in hunting, made even more noticeable in contrast to Figment's preference for lying in the sun.

   Palpable means _____.

9. The kids in our youth group at church are a fairly *pious* bunch, but we tend to be quiet about our beliefs.

   Pious means _____.

10. Figment has always been a *prodigious* eater. Marigold and Poucette eat sparingly, perhaps because they're good hunters who have a tasty morsel outdoors from time to time.

    Prodigious means _____.

11. Our cousin Frank talks for hours on *recondite* subjects. Jan and I listen politely, although his obscure topics are usually beyond our comprehension.

   Recondite means _____.

12. It's impossible to be *remiss* in our duties toward any of Marigold's family. Each cat meows loudly to remind us of attention due or meals that are behind schedule.

   Remiss means _____.

13. A man in our town wears a *sardonic* expression on his face that clearly expresses his disdain of fellow human beings.

   Sardonic means _____.

14. Jan sighed as she peered into the travel bureau's display window. "The *torrid* sands of Torremolinos look so romantic." I said that in summer those Spanish sands would be way too torrid for me.

   Torrid means _____.

15. The travel bureau's salesman slithered out the door and began recounting the joys of Torremolinos in *unctuous* tones, unaware that his ingratiating, overly sincere approach would turn Jan off.

   Unctuous means _____.

16. As we left the salesman, Jan hissed, "I can't stand people like that!" in a *vehement* whisper.

   Vehement means _____.

Word Study

The surest way to arouse and hold the attention of the reader is by being specific, definite, and concrete.
   —William Strunk Jr. and E. B. White, *The Elements of Style*

   Adjectives can be used with telling effect, or they can be squandered as excess fillers. A sentence loaded with adjectives overwhelms us and thereby loses effectiveness. Still, it's important to know many adjectives so that you can choose the one that is exactly right. And one is usually enough to describe the noun (or nounlike word) that you want your reader or listener to imagine.

   1. **evanescent** (ˌev-ə-ˈnes-ᵊnt) adj.   Short-lived, fleeting, transient; apt to disappear like vapor; from L. *evanescere*, to vanish

   And what are these fluxions? The velocities of evanescent *increments. . . . And may we not call them ghosts of departed quantities?*
      —George Berkeley, *The Analyst*

   Relatives: *evanescence, evanesce*
   Synonyms: *transient, ephemeral*
   Antonyms: *eternal, long-lived, lasting, enduring*

   2. **extenuating** (ik-ˈsten-yə-ˌwā-tiŋ) participial adj.   Tending to lessen the seriousness of by offering excuses or reasons; reducing in strength or effectiveness; literally, *to thin*, as *extenuating the broth;* from L. *ex + tenuis*, thin

   Team members are to swim in every meet unless *extenuating* circumstances, such as illness, prevent their participation.

   Relatives: *extenuate, extenuator, extenuatory*

3. **frugal** ('frü-gəl) adj.   Sparing, careful, economical in the use of resources; from L. *frugalis*, virtuous, frugal

O'erjoyed was he to find,
That, although on pleasure she was bent,
She had a frugal *mind.*
          —William Cowper, "John Gilpin"

Relatives: *frugality, frugally*
Synonym: *sparing*
Antonym: *wasteful*

4. **germane** ([ˌ]jer-'mān) adj.   Both fitting and appropriate, relevant; literally, *having the same parents;* from Middle E. *germain*

We excluded the problems with nuclear-generated fuels as they were not *germane* to our debate.

Relative: *germanely*
Synonyms: *relevant, material*
Antonyms: *foreign, alien, immaterial*

5. **inscrutable** (in-'skrüt-ə-bəl) adj.   Difficult to grasp, understand, or interpret, as *the Mona Lisa's inscrutable smile;* from L. *in + scrutari,* to search

Cruel, but composed and bland,
Dumb, inscrutable *and grand,*
So Tiberius might have sat,
Had Tiberius been a cat.
          —Matthew Arnold, "Poor Matthias"

Relatives: *inscrutability, inscrutableness, inscrutably*
Synonyms: *mysterious, enigmatic*

6. **intransigent** (in-'tran[t]s-ə-jənt) adj.   Unwilling to compromise or alter an opinion or custom, even though it may be extreme; uncompromising; from L. *in + transigere,* to transact

Mom and Dad are absolutely *intransigent* on the subject of drinking and driving; if we drink, we don't drive.

Relatives: *intransigent* (n., person), *intransigence, intransigently*
Synonym: *uncompromising*

7. **nether** ('ne<u>th</u>-ər) adj.   Placed below or under something else, lower; beneath the earth's surface, as *the nether world;* from OE *nither,* down

Alas! why gnaw you so your nether *lip?*
Some bloody passion shakes your very frame;
          —Shakespeare, *Othello*

Relatives: *nethermost, netherworld* (world of the dead or the criminal underworld)

8. **palpable** ('pal-pə-bəl) adj.   Noticeable or readily perceived; able to be felt or touched, tangible; from L. *palpare,* to stroke, feel

These lies are like the father that begets them; gross as a mountain, open, palpable.
          —Shakespeare, *King Henry IV, Part I*

Relatives: *palpability, palpably, palpate, palpation*
Synonym: *perceptible*
Antonyms: *impalpable, imperceptible*

9. **pious** ('pī-əs) adj.   Devout or worthy; self-consciously virtuous or religious in a hypocritical or conspicuous way, as *that pious soul who cheats when not in church;* from L. *piare,* to appease

The pious *ones of Plymouth, who, reaching the Rock, fell first upon their own knees and then upon the aborigines.*
     —William M. Evarts, in Louisville's *Courier-Journal*

Relatives: *piously, piety, piousness*
Synonym: *devout*
Antonym: *impious*

10. **prodigious** (prə-'dij-əs) adj.   Impressively large, enormous; calling forth wonder or amazement; from L. *pro-, prod-,* forth, + *agere,* to drive

All cultures have created heroes of *prodigious* strength, from Atlas, Hercules, and Samson to the more modern Paul Bunyan, Superman, Rambo, and lovable Mr. T.

Relatives: *prodigiously, prodigiousness*
Synonym: *awesome* (off the mark)
Antonyms: *tiny, insignificant, puny, infinitesimal* (none exact)

11. **recondite** ('rek-ən-ˌdīt, ri-'kän-ˌdīt) adj.   Difficult to understand, deep, as *a recondite subject;* of something obscure, generally unknown; from L. *recondere,* to conceal

The Druidic priests of old kept their knowledge secret, and so the *recondite* mysteries of their time have been lost forever.

Relatives: *reconditeness, reconditely*
Synonym: *abstruse* (first meaning)

12. **remiss** (ri-'mis) adj.   Showing lack of attention and care; lax, negligent, careless; from L. *remittere,* to send back

"I think we'd be *remiss* in our duty as friends if we failed to visit a classmate who's in the hospital," our adviser suggested.

Relatives: *remission, remissly, remissness, remissible*
Synonyms: *negligent, careless*
Antonyms: *attentive, dutiful, careful*

13. **sardonic** (sär-'dän-ik) adj.   Mocking or sarcastic; scornfully humorous or derisive, as *a sardonic expression of contempt;* from Sardinia (See Derivation.)

The *sardonic* smile on the terrorist's face told the captives that they had no hope of compassion from their captor.

Relatives: *sardonically, sardonicism*
Synonyms: *derisive, sarcastic* (neither exact)
Derivation: If you taste an acrid herb from Sardinia, it will cause convulsive facial movements that look like a terribly painful and nasty grin. The accompanying bitter laugh has been termed *rire sardonique* by the French, from whom we get our word. The Greek poet Homer was supposedly the first to use *sardonic* to describe an ugly smile of contempt.

14. **torrid** ('tȯr-əd) adj.   Intensely hot or parched by the heat, scorching; full of passion, ardent, as *torrid love scenes;* from L. *torrere,* to parch, burn

Give me more love or more disdain;
The torrid *or the frozen zone:*
Bring equal ease unto my pain;
The temperate affords me none.
     —Thomas Carew, "Mediocrity in Love Rejected"

Relatives: *torridness, torridly, torridity*
Synonyms: *scorching; passionate, ardent* (second meaning)
Antonyms: *gelid, icy, frigid*

15. **unctuous** ('əŋ[k]-chə[-wə]s) adj.   Showing a false warmth or sincerity in an oily-smooth way; being self-consciously virtuous, earnest, or spiritual; from L. *unctum,* ointment

If you want to describe an *unctuous* fellow, these lyrics from *My Fair Lady* are tough to beat: "He oiled his way across the floor, / Oozing charm from every pore. . . ."
Relatives: *unctuousness, unctuously*

16. **vehement** ('vē-ə-mənt) adj.   Full of emotion, feeling, passion; fervid, intense; expressed with force or animosity, as *a vehement denial;* from L. *vehement-,* impetuous, violent

James Michener's book *The Drifters* concerns the youth of the late sixties and early seventies who turned their backs on society in *vehement* protest against a system they believed to be fatally flawed.
Relatives: *vehemence, vehemently*
Synonyms: *impassioned, fervid, fervent*

Root Study

You will probably know most of these words derived from four of our most useful language roots.

1. HER and HES mean to stick, cling to.
   inherent—inborn, native, innate
   adhere—to stick to, abide by
   coherent—logically consistent, as *a coherent speech*

2. IT means to go.
   exit—v., to go out; n., a place of departure
   itinerary—planned outline of where you will go
   reiterate—to repeat, go over again; to restate
   initiative—drive, enthusiasm; colloquially "git up and go"

3. MISS and MIT mean to send.
   missive—a letter or note
   missionary—one sent to another place, usually with religious, educational, or medical knowledge
   remission—a period when something, usually a disease process, is inactive (not virulent)
   transmit—to send or give; literally, *to send across*

4. NOMEN, NOMIN, -ONYM, and ONOMA mean name.
   nomenclature—system of names, terms, or symbols
   nominal—small or insignificant, as *a nominal sum;* in name only, as *nominal head of the group*
   anonymous—literally, *without name*
   onomatopoeia—use of words that sound the same as the words' meanings, e.g., hiss, buzz, ding

Using the Words

List 23 Review

evanescent	inscrutable	pious	sardonic
extenuating	intransigent	prodigious	torrid
frugal	nether	recondite	unctuous
germane	palpable	remiss	vehement

Exercise I. Synonyms and Definitions. Write a synonym or brief definition beside each word, using your memory as much as possible, before referring to Word Study.

1. **unctuous** _____

2. **sardonic** _____

3. **recondite** _____

4. **prodigious** _____

5. **palpable** _____

6. **inscrutable** _____

7. **frugal** _____

8. **evanescent** _____

9. **extenuating** _____

10. **germane** _____

11. **intransigent** _____

12. **remiss** _____

13. **pious** _____

14. **nether** _____

15. **torrid** _____

16. **vehement** _____

Exercise II. Antonyms. Find an antonym or contrasting phrase for each word in bold type.

_____ 1. **remiss**
    (a) confused   (b) dutiful   (c) angry
    (d) energetic   (e) prompt

_____ 2. **evanescent**
    (a) eternal   (b) steamy   (c) dire
    (d) solid   (e) amorphous

_____ 3. **frugal**
    (a) meaty   (b) wasteful   (c) placid
    (d) weak   (e) extreme

_____ 4. **germane**
    (a) local   (b) vague   (c) immaterial
    (d) essential   (e) international

_____ 5. **palpable**
    (a) obvious   (b) intriguing   (c) vast
    (d) loathesome   (e) imperceptible

_____ 6. **prodigious**
    (a) monumental   (b) indescribable
    (c) serene   (d) fraudulent   (e) insignificant

_____ 7. **recondite**   (a) somewhat mistaken   (b) not suspicious
(c) unrecoverable   (d) readily
comprehensible   (e) vaguely contemptuous

_____ 8. **vehement**   (a) willy-nilly   (b) complacent   (c) dull
(d) repèntant   (e) lukewarm

_____ 9. **torrid**   (a) gelid   (b) acid   (c) fervid   (d) tepid
(e) rabid

_____ 10. **intransigent**   (a) difficult to explain   (b) easily swayed
(c) readily available   (d) hard to convince
(e) eagerly anticipated

_____ 11. **inscrutable**   (a) tired yet exhilarated   (b) tough but not
impossible   (c) open and easily interpreted
(d) discreet and secretive   (e) visible and real

_____ 12. **nether**   (a) either   (b) positive   (c) extreme
(d) upper   (e) escalated

Exercise III. Famous Descriptions. Use the words in List 23 to complete the following descriptions.

1. In Barrie's *Peter Pan*, the _____ fairy was Tinker Bell, who was on

   stage one second, gone the next.

2. Scrooge McDuck is a _____ fowl with every buck.

3. Fat Albert might be Skinny Albert if he didn't have a(n) _____ appetite.

4. Henry Clay, known as the Great Compromiser, could never be called

   _____ .

5. Ruler of Hades was Pluto, god of the _____ regions.

6. A dastardly enemy of Batman and Robin was the Joker, who perfected a sneering laugh and

   _____ smile.

7. Who has a more _____ face than the Sphinx?

8. Our forebears, the Puritans, known for their _____ ,

   Dressed with a sober regard for propriety.

   (This rhyme requires a noun form, not an adjective.)

Exercise IV. Know Those Roots. Knowledge of the roots in this lesson should enable you to match the words on the left with their meanings.

_____ 1. **adhesive**   (a) false, assumed name

_____ 2. **circuit**   (b) inborn, innate

_____ 3. **incoherent**   (c) drive, enterprise

_____ 4. **remit**   (d) projectile

_____ 5. **pseudonym**   (e) follower, believer

_____ 6. **itinerant**   (f) a course or route

_____ 7. **initiative**

_____ 8. **adherent**

_____ 9. **nominate**

_____ 10. **patronymic**

_____ 11. **missile**

_____ 12. **inherent**

(g) sticky

(h) name derived from a father or paternal ancestor

(i) going from place to place, roving, wandering

(j) babbling, illogical

(k) to send back

(l) to name, suggest, propose

Exercise V. Analogies. Complete each analogy with the best pair possible, using words from List 23 and Roots.

_____ 1. warm : torrid ::
  (a) difficult : recondite
  (b) tepid : lukewarm
  (c) nominal : insignificant
  (d) local : particular
  (e) coherent : distraught

_____ 2. unctuous : sincerity ::
  (a) upper : society
  (b) prodigious : behavior
  (c) sardonic : sympathy
  (d) frugal : economy
  (e) vehement : feeling

_____ 3. palpable : touch ::
  (a) legible : understand
  (b) credible : debate
  (c) attractive : see
  (d) audible : hear
  (e) distinctive : smell

_____ 4. irreverent : pious ::
  (a) adhesive : clinging
  (b) remiss : attentive
  (c) bitter : sardonic
  (d) great : prodigious
  (e) thinning : extenuating

_____ 5. annoyed : vehement ::
  (a) inherent : innate
  (b) antonym : synonym
  (c) frugal : miserly
  (d) intransigent : compliant
  (e) unctuous : smooth

Exercise VI. Word Analysis.

1. _Scrutinize_ is a verb that often pops up on standardized tests. You know its root. Define _scrutinize_, as in _he scrutinized the document at length before he gave an opinion._

   Scrutinize means _____

2. You know that context can change a word's meaning. In Arnold's poem (with word 5 in Word Study), what does _dumb_ mean?

   _____

3. In Virgil's _Aeneid,_ which traces the wanderings of Aeneas after the Trojan War, the hero often introduces himself with these words: _"Sum pius Aeneas,"_ meaning "I am the pious Aeneas." This phrase—always good for a chuckle in any advanced Latin class—tells us something about the word pious. What has happened to its meaning over time?

   _____

What expression is used to describe a word whose meaning has altered in a negative or disparaging way?

_____

4. What is a *misnomer?* _____

5. During a physical examination, the doctor may palpate your abdomen. If he says that you have a *palpable spleen,* what do you think he means?

_____

_____

6. Can you think of *extenuating* circumstances that might explain why your homework is late? Please be creative!

_____

_____

_____

The Low-Down Noun
NOUNS WITH A NEGATIVE CONNOTATION

In Context. Before studying the definitions, try reasoning out the meaning of each word, using context as your guide.

1. When we read Dickens's story, Andy wasn't worried by the four *apparitions* that appeared to Scrooge, but he found the TV version of those ghostly figures much more scary.

    Apparition means _____ .

2. If I were certain of my eventual career, I could view the next several years with less *apprehension*.

    Apprehension means _____ .

3. My cousin referred to his first college roommate as "that *churl*." When I met him, I agreed that he was quite rude.

    Churl means _____ .

4. "What do you do if the roommate you're assigned is a loser?" Jan asked with *consternation*.

    Consternation means _____ .

5. True to character as the family *cynic*, our cousin told Jan she could expect the worst. "But you'll have it sorted out by the second semester," he added in an unusually optimistic tone.

    Cynic means _____ .

6. Andy was downcast by the *demise* of his entire first litter of gerbils and only recovered his good spirits when the second litter survived.

    Demise means _____ .

7. Although a *detriment* to the appearance of the kitchen, Andy's cooking has done wonders for his confidence.

    Detriment means _____ .

8. Barry warned us that getting concert tickets required *guile*. "By now I know all the tricks," he said smugly.

    Guile means _____ .

9. The *infamy* of that crime was made clear to us by the shocking details related in the paper and on television.

    Infamy means _____ .

10. When he discovered that his hidden candy had melted all over his windowsill, Andy's mournful *lament* could be heard throughout the house.

    Lament means _____ .

11. We were in high gear for finals and graduation, but afterward we succumbed to *lassitude* and slept till noon for several days in a row.

      Lassitude means _____ .

12. "Miserable *miscreants!*" Mom hollered as she vigorously beat a wool rug infested with moths. "Only criminals would attack a good rug!"

      Miscreant means _____ .

13. "I'll never understand *parsimony,*" Dad commented. "We have to be thrifty to make ends meet, but I hope we're never downright stingy."

      Parsimony means _____ .

14. Mom sprayed her wool rug for moths, and said she felt not a single *qualm* as one bug after another dropped at her feet.

      Qualm means _____ .

15. "Our mother, the *sadist,*" Jan teased as Mom finished spraying the moths. "I swear you enjoyed killing those bugs." Mom nodded without a shred of remorse.

      Sadist means _____ .

16. "I'll visit you at school and take you out to dinner," Mom promised, "but college boys live in such *squalor* that I can't bear to see your room. Filth gives me a headache."

      Squalor means _____ .

Word Study

As you know, nouns and verbs are the building blocks of our language. *Birds fly* is a sentence. *Birds soar* is a better sentence because it has a more precise verb. *Eagles soar* is better still because both noun and verb evoke distinct images. The more you write and speak, the more you will want to be precise. Being misinterpreted or misunderstood is frustrating. This last lesson gives you more nouns to work with—nouns that will allow you to say **exactly** what is on your mind.

1. **apparition** (ˌap-ə-ˈrish-ən) n.   A specter or ghostly shape; appearance (in the sense that something has become visible); from L. *apparere,* to appear

   She was a phantom of delight
   When first she gleamed upon my sight;
   A lovely apparition, *sent*
   To be a moment's ornament.
         —William Wordsworth, "She Was a Phantom of Delight"
   (Note: *Apparition* is used in a positive sense here, which happens occasionally. Words are so sneaky.)
   Relative: *apparitional*
   Synonym: *ghost, phantom, specter* (none exact)

2. **apprehension** (ˌap-ri-ˈhen-chən) n.   Foreboding or fear of something bad to come; arrest, as *the swift apprehension of the suspect;* understanding or mental comprehension, as *a person of slow apprehension;* from L. *ad* + *prehendere,* to seize

   My apprehensions *come in crowds;*
   I dread the rustling of the grass;

The very shadows of the clouds
Have power to shake me as they pass.
      —William Wordsworth, "The Affliction of Margaret"
Relatives: *apprehend, apprehensive, apprehensible, apprehensively, apprehensiveness*

3. **churl** ('chər[ə]l) n.   Rude, loutish male or one typically in a bad mood; originally a peasant; from OE *ceorl*, man

"Peasant—lout—*churl!*" Carrie declaimed onstage. "I would rather live in the streets than in your house!"
Relatives: *churlish, churlishly, churlishness*
Synonyms: *boor, lout*

4. **consternation** (ˌkän[t]-stər-'nā-shən) n.   Surprise, often with dismay, that arouses worry or confusion; from L. *consternare*, to bewilder, alarm

We watched in *consternation* as one of the zoo's gorillas paced back and forth, betraying his distress at confinement.
Relative: *consternate*

5. **cynic** ('sin-ik) n.   A nitpicky critic of human nature who typically believes that people care only about themselves; from Gr. *kynikos*, like a dog (See Derivation.)

In Oscar Wilde's play *Lady Windermere's Fan*, Cecil asks, "What is a *cynic?*"
    "A man who knows the price of everything and the value of nothing," replies Lord Darlington.
Relatives: *cynical, cynically, cynicism*
Derivation: A student of Socrates began the school of the Cynics, an odd name considering its derivation from *dog*. The Cynics held that the only good was virtue, based in independence and self-control. Over time, this noble doctrine has been totally lost; today's cynics think that people are basely selfish.

6. **demise** (di-'mīz) n.   Final end or death; literally, to send down, smite; from L. *de* + *mittere*

The *demise* of ponderous or verbose prose is welcome to modern readers, who are fond of a leaner and cleaner style.
Relative: *demise* (v., to give over, as in a will or lease; to die, pass on by bequest)
Synonym: *death*
Antonym: *life*

7. **detriment** ('de-trə-mənt) n.   Harm or damage, as *the difficult work was a detriment to her health* (use with *to*); from L. *deterere*, to impair, wear away

The heavy rains that turned the flower beds into mud puddles were a *detriment* to our work in the gardens.
Relatives: *detrimental, detrimentally*

8. **guile** ('gī(ə)l) n.   Clever, artful deceit; duplicity, cunning; from OF *guile*, cunning
The infernal serpent; he it was, whose guile,
Stirr'd up with envy and revenge, deceived
The mother of mankind.
      —John Milton, *Paradise Lost*
Relatives: *guileful, guilefully, guilefulness, beguile, guileless, guilelessly, guilelessness*

9. **infamy** ('in-fə-mē) n.   Extreme disgrace or evil reputation (usually the result of something shockingly awful); from L. *in* + *fama*, fame

Yesterday, December 7, 1941—a date which will live in infamy—*the United States of America was suddenly and deliberately attacked by naval and air forces of the Empire of Japan.*
> —F. D. Roosevelt, War Message to Congress, December 8, 1941

Relatives: *infamous, infamously*

10. **lament** (lə-'ment) n.   A wailing, sorrowful cry or complaint; from L. *lamentum,* lament

When our dog Ruffles died, her mate uttered pitiful *laments* that we will never forget.

Relatives: *lament* (v.), *lamentable, lamentableness, lamentably, lamentation, lamented* (mourned)

11. **lassitude** ('las-ə-,t[y]üd) n.   Lack of energy, fatigue, weariness; languor; from L. *lassus,* weary

Overcome by *lassitude,* our cats sleep away the days in preparation for nights of exploration and hunting.

Synonym: *languor*
Antonyms: *vigor, dynamism*

12. **miscreant** ('mis-krē-ənt) n.   One who acts in a criminal or vicious way; villain, wrongdoer; from Middle F. *mescroire,* to disbelieve

To a chicken farmer, a fox in the hen house is a wretched *miscreant* never to be forgiven.

Relative: *miscreant* (adj., wicked, villainous)
Synonym: *villain*

13. **parsimony** ('pär-sə-,mō-nē) n.   Extreme thrift, often amounting to stinginess; niggardliness; from L. *parsimonia,* from *parcere,* to spare

Economy is a distributive virtue, and consists not in saving but selection. Parsimony requires no providence, no sagacity, no powers of combination, no comparison, no judgment.
> —Edmund Burke, letter, 1796

14. **qualm** ('kwäm, 'kwälm) n.   A pang of upsetting emotion, such as fear or remorse; an uneasy twinge on a matter of conscience, manners, or ethics; origin obscure

Poet James Naylor wrote that when King Solomon and King David wrote the Proverbs and the Psalms, they did so "with many, many *qualms*."

Relatives: *qualmy, qualmish, qualmishly, qualmishness*
Synonyms: *scruple, compunction*

15. **sadist** ('sād-əst, 'sad-əst) n.   One who enjoys cruelty or the infliction of pain; from the Marquis de Sade (See Derivation.)

The *sadist,* who delights in cruelty to others, and the masochist, who inflicts physical or mental pain on himself, are the subjects of many books and much psychological study.

Relatives: *sadistic, sadistically, sadism*
Derivation: The Marquis de Sade incurred infamy by torturing the women he loved. The French condemned him to death in 1772, but he escaped and fled to Italy, where he resumed his nasty old habits. He eventually landed back in France, in the Bastille. There he began writing lurid prose and never stopped, even when he was removed to the lunatic asylum where he died years later.

16. **squalor** ('skwäl-ər) n.   A state of disgusting filth, degradation, or both; from L. *squalidus,* squalid

In Port au Prince, Haiti, the contrast between the opulent homes of the wealthy and the appalling *squalor* of the poor has to be seen to be believed.

Relatives: *squalid, squalidly, squalidness*

Root Study

Let's hear it for the last roots to be learned—five of our best!

1. DOL means grief.
    doleful—sorrowful, full of grief, *dolorous*
    condole—to express sympathy in time of sorrow or grief
    Dolores—Spanish name honoring St. Mary of the Sorrows

2. MAL means bad, badly.
    malady—ailment or illness
    dismal—gloomy or depressing; without merit
    abysmal—incredibly great or profound, as *their abysmal ignorance*
    malfunction—to fail to function, to function improperly

3. MOB, MOT, and MOV mean to move.
    mobile—capable of being moved, *movable*
    motive—an impulse or incentive causing you to act; a recurrent theme or *motif* in a piece
        of music
    emote—to express emotion, especially when acting
    immovable—firm, fixed, stable

4. PHON means sound.
    phonograph—record player; literally, *written sound*
    phonetics—the system of spoken sounds of a language
    homophone—one of two (or more) words that sound the same but have different meanings
        and spellings, e.g., *to, too, two*

5. PREHEND, PREHENS, and PRIS mean to take or seize.
    apprehend—to seize, as you would a criminal; to grasp, perceive, understand,
        comprehend
    reprehensible—deserving blame or censure
    prison—place of confinement for those seized as criminals
    predatory—seeking to gain at the expense of others, as a predatory animal *preys* on others
        for its food and a predatory company may take over other companies for its own gain
    (Note: Remember *prehensile* from List 9?)

Using the Words

List 24 Review

apparition	cynic	infamy	parsimony
apprehension	demise	lament	qualm
churl	detriment	lassitude	sadist
consternation	guile	miscreant	squalor

Exercise I. Knowing the Words. Answer as many of these as you can before referring back to Word Study for help.

1. Write an *antonym* for each of the following words:

    a. **demise** _____

    b. **guile** _____

    c. **lassitude** _____

    d. **parsimony** _____

    e. **squalor** _____

2. Write a one-word *synonym* for each of the following words:

a. **apparition** _____

b. **churl** _____

c. **lament** _____

d. **miscreant** _____

e. **detriment** _____

3. Write a brief *explanation* of each of the following words:

a. **sadist** _____

b. **qualm** _____

c. **infamy** _____

d. **cynic** _____

e. **apprehension** _____

f. **consternation** _____

Exercise II. Switcheroo. Some words in List 24 frequently appear as verbs or adjectives, not just nouns. Match these other forms with their meanings or synonyms.

_____ 1. **apprehensive**   (a) to understand or to seize

_____ 2. **infamous**   (b) wantonly cruel

_____ 3. **parsimonious**   (c) to bemoan, regret exceedingly

_____ 4. **apprehend**   (d) sadly regrettable

_____ 5. **churlish**   (e) innocent, free of artifice

_____ 6. **sadistic**   (f) boorish

_____ 7. **lamentable**   (g) fearful of something ahead

_____ 8. **cynical**   (h) to please by charming

_____ 9. **guileless**   (i) stingy, niggardly

_____ 10. **detrimental**   (j) notorious

_____ 11. **beguile**   (k) harmful

_____ 12. **lament** (v.)   (l) distrustful of human nature

Exercise III. Fill-in Chart. Add the missing items to the chart. The first is done as an example.

	WORD	ROOT	DEFINITION	WORDS IN THE FAMILY
1.	telephone	phon	instrument to transmit distant sound	phonics, phone, phonetics, homophone
2.	predatory	_____	_____	prey, apprehend, comprehensive

	WORD	ROOT	DEFINITION	WORDS IN THE FAMILY
3.	_____	mot	impulse or incentive	_____ _____
4.	_____	mal	excessively great, profound	_____ _____
5.	condole	_____	_____ _____	dolorous, doleful, condolence
6.	_____	fama	utter disgrace	_____ _____
7.	_____	kynikos	_____ _____	cynical, cynicism, cynically
8.	_____	miss, mit	an ending, death	_____ _____
9.	squalor	_____	_____	squalid, squalidly
10.	_____	prehens	deserving of blame or criticism	_____ _____

Exercise IV. Substitution. Substitute words learned in List 24 and Roots for the phrases in italics. Write your words above the italicized word or phrase.

1. Knowing that I didn't have permission to take the car, I had *twinges of guilt* as I drove out the driveway.

2. "Rotten little *villain's* been in my cosmetics again," Jan grumbled as she pawed through her bureau drawer.

3. Mom explained that she'd had to give up jogging because the jarring of her feet against the pavement had been *harmful* to both her knees. (Hint: Use the adjective form.)

4. One night, to Marigold's *great confusion and dismay,* both of her kittens ran into the woods and stayed there.

5. Jan and Carrie confessed that they disliked being alone in the house at night. "We imagine there are strange *ghostly figures* lurking around outdoors," Jan said.

6. In spite of wanting to see the movie, I yielded to the *relaxed and languorous feeling* that overcame me.

7. If it weren't for the *cessation of publication* of that magazine, I'd have renewed my subscription.

8. Carrie doled out her candy so *stingily* that I could barely see the tiny pieces in my hand.

9. In *Four Seasons*, Stephen King tells a ghoulish story of a teenage boy whose morbid fascination with Nazi war criminals led him to become a *person who enjoys inflicting cruel suffering on others* and a murderer.

10. What often appears as *incredible filth* to a sanitized Westerner is apt to represent normal living conditions for some people who lack modern conveniences.

Exercise V. Find the Oddball. Select the one word in each group that does not fit with the others. Write its letter on the line.

_____ 1. (a) prehensile   (b) apprehend   (c) appreciate   (d) prey   (e) predatory

_____ 2. (a) impolite   (b) churl   (c) lout   (d) fool   (e) peasant

_____ 3. (a) impious   (b) evil-doer   (c) villain   (d) miscreant   (e) criminal

_____ 4. (a) pang   (b) wound   (c) qualm   (d) twinge   (e) scruple

_____ 5. (a) drowsiness   (b) unease   (c) lassitude   (d) weariness   (e) languor

_____ 6. (a) terror   (b) amazed concern   (c) consternation   (d) worry   (e) alarm

_____ 7. (a) emotion   (b) mobility   (c) immovable   (d) locomotion   (e) motley

_____ 8. (a) cynical   (b) sadistic   (c) satiated   (d) squalid   (e) lamentable

_____ 9. (a) Dolores   (b) guileless   (c) promote   (d) dismal   (e) life
(Tip: Check connotations.)

_____ 10. (a) ailment   (b) malady   (c) medical   (d) illness   (e) sickness

Exercise VI. Word Analysis.

1. What might you suspect of someone wearing a determinedly guileless smile?

_____

2. If the police have apprehended a suspect, where is that person apt to be? _____

3. How many homophones can you think of? _____

_____

4. What sort of person would you describe as *maladroit*? _____

_____

5. Oscar Wilde's definition of a cynic—a "man who knows the price of everything and the value of nothing"—falls into a distinct category in the list of literary terms. What is the term that classifies this witticism of Wilde's?

_____

Review

This final lesson reviews the words and roots in Lists 21–24. Read over all the words and roots, one by one. If a few have become fuzzy—not surprising at this point in the book—reread their definitions and example sentences before beginning the review exercises.

LIST 21	**LIST 22**	**LIST 23**	**LIST 24**
aria	amazon	evanescent	apparition
bravura	Attic	extenuating	apprehension
chiaroscuro	centaur	frugal	churl
concerto	hygiene	germane	consternation
diva	iridescent	inscrutable	cynic
dynamics	jovial	intransigent	demise
falsetto	myrmidon	nether	detriment
fresco	panacea	palpable	guile
frieze	Pandora's box	pious	infamy
libretto	phaeton	prodigious	lament
patina	pontoon	recondite	lassitude
rhapsody	procrustean	remiss	miscreant
sonata	stentorian	sardonic	parsimony
staccato	sylvan	torrid	qualm
vignette	tantalize	unctuous	sadist
virtuoso/a	Valkyrie	vehement	squalor
	zephyr		

ROOTS

DOL	MAL	-ONYM and ONOMA
DYN/DYNAM	MANU	PEND/PENS
GNOS/GNOM	MISS and MIT	PHON
HAL	MOB, MOT, and MOV	PREHEND, PREHENS, and
HER and HES	NOC/NOX	PRIS
IT	NOMEN and NOMIN	SPIR
LEG, LIG, and LECT		TANG, TING, TACT, and TIG

Using the Words

Exercise I. Antonyms. Select the word or phrase most nearly opposite in meaning to the word in bold type.

_____ 1. **dynamic**   (a) soft   (b) undecided   (c) lethargic
(d) striated   (e) pianissimo

_____ 2. **parsimony**   (a) stability   (b) philanthropy
(c) detriment   (d) notoriety   (e) frugality

_____ 3. **vehemence**   (a) approval   (b) intransigence   (c) calm
(d) emotion   (e) apathy

_____ 4. **remiss**   (a) scrupulously attentive   (b) quietly understanding   (c) reassuringly supportive (d) noticeably bold   (e) concisely stated

_____ 5. **intransigent**   (a) palpable   (b) profound   (c) tractable (d) tremulous   (e) lamentable

_____ 6. **germane**   (a) indigenous   (b) ingenuous   (c) sedate (d) irrelevant   (e) irretrievable

_____ 7. **evanescent**   (a) ethereal   (b) lingering   (c) placid (d) retreating   (e) pervasive

_____ 8. **stentorian**   (a) buoyant   (b) apprehensive   (c) callous (d) anomalous   (e) dulcet

_____ 9. **jovial**   (a) parsimonious   (b) squalid   (c) terse (d) choleric   (e) volatile

_____ 10. **procrustean**   (a) flexible   (b) debatable   (c) devout (d) complacent   (e) resourceful

Exercise II. Logic. From the words offered, select the most logical one to fit each phrase.

staccato	apparition	laments	sardonic
infamy	falsetto	hygiene	demise
panacea	consternation	frieze	arias
guile	amazon	sonata	

1. sure hate to meet one in a cemetery   _____

2. she'd stand out at a Munchkins' tea   _____

3. inappropriate for the "Hallelujah Chorus"   _____

4. an ingenuous soul wouldn't resort to this   _____

5. may be just the right pitch if you're a guy looking for laughs in a skit   _____

6. perfect ornamentation for a Greco-Roman building   _____

7. what Beethoven played in the moonlight   _____

8. intimidating tone for rapping out a sharp command   _____

9. the wrong sort of expression at a wedding   _____

10. what showed on your face when you discovered that the cat had her kittens in your bed   _____

11. a reputation to be avoided   _____

12. what Luciano Pavarotti, Jerome Hines, and Beverly Sills probably sing in the shower   _____

13. responsible for sweet breath, sparkling teeth   _____

14. what somebody ought to hurry up and find for the common cold   _____

15. may this never happen to your ambitions   _____

Exercise III. Synonyms and Definitions. Select the letter of the best synonym or definition for each numbered word.

_____ 1. **qualm**

_____ 2. **nether**

_____ 3. **inscrutable**

_____ 4. **torrid**

_____ 5. **miscreant**

_____ 6. **recondite**

_____ 7. **vignette**

_____ 8. **detrimental**

_____ 9. **pious**

_____ 10. **iridescent**

_____ 11. **churlish**

_____ 12. **rhapsodize**

(a) uncouth, rude

(b) a brief scene

(c) injurious

(d) evildoer

(e) brilliant, scintillating

(f) pang

(g) difficult to decipher

(h) lower

(i) talk or write in an ecstatic manner

(j) holier-than-thou

(k) steamy

(l) abstruse

Exercise IV. Truth or Fiction. Mark **T** for statements that express truth and **F** for those that are fiction.

_____ 1. A sadistic person is a likely choice for the main character in a morality play.

_____ 2. If Pandora had exhibited lassitude, she might never have opened her infamous box.

_____ 3. A smart salesperson cultivates an unctuous tone.

_____ 4. Those on diets had better have prodigious appetites.

_____ 5. Flimsy rubber pontoons would be risky underpinnings if you're planning to shoot the rapids.

_____ 6. A touch of Attic salt usually improves the stew.

_____ 7. To reach the bottom of Grand Canyon in safety, you'd choose a phaeton rather than a donkey.

_____ 8. Older brothers and sisters often delight in tantalizing a younger sibling.

_____ 9. An impalpable air of mystery or remoteness that often surrounds a film star may add to his or her appeal.

_____ 10. Portrayal of the squalid living conditions in much of Calcutta would detract from the authenticity of a film set in India.

Exercise V. Using the Roots. Use your knowledge of roots to answer the following questions and complete the statements.

1. What is a *condolence* call? _____

_____

2. A *suspension* bridge is (describe one) _____

_____

3. How are *contiguous* pieces of property situated? _____

_____

4. What is the body's *respiratory* tract? _____

_____

5. What is a *prognosticator?* _____

6. Why would you want to present a *cohesive* argument in a debate? _____

_____

7. The words *exit, circuitous, itinerant, initiate,* and *transit* share the root

_____, meaning _____ .

8. What are *noxious* fumes? _____

9. What is the best antonym of *diurnal* (of daytime)? _____

10. The root in *denominator* is _____, meaning _____ .

Exercise VI. Decoding with Roots.
a. Circle the root in each numbered word at the left.
b. Enter the meaning of the root on the line shown.
c. Consider any helpful prefixes.
d. Write a brief definition or synonym for each word.

WORD	ROOT MEANING	DEFINITION
1. **dismal**	_____	_____
2. **leguminous**	_____	_____
3. **emit**	_____	_____
4. **remote**	_____	_____
5. **homonym**	_____	_____
6. **misapprehension**	_____	_____
7. **extenuating**	_____	_____
8. **homophone**	_____	_____

Exercise VII. Common Sense Connections.
Join the vocabulary terms with the names, places, or ideas that make the best match. Write the letter of your choice on the line.

_____ 1. **fresco**   (a) oil   (b) design   (c) mural

_____ 2. **diva**   (a) prima donna   (b) basso   (c) concert

_____ 3. **bravura**   (a) Big Bird   (b) James Bond   (c) Carol Burnett

_____ 4. **libretto**   (a) composer   (b) W. S. Gilbert   (c) Howard Cosell

_____ 5. **chiaroscuro**   (a) darkness   (b) contrast   (c) brightness

_____ 6. **concerto**   (a) The Beatles   (b) Sondheim (c) Tchaikovsky

_____ 7. **patina**   (a) metals (b) rhythm (c) mercury

_____ 8. **sylvan**   (a) tract (b) nature trail (c) suburban

_____ 9. **Valkyrie** (a) Hindu (b) harpy (c) Valhalla

_____10. **zephyr**   (a) current (b) gentle (c) drafty

_____11. **frugal**   (a) economy (b) welfare (c) education

_____12. **virtuoso** (a) professional (b) instructor (c) member

_____13. **centaur** (a) settler (b) serf (c) cowboy

_____14. **myrmidon** (a) chief (b) henchman (c) duelist

_____15. **cynic**   (a) deity (b) devil (c) angel

UNIT IV
Your Best on the Test

All of the Above
ANSWERING THE FOUR MAIN TYPES OF VERBAL QUESTIONS ON THE PSAT AND SAT

The PSAT and SAT, plus all other standardized tests, ask questions to test your ability to work with words both in and out of context. Some people do well on standardized tests naturally, or so it seems. Others have trouble.

If you think you lack "test smarts" or test-taking techniques, this section is for you. Try the suggested approaches to each question type. See if these techniques work. If they don't, develop your *own* methods of attack. *Learn to use what works*—what leads you to correct answers—even if it sounds strange to somebody else.

Remember that standardized exams test your *developed ability,* not your *potential.* Think about that. If you can develop ability to one level, say an 80-percent level, then with work and determination, you can develop it to an even higher level. Now let's get at it.

Savvy Techniques for Getting More Answers Right Than Wrong

1. Never pounce on an answer like a cat on a tasty mouse. *Always eliminate the answer choices one by one,* as though you wore your head to the test. You know you had it on when you left the house.

Cross out wrong answers on any test, especially the PSAT and SAT. You are *supposed to write on your test booklet.*

2. Always make an educated guess. Do not leave any answer spaces blank on your answer sheet. Eliminate as many wrong answers as possible, then choose one lettered answer choice to record. Why? *Because probability is on your side.*

You have 5 answer choices for each question. You have 1 chance in 5, therefore, of getting a correct answer even if you *can't* eliminate some wrong answers. But you will *almost always* be able to eliminate some wrong ones.

Suppose you can eliminate 2 wrong answers for each question. Now, your odds of guessing the correct answer are 1 in 3. That's better. Keep reading!

Remember that only ¼ of a point is subtracted for a wrong answer. If you guess correctly on only 1 question, you can guess wrong on 3 others before you lose that correct answer. (When ¾ of a point is lost, you lose an entire question the way ETS scores.) Suppose that you are guessing 1 correct answer out of every 2 or 3 questions. That's more than enough to justify continued guessing. You will come out ahead.

Example: On a 10-question set of Sentence Completions, you got 6 correct *without guessing.* You missed 2 questions because you guessed and were wrong. (That's minus ½ of a point.) You got 2 questions right on which you made educated guesses. Your total of correct answers is 6 + 2 = 8 minus ½ point = 7.5. Scores are rounded upward, so you have scored roughly 80 points for this 10-question set. (Each correct answer is worth approximately 10 points.)

If you had left 4 questions blank, your score would have been only 60 points. Only the correct answers earn points.

NOW YOU SEE WHY IT'S SMART TO MAKE EDUCATED GUESSES.

3. Don't fall off the trolley. Check each question number to see that its answer is being recorded in the correct place on the answer sheet. If you discover you've written the answers in the wrong slots, you'll be frantic trying to repair your mistake.

Hot Tip: You may want to complete an entire section of the test and then record your answers in a batch. This method is preferred by many students. You will rarely put an answer in the wrong slot using this technique.

4. Keep track of the time. Wear a watch to the test. Some proctors forget (ahem) to remind you that time is flitting. Learn how long to spend on each batch of questions so that you have time to attempt an answer for each question.

Hot Tip: Learn how long each section takes you, and learn to work at maximum speed by practicing with actual SATs. Buy a copy of *10 SATs* at your bookstore today.

5. Know thyself. After some PSAT/SAT practice, or simply by taking other tests, you will learn which kinds of questions you answer best. *Do those first*. Then, do your next-best kind of question and so on, saving the ones you do poorly for the end.

Each answer is worth the same number of points (roughly 10), so you should collect as many right answers as possible before time runs out.

6. Save the stumpers. These tests are not the place to show the world you can stay-with-a-problem-come-hell-or-high-water. Stay with it too long, and even the proctors will abandon you and go home for lunch. But first, they'll take away your answer sheet.

Always save the stinkers for last. If they're that hard, chances are you may not do well on them. Make your best guess, enter your letter choice on the answer sheet, and think about something pleasant, like lunch.

7. What's done is done. Let your answers rest in peace. Change an answer only if you have plenty of time to reconsider, and be certain that the afterthought answer is the better one.

8. The unknown is sometimes the answer. Suppose you have eliminated all but one answer to a question, but that answer is a weird word, one you've never seen before. *Pick it anyway!* You eliminated the other answers because you knew they were wrong. Now you are left with the only correct answer. You did an intelligent thing, so enjoy it.

9. Avoid answers that aren't. In a guessing situation—but *not* when you're sure of yourself—avoid answers that read: *The answer cannot be determined*. Why, then, are they asking the question if it has no answer?

Rarely, a correct answer will read: *All of the above* or *None of the above*. Choosing one of these should mean that you have eliminated all of the more specific answers offered.

10. Direct, simple answers are preferred. Historically, makers of standardized tests prefer not to make up reams of long, involved answers. If 4 of 5 answer choices are fairly simple, avoid picking the one complex, wordy answer. It may have been designed to sound impressive, with the thought that you'd be so impressed you'd choose it. Now you will be a skeptic, right? *Distrust the highfalutin,* in other words.

REMEMBER, probability is on your side. Always make an educated guess.

A Word About Timing

You are in charge of your time on a PSAT or SAT exam. *You* decide how you will use each timed segment. *Make sure that you have read each question on the exam and recorded an answer*.

Suppose that you failed to attempt an entire section of analogies because you spent too long on the reading passages? *"Eeek!"* you say, as the proctor calls time. "I do my best work on analogies!" Remember the foregoing tips, and *always do your best kind of question first*. Then the next best, and so on.

Reading comprehension questions take just short of forever. For the amount of time spent, you have a chance to score fewer right answers for the reading comprehension section than for any other section. *Do the quick-answer types first, and save the slower reading passages for last.*

If you are particularly slow, careful reader, just ignore the last (and usually trickiest) reading passage altogether. That's right, ignore it! You will gain about 6–7 minutes that way, and you can use this time more profitably on other questions. You don't need those few answers from the last reading passage unless you're aiming to score over 650 on the verbal section.

When you see that time is running out, read the answers to the questions for the final reading passage and choose the answers that sound best to you. Do it quickly and forget about it.

If you want definite guidelines, here are suggestions that work for many students.

As a general rule, you should spend no longer than 5 minutes (30 seconds per question) on a test segment of 10 antonym questions. Timing for analogies should be roughly the same, allowing you a bit longer for the sentence-completion questions. *If you tend to do well on the reading passages, try to save half of the 30-minute limit on an SAT segment and half of the 50-minute limit on a PSAT for the reading comprehension questions.*

Facts About the PSAT

The full acronym for the PSAT (Preliminary Scholastic Aptitude Test) includes the letters NMSQT, which makes the whole title look like a minialphabet. The NMSQT part means that it is the qualifying test for students who want to take part in the nationwide competition run by the National Merit Scholarship Corporation.

Being a National Merit Finalist or Semifinalist, or receiving a Letter of Commendation, means a great deal at college application time. Doing well on the PSAT has grown into a significant topic and is certainly worth any extra effort you might put forth.

Stats: *Length:* 1 hour and 40 minutes
        Verbal Questions: 65 in 50 minutes
          20 Antonyms
          10 Sentence Completions
          15 Analogies
          20 Reading Comprehension Questions
        Math Questions: 50 in 50 minutes
          17 Quantitative Comparisons
          33 Problems in arithmetic, algebra, and geometry

Facts About the SAT

The SAT (Scholastic Aptitude Test) tests developed abilities in the areas of language and mathematics, with the same sorts of questions as on the PSAT. *In spite of its title, it is not a test of aptitude but of acquired knowledge.*

Stats: *Length:* 3 hours
        Verbal Questions: 85 in 2 test segments of 30 minutes each
          25 Antonyms
          15 Sentence Completions
          20 Analogies
          25 Reading Comprehension Questions
        Math Questions: 60 in 2 test segments of 30 minutes each
          20 Quantitative Comparisons
          40 Problems in arithmetic, algebra, and geometry
        Test of Standard Written English: 50 questions in 1 test segment of 30 minutes
        One set of Experimental Questions (May be a math, verbal, or TSWE segment):
          30 minutes

You can add up to 6, right? Six text segments of 30 minutes each make a very long test. There should be a recess in the middle, but somehow it's never enough. The best way to prepare for these tests is to practice your technique, memorize all the test directions, and practice.

How Can You Do Your Best?

You must know how the PSAT and SAT are written, what they look like, and what all of the directions say—*before you ever take a test* for the record.

So, right now, order the book titled *10 SATs* from your local bookstore, if it is not already on the shelves.

There is nothing like practice with THE REAL THING.

How to Answer Analogy Questions

An analogy is a relationship of one thing to another. When you say that your friend Brad is as crazy about skiing as you are about ice hockey, you are making an analogous comparison. In briefer language, it looks like this:

Brad : skiing :: I : ice hockey

In other words, *Brad feels about skiing just as I feel about ice hockey.* Each of us is related to the sport named in the same way—we're crazy about it.

Always express the relationship of the first pair in a sentence. The answer you seek must complement that sentence with another pair that expresses exactly the same relationship.

Note: The order of terms in analogies must be the same on both sides of the double colon. *Brad* and *I* must appear in the first slot and the sports we're mad about must appear in the second slot on each side. Positioning is critical. Move any item to another position and the analogy falls apart.

Common Analogous Relationships

Analogies fall into patterns or types that tend to repeat on tests. Being comfortable with some of the basic ones should prove helpful. (The PSAT and SAT rarely use type no. 1 or type no. 2 below, but these types illustrate correct analogous relationships.)

1. Antonyms

celestial : mundane :: pinnacle : nadir

Your sentence reads: *Celestial* is the direct opposite of *mundane,* just as *pinnacle* is the direct opposite of *nadir.* Total opposites on both sides.

2. Synonyms

stingy : miserly :: indigenous : native

Stingy means *miserly,* just as *indigenous* means *native.* Both sides of the analogy balance because both show synonyms.

3. Degree

warm : boiling :: cool : gelid

Warm is much less hot than *boiling,* just as *cool* is much less cold than *gelid* (frigid, frozen). Analogies of degree are favorite toys of people who make up tests. You'll get quite good at these with a bit of practice.

4. Person Related to Tool, Major Trait, or Skill/Interest

surgeon : scalpel :: bricklayer : trowel

A *surgeon* uses a *scalpel* as one major tool in his work, just as a *bricklayer* uses a *trowel* as one of his main tools.

orator : words :: artist : design

An *orator* is dependent upon *words* or uses *words*, just as an *artist* is dependent upon or uses a *design*. What is on the right side of each pair is that person's "stock in trade." These are popular analogous relationships on tests.

accountant : accurate :: judge : incorruptible

An *accountant* is expected to be *accurate*, just as a *judge* is expected to be *incorruptible*.

Note that a *noun* representing a person is in the first slot of each pair and the *adjective* we expect as the major describing trait is in the second slot of each.

Remember to make a sentence that states the relationship of the first pair, and make it as precise as possible.

5. Person Related to Least Desirable Characteristic or to Something Lacking

accountant : inaccurate :: judge : corrupt

The *last thing* an *accountant* should be is *inaccurate*, and the *last thing* a *judge* should be is *corrupt*. Again, the noun (person) is in the first slot, and the adjective naming the least desirable characteristic in the second slot of each pair.

liar : truthful :: lunatic : rational

A *liar* is not *truthful*, just as a *lunatic* is not *rational*.

bigot : tolerance :: dilettante : expertise

A *bigot* (prejudiced, opinionated person) lacks *tolerance*, just as a *dilettante* (dabbler) lacks *expertise*.

6. One of a Kind

petunia : flower :: maple : tree

A *petunia* is one kind of *flower*, just as a *maple* is one kind of *tree*.

7. Part of a Whole

verse : poem :: stanza : song

A *verse* is one part of a *poem*, just as a *stanza* is one part of a *song*.

8. End Product Related to Substance

car : metal :: furniture : wood

A *car* is typically constructed of *metal*, just as *furniture* is often constructed of *wood*.

9. Cause and Effect (or Typical Result)

aggression : war :: discord : altercation

Aggression can lead to (or result in) a *war*, just as *discord* (disagreement) can lead to (or result in) an *altercation* (heated angry argument).

10. Noun Related to Logical Action/Purpose

centrifuge : spin :: scissors : cut

A *centrifuge spins*, just as *scissors cut*.

stable : shelter :: warehouse : storage

The purpose of a *stable* is to provide *shelter*, just as the purpose of a *warehouse* is to provide *storage*.

11. Relationships of Location/Description

camel : desert :: alligator : swamp

A *camel* is an animal of the *desert*, just as an *alligator* is an animal of the *swamp*. (This does not mean that we only see camels in the desert or alligators in a swamp, merely that each is a natural denizen of the named areas.)

egg : oval :: brick : rectangular

An *egg* is often *oval*, just as a *brick* is usually *rectangular* in shape. (Again, not all eggs must be oval nor all bricks rectangular.)

12. Implied Relationships

clouds : sun :: hypocrisy : truth

Clouds hide (or block out) the *sun*, just as *hypocrisy* hides (or blocks out) *truth*.

Uncle Sam : United States :: John Bull : England

Uncle Sam is a *symbol* of the *United States*, just as *John Bull* is a *symbol* of *England*. (Ivan is the symbolic name for Russia.)

chauffeur : livery :: soldier : uniform

A *chauffeur* typically wears *livery* (as a uniform), just as a *soldier* wears a *uniform*.

Note: These implied relationships are the analogies most common on current PSATs and SATs.

When Working with Analogies, Remember:

1. Analyze the given pair as precisely as possible.
2. Express this relationship in a clause or sentence.
3. Choose your own idea of a good answer—your own pair of words—*before* looking at the answer choices.
4. *Eliminate* bad answer choices one by one. Cross them out on your answer sheet.
5. Keep *negative vs. positive* concepts in mind. If one or both sides of an analogy require a negative word, for instance, you can discard any answers that show positive words in that particular slot.
6. Keep *human vs. animal vs. plant vs. mineral* concepts in mind. Comparing a human worker to another human worker is a better analogy than comparing human to animal.
7. Be alert to *live vs. inanimate (nonlive)* distinctions. A comparison between a human and an animal is more accurate than one between a live thing and an inanimate thing. *A man uses a hammer just as an otter uses a rock,* for example, is a fair analogy that compares how one living thing uses a tool to the way another living thing uses a tool.
8. Use your knowledge of *prefixes* and *roots* to help decode a strange word. Negative or positive prefixes can be especially helpful. Also, if a word *sounds* very negative, it probably is. Words are funny that way; they often sound nice or nasty, and that may point toward their meanings. Your ear is a valuable language tool.
9. Select an answer and mark it on your answer sheet. Or circle it in your test booklet if you plan to record all of your answers to analogy questions at once. Guess if you need to, but *don't leave an answer slot blank.*

1. Practice Analogies

Complete each analogy with the best pair possible. Begin by making a sentence that clearly states the relationship in the given pair.

_____ 1. bee : honey ::
    (a) wolf : cub
    (b) spider : web
    (c) goat : cheese
    (d) ant : hill
    (e) human : child

_____ 2. transistor : radio ::
    (a) sound : stereo
    (b) sand : grains
    (c) awl : wrench
    (d) cement : driveway
    (e) spark plug : car

_____ 3. lace : gown ::
    (a) frosting : cake
    (b) zipper : coat
    (c) paint : enamel
    (d) tie : shoe
    (e) shag : carpet

_____ 4. captain : team ::
    (a) guard : forward
    (b) chef : menus
    (c) manager : policy
    (d) skipper : crew
    (e) overseer : concierge

_____ 5. client : lawyer ::
    (a) resident : apartment
    (b) patient : physician
    (c) devotee : opera
    (d) novice : expert
    (e) student : teacher

_____ 6. quibble : fight ::
    (a) inhibit : restrain
    (b) abash : embarrass
    (c) hesitate : pause
    (d) glance : inspect
    (e) protest : debate

_____ 7. trespass : property ::
    (a) ignore : license
    (b) intrude : privacy
    (c) evade : persuasion
    (d) extract : essence
    (e) demolish : building

_____ 8. dancer : lithe ::
    (a) bookkeeper : meticulous
    (b) gymnast : ambidextrous
    (c) musician : corpulent
    (d) manager : inept
    (e) hurdler : jovial

_____ 9. fat : congeal ::
    (a) hide : protect
    (b) water : liquidate
    (c) blood : coagulate
    (d) food : nourish
    (e) metal : temper

_____ 10. strength : debility ::
    (a) warning : awareness
    (b) humor : perception
    (c) meaning : incoherence
    (d) charity : virtue
    (e) candor : sanctity

Note: Although basic analogous relationships must be understood, remember that the SAT/PSAT favorite test type is _implied relationships_.

2. Practice Analogies

Complete each analogy with the best pair possible. Are you remembering to cross out answers as you eliminate them?

____ 1. beam : support ::
    (a) skin : pigment
    (b) shingle : shield
    (c) concrete : block
    (d) skeleton : size
    (e) partition : allot

____ 2. monarchy : government ::
    (a) anarchy : chorus
    (b) building : school
    (c) fruit : vegetable
    (d) sonata : music
    (e) despotism : economics

____ 3. article : newspaper ::
    (a) journal : ledger
    (b) account : diary
    (c) potato : field
    (d) egg : cake
    (e) scene : play

____ 4. orchestra : pit ::
    (a) skaters : rink
    (b) acting company : screen
    (c) troupe : podium
    (d) choir : rostrum
    (e) band : quartet

____ 5. hotelier : rooms ::
    (a) restaurateur : tables
    (b) proprietor : service
    (c) merchant : wares
    (d) clerk : sales
    (e) guide : maps

____ 6. eager : zealous ::
    (a) ecstatic : rapturous
    (b) inane : insipid
    (c) artless : ingenuous
    (d) bovine : perspicuous
    (e) generous : prodigal

____ 7. clumsy : movement ::
    (a) hastiness : retort
    (b) emulation : art
    (c) convoluted : writing
    (d) rashness : dancing
    (e) propriety : speech

____ 8. malign : vilification ::
    (a) appraise : confusion
    (b) deride : accreditation
    (c) castigate : reduction
    (d) satirize : mockery
    (e) embellish : austerity

____ 9. connoisseur : discrimination ::
    (a) monk : asceticism
    (b) gourmand : diet
    (c) bibliophile : stamina
    (d) novice : dedication
    (e) diplomat : style

____ 10. novel : review ::
    (a) class : study
    (b) court case : adjudication
    (c) product : sales plan
    (d) sculpture : evaluation
    (e) architectural design : approval

Check your answers against the key in the back of this book. Did you guess on some? How many of your guesses were correct? Remember to make a serious attempt at an educated guess for each question. This is a technique you can perfect only with practice.

3. Practice Analogies

Complete each analogy with the best pair possible.

_____ 1. kernel : ear ::
- (a) cake : dessert
- (b) potassium : mercury
- (c) ant : insect
- (d) sock : moccasin
- (e) curd : cottage cheese

_____ 2. vixen : fox ::
- (a) kitten : cat
- (b) mouse : rat
- (c) puma : cheetah
- (d) bitch : dog
- (e) heifer : mare

_____ 3. pioneer : apathy ::
- (a) designer : taste
- (b) envoy : diplomacy
- (c) disciple : rebellion
- (d) advocate : documentation
- (e) caterer : innovation

_____ 4. recruit : engage ::
- (a) oppose : rescind
- (b) acquire : reject
- (c) regard : exploit
- (d) air : expose
- (e) bedeck : strip

Tip: The answers always tell you what part of speech the words in the given pair must be. Here, the answer choices show *verbs* in the first slots, so *recruit* is being used as a verb, not a noun.

_____ 5. predator : claws ::
- (a) dinosaur : size
- (b) frontiersman : musket
- (c) equestrian : horse
- (d) analyst : statistics
- (e) simian : tail

_____ 6. dissension : harmony ::
- (a) obtuseness : perception
- (b) flattery : servitude
- (c) deception : reason
- (d) parasitism : host
- (e) malaise : thought

_____ 7. glut : satiation ::
- (a) force : condemnation
- (b) cheer : reparation
- (c) work : remuneration
- (d) height : exultation
- (e) anger : sensation

_____ 8. student : savant ::
- (a) instructor : teacher
- (b) archer : centaur
- (c) director : manager
- (d) knight : errant
- (e) tyro : master

_____ 9. toady : sycophant ::
- (a) mercer : assistant
- (b) storyteller : raconteur
- (c) guest : lampooner
- (d) elder : accomplice
- (e) novelist : playwright

_____ 10. wastrel : dissipation ::
- (a) recluse : isolation
- (b) fan : zealotry
- (c) warrior : exploitation
- (d) diva : imitation
- (e) coward : retribution

How to Answer Antonym Questions

An antonym question on a standardized test is purely a vocabulary problem. It stares you in the face and asks, "Do you know me or not?" And if you don't, finding the correct answer is *a royal pain*. A short word without a prefix or a fairly common root is the toughest.

Once upon a time, the antonyms on the PSAT and SAT were almost entirely Latinate. Those words had recognizable roots and prefixes, recognizable especially to a student population that had studied Latin in high school. For those pupils, the antonym section was not so tough, especially since they tended to read quite a bit.

Today's tests appear to me to be somewhat different. I find many short words (*eon, dour, quack, splice*), Anglo-Saxon or English words (*tarry, dither, loiter, patter*), and even colloquial expressions, such as *fly-by-night,* which appeared on an SAT in 1981. (I question whether knowing an antonym of *fly-by-night* is necessary for acceptance to college, but maybe I'm an irritable old bat.)

Nevertheless, I believe that the verbal sections of the PSAT and SAT, especially the antonym questions, are harder for today's students for three reasons:

1. Today's pupils read far less than their counterparts prior to 1960 and the television boom.

2. Students of the eighties rarely study Latin in high school, and both exams are still heavily Latinate.

3. The test questions themselves have altered somewhat and may demand an even broader vocabulary than previously.

What Can You Do?

You must read if you want a larger vocabulary. Read everything you can. Read the jam jar, the cereal box, the newspaper, books, and magazines. A book list of student favorites waits at the back of this text, just begging you to consult it for suggestions. Start now by showing that list to your favorite librarian or book-loving friend. Say, "Please, point out some good titles," choose a book, and turn to page one. *Today*.

And now for some "behind-the-wheel" practice.

Step-by-Step Approach to Antonym Questions

This approach is recommended whether you know the word in question or not.

Example: Select the word that is most nearly *opposite* in meaning to the word in bold type.

dormant   (a) thoughtful   (b) sluggish   (c) active   (d) aware   (e) permissible

Step 1. Examine the answers to determine the part of speech being tested. For this example, you see that the answer choices are *adjectives,* so even if you don't know *dormant,* you would know that here it is being tested as an adjective.

(What if you saw the word *air* in bold type? You would not know whether it was being tested as a noun or verb until you examined the answers.)

Step 2. Define the word in question as clearly as you can. Can you think of *synonyms* for it? *Related words?* Can you use the word in a sentence or remember hearing it used in a sentence?

Step 3. Look for a prefix that will tell you whether the word is positive, negative, or neutral in meaning (e.g., *trans = across* is neutral, as in *transmit, transfer*).

Step 4. How about a root? Here it must be **dor** or **dorm,** because *-ant* is a suffix. Words with this root include *dormitory, dormer* (bedroom window), and *dormouse*. All have something to do with sleeping or beds.

Step 5. Assume that dormant shares meaning with these known words; it probably refers to *sleeping, being asleep,* or *sleepy.*

(Your mind will do all this reasoning in seconds!)

Step 6. Eliminate answers one by one, systematically.

● Never grab for the first good-looking answer.

● Circle the answers to consider at final-choice time.

● Cross out each answer you decide is wrong.

   a̶. Is *thoughtful* the opposite of sleepy or drowsy? No. Off the mark. Cross out.

   b̶. Is *sluggish* the opposite? No, too close to the idea of sleepy. Cross out.

   ©. Is *active* the opposite? Yes. Circle the answer.

   ⓓ. Is *aware* an opposite? Sort of. Circle the answer.

   e̶. Is *permissible* an opposite? No, because we are not concerned with permission or its lack. We are talking about awake vs. asleep.

Now you have *answer c* and *answer d* as keepers. Of the two possible answers—a typical situation—*which one is more specific?* Which answer is a more direct opposite of the idea of being sleepy, sluggish, drowsy, or in bed?

Answer c, active, is the best opposite of *dormant,* which means *inactive, temporarily devoid of life*—like the bears who go night-night every winter.

You can use this step-by-step approach for all antonym questions. Many words you will recognize immediately, and you can begin eliminating answers (Step 6).

Should You Guess?

Yes, you should guess. As explained on page 291 of this unit, the odds are in your favor. You will nearly always be able to eliminate 2 or 3 answer choices, and then your chances of choosing the correct answer will be quite good.

Even if you can eliminate only one answer as being wrong, go ahead and guess. If you guess correctly on only one out of every four puzzlers in this situation, you'll be even. If you learn to guess more accurately—and you will by practicing the technique—you'll be points ahead.

If you doubt, ask a math whiz to explain probability.

Prefix Alert

Prefixes are treated at length earlier in this text, but, as a reminder, here are some of the most helpful ones for decoding a mystery word.

Prefixes That Are Usually Negative

a, an	*a*typical
ab, abs	*abs*tain
anti	*anti*dote
contra	*contra*dict
counter	*counter*act
de	*de*mise
dif, dis	*dif*fer
for	*for*sake
im, ir	*im*pale, *ir*regular
in, il	*in*ept, *il*legal
mis	*mis*spell
non	*non*sense
ob	*ob*tuse
of, op	*of*fend, *op*pose
un	*un*ready

Prefixes That Are Usually Positive

bene	*bene*fit
bon	*bon*us
col, con, cor	*col*laborate
com, co	*com*ply, *co*operate
eu	*eu*logy
pro	*pro*mote

Try putting the step-by-step method into practice with a few sets of antonym questions.

1. Practice Antonyms

For all antonym exercises, select the word or phrase most nearly *opposite* in meaning to the word in bold type. Use roots or prefixes as clues to meaning whenever possible. As you reason through each problem, repeat, "WORD is the opposite of . . ." so that you remember you are hunting an *antonym*.

_____ 1. **vital**
(a) acute   (b) misleading   (c) redundant
(d) stolid   (e) retiring

_____ 2. **focus**
(a) alter   (b) disperse   (c) discourage
(d) refer   (e) mislead

_____ 3. **mollify**
(a) irritate   (b) disengage   (c) deploy
(d) scatter   (e) thwart

_____ 4. **puny**
(a) minor   (b) correct   (c) weird
(d) firm   (e) great

_____ 5. **seasoned**
(a) having power   (b) acquainted with evil
(c) dependent on others   (d) wanting
courage   (e) lacking experience

_____ 6. **bias**
(a) charisma   (b) openness   (c) logic
(d) impartiality   (e) authenticity

_____ 7. **plethora**
(a) modicum   (b) paucity   (c) variety
(d) understatement   (e) aggravation

_____ 8. **blatant**
(a) subtle   (b) complex   (c) asinine
(d) unrepentant   (e) ingratiating

_____ 9. **harbinger**
(a) dullard   (b) envoy   (c) wastrel
(d) laggard   (e) dictator

_____ 10. **asymmetry**
(a) eagerness   (b) void   (c) balance
(d) perception   (e) beneficence

2. Practice Antonyms

_____ 1. **moist**
(a) clammy   (b) ebullient   (c) arid
(d) equable   (e) temperate

_____ 2. **quell**
(a) observe   (b) accord   (c) instigate
(d) erode   (e) enlarge

_____ 3. **naive**
(a) inept   (b) skilled   (c) alert
(d) bumptious   (e) sophisticated

_____ 4. **ineligible**
(a) suitable   (b) practiced   (c) useful
(d) practical   (e) orthodox

_____ 5. **sever**
(a) weaken   (b) unite   (c) disavow
(d) pacify   (e) ameliorate

_____ 6. **incongruous**
(a) commodious   (b) lofty   (c) attractive
(d) compatible   (e) pleasant

_____ 7. **assuage**
(a) pacify   (b) aggravate   (c) inundate
(d) begrudge   (e) inflate

_____ 8. **rancor**
(a) fondness   (b) acrimony   (c) dryness
(d) meagerness   (e) insignificance

_____ 9. **burgeon**
(a) retire   (b) approximate   (c) wither
(d) rectify   (e) mitigate

_____ 10. **saturnine**
(a) brawny   (b) mercurial   (c) ashen
(d) earthly   (e) blithe

3. Practice Antonyms

_____ 1. **retain**
(a) deter   (b) release   (c) extract
(d) permeate   (e) misdirect

_____ 2. **servile**
(a) frivolous   (b) restrained   (c) haughty
(d) boorish   (e) impatient

_____ 3. **smug**
(a) merry and unconcerned   (b) free from
blame   (c) fair and equitable   (d) loose or
unfettered   (e) insecure and unsure

_____ 4. **splice**
(a) separate   (b) coerce   (c) enjoin
(d) escalate   (e) rewire

_____ 5. **covert**
(a) aboveboard   (b) silent   (c) base
(d) honest   (e) frequent

_____ 6. **deft**
(a) sane   (b) keen   (c) inept   (d) rangy
(e) unwilling

_____ 7. **acrid**
(a) similar   (b) energetic   (c) decent
(d) sweet   (e) genteel

_____ 8. **strident**
(a) noisy   (b) relaxed   (c) meandering
(d) unremarkable   (e) unobtrusive

_____ 9. **goad**
(a) misalignment   (b) deterrent
(c) inundation   (d) disparity   (e) drain

_____ 10. **predilection**
(a) misinterpretation   (b) despair
(c) boredom   (d) attainment
(e) disinclination

How to Answer Sentence Completion Questions

Sentence completion questions ask you to select the word or words that best complete the meaning of a sentence. Students who read a great deal do well on this question type. The reluctant reader has more trouble, but practice makes a big difference, so let's get on with it.

"Test Smarts" You Can Use

Key Words point to the answer you want in every sentence.

Note the italicized words in the following examples. They are your clues to the needed words and to sentence type.

Example 1. *Although* Janie was *normally* _____, *she became* extremely _____ when it was time to get out of the pool, *insisting* that she needed more practice with the kickboard.

  a. Is Janie behaving normally?
  b. How is she behaving? Is she being insistent?
  c. Is she normally the insistent type?
  d. Is Janie's normal behavior the opposite of how she's acting now? Yes.
  e. *This is a sentence of contrast:* one behavior contrasted with (opposed to) another.
  f. The answer will be opposing words, such as *docile . . . stubborn.* Try reading the sentence with those words inserted. It makes complete sense, doesn't it?

Example 2. The critic labeled the film _____, saying that *it was poorly cast and lacked substance.*

  a. Why so many key words in a row?
  b. Do the italicized words after the blank act as a definition of the unknown word? Yes.
  c. *This is a definition sentence:* the key words explain, amplify, or define the missing word.
  d. Try plugging in a word that fits the definition, such as *shallow* or *tasteless.* Now the sentence makes complete sense.

Example 3. The *aggressive* _____ *and commitment* to opening the American West are *reflected* today in the _____ of modern business entrepreneurs.

  a. Is that little word *and* really significant? You bet it is.
  b. *And* links *similar* words, certainly not opposites.
  c. The missing word and *commitment* must be closely linked and well described by *aggressive* to make logical sense.
  d. These two nouns, *blank* and *commitment,* are *reflected* (they show up again) in modern business entrepreneurs—today's pioneers in the business field.
  e. *This is a sentence of comparison or coordination of similar ideas:* the key words told you so.
  f. Try reading the sentence again, with words inserted:

  The aggressive *drive* and commitment to opening the American West are reflected today in the *actions* of modern business entrepreneurs.

  or: The aggressive *drive* and commitment to opening the American West are reflected today in the *thrust* of modern business entrepreneurs.

Example 4. *Due to* the _____ of qualified instructors, the obvious *concern* of modern education *is not the curriculum but* the _____ required to give it life.

  a. *Due to* means *because of,* right?
  b. *Because of* some problem with qualified instructors, the *concern* (worry) in education is *not* curriculum (what is being taught) *but* that problem with teachers.
  c. *This is a cause and effect sentence* or *cause and result:* the key words tell you that one thing/situation is resulting in another.
  d. Go ahead now and plug in your own words. Write your complete sentence here: _____

  _____

  e. Did you come up with something like this? Due to the *lack* of qualified instructors, the obvious concern of modern education is not the curriculum but the *personnel* required to give it life.

Key Word Alert! Certain words in sentence completion questions should grab you. Words indicating a **contrast** include *but, although, nevertheless, on the other hand, atypically, uncharacteristically, abnormally, illogically, yet, however, curiously, even though, except, strangely, oddly, ironically,* etc.

Words that hint at **similar** or **like ideas being compared or coordinated** include *and, moreover, like, always, ever, faithfully, reflected, echoed,* etc.

Words that suggest a **cause and effect** sentence include *so, because, result, since, unless, except, but,* etc.

These are the so-called "little words," but they are the *big words* when it comes to determining the feeling of any sentence. You must take the pulse of your sentence by noting these key words right away. Many will be conjunctions or adverbs. Others will be verbs such as *echoed* or *reflected.*

Certain sentence types repeat. Learn these sentence types.

1. Contrast of one thing/situation with another. (Read Example 1 above.)
2. Definition or explanation. (Read Example 2 above.)
3. Comparison/coordination of similar ideas. (Read Example 3 above.)
4. Cause and effect/result. (Read Example 4 above.)

Knowing what sentence type you are working with will tell you what sort of words must be used to complete the meaning. Although not all sentences on standardized tests fit into these categories, you'll be surprised at how many do.

Negative vs. positive concepts abound. Remember this example? *The critic labeled the film _____, saying that it was poorly cast and lacked substance.* Did the critic like the film? No. The word for this blank must be a *negative* word. Any positive or even neutral word offered as an answer choice will be wrong and can be crossed out immediately.

How about this example? *The aggressive _____ and commitment to opening the American West are reflected today in the _____ of modern business entrepreneurs.* Is this a negative sentence as a whole? No, it appears to be fairly positive. Any negative answer choices can be eliminated immediately. *Commitment* is a fairly positive word, and the word linked to it by *and* must also be positive. For the second blank, a positive word or one with no negative connotations is a must. Why? Because the two nouns (*blank* and *commitment*) are *reflected* today. They show up again in modern business pioneers, and they are still positive qualities.

Be alert for negative and positive word requirements. Ask yourself whether you want good words or bad ones? Is the general idea nice or nasty?

The last sentence completion questions are usually the hardest. In a set of five questions of this type, the first two are apt to be relatively simple. One-word completions are the easiest and will take you only a few seconds. As you work through the problem set, however, the going may get rougher, and the answer choices may be words you've rarely seen. As a general rule, the more difficult the question, the more sophisticated the answer choices. Eliminate all the answers you *know* to be wrong. Then choose the best of those remaining.

Reasoning Your Way Through to the Answer

Let's work through a question of medium difficulty to demonstrate the reasoning process. This always looks long in print, but your mind is the best computer ever made and it will do all this work in seconds.

Example: Choose the word or words that best complete the meaning of the entire sentence. The bygone belief that education was the province of the _____, and not required by the masses, has been supplanted by our conviction that education is absolutely _____ for everyone if our nation is to progress.

(a) monarchy ... logical

(b) church ... impossible

(c) populace ... desirable

(d) elite ... mandatory

(e) educators ... required

Step 1. Read the sentence carefully. Read it again.

Step 2. Note key words pointing to the required answer: *not required by the masses* sets up a contrast with the first clause; *supplanted by* (replaced) further emphasizes the contrast with *bygone belief. Conviction* and *absolutely* are strong words, pointing to a strong word for the second blank.

Step 3. Sentence type? An obvious contrast—old with modern. Education long ago compared with now.

Step 4. Whomp up the answer. Let's try: *The bygone belief that education was the province of the wealthy or upper class, and not required by the masses, has been supplanted by our conviction that education is absolutely necessary for everyone if our nation is to progress.* Does the "guess" answer make total sense?

Step 5. Eliminate answers.

(a) monarchy ... logical No. Factually wrong, as the wealthy were also educated. And *logical* makes little sense in the second slot. This sentence poses the problem of *who* must have an education, not whether it is logical or illogical.

(b) church ... impossible True, the church once did most of the education, but *church* is not an opposite of *the masses,* which is required in this sentence. *Impossible* makes no sense in the second blank. No. Cross out.

(c) populace ... desirable *Populace* is a good synonym of *the masses,* not the contrasting word we need. *Desirable* works, but is very weak when you remember the strong words: *conviction, absolutely.* No. Cross out.

(d) elite ... mandatory *Elite* would include the monarchy and the wealthy, who were educated in bygone days, and *mandatory* (essential, vital) completes the idea of contrast between then and now. Circle this one to KEEP.

(e) educators ... required *Educators* is not an opposite of *the masses* and makes little sense, although it's vaguely possible. *Required* works well in the second blank. KEEP, for now.

You are left with *answer d* and *answer e.* Which one is *more specific?* Which one is closer to your idea of a good answer? Because *elite* fits so much better in the first blank, and because *mandatory* is a stronger word than *required,* you should choose *answer d. Answer d* is correct for this sentence.

Once More, with Feeling

1. *Read and reread the given sentence.* Examine it like a bug under a microscope. Circle key words if it helps you.

2. *Note the key words as clues, especially the "little words"* : so, because, and, yet, since, most, least, although, enough, moreover, typically, normally, curiously, however, uncharacteristically, unless, even though, nevertheless, etc. Note all *adverbs.*

3. *Decide on sentence type*—is it one of these?
   a. *Contrast* of one thing with another?
   b. *Definition*—with the word you're looking for defined or explained in the sentence?
   c. *Comparison* or *coordination* of similar ideas?
   d. *Cause and effect or result?*

4. *Whomp up your own answer for the fill-in word (or words)* **before** *looking at the answer choices.* Do you want a positive or negative word? Positive word in the first blank and negative word in the second blank? What does the sentence *need* to make absolute logical sense?

5. *Eliminate answer choices systematically,* one by one. Cross out the wrong ones in your test booklet, and circle the answers to keep for final decision time.

   Note: *Management of your time* is a critical factor on any test. Remember to check the wall clock or your watch frequently during each timed test segment. For these sentence completion questions, allow yourself 30–60 seconds for each, so that a section of five questions will not gobble more than 3–4 minutes. Easy fill-ins take only a few seconds, and you can ponder longer on the stinkers.

1. Practice Sentence Completions

Directions for all practice exercises: Circle the word or words that best complete the meaning of the entire sentence.

1. Can we restructure education so that it teaches logic and _____, rather than the collection and recitation of facts divorced from useful application?
   (a) cohesiveness
   (b) reasoning
   (c) problem-solving skills
   (d) proven data
   (e) historical precedent

2. Popular in the seventies, the young adult problem novel, as it was known in the publishing trade, was essentially _____ in nature, bent on conveying a moral lesson in modern slang.
   (a) frivolous
   (b) boring
   (c) modern
   (d) equivocal
   (e) didactic

3. Her school performance was consistently _____; in conferences, her parents debated with the instructors as to whether she was _____ or just plain bored.
   (a) lackluster ... incapable
   (b) insipid ... gifted
   (c) meteoric ... attentive
   (d) slow ... bright
   (e) erratic ... deficient

4. The job of the linguist must be to discriminate between what is merely a fad and what qualifies as an actual change in language usage, to _____ the former and accurately _____ the latter, regardless of personal preferences.
   (a) despise ... reflect
   (b) disregard ... transcribe
   (c) enhance ... repeat
   (d) enjoy ... deplore
   (e) record ... expunge

5. An optimist by nature, Harold faced a difficult adjustment when his investments turned sour, and he was slow to regain his customary _____ after the _____.
   (a) cheer ... process
   (b) hardiness ... event
   (c) wariness ... disaster
   (d) sanguinity ... debacle
   (e) outlook ... result

6. Because the front-runner in a state election focused on _____ interests rather than the parochial ones of his constituency, he lost to a _____ who told the citizens what they wanted to hear about their own narrow concerns.
   (a) private ... campaigner
   (b) catholic ... demagogue
   (c) wide-ranging ... pioneer
   (d) specific ... candidate
   (e) centralized ... politician

7. For the author, composer, and painter who must work alone, an occasional, stimulating meeting with others in the solitary arts serves to _____ their self-imposed _____.
   (a) combat ... isolation
   (b) expand ... endeavors
   (c) mitigate ... agony
   (d) destroy ... talent
   (e) allay ... fears

8. Although E. B. White enjoyed the success of his children's novel *Charlotte's Web,* he was _____ to have it translated into a movie, which he feared might _____ the book.

   (a) resigned … reproduce   (d) hesitant … skillfully depict

   (b) delighted … magnify   (e) ecstatic … lampoon

   (c) reluctant … inaccurately reflect

9. Many of the antique "finds" she holds most dear have been strictly _____, the result of happenstance or what is often termed serendipity.

   (a) characteristic   (d) immaculate

   (b) preposterous   (e) fortuitous

   (c) brilliant

10. Knowing that Aunt Jo was customarily well-groomed and _____, we were caught off guard when we arranged to pick her up and found her not only _____ but unready.

   (a) coiffed … late   (d) punctual … disheveled

   (b) distraught … prepared   (e) imperturbable … jaunty

   (c) particular … loquacious

2. Practice Sentence Completions

1. Proponents of women's liberation often feel that the name of the movement is no longer accurate, because it suggests a need for _____ rather than for the equality they seek in jobs, pay scale, and opportunity in the working world.

   (a) peace   (d) femininity

   (b) freedom   (e) honor

   (c) self

2. Although the _____ of nuclear power has yet to be fully realized, humans are as aware of having a "tiger by the tail" as they were when they discovered fire, eons ago.

   (a) fear   (d) potential

   (b) limitation   (e) awe

   (c) amazement

3. Rhonda's belief that people's lives are predestined, determined by God or perhaps fate, makes her championship of free will and independence especially _____.

   (a) understandable   (d) suspect

   (b) incongruous   (e) reprehensible

   (c) specious

4. Ralph's young, ingenuous appearance belied his _____ bargaining skill in awkward negotiations, so that opponents were often surprised by his _____.

   (a) honest … approach   (d) innovative … retreat

   (b) clever … failures   (e) plausible … illogic

   (c) canny … acumen

5. As anyone who watches TV can _____, the determination of advertisers to feed us their messages along with our entertainment continues _____.

   (a) attest … unabated   (d) deny … as before

   (b) reveal … to diminish   (e) verify … to wane

   (c) state … to be mystifying

6. Emily found that her pet monkey had not only a _____ tail but a mind to match it; his inventive exploits displayed a _____ intelligence far beyond what she had expected in so young an animal.

   (a) talented … kind of   (d) prehensile … precocious

   (b) simian … destructive   (e) clever … malicious

   (c) sedulous … brief

7. In times past, society suffered from a _____ of information about diet and exercise, but recently we have been _____ reams of information on both topics.
    (a) deluge ... deprived of
    (b) dearth ... inundated with
    (c) paucity ... denied the
    (d) plethora ... showered with
    (e) misdirection ... given

8. Known for her _____ and generosity, Mavis astonished her community by withdrawing her customary support from a charity and establishing a rival one in her own name, a gesture labeled as pure _____ by disgruntled former associates.
    (a) keenness ... philanthropy
    (b) aggressiveness ... conceit
    (c) geniality ... insensibility
    (d) idealism ... rudeness
    (e) altruism ... narcissism

9. Because of our cherished conception of the friar as an honest _____ who has no need of worldly goods, Chaucer's portrayal of the _____ and mendacious cleric comes as a shock.
    (a) priest ... perspicacious
    (b) cleric ... efficacious
    (c) ascetic ... avaricious
    (d) fanatic ... grasping
    (e) lunatic ... craven

10. When informed that their ideas are _____, many people both old and wise have refrained from sharing their patiently garnered knowledge with the young and smug whom they deem too _____ to appreciate it.
    (a) perceptive ... conceited
    (b) ludicrous ... grateful
    (c) revolutionary ... hidebound
    (d) vicarious ... insular
    (e) obsolescent ... myopic

STOP! Are there, by any remote chance, some words given as answer choices in these exercises that you *didn't know??* If so, you'd better check on their meanings. These words were taken from PSATs and SATs of recent years, and many are repeat offenders.

3. Practice Sentence Completions

1. Americans seem committed to the exploration of space, aware that the variety of information gained in the attempt is of _____ value—beyond precise calculation.
    (a) dubious
    (b) medical
    (c) inconclusive
    (d) inestimable
    (e) calculable

2. James was _____ about joining a fraternity; yes, he wanted the society of compatible, like-minded friends, but he also craved _____.
    (a) confused ... education
    (b) ambivalent ... diversity
    (c) delighted ... companionship
    (d) determined ... solitude
    (e) uninformed ... knowledge

3. The principle behind mediation is _____, wherein people with _____ goals or philosophies reach agreement on common ground, with each side conceding a point now and then.
    (a) arbitration ... identical
    (b) historic ... similar
    (c) compromise ... disparate
    (d) modern ... current
    (e) dissension ... divergent

4. Although Larcenous Louie _____ his escape from jail in an innovative manner, of which he was justly proud, none of his underworld associates could _____ the details from him.
    (a) effected ... elicit
    (b) bungled ... learn
    (c) managed ... suppress
    (d) aborted ... force
    (e) deferred ... prize

5. Patience, who possessed a(n) _____ temperament at odds with her name, learned that office work was too repetitive and predictable for one of her nature.
   (a) placid
   (b) volatile
   (c) remote
   (d) benevolent
   (e) amicable

6. A dedicated sculptor, Wharton found himself _____ with his new acquaintances because they valued him more for his ability to regale them with _____ at endless parties than for his hard-won artistic achievement.
   (a) conversant ... grisly details
   (b) incompatible ... witty repartee
   (c) blessed ... professional skills
   (d) disgusted ... information
   (e) malcontent ... frivolity

7. It is an unfortunate _____ that the countries most in need of restructuring their economic systems are the ones whose history, customs, or rulers have _____ the acquisition of modern education and technology.
   (a) situation ... encouraged
   (b) error ... frustrated
   (c) paradox ... inhibited
   (d) concern ... realized
   (e) contretemps ... promoted

8. Possessed of an _____ desire to ride in the red helicopter, Jane stared silently at the glorious machine, willing someone to look her way and _____ the longing she was unable to express.
   (a) insane ... suggest
   (b) insatiable ... refute
   (c) incredible ... deny
   (d) inarticulate ... divine
   (e) inner ... relieve

9. Tourists in _____ countries, where so many eke out their existence by begging, note that the poor never _____ when the traveler makes an overly generous contribution, but they're apt to object mightily when none is made at all.
   (a) foreign ... accept
   (b) affluent ... reply
   (c) indigent ... demur
   (d) respectable ... respond
   (e) mendicant ... harangue

10. Literary styles change, and Dickens or Hawthorne would be as astonished by the deliberate _____ of Hemingway, as Hemingway was appalled by their _____ of words.
    (a) terseness ... welter
    (b) prose ... paucity
    (c) approach ... variety
    (d) morass ... style
    (e) passages ... mastery

How to Answer Questions on Reading Passages

A written passage followed by questions is designed to test your reading comprehension. The tester wants to know if you understood everything in the passage, not only what was stated but also what was implied.

The majority of reading samples on standardized tests read like textbook material or articles in good magazines. But occasionally you will find some reading passages on standardized tests to be both boring and convoluted. (Only the test makers know why these writing samples have been allowed out in public.) You need to know that none of your college textbooks will be written as poorly as those few stinkers on tests. But—they exist.

How can you triumph over these reading passages?

Suggested Strategy

1. **Practice the art of involved reading—with total concentration.** You can read a Garfield cartoon book in one way, but you must read textbook material in a totally different way.

Blank out the world. Immerse yourself in the material to the exclusion of everything else. Only in that way will it make sense and stay in your mind.

The more you practice being involved with what you are reading, the better you will get. This technique is invaluable for success with reading passages on most standardized tests.

2. **Read the questions first, so that you know what you're looking for as you read the passage.**

3. **Know the kinds of questions that can be asked.** On a sample 30–60 lines long, only certain questions can be asked about the material:
   a. Logical title/main theme?
   b. Facts?
   c. Author's mood or attitude toward the material?
   d. Tone of the piece?
   e. Inferences, e.g., what logically preceded or would follow this material?
   f. Conclusions regarding the information itself—what consequences or implications could it have?

4. **Mark the passage for later reference, as follows:**
   ** Asterisks by *meaty sentences*.
   F Put F in the margin or underline for *facts*.
   O Circle words that indicate *tone, mood, author attitude, contrast*—note all words that hint at *change or contrast,* (e.g., however, but, even though, although, nevertheless, except, on the other hand) plus all adverbs that qualify what has been said (curiously, oddly, and so on).
   C *Cause and effect* relationships must be noted, as they are a great source of questions.

5. **Read the passage once, quickly,** for an overall picture and a good crack at answering any question on central idea or main theme. Read again, slowly, with the questions in mind, marking the passage as you go, if you find that this technique works for you.

6. **Eliminate answer choices one by one.** You will almost always be able to eliminate 2 of the 5 answer choices. One answer is usually too broad and all-encompassing, and another answer is typically off the wall—a joke perhaps on the part of the test makers.

Now you have 3 answer choices. If you are unsure, make your best guess, record the answer, and go on. Don't dither too long on any question, and *don't worry about it.* (You wouldn't believe how many successful professionals had low test scores and it didn't stop them.)

Do You Want to Score over 650?

Now stop chuckling. People do score over 650 for the verbal SAT (65 for the PSAT). If that's your goal, you must make a decidedly serious attempt to answer every single question.

If you wish to make a respectable score, here's a tip: *Skip the most difficult reading passage entirely.* That's right. Scan the passages quickly to determine which is the most abominable one for you, and don't even *attempt* to read that passage. You do not have to work with it unless you're trying for a nearly perfect score. *By skipping this passage you will buy yourself 5–7 extra minutes, which you can use more profitably by scoring right answers to all the other questions on that timed segment.*

Repeat this procedure for every 30-minute verbal segment of your exam. At the most, for two verbal segments (all that can count toward your final score), I am suggesting that you avoid 10 questions at the most, or roughly 100 points of the total.

Save a couple of minutes at the end of each timed segment for that passage you decided to ignore earlier. Read its questions quickly and pick answers that sound logical. Record them and forget about them.

If this idea of last-minute guessing bothers you, don't do it. But first, check yourself by guessing the answers to some passages you haven't even read. If you're a dreadful guesser, you might as well leave those answers blank.

Why Are Reading Passages Such a Big Part of a Verbal Test?

College entrance exams like the SAT and ACT are developed at the request of colleges themselves. They are designed to discover how well you will do with college-level reading materials. Some authorities have stated that as much as 90 percent of your college studies will be reading.

So—you must learn to read in an involved way, *not just for a test* but because you will need to read the same way as a college student.

Once More About Timing . . .

Because 25 of the 85 verbal questions counted for score are questions on reading passages, you need to save as much time as is comfortable for you for this portion of an SAT. If you can save half, 15 minutes, of every verbal test segment, you can make a fairly careful study of each reading passage and answer nearly every question correctly. After all, *the answers have to be in the reading passage itself.*

And now, review the suggested strategy for reading comprehension passages and practice . . . practice . . .

1. Practice Reading Passage

The general public is sometimes suspicious about the motives of therapists and curious about why someone would choose to work in this field. The old gag that "you don't have to be crazy to work here, but it helps" has more application to doing therapy than to, say, selling shoes. But I won't pretend to understand why therapists
5 end up therapists or, for that matter, why shoe salesmen end up selling shoes. Still, having worked for many years now with all kinds of therapists, I'm convinced that many of them took an interest in psychology for purely personal reasons.

In some cases, they may have felt their own psyches weren't wrapped all that tight and hoped that by taking a freshman primer in general psychology they would learn
10 something about just how tight a psyche should be wrapped. Or they may have taken that first course because it was a requirement and discovered that what they thought was tightly wrapped had actually come loose and was waving in the breeze. Or they may have taken Psychology 101 in the hope that now, at last, Uncle George's bizarre fetish for cowboy boots could be explained to the family over Christmas vacation, and
15 Dad's underwriting of a college education could be justified. For all these motives and more, rarely is this thirst for knowledge quenched by a first psychology course. If anything, the effect can be like salted peanuts.

For whatever reasons people take an interest in human behavior, it strikes me as unfair that they should be automatically suspect for taking a *serious* interest. A seri-
20 ous interest would, after all, lead to more classes in the field, a major, graduate training, and eventually a job as a therapist. The fact is, college courses in psychology have been at the top of the popularity poll for several years and psychology has been the number one major for undergraduates across the nation. Are all these people a little unhinged?

Circle the best answer choice based on material stated or implied in the passage.

1. The passage best answers which one of the following questions:
   (a) What is the purpose of psychotherapy?
   (b) When is a therapist most useful?
   (c) Why do people decide to become psychotherapists?
   (d) What is the most popular major on college campuses today?
   (e) How can a study of psychology help you?

2. It can be inferred from the passage that
   (a) most people who take a course in psychology want to take additional courses.
   (b) most people do not have time to take college-level courses in psychology.
   (c) all psychology majors are "a little unhinged."
   (d) all psychology majors find themselves in need of therapy sooner or later.
   (e) the purpose of a psychology course is to explain various familial eccentricities.

3. The clearest way to describe the author's attitude toward his subject, given this limited sample, is
   (a) unbiased and clearly detached.
   (b) knowledgeable, but slightly defensive.
   (c) clinical, yet intensely personal in nature.
   (d) resentful of popular opinion about psychologists.
   (e) blasé and weary of the entire topic.

4. What does the author mean with his phrase "what they thought was tightly wrapped had actually come loose and was waving in the breeze"?
   (a) The students' clothes were no longer in proper order.
   (b) The students' mental attitudes toward psychology had changed.
   (c) The students' attitudes toward school had undergone a profound change.
   (d) The students were unfettered and free at last.
   (e) The students were no longer as mentally stable as they'd thought they were.

2. Practice Reading Passage

Seeing in the universe a wonderfully designed organism, in which each member held its proper place and fulfilled its God-given function by virtue of a "pre-established harmony," Leibniz had designated the world we know as "the best of all possible worlds." (Arthur) Schopenhauer (1788–1860), on the other hand, weighing the ac-
5 tual amount of good and evil in the world against each other, arrived at the pessimistic conclusion that life was "a business whose profits do not nearly cover its expenses" and that therefore this world of ours was "the worst of all possible worlds." For him the prevalence of evil was the most obvious of facts and he considered the supposed rationality of the universe as an assumption and a product of the wishful thinking of
10 armchair philosophers.

Schopenhauer was a native of Danzig. He traveled in France, England, and Italy for some time to acquire cosmopolitan tastes and to perfect his natural ability in the command of foreign languages. He was a great admirer of Lord Byron, but envied the English poet his luck with women and therefore refused to make his personal acquain-
15 tance. As a student of philosophy he attended Fichte's and Schleiermacher's lectures in Berlin and was so unfavorably impressed that he developed a lifelong antagonism against all the representatives of idealistic philosophy.

When he temporarily settled down in Berlin as a *Privatdozent,* Hegel and Schleiermacher had become the favorites of the academic world, while Schopenhauer's lec-
20 tures and writings found no response. He gave vent to his disappointment in bitter attacks against "the professorial philosophy of the philosophy professors" in general

and against Hegel in particular, whom he dubbed a quack, a charlatan, and a servile creature of the Prussian government. The cholera epidemic of the year 1831, which claimed Hegel as one of its victims, caused Schopenhauer to move to Frankfurt,
25 where he spent the rest of his solitary life, with his faithful black poodle as his only companion.

Circle the best answer choice based on material stated or implied in the passage.

1. We can assume that the material directly preceding our sample was concerned with
    (a) the universe as a well-designed organism.
    (b) a preestablished harmony ordained by God.
    (c) Lord Byron and Schopenhauer.
    (d) the philosopher Leibniz.
    (e) all other German philosophers.

2. It can be inferred from the passage that Schopenhauer's personality included which of the following?
    I. jealousy   II. bitterness   III. conviviality   IV. great intelligence   V. diffidence
    (a) I and II
    (b) II, IV, and V
    (c) I, III, and V
    (d) II, III, and IV
    (e) I, II, and IV

3. A suitable title for the passage would be
    (a) The Many Gifts of Schopenhauer
    (b) German Philosophers of the Nineteenth Century
    (c) Schopenhauer and Leibniz, German Antipodes
    (d) Schopenhauer: Philosopher at Odds
    (e) Study of a German Native

4. According to the passage, Schopenhauer experienced all of the following in his life *except*
    (a) admiration of Lord Byron.
    (b) rejection of Leibniz's philosophy.
    (c) academic acceptance and recognition.
    (d) solitude.
    (e) extensive travel and education

5. The passage states that Schopenhauer became a lifelong antagonist toward
    (a) Germany, and Berlin in particular.
    (b) idealistic philosophers.
    (c) his fellow man.
    (d) only Hegel and Schleiermacher.
    (e) the academic establishment in nineteenth-century Germany.

3. Practice Reading Passage

I try to clean the language up and give words back their original meaning, not the one that's sabotaged by constant use, so that "chaste" means what it meant originally. I try to do that by constructing sentences that throw such words into relief, but not strange words, not "large" words. Most large words are imprecise. They are useful
5 because of their imprecision. If you work very carefully, you can clean up ordinary words and repolish them, make parabolic language seem alive again.

Dialogue done properly can be heard. Somebody in London told me I seldom use adverbs in my dialogue, that I never have a character say such-and-such *loudly*. But that he always knew how something is said. When I do a first draft, it's usually very
10 bad because my tendency is to write in the language of everyday speech, which is the

language of business, media, the language we use to get through the day. If you have friends you can speak to in your own language, you keep the vocabulary alive, the nuances, the complexity, the places where language had its original power; but in order to get there, I have to rewrite, discard, and remove the print-quality of lan-
15 guage to put back the oral quality, where intonation, volume, gesture are all there. Furthermore, the characters have to speak their own language. Novice writers, even when they get a good dialogue style, frequently have everybody talking the same way. If they didn't identify the speaker, the reader wouldn't know. You've got to be able to distinguish among your characters. Sula doesn't use the same language Eva does be-
20 cause they perceive things differently. If the reader feels he or she can visualize a character, in spite of the fact no one has said what the character looks like, that's it! All I have to do as a writer is *know* it in my mind. I don't have to write every piece of it. I give a few clues, some gestures. . . .

   I try to avoid editorializing emotional abstractions. I can't bear to read any more of
25 those books where there is this hopeless, labored explanation of a simple thing. If you can see the person experiencing the thing, you don't need the explanation.

Circle the best answer choice based on material stated or implied in the passage.

1. According to the narrator of the passage, words
   (a) that are deliberately imprecise are the most useful.
   (b) in constant use tend to lose their original meanings.
   (c) that are large are more precise.
   (d) are the basis for parabolic language.
   (e) acquire more interesting meanings with usage over time.

2. Based on material in the passage, we can assume that
   (a) the narrator is an experienced editor.
   (b) the narrator is an enthusiastic, beginning writer.
   (c) the narrator is lecturing to a college audience.
   (d) the narrator is drawing on experiences of many like himself or herself.
   (e) the narrator is an experienced writer.

3. The narrator's attitude toward his or her work can best be expressed as
   (a) casual and unassuming.
   (b) dedicated, yet occasionally diffident.
   (c) perceptive and professional.
   (d) authoritative, even pedantic.
   (e) detached and judgmental.

4. Which of the following would be abhorrent to the narrator of this passage?
   (a) careful exposition of a character's feeling of joy
   (b) writing a first draft in ordinary language
   (c) a number of rewrites
   (d) in-depth analysis of each character prior to and during the writing process
   (e) frequent cutting/discarding of written material

4. Practice Reading Passage

   The central mystery of the Celtic religion, and the ceremonial rituals which embodied its essence, will always be elusive. For many the Celtic mystique, with its romantic emphasis on the fairy and the spirit-world, has obscured the spirituality of these warrior peoples and the fact that they even had a religion. The ancient oral tra-
5 dition that perpetuated the laws, legends and the tribal teachings, through the trained memories of a group of poets and priests, made the act of writing unnecessary. And,

much like the prohibitions laid on the Celtic warrior heroes, which predestined their lives and actions, the taboo on writing continued as long as the old religion lasted.

The earliest remnants of Celtic culture in Central Europe are usually dated be-
10 tween 800 and 450 BC and assigned to the Hallstatt culture, after the metal artifacts found in a cemetery at Hallstatt in Austria, a centre for salt and copper mining. The later Celtic phase, the La Tène, named after a village site in Switzerland, continued in Continental Europe until Roman times. The style of ornament associated with the La Tène culture, with its wild, imaginative but formalized decoration of floral patterns
15 and abstract symbols, was still the dominant characteristic of Celtic metalwork, stonecarving and manuscript illumination in Britain and Ireland a thousand years later.

The Celts emerged from the Rhinelands of Central Europe as a distinctive group of clans or tribes between 1000 and 500 BC. Their language, religion, social organiza-
20 tion and customs were different from those in the Mediterranean south, or further east by the Danube. In general the Celts seem to have many affinities with Indo-European warrior groups who had overrun the Indus Valley civilizations a millennium or so earlier. A number of archaic linguistic forms, such as *raja,* king (Latin *rex,* Irish *ri* and Gallic *-rix)* or *rigu,* queen, as well as many others connected with sacred customs
25 and social organizations, are shared by Indo-European languages in Asia and Europe. Cultural affinities between the Celts and India can be also traced in the animal rituals in which the spirit of the new king or queen is rendered incarnate with that of a bull or horse; in the act of fasting to gain recognition for a grievance; in the position of women and the fact they were accorded parity with men (Boadicea in Britain
30 and the legendary Maeve in Ireland) in the warrior class; in metric forms, which in the *Rig Veda,* oldest and most important of the sacred books, are similar to some early Irish and Welsh verse; and in the close relationship between teacher and pupil which is still such a feature of Indian religious life and which was an essential part of the Celtic oral tradition.

Circle the best answer choice based on material stated or implied in the passage.

1. The passage states that the *Rig Veda* is the sacred book of
   (a) Continental Europe.
   (b) India.
   (c) the Celts.
   (d) Ireland.
   (e) Wales.

2. According to the passage, the distinctive and imaginative ornamentation produced by the Celts
   (a) was still their hallmark in the British Isles 1,000 years after the Roman occupation.
   (b) was a product of the Celtic culture known as Hallstatt in Austria.
   (c) was unique but so wildly imaginative that it never found lasting favor.
   (d) dates to the era between 800 and 450 BC in Switzerland.
   (e) adorned jewelry and personal belongings, which are the artifacts most commonly unearthed today.

3. The author of the passage wishes to emphasize
   (a) the artifacts left by the various Celtic cultures.
   (b) the oral tribal teachings of the two separate but related Celtic cultures.
   (c) the dominant characteristics of Celtic art.
   (d) similarities between Indo-European warrior groups and the Celts.
   (e) the elusive ceremonial rituals of the Celtic religion.

4. According to the author, the reason Celtic culture is essentially elusive is that
   (a) there are relatively few artifacts of the Celts.
   (b) the Celtic traditions were mingled with those of Wales and Ireland.

(c) other related groups of warrior peoples added their beliefs to those of the Celts.

(d) few archaeologists and historians have been properly trained to sift the available material for facts.

(e) written records are nonexistent.

5. The passage states that cultural affinities between the Celts and India include all of the following *except*

(a) the position of women.

(b) animal rituals involving a bull or horse.

(c) ceremonial feasts as acts of recognition.

(d) forms of language.

(e) metric forms.

5. Practice Reading Passage

A 1979 study by James Ruchti showed forty-three positions in the State Department requiring professional proficiency in Russian and thirty-five Foreign Service officers with that proficiency; a total of 4,943 positions in the federal government require Russian proficiency, but there are only 3,206 persons who can fill that need; of
5 the 4,576 positions in "defense-security" requiring knowledge of Russian, 3,039 persons in these jobs know the language. The Russian language capabilities of our federal government are limited—and our knowledge of the languages in some of the non-Russian republics of the Soviet Union is almost nonexistent. We do not have the language capacity to match our incredible technical knowledge of the Soviet Union, knowledge
10 gained, in large measure, by satellite movements of men and military equipment; and infrared satellite exposure that reveals locations of missile installations by plotting areas in the earth from which heat is escaping. We have no comparable wealth of understanding between the leaders and peoples of the United States and the Soviet Union, ultimately more important to the security of both nations than the mountains
15 of data and pictures we collect on each other.

While U.S. and Soviet expenditures for armaments increase, the number of students of the Russian language in the United States declines—which seems absolutely irrational whether from the viewpoint of the hard-liners who expect to fight or from the viewpoint of those of us who hope to avoid such a disaster. There are more
20 teachers of English in the Soviet Union than there are students of Russian in the entire United States. But this is only part of the story. During the academic years 1975–76 to 1978–79, 52 colleges and universities in the United States dropped the teaching of Russian. I visited the University of North Carolina at Charlotte recently, with its above-average language program—fewer than fifteen students were enrolled in Rus-
25 sian.

In the entire Southeastern United States, only one school, Florida State University, offers a master's degree in Russian. Nationally, Russian language courses are fewer and poorly attended, and Soviet study programs are suffering.

We [in the United States] seem to believe that if an emergency arises, we can turn
30 on a spigot somewhere and the knowledge and expertise we need will spout forth. There is no such spigot or computer or sudden fount of knowledge. We must begin to "stockpile" language and area resource personnel as we have stockpiled strategic metals. Rarely in the history of nations do we find that it did any harm for the leaders and peoples of two nations to talk to one another. The lesson of history is that the dangers
35 almost always exist in not talking.

Circle the best answer choice based on material stated or implied in the passage.

1. According to the author, one major difference between the United States and Russia is
   (a) the U.S. possession of incredible technical knowledge of the Soviet Union.
   (b) the Soviet's heavy expenditure for armaments.
   (c) the size of the U.S. State and Foreign Service departments.
   (d) the number of students preparing for foreign service.
   (e) the U.S. lack of language skills.

2. Statistics cited in the passage allow us to conclude
   (a) that the federal government needs roughly 30 percent more people to fill its various posts.
   (b) that the federal government has roughly 75 percent of the Russian-speaking people it requires.
   (c) that the Russian government posts are 100 percent filled with people proficient in English.
   (d) that 50 percent of U.S. college and universities have stopped teaching Russian.
   (e) that only 45 percent of U.S. "defense-security" positions have been filled by employees knowing Russian.

3. We can infer from the writer's presentation of material that he or she believes
   (a) that war is inevitable, given our present knowledge.
   (b) that nations have stopped talking to one another.
   (c) that nations must communicate with one another.
   (d) that the stockpiling of strategic metals must never be abandoned.
   (e) that satellite tracking and recording of technical data are irrelevant.

4. The author states that the security of the United States and the Soviet Union is dependent upon
   (a) a wealth of cultural understanding to match our technical knowledge of one another.
   (b) mutual willingness to abandon the stockpiling of arms.
   (c) the number of students studying languages in our country, especially the Russian language.
   (d) insistence by colleges and universities that students master foreign languages.
   (e) the U.S. determination to learn the Russian language.

5. The best interpretation of "hard-liners" in the second paragraph would be
   (a) difficult, annoyingly belligerent people.
   (b) unpleasant, irritatingly rude people.
   (c) conservative, definitely traditional people.
   (d) unyielding, persistently firm people.
   (e) liberal, regularly tolerant people.

6. Practice Reading Passage

Securing the rights of newly emancipated blacks in a practical way was a cardinal objective of the Reconstruction Congresses. For this reason, the thirteenth, fourteenth and fifteenth amendments were drafted and offered to the states; they were ratified in 1865, 1868 and 1870, respectively. Theoretically, of course, the rights
5 enumerated in the Bill of Rights would have sufficed to do the job of implementing full citizenship for former slaves. But the circumstances were special, and obviously Jefferson's moral universalism had never been put to this particular test. The thirteenth amendment abolishing slavery, the fourteenth amendment guaranteeing privileges and immunities, due process, and equal protection of the laws, and the fifteenth
10 amendment prohibiting denial or abridgement of the right to vote took long further

steps toward realization of equal treatment for all Americans. More than a century later, that ideal has not been fully reached. Yet the Republic has come a considerable distance from the colonial period, in which rights were accorded primarily to land- and slave-owners.

15   Legal scholars dispute the original intention of the framers of the fourteenth amendment. Indeed, "theories of legislation" in general are disputed in American jurisprudence. If a statute enacted by Congress unambiguously specifies rights and duties and if it embodies a reasonable political goal, then few problems of interpretation arise because there is substantial agreement about new obligations to be enforced

20 by the courts. Several factors must combine if a statute is to achieve unambiguous clarity. In older days, a preamble set forth the intent of the legislation, and the language became an official part of the new law itself. Sometimes now a committee report serves the same function, as do floor speeches of legislators who are acknowledged sponsors of a given bill. These factors, along with other more amorphous ingre-

25 dients, such as dicta and opinion among debators of a bill, comprise the "legislative history" of a statute, what is often called by lawyers the "original understanding." Clarity and binding force of interpretation are further enhanced if good political arguments are available justifying policies or principles advanced by the new law.

Unfortunately, with some legislation no agreed-upon original intention stands out,

30 no general collective understanding of a bill's aim finds consensus, and possible justifications collide. Cases involving the fourteenth amendment and the 1871 Civil Rights Act designed to enforce it tend to fall into this latter category, and no important decisions have escaped argument based on differing readings of legislative history and on projections of various conceivable principles and policies.

Circle the best answer choice based on material stated or implied in the passage.

1. One purpose of the amendment passed in 1868 was
    (a) to abolish slavery.
    (b) to guarantee the right to vote.
    (c) to guarantee equal protection of the laws.
    (d) to set a precedent later followed by Jefferson.
    (e) to abolish due process.

2. According to the passage, a statute will lack ambiguity if
    (a) a preamble is attached, defining the legislators' intent.
    (b) it has clarity.
    (c) it is sponsored by a number of legislators.
    (d) that is the intent of the legislators.
    (e) possible justifications collide and the statute is then tested exhaustively in court.

3. The author believes that the failure of the Bill of Rights to secure proper freedoms for the slaves was due in part to
    (a) Thomas Jefferson and his philosophy.
    (b) moral universalism.
    (c) the Congresses at the time of Abolition.
    (d) special circumstances at the time.
    (e) errors in the Bill of Rights itself.

4. The real difficulty with the Fourteenth Amendment, as the author sees it, is
    (a) its general collective understanding.
    (b) its historic lack of original understanding.
    (c) its various readings throughout legislative history.
    (d) insurmountable, and that is why it is continually being tested in the courts.
    (e) the law itself, with its attendant ramifications.

5. In order that a statute achieve unambiguous clarity, which of these factors should exist, according to the passage?
   - I.   specification of rights and duties
   - II. clear outline of the courts' obligations
   - III. avoidance of any political goal
   - IV. an original understanding or legislative intent
   - V.   acceptance within our Constitutional framework
   - (a) II, III, and V
   - (b) I, III, and IV
   - (c) I, II, and IV
   - (d) II, III, and IV
   - (e) I and IV

A Book List You Can Love

VOCABULARY BUILDERS THAT ARE FUN TO READ

The following list was compiled from student recommendations. No book list is ever complete, but this one can suggest many enjoyable titles for you. Nearly all book lists for college-bound students are pretty similar, but this list is different.

Note that only one or two books are suggested for most authors. If you like one of an author's books, try others!

Books Featuring Teenagers or Young People

Alexander	*Westmark*
Baldwin	*Go Tell It on the Mountain*
Bradford	*Red Sky at Morning*
Burns	*Cold Sassy Tree*
Conford	*Dear Lovey Hart, I Am Desperate*
	We Interrupt This Semester for an Important Bulletin
Duncan	*Stranger with My Face*
	The Third Eye
Ellison	*Invisible Man*
Frank	*The Diary of a Young Girl*
Godden	*The River*
Greenwald	*Blissful Joy and the SATs*
Gunther	*Death Be Not Proud*
Hentoff	*Does This School Have Capital Punishment?*
Kerr	*Little, Little*
	Gentlehands
LeGuin	*Very Far Away from Anywhere Else*
Lipsyte	*The Contender*
	One Fat Summer
Michener	*The Drifters*
	Caravan
Mohr	*In Nueva York*
Peck	*The Ghost Belonged to Me*
	Ghosts I Have Been
Salinger	*The Catcher in the Rye*
Taylor	*Roll of Thunder, Hear My Cry*
Walter	*The Girl on the Outside*
Watson	*Lightning Bird*
Wersba	*Tunes for a Small Harmonica*
Westall	*The Machine Gunners*
Wojciechowska	*Till the Break of Day*
	Shadow of a Bull
Zindel	*Confessions of a Teenage Baboon*

Humor and Satire

Benchley, R.	*My Ten Years in a Quandary*
Brinkley	*Don't Go Near the Water*
Cuppy	*The Decline and Fall of Practically Everybody*
Day	*Life with Father*
Dennis	*Auntie Mame*

Durrell, G.	*My Family and Other Animals*
	Birds, Beasts and Relatives
Ephron	*Crazy Salad*
	Scribble Scribble
Gilbreth and Carey	*Cheaper by the Dozen*
	Belles on Their Toes
Hyman	*No Time for Sergeants*
Kimbrough	*The Innocents from Indiana*
Leacock	*Literary Lapses*
MacDonald	*The Egg and I*
	The Plague and I
Marquis	*Archy and Mehitabel*
McKenney	*My Sister Eileen*
Rosten	*The Education of Hyman Kaplan*
Shulman	*Guided Tour of Campus Humor*
Skinner and Kimbrough	*Our Hearts Were Young and Gay*
Thurber	*A Thurber Carnival*
Viorst	*People and Other Aggravations*
	Love and Guilt and the Meaning of Life
Wodehouse	*Leave It to Psmith*
	Carry On, Jeeves

Mysteries and Adventure / Suspense and Science Fiction

Beach	*Run Silent, Run Deep*
Bradbury	Short stories and science fiction novels
Burdick	*Fail-Safe*
Christie	Mysteries
Collins	*The Moonstone*
Cook	*Coma*
	Brain
Crichton	*The Andromeda Strain*
Daniken	*Chariots of the Gods?*
Doyle	*The Adventures of Sherlock Holmes*
Dumas	*The Count of Monte Cristo*
Fleming	*Moonraker*
	Goldfinger
Forsyth	*The Day of the Jackal*
	The Odessa File
Francis	*Bonecrack*
	Whip Hand
Herbert	The *Dune* books
Jones	*From Here to Eternity*
King	*The Stand*
	Firestarter
Leroux	*The Phantom of the Opera*
London	*The Call of the Wild*
MacLean	*H.M.S. Ulysses*
	Ice Station Zebra
	The Guns of Navarone
Monsarrat	*The Cruel Sea*
Moore	*The Green Berets*
Sabatini	*Scaramouche*
Shute	*On the Beach*

Stewart	*Airs Above the Ground*
	This Rough Magic
	The Ivy Tree
Stoker	*Dracula*
Tey	*Brat Farrar*
	The Franchise Affair
Uris	*Battle Cry*
Verne	*20,000 Leagues Under the Sea*
Vonnegut	*Galapagos*
	The Sirens of Titan
Wells	*The Time Machine*
	The War of the Worlds
Wouk	*The Caine Mutiny*
	The Winds of War
Wren	*Beau Geste*

Not-So-Sappy Romances

Alcott	*Little Women*
Aldrich	*Lantern in Her Hand*
Austen	*Pride and Prejudice*
	Emma
Bristow	*Jubilee Trail*
	This Side of Glory
Brontë, C.	*Jane Eyre*
Brontë, E.	*Wuthering Heights*
De la Roche	The *Jalna* series
Du Maurier	*Rebecca*
	My Cousin Rachel
	Frenchman's Creek
	The King's General
	Jamaica Inn
Emecheta	*The Bride Price*
Ferber	*So Big*
	Cimarron
	Show Boat
Freedman	*Mrs. Mike*
Godden	*The Peacock Spring*
Hilton	*Lost Horizon*
Holland	*Great Maria*
Marshall	*Christy*
Mishima	*The Sound of Waves*
Seton	*Katherine*
	Devil Water
	Green Darkness

Fantasy

Adams	*Watership Down*
Bach	*Jonathan Livingston Seagull*
Ehrlich	*The Reincarnation of Peter Proud*
Le Guin	*A Wizard of Earthsea*
Lewis, C. S.	*All novels*
Stewart	*The Crystal Cave*
Thurber	*The White Deer*

Tolkien	*The Hobbit*
	Lord of the Rings trilogy
Wangerin	*The Book of the Dun Cow*
White, T. H.	*The Once and Future King*

Historical Novels / Biography / Great Big Sagas

Abdul	*Famous Black Entertainers of Today*
Clavell	*Tai-Pan*
	ShōGun
	King Rat
Costain	*The Black Rose*
	Below the Salt
Gilliam	*Paul Robeson*
Haley	*Roots*
Hugo	*Les Misérables [The Unfortunate Ones]*
Kingston	*Warrior Woman*
Markham	*West with the Night*
McCullough	*The Thorn Birds*
Meltzer	*Langston Hughes*
Michener	*Hawaii*
Mitchell	*Gone with the Wind*
Roberts	*Northwest Passage*
	Rabble in Arms
	Lydia Bailey
Undset	*Kristin Lavransdatter*
Uris	*Exodus*
Walker	*The Color Purple*
Waltari	*The Egyptian*
Wright	*Black Boy*
	American Hunger

More Nonboring Nonfiction

Angelou	*I Know Why the Caged Bird Sings*
Berne	*Games People Play*
Brown	*I Married a Dinosaur*
Burdick and Lederer	*The Ugly American*
Corbett	*Man-Eaters of Kumaon*
De Kruif	*Microbe Hunters*
	Hunger Fighters
Ellis	*The Brooks Legend*
Francis	*The Sport of Queens*
Greenfeld	*Gypsies*
Griffin	*Black like Me*
Hall	*Possible Impossibilities: A Look at Parapsychology*
Hayes and Hoffer	*Midnight Express*
Kanin	*Tracy and Hepburn*
McKenney and Bransten	*Here's England*
Mead	*Blackberry Winter*
Mowatt	*Never Cry Wolf*
	The Dog Who Wouldn't Be
Murray	*The Kings and Queens of England*
North	*Rascal*
Pirie	*Down These Mean Streets*

Shaw	*Gentlemen, Start Your Engines*
Stevenson	*A Man Called Intrepid*
Stinetorf	*Beyond the Hungry Country*
	White Witch Doctor
Taylor	*Zoo Vet*
Thomas, L.	*The Lives of a Cell*
	The Medusa and the Snail

Books with Universal Appeal

Adamson	*Born Free*
Braithwaite	*To Sir, with Love*
Burnford	*The Incredible Journey*
Caldwell	*Testimony of Two Men*
Cronin	*The Citadel*
Herriot	*All Creatures Great and Small*
Hilton	*Goodbye, Mr. Chips*
Irving	*The Legend of Sleepy Hollow*
Kantor	*The Voice of Bugle Ann*
Kaufman	*Up the Down Staircase*
Kesey	*One Flew over the Cuckoo's Nest*
Kipling	*The Jungle Books*
Lee	*To Kill a Mockingbird*
Milne	*Winnie the Pooh* (Have you read this, now that you're older? Hilarious.)
Moody	*Little Britches*
Poe	Short stories, especially his mysteries, which sometimes get overlooked
Rand	*The Fountainhead*
	Atlas Shrugged
Saki	Short stories
Smith	*A Tree Grows in Brooklyn*
Steinbeck	*Travels with Charley*
Twain	*The Adventures of Huckleberry Finn*
	The Prince and the Pauper

Dear Reader,

I may have left your favorite book off the list, and if so, please share it with me by writing to the publisher. Let me know *all titles* that should be added, plus the titles of any books so dreadful that we should turn them into confetti. Now—happy reading!

Joan Carris

P.S. If a book hasn't turned you on after 50–75 pages, get out another book. You can go back to the one that seemed slow when you're in the mood. It's better to be reading something you enjoy than not reading at all.

The Answer Section

Unit I. What You Already Know

List 1

A. Basic Roots

1. AQUA, AQU = water
2. HYDR = water
3. BIO = life
4. CHROM = color
5. CORP = body
6. EGO = self
7. GE/GEO = earth
8. BIBLI/BIBLIO = book
9. AGR = field
10. MATER/MATRI = mother
    PATER/PATRI = father

B. No Surprises

1. AUD/AUDIT = hear
2. COGN = know
3. DICT/DIC = speak, say
4. DORM = sleep
5. ERR = wander
6. FLECT/FLEX = bend
7. LABOR = work
8. SCI = know
9. SCRIB/SCRIPT = write
10. VID/VIS = see
11. SENS/SENT = feel

C. More Roots You Know

1. CHRON = time
2. COSM = universe, world
   (sometimes, harmony)
3. CIV = citizen
4. PED and POD = foot
5. PSYCH = mind
6. PED = child
7. VIA = way
8. URB = city
9. TEMP (tempor) = time
10. ZO = animal
11. EQU = horse

D. Roots One More Time

1. CYCL = circle   a. (2)   b. (3)   c. (1)
2. FALS/FALL = deceive   a. (2)   b. (1)   c. (3)
3. GRAV = weigh, heavy   a. (2)   b. (3)   c. (1)
4. AM (AMI) = love, like   a. (2)   b. (3)   c. (1)
5. NEG = deny   a. (2)   b. (3)   c. (1)
6. NOV/NEO = new   a. (4)   b. (2)   c. (1)   d. (3)
7. VAC = empty   a. (1)   b. (3)   c. (2)
8. EQU = equal   a. (3)   b. (1)   c. (2)
9. FRAG/FRACT = break   a. (2)   b. (4)   c. (3)   d. (1)
10. MIN/MINIM = little, least, or
    smallest   a. (2)   b. (3)   c. (1)   d. (4)

I. Fill-ins

1. corpulent
2. amorous
3. dissension
4. biopsy
5. matron
6. Trivial
7. fraction
8. hydroponics
9. dormant
10. audience
11. podium
12. novice
13. collaborated
14. temporal
15. pedant

II. Antonyms

1. (c) unsophisticated
2. (d) attentive care
3. (b) impolite
4. (i) bright, intelligent
5. (f) huge or vast
6. (e) correct
7. (g) ignorant
8. (j) narrow in scope
9. (a) patriarchal
10. (h) regular, dependable

III. Fill-ins

1. anachronism
2. geological
3. equestrian
4. dictatorial
5. patrimony
6. envision
7. grave
8. polychrome
9. agrarian
10. psychology
11. precognition
12. equivocal
13. cyclic
14. inscription
15. protozoans
16. deflect
17. egotistical

List 2

A. Number Roots

1. DEMI/SEMI/HEMI/MED = half
2. UNI/MONO/SOL = one

3. SESQUI = one and a half
4. DI/BI/DU/DUO/DIPLO = two
5. TRI/TER = three
6. QUADR/TETR = four
7. PENTA/QUINT/QUINQUE = five
8. SEX/HEX = six
9. SEPT/HEPT = seven
10. OCT/OCTA/OCTO = eight
11. NON/NOVEM/ENNEA = nine
12. DEC = ten

B. Number Roots Again

1. DUO and DO have been added to *dec,* which means *ten. Duodec/dodec* = twelve; twelve faces.
2. Ten and is written -teen.
3. Times ten is written -ty.
4. CENT/HECTO/HECATO = 100
5. MILLI/KILO = 1,000
6. MYRIA = 10,000 or great, vast
7. MEG/MEGA = million or great, large
8. ARCH/PRIM/PRIN/PROTO = first
9. AMBI/AMPHI = both, around
10. OLIGO/PAUCI = few
11. MULTI/MYRIA/POLY = many
12. OMNI/PAN/PANTO = all

I. Matching

1. (g) in all places all the time
2. (e) times ten
3. (k) two letters pronounced as one sound, e.g., *ch*orus, br*ea*d
4. (h) great slaughter
5. (i) model or prototype
6. (j) four plus ten
7. (c) 500th anniversary
8. (l) paralysis of one side of the body
9. (a) speaker using lengthy words
10. (b) one great stone, or a single impressive structure
11. (d) first seven books of the Bible
12. (f) scanty quantity

II. Fill-ins

1. megalomaniac
2. multitudinous
   (or myriad)
3. triad
4. sextet
5. millipedes
6. octet
7. pandemonium
8. ambivalent
9. solitude
10. omnivorous
11. ennead
12. myriad
   (or multitudinous)
13. principal
14. dodecahedron
15. decennial
16. one

III. Logic

1. An octogenarian is eighty or in his eighties.
2. Because a few people share the rule in an oligarchy, it is difficult to keep the balance of power equal. A group of 4 or 5 people who can consistently agree on policy is extremely rare. Humankind's basic nature is egocentric; one person wants to have final say. Even the old Roman triumvirate (3 joint rulers) had a short life.
3. A pentavalent element has a valence of 5.
4. The thigh's quadriceps is divided into four parts.
5. An ambiguous answer lacks focus, may present too many points of view, or may "beat around the bush." It is anything but definite.
6. The ancients thought that the Mediterranean Sea was in the middle of the Earth. On a map you can see that it is almost entirely surrounded by land, literally *in the middle of land.*
7. *Two-faced* people are guilty of duplicity—literally *double fold.*
8. There are 6 metrical feet to most lines in *The Aeneid.*
9. A millennium is a period of 1,000 years.
10. A triptych has *three* folding panels. A *tripod* supports a movie camera, and many still cameras also.

List 3

A. Prefixes

1. a. to view or go over again
   b. to put back
   c. It fires in the reverse direction to the motion of the aircraft.
   d. *retro*spectively
   e. to put it off, to set a later date for it
   f. postbellum = after the Civil War
2. a. not sociable or congenial; not fond of people
   b. literally *against aircraft,* usually referring to a defense system set up to detect aircraft
   c. literally *against the thesis;* the exact opposite
   d. bad luck, ill fortune
   e. lacking sense; illogical
   f. mentally uncomfortable; upset or apprehensive
   g. to act against or contrary to
   h. to function improperly or badly
   i. not irritating to allergies, as, *nonallergenic makeup*
   j. to speak against or in opposition, to disagree
3. a. large or great in size or importance
   b. enlarges objects so that we may see them
   c. extremely tiny or invisible to the naked eye
   d. minuscule (tiny) organisms or germs
4. a. forward
   b. in favor of it
   c. in favor of liberal causes
5. a. autodidact
   b. auto; automobile = self-propelled
   c. autonomous

B. Yes, More Prefixes

1. a. circumference = the distance around a circle
   b. circumnavigate = to sail or travel around the globe
   c. circumvent = to get around someone or something, as *he circumvented his friend's plans by making a good plan of his own*
2. a. introspective
   b. intramural
   c. intramolecular
   d. introvert
3. a. warned ahead of time
   b. in the front of a picture, closest to the viewer
   c. going before, preceding
   d. *fore*tell it, *pro*gnosticate it, or *pro*phesy it
   e. An idea that takes precedence over another comes before it in rank or importance.
4. a. beyond the ordinary; therefore, special
   b. external
   c. extrovert
   d. ESP refers to perceptions, knowledge, or feelings (vibes) attained in some inexplicable way outside the scope of the five senses.
5. a. between (rex, regis = ruler)
   b. between
   c. between
6. a. overcooked
   b. overlord
   c. hyperactive
   d. hyperbole
   e. superimpose
   f. supranational
   g. surmount
7. a. something beyond rage—causing profound anger, even disgust or contempt
   b. supposed to be as pure as possible
   c. way beyond the norm, far out, exotic

I. Antonyms

1. (i) antitoxic
2. (h) regress
3. (g) agree with
4. (a) prospect
5. (c) preliminary study
6. (e) antagonist
7. (d) outré
8. (b) normal
9. (f) dependent on others
10. (j) conservatism

II. Chart Completion

1. [example]
2. misbegotten
3. contra; to go against, contradict, or deny
4. non; nonreader
5. galact (Gr. *milk,* as in Milky Way); intragalactic
6. micro; cosm; a tiny portion typical of the whole
7. magniloquent; speaking in a very grand manner
8. mal; maladroit
9. circum; scrib; to encircle, mark off, or limit
10. ballein (Gr. *to throw*); hyperbole

III. Fill-ins

1. recurrent
2. postmortem
3. counteract
4. malevolent
5. profusely
6. superhuman
7. extrajudicial
8. misnomer
9. foregone
10. unassuming

Unit II. Vocabulary In and Out of Context

List 1

I. Antonyms

1. (b) refined, sensitive, polite
2. (a) major, important
3. (f) timidity, lack of nerve
4. (i) lacking zest or flavor
5. (h) youthful
6. (j) absent
7. (e) full of body, springy
8. (c) straight (not winding)
9. (d) restrained
10. (g) noticeably bright or interesting

II. Logic

1. A *petty* act is mean-spirited or spiteful, and atypical of someone normally well-behaved and considerate.
2. *Lank* hair often appears stringy, dirty, and unkempt. Its lifelessness is unappealing, as it indicates lack of care.
3. A brain *teeming* with ideas is stuffed full of ideas.
4. Other words ending in *-ling*, where the suffix indicates young or little include *yearling, gosling, duckling, foundling, fledgling, fingerling* (young fish), *nestling,* and *sapling*.
5. Ask any mother of five under the age of 5!

III. Fill-ins

1. lucrative
2. paltry
3. haggling
4. rift
5. teeming
6. puling
7. dank
8. pestilence
9. reverie
10. petty
11. ubiquitous
12. stripling
13. crass
14. sinuous
15. vapidly

List 2

I. Fill-ins

1. razed
2. scrutiny
3. capitulation
4. pert
5. tyro
6. smirk
7. rapture
8. filching
9. bizarre
10. vacillating

II. Thinking About the Words

1. A *salutatory* address is given by the second-ranked senior at graduation. *Salutary* means promoting good health and derives from salut, salus = *health*, which also happens to mean *greeting*. When we salute someone, we are really saying, "to your health," if we remember our roots.
2. A typical ranking of these adjectives would begin with *contentment* first, then *happiness, delight, exultation,* and finally *rapture,* as the utmost in joy. (Any group that wishes may debate this ranking!)
3. In the phrase "only a semblance of her former self," *semblance* means a faint reminder—an appearance we recognize, yes, but just barely. She *resembles* herself, but she is not herself.
4. The *sloth* is a lazy creature, often taking hours to move an inch or two. Indolence, sloth, laziness, and idleness are often given as synonyms, yet each word has slightly different connotations. Sloth is the most negative one, as it suggests ideas like a dirty house, an unkempt appearance, etc.
5. Synonyms for *ruse,* each with slightly different connotations, include trick, stratagem, artifice, subterfuge, ploy, hoax, deception, dodge, flimflam, humbug, pretext, feint, gimmick, snare, trap, and game.
6. *Marauding* means plundering or thieving.

III. Antonyms

1. normal, commonplace, everyday, customary, accepted
2. sophisticate, an urbane man, a learned or erudite person, a cosmopolitan individual, a savvy person
3. to refuse to budge, be adamant or stubborn, refuse to yield, "dig in," plant your heels
4. energy, dynamism, get-up-and-go, activity, drive, ambition
5. detrimental to health, harmful, injurious
6. to remain static, to be unwavering or steady
7. to build, construct, restore, institute
8. to tell the truth, be honest and trustworthy
9. one who is truthful, honest, straightforward; an ingenuous person who is without guile
10. cheerful, jovial, optimistic, jolly, sunny, merry, sociable, convivial
11. a purifying substance
12. droopy, lifeless, drab, lank (referring to a hairstyle); if referring to behavior or remarks, antonyms could include polite, respectful, deferential, well-mannered
13. disagreement, noncompliance, refusal to accede to the wishes of another, lack of consent, demurral
14. despair, despondence, misery, grief, woe
15. to give only a cursory look, glance over

Unit III. The Vocabulary Lists

List 1

I. Definitions

1. stigmatize
2. perpetrate
3. relinquish
4. truckle
5. nurture
6. evince
7. intimate
8. defile
9. feign
10. entice

II. Switcheroo

1. (g) force
2. (e) lure
3. (f) urgent appeal
4. (j) hint, suggestion
5. (a) reparation or satisfaction
6. (i) one who commits a foul deed
7. (b) downgrading
8. (h) compensation or correction
9. (d) brand of infamy
10. (c) one who profanes or desecrates

III. Analogies

1. wax : wane :: burgeon : wither (Antonyms)
2. nurture : growth :: exhort : action (Cause and effect)
3. philosopher : wisdom :: Anglophile : England (Person related to thing he or she is most attracted to)
4. disparage : praise :: truckle : command (Antonyms)
5. evince : interest :: redress : wrong (Implied relationship)

IV. Fill-ins

1. redress (*to atone* is also possible)
2. medieval
3. truckle
4. stigmatized
5. relinquishing
6. philologist
7. enticed
8. *Invincible*
9. coerced
10. perpetrated

V. Antonyms

1. (b) citation
2. (c) philanthropist
3. (a) futuristic
4. (d) conceal
5. (d) cajole
6. (a) stunt
7. (c) be truthful
8. (c) respect
9. (b) brevity
10. (a) proclaim

VI. Word Analysis

1. Possibilities are nearly endless. Some of the more well-known include Kipling's *Just So Stories, Alice in Wonderland, Charlotte's Web, Stuart Little, Trumpet of the Swan,* most Disney cartoons, *The Wizard of Oz,* Aesop's *Fables,* the *Nutcracker* ballet, *The Wind in the Willows, Rabbit Hill, Uncle Remus* tales, *Knight Rider* (TV), *Christine,* and so forth.

2. a. 1. hard-fought (it was a tough election)
    2. barely or not at all
   b. 1. make me feel awful
    2. push down
   c. 1. sloped upward
    2. apt or likely
   d. 1. stick together
    2. break asunder, divide, split
   e. 1. absolutely, totally
    2. examine in careful detail
   f. 1. hint or suggest indirectly
    2. close, well-known

3. *At one in harmony* suggests the accord (as well as the feeling of self-satisfaction) that comes from atoning for a wrong. You have "paid the price," whatever it was, and now feel harmonious within, not divided by anxiety or guilt.

4. *Yield, surrender, abandon, resign,* and *waive* all share the idea of giving up completely. *Yield* suggests that you have given way after being forced to do so, as a team is forced to *yield yards to the opposition,* or a driver is compelled by law to *yield right of way.*

   Surrender implies that somebody on an opposing side resisted for a while, as *he surrendered to the impassioned pleas of his constituents.*

   Abandon is a term of finality and suggests a complete giving up, as *she abandoned her child, knowing she could not care for him.*

   Resign is used in more formal contexts, such as *resigning a position* or *he was resigned to defeat,* meaning that he had given himself up to defeat and had come to terms with it.

   Waive implies less force and more willingness to concede, as *they waived their right to the beach property.* Signing a *waiver* means that you sign a legal document giving over a right or claim.

5. A person who "insinuates" himself into a group was not *invited* to join. He wormed his way in through devious means, clever enough that no one is absolutely sure how he did it.

Teacher Note: This lesson contains a number of meaty quotes that spark good classroom discussions. You might wish to consider the quotes used in "Word Study" for sentences 1, 6 (interesting word order, too), 13, and 14.

List 2

I. Fill-ins

1. Gothic
2. free verse
3. classic
4. travesty
5. genre
6. denouement
7. protagonist
8. thespian
9. rococo
10. lampoon

II. Matching

1. (h) elaborate seventeenth-century artistic style
2. (c) a medieval architectural style
3. (j) a tale using figurative characters and language
4. (a) the opposite of tragedy
5. (i) mockery through caricature
6. (b) illogical, often unrealistic slapstick comedy (i is possible)
7. (d) wit used as a weapon to evoke scorn or contempt
8. (e) low or distorted imitation of the real thing
9. (f) ridiculing verbal portrait of a person (i is possible)
10. (g) high burlesque ridiculing a literary work or well-known literary style

III. Analogies

1. thespian : comedian :: doctor : pediatrician (One of a kind)
2. Notre Dame Cathedral : Gothic :: Parthenon : classical (Implied relationship—building to predominant architectural style)
3. classical : Attic :: genre : category (Synonyms)
4. prologue : denouement :: beginning : culmination (Antonyms)
5. comedy : amusement :: satire : contempt (Cause and effect/result)

IV. Identification

1. satire (also classical)
2. thespian
3. allegory (also classical)
4. Gothic
5. farce (also comedy)
6. (fantasy) genre
7. allegory (also fantasy genre)
8. protagonists
9. classical
10. free verse
11. classical
12. (fantasy) genre; classical; allegorical in part
13. free verse
14. classical
15. thespian
16. Gothic (novel); classical
17. protagonist
18. classical
19. satire (also classical)
20. Gothic

V. Word Analysis

1. Literally, *belles lettres* means *fine letters*. This term refers to literature written as "pure" literature, not as informative or instructive material. It is typically light, sophisticated writing meant for the reader's aesthetic pleasure. Popular, current fiction, concerned primarily with plot or satisfying readers of a particular genre (e.g., mysteries or Gothic novels) is *not* considered *belles lettres*. Essays by E. B. White, however, fit this description, as do the short stories of Flannery O'Connor and other accomplished modern authors.

2. a. photogenic
   b. genus
   c. gentleman
   d. genius
   e. genesis
   f. gene
   g. genetic
   h. engender
   i. indigenous
   j. ingenue

3. *Arts Antonyms*
   1. protagonist—(d) antagonist
   2. tragedy—(g) comedy
   3. assonance—(e) dissonance
   4. realism—(a) romanticism
   5. hyperbole—(j) understatement
   6. travesty—(b) honest representation
   7. overture—(c) finale
   8. ancient—(i) modern
   9. ingenue—(f) sophisticate
   10. rococo—(h) classical

4. *Divers* means *various* or *several* and refers to number.
   Diverse means *unlike* or *different,* also having various shapes or characteristics.

   If you are studying this course on your own, please show your sentences to a teacher or helpful friend. In class, judgment of students' sentences may be at teacher's discretion.

5. *Fill-ins*
   a. bona fide
   b. benefactor
   c. bons mots
   d. bon voyage
   e. benediction
   f. bonhomie
   g. beneficiary
   h. benefit

6. A *protagonist* is depicted as someone struggling to achieve something, often a victory, in personal terms, over his own character. Usually, he must struggle to surmount some difficulty, solve some problem. Opposing him in the struggle is an *antagonist,* usually a person, sometimes an entire political body or government, that seeks to defeat the protagonist.

VI.
Current examples are best judged by the individual teacher, as new books, movies, and television productions will be different from year to year. If you are studying on your own, show your list to any knowledgeable person.

List 3

I. Fill-ins

1. dupe	5. flayed	8. gibes
2. sect	6. warily	9. rank
3. coup	7. crux	10. whit
4. abuts		

II. Synonyms

1. (b) attest, (c) avow
2. (a) jargon, (c) argot
3. (c) distribute, (d) parcel (out)
4. (a) bog, (d) entangle (Note that one synonym is a noun for the noun meaning of mire; the other synonym is a verb for the verb meaning.)
5. (a) gross, (b) excessive
6. (a) feign, (d) hypocrisy (Again a verb for the verb meaning, a noun for the noun meaning.)
7. (b) guile, (c) entice (Same explanation as with 4 and 6)
8. (a) decree, (b) edict
9. (c) faction, (d) party
10. (b) complete, (d) flagrant

III. Analogies

1. truth : sham :: honesty : guile (Antonyms)
2. gull : dupe :: touch : abut (Synonyms)
3. sect : political :: verdict : guilty (One of a kind)
4. coup : downfall :: credentials : employment (Cause and effect/result. One may lead to the other.)
5. noticeable : rank :: wily : ingenious (Degree)

IV. Famous Fill-ins

1. mire	4. cant	7. verisimilitude
2. wiles	5. rank	8. gibes
3. shamming	6. flayed	9. coup

V. Antonyms

1. (f) commend (or b, praise)
2. (h) nervousness
3. (j) foolhardy
4. (e) disclaim
5. (i) extraneous detail
6. (a) circumspect
7. (b) praise, or (f) commend
8. (d) reality
9. (c) large amount
10. (g) unbelievable

VI. Word Analysis

1. Because prefixes *in-* and *dis-* most often mean *not,* the attachment of them makes a word opposite to its original meaning. *Incredible* means not believable or exceedingly difficult to credit as truth. *Discredit* means lack of credit or esteem. A discredited story is one no longer believed.
2. a. (4) sacred choral music, usually with accompaniment
   b. (3) musical direction: in a singing manner
   c. (5) a religious song from the Bible
   d. (1) one segment of a long poem
   e. (2) a singer or chanter in a synagogue
3. The root **crux** means *torture,* and *excruciating* refers to something intensely painful, with a synonym of torturous. One favorite old method of execution was death on the *cross,* the other meaning of **crux.**
4. Modern uses of *crusade* can refer to anything from a determination to sell play tickets (I'm on a crusade to fill the house opening night) to a weight-loss crusade. As soon as Crusade is capitalized, however, it refers to Christian religious/military expeditions in the eleventh, twelfth, and thirteenth centuries to fight the Muslims in the Holy Land.
5. a. (5) sudden, violent overthrow of government
   b. (4) a fatal blow or finishing event

   c. (1) two-door automobile
   d. (6) theatrical success
   e. (3) detachable ticket, certificate
   f. (2) to deal with successfully
6. *Nonsectarian* suggests a much broader outlook on issues (or an issue in particular) than that held by the narrow-minded *sectarian*. A *nonsectarian* group is not affiliated with any specific religion, for instance, but can be composed of people of many religious faiths.

List 4

I. Fill-ins

1. titan
2. somnolent
3. mnemonic (seventeenth-century Dutch painters: Hals, Rembrandt, Rubens, Terborch, Vermeer)
4. nemesis
5. mentor
6. ethereal
7. hierarchy
8. narcissistic
9. bacchanal (or saturnalia)
10. cynosure
11. terpsichorean
12. stygian
13. Promethean
14. mercurial
15. theology
16. cupidity, saturnine
17. solons
18. draconian

II. Analogies

1. titan : weakling :: giant : midget (Size)
2. saturnine : dour :: mercurial : inconstant (Synonyms)
3. deity : Zeus :: nymph : Echo (One of a kind)
4. miser : cupidity :: mentor : leadership (Type related to main characteristic)
5. alert : somnolent :: selfless : narcissistic (Antonyms)
6. Cynosure : sky :: Styx : underworld (Location)
7. physician : medicine :: solon : law (Person related to field)
8. religion : Deism :: Muse : Terpsichore (One of a kind)
9. daringly inventive : Promethean :: brutally harsh : draconian (Synonymous relationship)
10. *The Mikado* : opera :: "The Raven" : poem [One of a kind; answer (a) is incorrect since *The Iliad* is a narrative poem, and a *saga* is a form of prose.]

III. Antonyms

1. (c) soft, lax, weak
2. (h) steady, constant
3. (f) responsible government
4. (i) extend, lengthen
5. (a) funeral
6. (b) cheerful, pleasant, bright
7. (d) deadening (Promethean does mean life-giving)
8. (b) cheerful, pleasant, bright
9. (e) hellish
10. (g) generosity

IV. Word Analysis

1. a. (5) capable of walking
   b. (4) stroll idly
   c. (1) vehicle for moving those who cannot walk
   d. (6) walk on an inspection
   e. (3) introductory remarks
   f. (2) baby carriage
2. a. protean b. junoesque c. Uranus d. aeolian e. erotic f. martial g. Olympian
3. a. complete, unobstructed view of an entire region
   b. referring to all North and South American republics
   c. wild tumult, uproar, uncontrolled behavior
   d. relating to all Greece or Greeks
   e. relating to all humanity
   f. a mime show, with no talking
   g. a cure-all, perfect remedy
4. a. short poem, epigram, or any abbreviated piece of writing
   b. alert, "bright-eyed and bushy-tailed," peppy
   c. cheerful, optimistic, bright, pleasant
   d. selflessness, concern for (and interest in) others
   e. steady, constant, dependable, changeless
   f. weak, lax, loose, mild
   g. generosity
5. *Planets:* Mercury, Venus, Mars, Jupiter, Saturn, Uranus, Neptune, Pluto.
   Constellations (zodiacal): Aries, Taurus, Gemini, Cancer, Leo, Virgo, Libra, Scorpio, Sagittarius, Aquarius, Capricorn, and Pisces.

Constellations (partial list): Ursa Major, Ursa Minor (Cynosura), Cassiopeia, Andromeda, Cepheus, Pegasus, Perseus, Orion, Cygnus, Pleiades (Seven Sisters, the daughters of Atlas), Draco, Boötes, Aquila.

Ceres, goddess of agriculture, leaves her name in the asteroid Ceres, a minor planet revolving around the sun.

Review. Lists 1–4

I. Fill-ins

1. coup	6. whit	11. cynosure
2. mnemonic	7. titan	12. wiles
3. relinquished	8. satire	13. dole
4. sect	9. atoned	14. thespian
5. feign	10. classic	15. defile

II. Analogies

1. genre : Gothic :: disposition : mercurial (One of a kind)
2. nemesis : jinx :: coercion : force (Synonyms)
3. dim : stygian :: smelly : rank (Degree)
4. books : bibliophile :: French : Francophile (Person related to outstanding trait; *stampophile* is a made-up word)
5. classic : rococo :: complimentary : disparaging (Antonyms)
6. dupe : credulous :: Prometheus : inventive (Character related to outstanding trait)
7. episode : saga :: Norman Conquest : Dark Ages (Part of a whole)
8. somnolence : yawn :: burlesque : laughter (Cause and effect)
9. satirist : words :: philosopher : wisdom (Person related to significant tool of the trade)
10. mire : entanglement :: lampoon : ridicule (Synonyms; also, cause and effect/result)

III. Find the Oddball.

1.	(c) omnipresent	Others are synonyms.
2.	(d) duplicity	Others share *arch-* prefix.
3.	(e) heavenly	Others share a root meaning *god*.
4.	(b) laud	Others are synonyms.
5.	(a) disclaim	Others are synonyms.
6.	(a) allegory	Others are types of comedy.
7.	(d) baroque	Others are literary/theatrical terms.
8.	(e) germane	Others share the root *gen*.
9.	(c) nursery	Others are synonyms.
10.	(b) solon	Others are gods/goddess in Roman mythology.
11.	(a) nemesis	Others are synonyms.
12.	(d) bond	Others share the root *bon, bene.* (*Bond* is English and Norse.)
13.	(c) whim	Others are synonyms.
14.	(c) assist	Others are synonyms.
15.	(b) vestments	Others share the root *vers, vert.*

IV. Antonyms

1. nurture	6. cupidity	11. brevity
2. evince	7. verify	12. coerce
3. abutted	8. animated	13. somnolence
4. gibe	9. denouement	14. narcissism
5. wary	10. invincible	15. free verse

V. Fill-ins

1. baroque	5. Flayed	9. crux
2. fiat	6. perpetrated	10. exhorted, redress
3. truckles	7. anthropomorphic	11. ethereal
4. cant	8. mentor	

List 5, Part 1

I. Antonyms

1. postpone	3. postpartum	5. anticipate
2. preliminary	4. predate, antedate	6. microcosm

7. paucity   9. illiterate   10. offense
8. miniature

II. Fill-ins

1. misanthrope or misanthropist
2. ob-, to disagree, voice a contrary opinion
3. unfeigned
4. im-, stolid, revealing no emotion
5. foresee
6. pan-, the gods of a people or a temple of the gods
7. ambi-, ambidextrous
8. for-, to give up, renounce
9. nonentity
10. omni-, literally, all-knowing

III. Definitions

1. bonny = attractive or appealing; good (Scots)
2. discredit = to cause loss of belief or trust; doubt, loss of reputation
3. invalidate = to render not valid, to discredit
4. irrational = not rational or logical, not sensible
5. atheism = lack of belief in God; denial of God's existence
6. eurythmic = harmonious
7. proclivity = tendency toward, leaning, natural inclination
8. antithesis = an opposite; direct contrast
9. apolitical = not connected with politics
10. counteract = to go (or work) against, to offset

IV. Find the Oddball.

1. (d) quinine   6. (b) trip   11. (e) mulct
2. (a) semantic   7. (a) equestrian   12. (c) hepatoma
3. (b) decant   8. (d) prim   13. (b) squadron
4. (c) monetary   9. (c) hector   14. (a) sexton
5. (e) oculist   10. (e) novel   15. (d) ominous

V. Missing Prefixes

line 1. excited, anticipatory
line 2. forward
line 3. Presently, into, forehead
line 4. irritated, again, intoned, opposed
line 5. unless, experienced, beside
line 6. Uncomprehending, confusion, retorted, dismay
line 7. object, accused
line 8. destroyed, replied
line 9. Distraught, automobile
line 10. Understanding, replaced, confusion, recognized
line 11. postponing, enjoyment, exactly
line 12. belongs, mistake

List 5, Part 2

I. Fill-ins

1. de-, defame
2. se-, segregate
3. em-, path; the sharing of another's feeling; knowing exactly how he or she feels
4. e-, emit
5. gen (type, kind), homogeneous
6. apo-, apogee
7. ad-, her/hes (cling, stick to); to cling to, stick with
8. fer (carry, bear), transfer
9. para-, paradigm
10. ana-, chron (time); something out of place in time

II. Antonyms

1. (f) orthodox
2. (j) endoderm
3. (d) emerge
4. (h) epilogue
5. (g) include
6. (k) refutable
7. (a) extramundane
8. (c) reject
9. (e) extramural
10. (b) asymmetry
11. (l) antithesis
12. (i) synthesis

III. Analogies

1. disaster : catastrophe :: permeation : seepage (Synonyms)
2. submarine : periscope :: tank : turret (Implied relationship)
3. interjection : between :: epilogue : end (Implied relationship of location)
4. apocryphal : doubtful :: eccentric : odd (Synonyms)
5. orthopedist : skeleton :: orthodontist : teeth (Person with major concern/focus)

IV. Add-a-Prefix

1. ob + ject = object
2. tra + jectory = trajectory
3. re + ject = reject
4. e + ject = eject
5. con + jecture = conjecture
6. e + jaculation = ejaculation
7. pro + ject = project
8. ad + jective = adjective
9. de + jected = dejected
10. ab + ject = abject

V. Fill-ins

1. contingent
2. alleged
3. suffused, writhed
4. metamorphosis, wrought
5. effected
6. effaced
7. correlation
8. annealing
9. aberration, diaphanous

List 6

I. Fill-ins

1. stolid
2. requisite
3. nebulous
4. plausible
5. lithe
6. incumbent
7. eldritch
8. diffident
9. brusque or brazen
10. astringent

II. Synonyms

1. pastoral = bucolic, rural
2. pristine = fresh, uncorrupted
3. expedient = advisable, politic
4. incorrigible = uncontrollable, delinquent
5. catholic = comprehensive, wide-ranging
6. diffident = shy, unassertive
7. eldritch = weird, eerie
8. astringent = dry, puckery
9. brusque = bluff, curt
10. brazen = forward, insolent

III. Analogies

1. rabbi : synagogue :: pedagogue : school (Implied relationship, of leaders and their locations)
2. dog : fidelity :: cheetah : speed (Noted characteristic of each)
3. diffident : gregarious :: timorous : brazen (Antonyms)
4. catholic : parochial :: open : restricted (Antonyms)
5. repeated offender : incorrigible :: impassive judge : stolid (Implied relationship, most appropriate adjective for each person)

IV. Fill-ins

1. incorrigible
2. pristine
3. astringent
4. incumbent
5. nebulous
6. egregious
7. demagogue
8. brazen
9. infidel
10. expedient

V. Antonyms

1. Plausible is the opposite of implausible, unbelievable.
2. Incorrigible is the opposite of compliant, docile, amenable.

3. Catholic is the opposite of parochial, narrow, provincial.
4. Diffident is the opposite of confident, sure, aggressive, brazen, bold, assertive.
5. Lithe is the opposite of inflexible, rigid, stiff.
6. Pastoral is the opposite of urban, metropolitan.
7. Pristine is the opposite of impure, sullied, tainted, stale.
8. Requisite is the opposite of unneeded, unnecessary, extra.
9. Stolid is the opposite of sensitive.
10. Stringent is the opposite of lax, weak, lenient, relaxed.

VI. Word Analysis

1. Roman Catholic schools are often called parochial schools, and thus the words catholic and parochial have joined hands in our minds. Instead, we should remember that *parochial* means limited or restricted, provincial. Parochial schools are normally supported by private, not public, funds, and managed privately as well.
2. Works that show country or rural life as peaceful, innocent, and idyllic are the ones that qualify as pastoral or bucolic. Students working alone should share their lists with any knowledgeable adult.
3. Simpler, usually Anglo-Saxon, words as substitutes for the Latinate/Greek words include *dry,* for astringent; *shy,* for diffident; *needed,* for requisite; *harsh,* for stringent; *teacher,* for pedagogue; *gather,* for congregate; *broad,* for catholic; *sure,* for confident; and *church,* for synagogue. As noted, however, these are rarely exact synonyms, which explains why the English dictionary keeps growing.

    The point, of course, is that writing composed of entirely Latinate words becomes ponderously slow going at times. The briefer, punchier words give life to prose. (Remember List 3, "Four-Letter Words"?)
4. The most appropriate tone is humorous. In this context, the journalist didn't "keep faith" with the old saw "never split an infinitive," and therefore he was an unbeliever, an infidel. In fact, splitting infinitives has never been *grammatically* wrong; it used to be considered *stylistically* incorrect. This old view is changing as modern grammarians urge common sense. When the phrase *sounds* better with the adverb inserted mid-infinitive, leave it there.

List 7

I. Synonyms

1. sangfroid
2. concierge
3. insouciance
4. dossier
5. rapport
6. entrepreneur
7. précis
8. debacle
9. avant-garde
10. détente
11. echelon
12. ménage
13. outré
14. soupçon
15. ennui
16. pique

II. Antonyms

1. (d) agitation
2. (c) large amount
3. (e) follower
4. (c) success
5. (a) heightened tension
6. (c) common
7. (d) discord

III. Fill-ins, Parisian Dream

1. concierge
2. ménage
3. ennui
4. Dossier
5. insouciance
6. piqued
7. soupçon
8. précis
9. (an) entrepreneur

IV. French in Print

1. (d) select group, set
2. (g) unpleasantly familiar, known or seen before
3. (e) proper, what is required by society's rules of behavior
4. (k) a social false step, a boo-boo
5. (i) an accomplished fact, usually unchangeable
6. (b) the responsible obligations of those with rank, nobility, position
7. (l) outstanding item, the showpiece
8. (j) special, favored pupil
9. (c) savvy, know-how, social competence
10. (h) private conversation between two
11. (a) feat of strength, skill, ingenuity
12. (f) related to, compared with

V. Roots of Derived Words

1. **tent,** prefix *re-*
2. **port,** prefix *sup-*
3. **tent,** prefix *dé-*
4. **dos** (from dors)
5. **port,** prefix *rap-*

6. **tens**
7. **port,** prefix *com-*
8. **tend,** prefix *ex-*
9. **dors,** prefix *en-*
10. **port,** prefix *de-*

11. **dors**
12. **port,** prefix *ex-*
13. **tent,** prefix *at-*
14. **port,** prefix *im-*
15. **dors** (root as prefix)

VI. Word Analysis

1. Sans Souci means *without care,* which is how people wish to feel on vacation at the seaside.
2. As they say in England, there's a "bloody great" difference between *sanguine,* meaning optimistic and confident, and *sanguinary,* meaning bloody, bloodthirsty, or murderous. As for *exsanguinate,* it means to bleed to death. Note that helpful prefix *ex-* as a key to the meaning of this word.
3. a. 4, middle-class, common
   b. 5, expert, specialist, or professional
   c. 1, meeting, usually secret
   d. 3, young woman formally entering society
   e. 2, trite remark.
4. A Francophile is a lover of (*phil*) France and things French, while the Francophobe strongly dislikes things French; he or she has a *phobia* (fear or hatred) of everything French.
5. Webster tells us that our modern meaning of *canard,* a false or unjustified story, or trumped-up report, derives from the Middle French language period when the phrase *vendre des canards à moitié* meant to cheat, literally *to half-sell ducks.*
6. Words come into the language through need. For example, the phrase *a little bit* is not as precise as *soupçon,* which is a hint or suggestion of something, actually *less* than a little bit. We needed *soupçon* (or a word like it) to describe more accurately what we wanted to say. Likewise, we needed the word *astronaut,* with its solid Latin base, once we began to have such a person as an astronaut. Before that, there was no need. Moreover, words that are better than the English equivalents come into the language so that writers and speakers can express themselves with greater clarity and precision. We have no exact equivalent for *ennui,* a brief word that suggests boredom, dissatisfaction, and a yearning for something exciting—all in five letters!

    Lastly, words enter the language through popular usage. The word *swivet,* derivation unknown, did not appear in *Webster's Collegiate Dictionary* as published in the early fifties, yet it is lined up with fellow respectable words in the 1983 edition of this same dictionary. *Her announcement struck him forcibly, leaving him in a perfect swivet. What should he do now?* Obviously, we can use the word *swivet,* and we did—enough to bring it formally into the language.

List 8

I. Synonyms

1. (b) stale and (d) hackneyed
2. (a) redundancy and (d) repetition
3. (b) cite and (e) set forth as possible
4. (c) understandable and (e) intelligible
5. (a) loquacious and (c) voluble
6. (b) terse and (c) concise
7. (d) retort and (e) rejoinder
8. (a) chatter and (e) babble
9. (b) repartee and (d) banter
10. (c) sarcasm and (d) wit

II. Analogies

1. anecdote : book :: epigram : monologue (Part of a whole)
2. laconic : garrulous :: novel : trite (Antonyms)
3. Oscar Wilde : raconteur :: Mark Twain : satirist (Example of general type)
4. repetition : speech :: tautology : writing (Implied relationship)
5. malapropism : words :: gibbering : speech (Implied relationship)

III. Fill-ins

1. cliché
2. repartee
3. double entendre
4. raconteur

5. riposte
6. malapropism
7. banal

8. persiflage
9. badinage
10. bon mot (pl. bons mots)

IV. Terms in Use

1. anecdote
2. malapropism (He meant *varicose* veins, not warlike ones.)
3. double entendre
4. irony, and an epigram as well
5. etymology (example of entry)
6. irony
7. riposte, and a double entendre
8. tautology (This sentence needs to be cleared of clutter. "The frisky foal romped in the pale green meadow fragrant with spring grass," or "The foal gamboled in the meadow fragrant with spring grass.")

V. Roots. Matching

1. (k) disparaging
2. (m) inherited trait, possession, privilege
3. (f) extremely vivid and clear
4. (h) to move or bend
5. (i) unyielding
6. (n) record player
7. (a) special right or privilege
8. (j) thought or image
9. (b) story of a life
10. (c) to turn aside or away
11. (d) to question
12. (g) easily bent, yielding
13. (e) study of handwriting
14. (o) to enact laws
15. (l) not lawful

VI. Word Analysis

1. a. actual, real, verifiable
   b. inarticulate, mute, silent
   c. laconic, terse, concise
   d. fresh, novel, original
   e. garrulous, talkative, loquacious, verbose, voluble
2. Badinage, repartee, banter, persiflage, *possibly* raillery, epigrams; irony also possible; a riposte is often witty enough to be termed a bon mot.
3. *Apropos* means *fitting, suitable,* or *opportune,* depending on the context. Additionally, as illustrated by example *b,* it means *relevant.*
4. Voices change in both pitch and loudness to reflect feelings such as fear, sorrow, joy, and anger. The need for secrecy usually brings on a whisper or lowered volume. Psychologists have confirmed that much of our opinion of people is based on their voice characteristics—their inflection, in other words. A newscaster with a whiny, high-pitched voice might never land a job.

VII. Stinky Pinkies

a. fly guy
b. jet set
c. glad dad or happy pappy
d. fryer buyer
e. pink sink
f. mouse house, mole hole
g. shivery delivery
h. jerky turkey
i. dramatic fanatic
j. sunk monk

Incidentally, what would be the definition given for the name of the game itself, Stinky Pinkies? Smelly hands? Warning: This game can degenerate!

Review. Lists 5–8

I. Know Those Roots and Prefixes.

1. Root = *bon;* an extra, unlooked-for reward
2. Prefix = *inter;* root = *rog;* to question, often with persistence
3. Prefix = *rap* (from *re*); root = *port;* accord, mutual understanding
4. Prefix = *mal;* root = *a + propos;* humorous misuse of words
5. Prefix = *in;* root = *flect;* change in pitch or loudness of voice
6. Prefix = *epi;* root = *gram;* short, witty saying
7. Prefix = *al;* root = *leg;* to presume or assume without proof; to offer as a reason or excuse
8. Prefix = *de;* root = *tent;* suspension of tension or relaxation of mutual distrust or animosity
9. Prefix = *in;* root = *souci;* cheerful nonchalance, lack of care
10. Prefix = *ex;* root = *ped;* advisable, practical; what will "get the job done"—even if not moral or honorable

II. Antonyms

1. (g) macrocosm
2. (d) shy
3. (i) parochial
4. (a) extra, superfluous
5. (k) agitation, nervousness
6. (b) ordinary
7. (n) success
8. (m) concise thought
9. (c) gibber
10. (e) original
11. (o) urban
12. (h) definite
13. (f) amenable
14. (j) bold
15. (l) laconic

III. Fill-in Chart

1. Prefix = *re;* root = *strict;* bound by law or convention or kept within boundaries; confined
2. demagogue
3. Prefix = *in;* root = *fid;* an unbeliever
4. Prefix = *en;* endorse
5. Prefix = *de;* root = *port;* to send away/out of the country legally
6. metamorphosis
7. Prefix = *de;* derogatory
8. Root = *gram;* epigram
9. Prefix = *a;* root = *string, strict;* dry, as *an astringent comment* (also, wry); drying, as a styptic pencil
10. Prefix = *se;* segregate

IV. Sentence Completion

1. incumbent	5. pristine	9. plausible
2. irony	6. anecdotes	10. précis
3. dossier	7. brusquely	11. eldritch
4. avant-garde	8. raconteur	12. badinage

V. Analogies

1. dancer : lithe :: entrepreneur : resourceful (One desirable characteristic for each)
2. stolid : impassive :: ironic : sarcastic (Synonyms)
3. enthusiasm : ennui :: plausibility : illogic (Antonyms)
4. repartee : riposte :: détente : compromise (Implied comparison—one logically leads to the other, and one is implicit in the other)
5. words : etymology :: mind : psychology (Implied comparison)

VI. Word Analysis

1. See Answers for List 7, part VI, question 6.
2. The root of *echelon* means rung(s) of a ladder, which corresponds directly to our current meaning of level or rank.
3. *Good, Well, Favoring:* bene-, bon-, eu-, and pro-.
   Bad, Negative, Not: a-, anti-, ant-, dif-, dis-, in-, il-, im-, ir-, non-, un-, mal-, mis-, de-, cata-.
   Above, Over: over-, super-, ultra-, hyper-, exter-, extra-, extro-.
   Out/Away: for-, ab-, abs-, apo-, ap-, e-, ex-, ec-, ef-, de-, cata-.
   Below, Under: Sub-, suc-, suf-, sug-, sum-, sup-, sus-, hyp-, hypo-.
   With, Together: com-, co-, col-, con-, cor-, syn-, syl-, sym-, sys-, sy-
   Indicating Time/Place: amphi-, circum-, peri- (around); epi-, ecto- (outer); ab-, abs-, apo-, ap- (from, away, down); se- (away, apart); inter- (within); tele- (far, distant); anti-, ante- (before); ex- (former); fore- (before); pre- (before); post- (after).
   Size/Amount: micro-, min-, pan-, panto-, omni-.
   In, Into, Within: In-, im-, ir-, il-, endo-, en-, em-, intro-, intra-.
4. Each person's description of his or her household will be different.
5. In sentence (a), *pique* means annoyed or peeved. In sentence (b), it means aroused or awakened.
6. At teacher's or student's discretion.
7. A *soupçon* of chili powder would result in bland Mexican food, and those who love it tend to love it hot.

List 9

I. Definitions

1. hirsute	7. simian	12. vivisection
2. prehensile	8. fodder	13. whelp
3. asinine	9. spoor	14. fledgling
4. leonine	10. porcine	15. vixen
5. ruminate	11. bovine	16. reptilian
6. denizen		

II. Adjectives, Fill-in

1. piscatory	6. feline	11. leonine
2. elephantine	7. lupine	12. porcine
3. canine	8. simian	13. equine
4. taurine	9. asinine	14. bovine
5. ursine	10. reptilian	15. ovine

III. Antonyms

1. (h) celestial
2. (e) intelligent
3. (j) alien
4. (b) whelp
5. (i) hirsute
6. (a) ace
7. (c) variable
8. (f) nebulous
9. (g) stable
10. (d) to dig up

IV. Fill-ins

1. vixen
2. vivisection
3. whelp
4. viviparous mammals
5. disinter
6. carnage
7. meat *and* vegetation (everything)
8. vixen
9. ruminants
10. simians

V. Word Analysis

1. Fishing is the piscatorial art. (*Pisces* = fish)
2. Astrologers say that Leos are the "kingly" ones, like their namesake, the lion. Pride and a love of being the center of attention are common traits. Many Leos are stage actors, film stars, and professional speakers. (Those who become teachers enjoy having all those captive audiences, day after day.) Leos like bright, true colors, sunshine, and parties. They tend to have flashing tempers, especially if their pride is wounded, but they are staunch friends as they value friendship highly.
3. *Matching*
   a. (3) swan
   b. (5) fox
   c. (6) dog (canine)
   d. (2) horse (equine)
   e. (1) calf
   f. (4) kangaroo
4. An aviary is a "bird zoo" or enclosure to preserve/protect/display birds. A *rara avis*, literally rare bird, is a rare (unusual) person, a character. *Rara avis* can also refer to any rare thing.
5. A pussycat should come to the French girl's call. This Anglicized usage is modern slang and won't appear in many dictionaries, but it typifies the words that the French have adopted from English: *pullover* (sweater) and *l'uppercut* (uppercut) are other examples.
6. *Matching*
   a. (4) words
   b. (1) birds
   c. (5) insects
   d. (2) mind and behavior
   e. (3) mammals
7. Educational fodder is the food that school offers: math, science, languages, etc., plus any information that adds to our store of knowledge.
8. At teacher's and student's discretion. It might be fun to compile a group list and discover how many animals have found their way into common sayings/old saws.

List 10

I. Synonyms

1. (a) whims, (d) caprices
2. (b) enmity, (c) animosity
3. (d) tenacity, (e) perseverance
4. (c) double-dealing, (e) hypocrisy
5. (a) behavior, (b) appearance
6. (c) trifle, (d) trinket
7. (a) keen, (c) shrewd
8. (b) precise, (d) clear
9. (b) persistent, (e) determined
10. (a) atmosphere, (d) environment

II. Antonyms

1. honesty, straightforwardness, openness, frankness
2. caution, circumspection, timidity, timorousness
3. accord, friendship, harmony
4. modesty, restraint, humility, reserve, unpretentiousness
5. normal, regular, customary, expected, typical

III. Fill-ins

1. ambience
2. pertinacity
3. demeanor
4. respite

5. bigot
6. attrition
7. exigency

8. quisling
9. vagaries
10. anomaly

IV. Analogies

1. amenities : desirable :: vagaries : unpredictable (Implied relationship)
2. attrition : reduction :: bearing : demeanor (Synonyms)
3. bigoted : tolerant :: ostentatious : modest (Antonyms)
4. temerity : effrontery :: pertinacity : obstinacy (Synonyms)
5. annoyance : rancor :: display : ostentation (Degree)

V. In Your Own Words

At teacher's discretion. If working on your own, consult with a knowledgeable adult about your sentences. Also, reread the sentences using these words in your lesson.

VI. Word Analysis

1. logistics
2. a. buddy, pal, companion, crony, confidante, soulmate, alter ego, comrade, sidekick, classmate, roommate
   b. Make of car specifically named; auto, machine, motor, tin can (to suggest cheap construction), jalopy, buggy, convertible, station wagon, sedan, vehicle
   c. odor, stench, stink, reek, foulness, fetidness, must, mustiness, moldiness, mildew, etc. (bad smells) —fragrance, perfume, scent, aroma, redolence, bouquet, spiciness, muskiness, sweetness (good smells)
   d. sandals, loafers, brogues, wingtips, tennies, sneakers, trainers (e.g., running shoes), pumps, slingbacks, huaraches (Mexican woven-leather sandals), flats, duckboots, oxfords, boots (specific boot varieties perhaps)
   e. tension, anxiety, apprehension, strain, stress, misgiving, "the willies," distress, unease, jumpiness, agitation, disquiet, malaise, "the jitters," plus any current, appropriate slang expressions
3. Some nouns always appearing in plural form are news, trousers (or pants), scissors, molasses, mathematics, measles, mumps, economics (the study), politics, alms, hysterics, headquarters, and vermin.
4. *Vagariously* is an adverb meaning capriciously, or in a whimsical way, therefore unpredictable. *Vicariously* refers to something experienced secondhand, as through reading or watching a movie. A vicarious experience is *felt,* not actually lived.
5. Annoyance or harassment requires constant rubbing interaction by persons determined to wear each other down through persistence—just as the stones are worn down tumbling against one another in the rock polisher. The current, popular usage of attrition to mean reduction in work force seems (to me) to be more related to the action of stones, pebbles, or shells near the seashore. Gradually, many are moved up onto the shore or beach by the action of the other stones and the waves. Those that are beached are, in a sense, cast off or discarded. Those members of a work force who retire, resign, or die, have also moved out of their system in a gradual, natural manner.
6. A few examples from *plex, plic, -ply* are complex, Plexiglas, duplex, perplex, complicate, explicit, replica, replicate, duplicate, imply, implicate, reply, multiply, supplicate, complexion, and duplicity.

   From *spec, spic, spect:* spectator, speculate, inspect, respect, disrespect, inspector, perspicacity, specimen, spectacles, species, aspect, special, specter, circumspect, expect, introspection, prospect, suspect, auspice(s), conspicuous, despicable, etc.

   From *ten, tin, tain, tent:* tenacious, tenacity, tenable, tenant, tenement, tenet, tennis, tenor, tenure, abstinence, abstain, attain, contain, detain, maintain, obtain, pertain, retain, sustain, abstention, attention, etc.

List 11

I. Synonyms

1. connive
2. discern
3. improvise
4. adulterate

5. extrapolate, infer
6. peruse
7. promulgate
8. succumb

9. succor
10. ascertain
11. inundate
12. portend

II. Antonyms

1. spurn
2. adulterate
3. exacerbate
4. connive

5. conciliate
6. improvise
7. extrapolate

8. vilify
9. succor
10. succumb

III. Switcheroo—Verbs into Nouns

1. (g) omen
2. (k) corruption
3. (n) spontaneous creation
4. (h) deduction
5. (a) appeasement

6. (c) discrimination
7. (b) declaration
8. (l) relief, help
9. (e) consent to wrongdoing
10. (m) abuse, defamation

11. (d) aggravation
12. (o) examination
13. (i) flood
14. (f) discovering beyond doubt
15. (j) prediction based on past knowledge or experience

IV. Analogies

1. criticism : vilification :: shower : inundation (Degree)
2. spurn : hanker for :: exacerbate : relieve (Antonyms)
3. improviser : ingenuity :: conciliator : diplomacy (Person related to most desirable characteristic)
4. ascertainment : conclusion :: perusal : knowledge (Cause and effect or result)
5. discern : differences :: infer : conclusions (Implied relationship, as one leads to the other)

V. Fill-ins

1. incubate
2. recumbent
3. confer
4. acrimonious

5. cursory
6. acumen
7. defer

8. deference
9. acrid
10. recourse

VI. Word Analysis

1. To *infer* is to draw conclusions based on evidence. To *imply* is to hint or suggest, often in a negative or critical manner; something implied is hinted or suggested, never stated directly. To *intimate* is to hint or suggest indirectly, and it often substitutes for the word *imply*. All of these words can mean suggest or hint, but *anything inferred involves conclusions drawn from somewhere*. To *impute* means (1) to blame unfairly and (2) to attribute, as *many qualities that now seem extremely fanciful were once imputed to the Greek gods*. Ascribe or *assign* are good synonyms for impute.

    Sentences at the instructor's discretion. If you are working alone, share your sentences with a knowledgeable adult.
2. A *cursory inspection* is not really an inspection, as it is hasty and not thorough, whereas *perusal* means careful study.
3. Words derived from *fer* include transfer, transference, conference, refer, reference, inferential, prefer, preference, suffer, indifferent, indifference, referendum, circumference, vociferous, odoriferous, coniferous.
4. a. ascertain
   b. improvise, extemporize
   c. peruse
   d. connive
   e. inundate
   f. spurn
   g. succumb
   h. confer
   i. defer
   j. adulterate
5. *Aggravate* is most commonly used to mean annoy or irritate, as *Her violin practicing aggravated her tired father*. This usage is considered *wrong*, no matter how common. However, the sentence *Don't aggravate the situation any further* is correct usage.
6. *To course* is *to run* and is a direct translation of the Latin root, *currere*. Coursing with hounds, therefore, is running with them and is popular in several parts of the world. Hounds of small size, known as beagles, course after hares in England, and the accompanying runners charge along after them. A beagle pack flourishes in Pennsylvania, and the sport is popularly called "beagling." Foxhounds course after a fox, while their human companions ride horses. Fox hunting continues in parts of America, notably the East and South, as well as in England.
7. Working with prefix and root meanings usually gives a student a close idea of word meaning, especially if the word in question is in context. In context, *refer*, literally *to carry back* or *to bear again (over)*, will be quite clear in meaning, as will *confer*, literally *to bear or carry with (someone else)*. But *defer* would elude quick definition as it has more than one meaning and would be even more dependent upon context for definition. Its meaning of *put off, postpone*, literally *carry down, off, away*, is usually clear in context. To *defer* to another's wisdom or superior position seems further away in meaning from the original root and prefix. No wonder we have to study the meanings of words.

List 12

I. Substitution

1. vascular
2. resuscitating
3. phobia
4. lesion
5. carcinogen
6. euthanasia
7. Gastric
8. paranoia
9. salutary
10. cardiac

II. Matching

1. obstetrician
2. cardiologist (also internist)
3. toxicologist/internist
4. psychiatrist
5. oculist or ophthalmologist
6. dermatologist
7. pathologist (possibly, an internist skilled in diagnosis)
8. vascular specialist
9. podiatrist or chiropodist
10. psychiatrist
11. internist
12. pediatrician
13. physical therapist
14. podiatrist or chiropodist
15. orthodontist
16. neurologist

III. Chart Fill-in

1. in-; cide/cis; a surgical cut
2. em-; empathy
3. derm; hypodermic
4. anti-; antidote
5. fratri-; cide/cis; the killing of a brother
6. virulent
7. mania; megalomania
8. eu-; thanatos; mercy killing or allowing the death of someone terminally ill
9. suscitare; resuscitate
10. anti-; antitoxin

IV. Antonyms

1. (a) incisive, (e) clear-cut
2. (b) toxic, (d) harmful
3. (b) soothe, (e) alleviate
4. (c) vivacious, (d) sparkling
5. (a) sane, (c) composed

V. Definitions

Refer to the definitions given earlier in List 12.

VI. Word Analysis

1. A *carcinoma* is a cancerous tumor.
2. Patients who abandon orthodox medical treatment usually do so for religious reasons or because traditional forms of treatment have been unsuccessful. Those patients with intractable or incurable illnesses are most prone to seek an alternative.
3. a.(5), b.(4), c.(7), d.(6), e.(2), f.(l), g.(3)
4. A *salutation* is a greeting, and its root is **salut, salus,** which means health, safety, and also *greeting*. In Italian, *saluto* is a salutation or salute; *saluer* means to salute, greet, or bow in French; and *to your health* in Spanish is ¡*a su salud*! A friendly greeting is also a wish for good health, the ancient root meanings well intact in modern usage.
5. a. tonsils (removal of)
   b. lobe of the brain, usually an operation that severs nerve fibers for relief of mental illness or tension (Have you read Kesey's *One Flew over the Cuckoo's Nest,* in which a lobotomy was performed on any mental patient "out of control" according to the authorities? Thought-provoking book.)

  c. appendix (removal of)
  d. uterus (removal of)
  e. stomach (removal of diseased portion)
  f. breast (removal of)
6. To *exsanguinate* is to die as result of excessive blood loss.
7. Death is the subject; root, **thanatos.**
8. a. (5) surgical cut
  b. (9) outer skin layer
  c. (7) compulsion to steal
  d. (6) lack of feeling or interest
  e. (2) cause of infectious disease
  f. (8) irritation or disease of skin
  g. (10) study of viruses
  h. (1) optimistic, cheerful
  i. (4) science of nervous system
  j. (3) division into two parts

Review. Lists 9–12

I. Antonyms

1. (g) judicious
2. (c) honesty
3. (j) to purify
4. (e) to mollify, appease
5. (a) to welcome
6. (h) parent
7. (d) hairless
8. (f) alien
9. (b) variable
10. (i) to antagonize

II. Analogies

1. rumination : idea :: mutation : anomaly (Cause and effect or result)
2. whims : vagaries :: trinket : bagatelle (Synonyms)
3. bovine : herbivorous :: leonine : carnivorous (General kind plus typical characteristic)
4. dismay : phobia :: glance : perusal (Degree)
5. spoor : pawprint :: temerity : backtalk (General category plus specific example [or one of a kind])
6. grain : fodder :: anemia : illness (Specific example of a general category. Answers *a* and *c* show exact synonyms.)
7. duplicity : truth :: confusion : logic (Implied relationship—the one impedes or prevents the other)

III. Definitions

1. prehensile
2. vivisection
3. vascular
4. torso
5. therapeutic
6. paranoia
7. lymph
8. cardiac
9. ambience
10. logistics
11. ascertain
12. extrapolate
13. improvise
14. gastric
15. euthanasia

IV. Fill-ins

1. portends
2. connived
3. succor
4. antidote
5. infer
6. salutary
7. Succumbing
8. vilifies
9. resuscitate
10. attrition
11. Promulgation
12. carcinogens
13. lesion, discern
14. fester

V. Remembering Roots

1. spec, spic, spect meaning to look
2. plex, plic, ply meaning to fold
3. cid, cis meaning to cut, to kill
4. cur, curr, curs, course meaning to run
5. ten, tin, tain, tent meaning to hold
6. ac, acr meaning bitter, sharp, sour
7. fer meaning to carry, bear
8. ter, terr meaning earth, land
9. vita, viv meaning life
10. path meaning feeling, suffering, disease

VI. Find the Oddball.

These are the words crossed out, the oddballs.

1. needle
2. idea
3. thought
4. health
5. mask
6. taste
7. indigence
8. timorousness
9. alteration
10. accord

List 13

I. Antonyms

1. (b) sober
2. (e) flawed
3. (a) morose
4. (b) revulsion
5. (d) boorish
6. (c) humorless: Answers (a) and (b) may be momentarily tempting, but they lack reference to humor, which is necessary for an antonym of jocular.
7. (a) apathetic
8. (e) ill-fitting
9. (d) credulous
10. (d) ill-omened: Answers (a), (b), and (e) are all wide of the mark.

II. Analogies

1. friend : congenial :: Daffy Duck : zany (Individual related to logical or expected trait)
2. temperament : sanguine :: writing : belles lettres (One of a kind or general type)
3. happiness : exhilaration :: naughtiness : rebellion (Degree)
4. homage : respectful deference :: calmness : placidity (Synonyms)
5. fortress : indomitable :: warrior : bellicose (Thing/person related to logical characteristic)

III. The Right Word

1. belle
2. docile
3. postbellum
4. homo sapiens
5. levity, jocularity, or jocosity
6. levitate
7. sanguine
8. impeccable
9. congeniality (Jocularity, jocosity, jocundity, or levity are also possible, but not as precise. A *close* friend is usually a kindred soul, one like you.)
10. adulation
11. astute (perhaps impeccable)
12. exhilaration
13. felicitous
14. homage
15. fervent

IV. Switcheroo

1. (c) boding ill
2. (e) state of delight
3. (g) enliven, excite, refresh
4. (h) unconquerably
5. (b) merry, jolly
6. (j) serenely
7. (i) in a polished manner
8. (f) relief
9. (a) teach with a definite opinion/point of view
10. (d) adorned, decorated

V. Truth or Fiction

1. F
2. T
3. T
4. F
5. F (Bloodthirsty is a synonym for *sanguinary*.)
6. T
7. F
8. F
9. F
10. T

VI. Word Analysis

1. Usually the context will tell the reader whether the subject refers to war *(bellum)* or to something beautiful *(bell)*. However, hunters refer to their weapons as beautiful pieces, so the chance for confusion certainly exists. Alas, there is no substitute for a large working vocabulary.

2. (a) At teacher's discretion. Most students will think of moth*er*, fath*er*, broth*er*, and sist*er* at least. Maybe even teach*er*. If you are working alone, show your list to any knowledgeable adult.
   (b) When you are faced with a strange word on a standardized test, it may be very helpful to use the suffixes *-or* and *-er* to denote a person, perhaps even an animal (otter). That basic knowledge might help to begin the logical deduction process leading toward a word's meaning.

3. (a) Pug, pugn- means *to fight*. A *pugilist* is a boxer or prizefighter, who is probably *pugnacious*, at least when in the ring. If not, his career is apt to be short. The words *pugnacious, truculent,* and *belligerent* are nearly interchangeable.
   (b) The *pug dog* got his name from a seventeenth-century word, *pug,* meaning imp or monkey, according to the O.E.D. By the eighteenth century, pug referred to the small breed of dog we know now—the short, stubby fellow with a curled tail and funnily wrinkled face who originated in Asia.

4. At teacher's discretion. If you are working alone, discuss these girls' names with your friends or any adult.

5. (a) To *placate* someone is to mollify, soothe, or appease that person, typically by promising to be good eternally: to carry out the trash, to write faithfully once a week, or to remember all of those things that you have no hope of remembering. (A person in need of placating someone else will promise the most outlandish things.)

6. Words from the root stup include *stupefy, stupor, stuporous, stupid, stupidity, stupendous,* and the colloquial *stupe,* meaning a dope.

List 14

I. Definitions

1. morbid	5. heinous	9. captious
2. pompous	6. inimical	10. atrocious, execrable
3. scurrilous	7. furtive	11. ludicrous
4. specious	8. choleric	12. plaintive

II. Fill-ins

1. (d) lurid	5. (b) intercept	8. (c) captivate
2. (c) nefarious	6. (c) mortal	9. (a) obdurate
3. (a) sordid	7. (d) duress	10. (b) specious
4. (b) macabre		

III. Antonyms

1. (a) placid	5. (e) genuine	8. (d) aboveboard
2. (b) admirable	6. (c) self-effacing	9. (a) congenial
3. (c) buoyant	7. (b) cheerful	10. (a) accepting
4. (d) not fatal		

IV. Analogies

1. pollute : waterway :: desecrate : temple (Implied relationship)
2. slander : scurrilous :: enemy : inimical (Concept or person related to logical characteristic)
3. sacrilege : heinous :: squalor : sordid (Concept related to logical characteristic)
4. deed : nefarious :: motion : furtive (Concept related to logical characteristic)
5. moribund : ill :: atrocity : misdeed (Degree)

V. Matching

1. (g)	5. (b)	8. (e)
2. (i)	6. (d)	9. (f)
3. (a)	7. (c)	10. (h)
4. (j)		

VI. Word Analysis

1. A *heinous crime* is one that appalls or shocks. Unfortunately, the theft of a pencil is rather common and not particularly shocking—unless it's your best pencil.

2. *Derisive laughter* (at something ludicrous) is scornful laughter. You feel superior to or in some way better than that which is merely ludicrous. Therefore, both *superiority* and *scorn* figure in derisive laughter, whereas we laugh with simple pleasure at beloved comedians. (They'd be upset if we didn't!)

3. *Matching*
    - a. (3) lacking necessary possessions or resources
    - b. (5) morally loose, unrestrained
    - c. (6) unable to be consoled, downcast
    - d. (8) notorious
    - e. (1) utter shame or disgrace
    - f. (4) worn out, useless, dead
    - g. (7) foul, rotten, malodorous
    - h. (2) base, low, contemptible
4. A crime may be of various degrees, some not terribly serious, but an *atrocity* is an *outrage,* an affront to our sense of morality and humanity. The torture of prisoners of war, murder, and genocide qualify as genuine atrocities.
5. *Furtive* means *stealthy* or *sly,* and sometimes *stolen.* Anything you do furtively is done with the hope that no one will see you. *Wary* implies both *caution* and *careful watchfulness,* not deliberate secretiveness.

List 15

I. Synonyms

All definitions and synonyms found in "Word Study."

II. Substitution

1. spores
2. antipodes
3. refraction
4. Axis (The three powers, Germany, Italy, and Japan, in World War II get a capital letter to distinguish them from any other axis.)
5. laser
6. centrifugal
7. shards
8. inertia
9. dross
10. fusion; also, axis is possible but not preferred.

III. Analogies

1. washing machine : centrifuge :: plant stem : axis (One example of a general type)
2. biology : life systems :: anthropology : humankind's development (The study related to what it studies.)
   Note: Don't be tempted by answer (a), which is off the mark. Science is a collection of facts, as well as unproven hypotheses and theories, but not a study of facts per se. Answer (d) is too narrow.
3. wine : dregs :: metal : dross (Implied relationship—the impurities of each general type)
4. Dark Ages : unenlightened :: tyrannosaurus : antediluvian (Implied relationship—the most typical adjective applied to each)
   Note: Anyone tempted by answer (e) should remember that not all fossils are by definition prehistoric.
5. concave : convex :: invigorated : inert (Antonyms)
6. axis : periphery :: tree heart : twig (Location)
7. shower : deluge :: pause : doldrums (Degree)
8. medicine : antibiotic :: rock : igneous (One of a kind/general type)

IV. Matching

1. (c) violation	5. (a) resistant single cell	9. (l) to wash
2. (d) opposite	6. (j) the study of rocks	10. (h) rapidity
3. (i) splitting into parts	7. (k) kindling	11. (b) hollow, depression
4. (f) bending of light	8. (e) unruly	12. (g) separatist

V. Completion

1. biomedicine	5. igneous	8. doldrums
2. alluvial	6. fusion	9. antipodes
3. paleontologist	7. axis	10. laser
4. pyre		

VI. Word Analysis

1. *Velocipede* is an old term for a wheeled vehicle propelled by a rider, such as a bicycle or even a tricycle. The term is still in use to refer to a railroad handcar with three wheels.

   A *velodrome* is a racing track for cyclists and may be enclosed or out of doors.

2. At teacher's discretion. If working alone, you decide which quotation you prefer and why. *Both* are worth thinking about.

3. EC- or ECO- is Greek for *habitat* or *environment;* thus, ecology studies the habitats or environments of organisms and their interrelationship.

4. *Matching*
   a. (5) the study of Earth's history, makeup, etc.
   b. (6) the study of crime and criminal behavior
   c. (4) the study of civilizations' artifacts or remains
   d. (10) the study of bacteria
   e. (3) the study of the nature and cause of diseases
   f. (9) the study of viruses
   g. (2) the study of mammals
   h. (8) the study of insects
   i. (1) the study of birds
   j. (7) the study of the origin and history of words

List 16

I. Fill-ins

1. cabana
2. siesta
3. presto
4. portfolio
5. quixotic
6. vendetta
7. bonanza
8. imbroglio
9. sierra
10. mañana
11. salvo
12. sotto voce

II. Synonyms and Definitions

1. (b) outdoors and (c) in the open air
2. (a) coalition with a definite purpose and (c) plotters [As to (e), remember that a faction is within the political party and not representative of the whole.]
3. (c) dabbler and (d) one lacking commitment
4. (b) fan and (d) devotee [Are you familiar with the word *swain,* answer (c)?]
5. (c) chaperone and (d) companion
6. (a) experts and (d) connoisseurs
7. (b) outstanding and (c) of major importance
8. (b) easily molded and (e) malleable
9. (a) sham and (c) artificial
10. (c) embroilment and (e) hostile, confusing argument

III. Logic

1. duenna   2. vendetta   3. dilettante   4. aficionado   5. quixotic or quixotism

IV. Contrasting Ideas

1. (i) indoors
2. (f) tyros
3. (h) fortissimo
4. (l) andante
5. (a) meager amount
6. (c) mansion
7. (m) entire political party
8. (b) yesterday
9. (e) desert
10. (o) unaware
11. (j) introduce
12. (n) honor, praise
13. (k) fact
14. (d) reduce
15. (g) single shot

V. Logic

1. Almost anyone would enjoy receiving a leather portfolio as a gift, but especially an artist or anyone in business or record keeping who must tote papers around.

2. Siestas and warm climates seem to go together, as people naturally seek to escape the fierce heat of midday. Over time, the life-style of an entire country logically revolves around the siesta, and business is conducted during cooler hours. Evening meals are typically late, when it is cooler and people feel more like eating. England's weather stands in direct contrast, as does weather in any of the more northern countries. There, business is often transacted over long lunches, leaving no time for the luxury of a siesta.

3. *Sierra,* by derivation, refers to jagged or saw-toothed mountains, whereas *mountain* can refer to any of the rather worn-down humps we fondly think of as mountains, such as the Sourland Mountains in central New Jersey. Geologically, sierras are younger mountains, less eroded by weather and time than older ones like the Appalachians or Sourlands.

4. The practical, sober nondreamer is the opposite of the quixotic person.

5. Women's liberation, which has come in moderate form even to Spain and Portugal, means that young women have freedoms formerly denied them, thus eliminating the cultural need for a constant chaperone prior to marriage.

6. Even in America, where teenagers have unusual freedom, we have kept the idea of chaperonage at dances and parties for young people. In college dorms and fraternities and sororities, we have a housemother, hoping that she will maintain a respectable level of decorum and act as an older adviser.

7. A *vendetta* or blood feud always demands retribution. As soon as one person is killed, another on the opposite side will be killed, and then it starts all over, never ending, as a circle never ends.

8. An *imbroglio* is always complex, usually quite hostile or bitter. Chances for one side misunderstanding the other are great, because of the complexity of the difference between them. An *argument,* on the other hand, can be quite straightforward and simple.

9. The *dilettante* dabbles, typically in one of the arts, and lacks serious commitment, therefore accomplishing nothing of worth. Many flit from one art to another. But America, established by the rigid Puritans, admires stick-to-it-iveness and commitment. They are major ingredients of the Protestant work ethic, still firmly in place. A dilettante may be a fine, upstanding person without a mean bone in his or her body, but someone *is* going to inquire, "And what do you plan to *do with yourself,* dear?"

10. A *general factotum* around the office is one who fetches and totes, who often does the jobs no one else will or can do. The factotum usually can turn a hand to anything and everything. No wonder the office is a gloomy place when that person goes on vacation.

VI. Word Analysis

1. A *junta* is a council or deliberative body for the purpose of government and is explained in Word Study. *Junto* is a group joined for a common purpose.

2. *Peccadillo* means a small sin, a slight fault.

3. Rephrasing Irving is a bit presumptuous, but to aid understanding, here is one suggestion: *There is no chaperone as rigidly cautious and unfailingly proper as an old flirt.*

4. At teacher's discretion. The dictionary definitions are helpful, but examples worked out within the class will be even more so. If you are working alone, consult with any knowledgeable adult about the material contained in your dictionary.

Review. Lists 13–16

I. Analogies

1. connoisseur : dilettante :: neighbors : antipodes (Antonyms)
2. sanguine : exhilarated :: satisfied : pompous (Degree)
3. sluggish : inert :: bad : heinous (Degree)
4. presto : music :: rushing : current (Implied comparison—the rapidity in music compared to the rapidity of moving water) [Answer (d) will not work, because friendship is by definition between congenial people.]
5. saleswoman : portfolio :: aficionado : scrapbook (Person related to logical possession)
6. plaintive : sentence :: morbid : outlook (One of a kind)
7. shard : pottery :: ethic : doctrine (Part of a whole)
8. sophistication : suavity :: chaperone : duenna (Synonyms)
9. stance : ludicrous :: attitude : inimical (One example or description of a general type, or one of a kind)
10. cognoscente : respect :: murderer : execration (Person related to logical/expected attitude from the public)

II. Fill-in Chart

1. em-, embellish
2. re-, bell, characteristic of a rebel, resisting control or discipline, unruly, refractory
3. indoctrinate
4. al-, alleviate
5. anti-, anticipate
6. ob-, dur, stubborn, unwilling to yield or give way
7. mort, immortal
8. desecrate
9. anti-, antibiotic
10. refractory
11. re-, ign, to light or fire again
12. petrology, the study of rocks
13. de-, deluge
14. re-, capit, to review the main points or summarize
15. duc, traduce

III. Affect and Effect

1. affects
2. effected
3. effects
4. affected
5. effect
6. Affecting
7. effect
8. effected

IV. Antonyms

1. (d) discourage
2. (b) practical
3. (e) accord
4. (e) current
5. (a) open
6. (c) cheerful and jocular
7. (b) noble
8. (c) sordid
9. (a) above suspicion
10. (b) fervent
11. (d) toward a center
12. (d) placid

V. Story Fill-in

1. auspicious
2. felicitous
3. nefarious
4. impeccable
5. sanguine
6. pompously
7. inimical
8. placid
9. choleric
10. fusion
11. velocity
12. shards

VI. Substitution

1. plaintive
2. cabana
3. mañana
4. ludicrous
5. execrable
6. homage
7. dilettante
8. captious
9. zany
10. siesta
11. indomitable, exhilarating
12. fission, fusion
13. spores
14. salvo

List 17

I. Identification

1. solecism
2. pun
3. hyperbole
4. aphorism (also an epigram, if anyone is fortunate enough to remember an earlier lesson)
5. innuendo

II. Definitions

1. bombast
2. rhetoric
3. vociferous
4. spiel
5. construe
6. terse
7. prate (or prattle)
8. soliloquy
9. dissent
10. reticent
11. glib

III. Aphorisms

1. Birds of a feather flock together.
2. Beauty is only skin deep.
3. The pen is mightier than the sword.
4. Beginner's luck.
5. People in glass houses shouldn't throw stones.
6. Sticks and stones may break my bones, but names can never harm me.
7. You can't teach an old dog new tricks.
8. Dead men don't talk.
9. Too many cooks spoil the broth.
10. A rolling stone gathers no moss.

Note: At this point you might think about *conciseness* in speech and writing, exemplified here by the old, simple adages. Our finest language critics and writers, such as E. B. White, William Safire, and Edwin Newman, have repeatedly implored us to use direct, uncluttered English if we wish to make our meanings absolutely clear.

IV. Antonyms

1. (g) dissent
2. (j) lacking fluency
3. (i) hyperbole
4. (a) accusation
5. (c) reticent
6. (h) wordy, verbose
7. (b) vociferous
8. (e) unintelligible
9. (f) dull, insensitive
10. (d) establish

V. Analogies

1. construe : gesture :: interpret : language (Implied comparison)
2. prate : speak haltingly :: run : stumble (Implied comparison)
3. play on words : pun :: grammatical error : solecism (One the definition of the other)
4. demagogue : rhetoric :: door-to-door salesperson : spiel (Person related to appropriate form of speech delivery, i.e., stock in trade)
5. bombast : lucubration :: innuendo : insinuation (Synonyms)
6. compassion : Lucifer :: mortality : deity (Person related to what he or she does not have)
7. presentiment : future :: review : past (Implied comparison)
8. thespian : soliloquy :: minister : invocation (Person related to one probable form of speech)

VI. Word Analysis

1. Your *avocation* is what you do for a hobby. Some, like Charles Schulz, creator of Peanuts and Snoopy, are fortunate to have combined both vocation and avocation.
2. Sentimentality is thought of as too much sentiment, an excess of gooey emotion, which would mar any book for current readers.
3. Anyone described as "not lucid" is incapable of intelligent speech or understanding. A person in shock or recovering from anesthesia or a blow on the head is often not lucid for a short time afterward.
4. Just for starters: dispose, depose, impose, imposition, juxtaposition, position, expose, exposition, repose, appose, apposite, apposition, appositive, suppose, supposition, presuppose, exponent, and exponential.
5. A *rhetorical question* is usually one asked for effect, with no reply expected or possible. People often ask a rhetorical question because they feel it is something that should be raised, an important matter to consider, perhaps with the hope of eventually securing an answer.
6. *Aphorisms.* Students will undoubtedly be more creative than these suggestions, but here they are.
   a. *Reticence is auriferous.* Note the root fer in this last word. It also occurs in *coniferous* (cone-bearing, which refers to some evergreens), *odoriferous,* and *vociferous.* Remember that fer means *to carry, bear.*
   b. *Prating involves negligible pecuniary expenditure.*
      Prattle requires negligible pecuniary expenditure.
   c. *It is inadvisable to postpone until mañana that which could conceivably be expedited precipitately.*
7. *Paronomasia* is from the Greek word *paronomazein,* to call with a slight change of name. It is now simply a pun, a play on words.

List 18

I. Definitions

1. subpoena
2. ad hoc
3. in extremis
4. magnum opus
5. sine qua non
6. alter ego
7. non sequitur
8. quid pro quo
9. caveat emptor
10. ex post facto
11. extempore
12. bona fide

II. Fill-ins

1. quid pro quo
2. ex post facto
3. ad hoc
4. status quo
5. magnum opus
6. in extremis
7. caveat emptor
8. sine qua non
9. alter ego
10. habeas corpus
11. extempore
12. subpoenaed
13. corpus delicti
14. bona fide
15. non sequitur
16. persona non grata

III. Logic

1. You could be served a writ of habeas corpus if you were required to appear in court.
2. If you felt that illegal, unjust imprisonment faced you, then you might secure a writ of habeas corpus as protection against imprisonment until you'd had a chance to testify in court, or produce exonerating documents and/or witnesses.
3. Welcome, acceptable persons would include all regular governmental employees and elected or appointed officials. Also, those officials in good standing from other countries would be persona grata. Any in disgrace or under suspicion would, of course, be persona non grata.
4. Corporeal beings are material ones that have earthly substance, as opposed to spiritual beings, who exist only in our minds or imaginations.
5. Progress inevitably brings change, and change disturbs the status quo, which requires that everything stay the same.

IV. Matching

1. (i) to go before
2. (g) to interpose
3. (k) an act of repentance
4. (l) unformed, vague, shapeless
5. (h) to play for time
6. (j) current
7. (a) change of form, type
8. (c) earthly
9. (b) withdrawal
10. (d) language unit
11. (f) contrite
12. (e) movement

V. Useful Latin Bits

1. *Abbreviations:* a. ibid.   b. i.e.   c. e.g.   d. N.B.   e. et al.
2. *Story.* In order: per annum, per se, per capita, and per diem.
3. *Matching opposites:* a. (5) bogus   b. (2) ex post facto   c. (1) rehearsed, planned   d. (3) welcome   e. (4) sine qua non
4. Graduating magna cum laude, with great distinction, or summa cum laude, with highest distinction, certainly would be worth considering.

VI. Word Analysis

1. Pro tem is the abbreviated form of pro tempore.
2. *Latin phrases.*
   a. in loco parentis = in place of the parents, or as foster parents
   b. in toto = in total, in all
   c. mirabile dictu = marvelous (or miraculous) to tell (or relate)
   d. pax vobiscum = peace be with you
   e. sub rosa = in secrecy is the idea; literally, under the rosebush
   f. tempus fugit = time flies (or flees)
   g. terra firma = solid earth, or firm ground
3. Penance, or the idea of atoning for a wrong, is the same as an act of contrition. One can do penance mentally as well as through some overt act.
4. Penitent and contrite are fine synonyms as both indicate sincere sorrow or regret for something one has done.
5. Latinate words often have longer root stems to begin with than many of the short Anglo-Saxon words. We tend to add prefixes and lengthy suffixes to these roots, expanding the whole business. *Destine,* for example, is not long, but by the time we add *pre-* and *-ation* to form *predestination,* we have an extremely healthy word. *Fer* is brief, but we make *transference* and *interference* out of it, and so on. Anyone familiar with the German language will be aware that it adds suffixes and prefixes with even greater abandon than English.

List 19

I. Definitions

Refer to "Word Study."

II. You're the Lawyer

1. commuted
2. law of torts
3. perjury (I had sworn to tell the *whole* truth.)
4. verdict
5. an annulment
6. injunction
7. larceny (petit larceny)
8. vagrant
9. lawyer, advocate
10. sanctions
11. misdemeanors, felony
12. extortion
13. forensic
14. malfeasance
15. litigation
16. adjudicates
17. extradite
18. indicted
19. acquitted
20. jurisdiction

III. Antonyms

1. (c) to sanction
2. (f) to abrogate
3. (h) disapprove of, also (i) to discourage, go against
4. (a) to indulge in
5. (b) to absolve, acquit
6. (i) to discourage, go against; (h) disapprove of also okay
7. (d) stable, fixed
8. (e) dictatorship
9. (j) to beg, plead with
10. (g) separation

IV. Analogies

1. felony : indictment :: libel : litigation (Cause and logical effect or result)
2. death : legacy :: trial : verdict (Cause and effect or logical outcome)
3. noble : plebeian :: fixed : vagrant (Antonyms)
4. curse : malediction :: interdict : prohibition (Synonyms)
5. oath : perjury :: public office : malfeasance (Implied comparison. Perjury is a serious offense while under oath just as malfeasance is a serious offense while in office.)

V. The Root of It All

1. Other words from *tor-* include torture, torturous, tortuous, retort, distort, distortion, contort, contortion, contortionist, torment, tormentor, torque, torsion, etc.
2. Words from *dict-* include dictate, dictation, dictatorial, predict, prediction, edict, dictaphone, diction, abdicate, dedicate, indicate, predicate, vindicate, addict, addiction, benediction, dictionary, etc.
3. A *plebe* is the lowest of the low at West Point, and since it is rooted in the word meaning common people, with modern connotations of low, coarse, vulgar, the label of plebe for the freshman suits the upperclassmen just fine.
4. The *conjunction* is a function word in the English language, serving as a go-between to link portions of a sentence or phrase. A conjunction is a joiner, which is its root meaning. Literal meaning = *join with*.
5. *Pandemic* refers to anything occurring throughout a large area and affecting a high proportion of the population. In contrast, an *epidemic* is an outbreak (typically of disease) within a more localized area, which is short-lived and affects a smaller percentage of people.

VI. Word Analysis

1. A civil lawsuit takes place between one citizen and another to determine each person's rights under the law. A criminal lawsuit involves a citizen and the state or federal government in such crimes as treason, hijacking a vehicle, corporate misbehavior (e.g., monopolistic practices), the abducting of a minor across state lines, homicide, etc.
2. At teacher's discretion. If working on your own, discuss Descartes's quote with any knowledgeable adult.
3. Quincy, or any doctor whose specialty is forensic medicine, must be able to present his facts in a court of law. In a case of murder or grave bodily damage, the doctor's factual findings will become part of the evidence collected on the case and may be used during a trial.
4. *Vagabond, rover,* and *wanderer* can be used in a positive way, or at least a neutral manner. *Vagrant* and *tramp* have fairly strong negative connotations. For most people the word *vagabond* (or perhaps *rover*) suggests someone who is independent and carefree, bouncing from place to place by choice.
5. A larcenous thought comes to all of us at times, if we admit the truth. Most young children have gazed a bit avidly at the collection plate in church, wondering what it would be like to have all that money to do with as they please. Most people don't give in to thoughts of theft, however minor, but now and then weak human natures are subject to fleeting temptations.

List 20

I. Substitution

1. suffused
2. vindicated
3. expurgate
4. suffice
5. imputed
6. remonstrate
7. tempered
8. instigate
9. extricate
10. imbibe

II. Fill-ins

1. admonished, abstained
2. sated, premonition
3. divulged, condescend
4. annihilating
5. influx, supplanted

III. Switcheroo

1. (h) self-indulgent
2. (d) unaffected, natural, not superior in manner
3. (g) concealed
4. (j) lacking
5. (a) exuded
6. (c) able to be fulfilled or satisfied
7. (b) drained
8. (i) weakened
9. (e) agreeable
10. (f) unavenged

IV. Rhyme Completion

1. satiety
2. temper
3. abstention
4. expurgation
5. instigation
6. extrication
7. compulsion
8. condescension
9. annihilations
10. imputation

V. Find the Oddball.

(These are the words to be crossed out in each question.)

1. imbed	6. suffice	11. trickle
2. defy	7. annoy	12. dispute (All others are
3. maintain	8. remonstrance	synonyms of the verb
4. discuss	9. revile	*temper*.)
5. expel	10. precipitate	

VI. Word Analysis

1. *Nihilism* rejects the idea that there is an objective ground for truth, especially moral truth. Nihilists say that the world is such a total mess that we should give up and wipe ourselves off the face of the earth. To them, annihilation seems like a desirable thing, and if war would accomplish that goal, they'd be in favor. An alarming number of terrorists are nihilists; others are blind idealists who will stop at nothing to achieve their goals.

2. A *confluence* is a junction where two or more streams or bodies of water join each other. *Junction, conjunction,* and *confluence* can often be used interchangeably.

3. A *vindicatory* remark might be said in justification of something done, an opinion held, an action taken, etc. Also, it might be a "gotcha" comment in retribution or as verbal punishment.

   A *vindictive* remark is a vengeful one, made by someone seeking revenge. Vindictive statements are spiteful, meant to wound the listener. (The second sense of vindicatory is close to this meaning, though not exact.)

4. *Precognition* refers to knowledge gained ahead of time, before the knowledge should logically be known. It does not necessarily refer to anything ill-omened.

   A *premonition* is a foreboding that something bad is going to happen, but it is not knowledge. Often, a premonition is unfounded and does not come to pass.

5. At teacher's discretion. If you are working alone, compare your answer to the definition of *intricate* found in a dictionary.

6. Because there are several hundred words in current use that are exactly the same as the Latin words, we can't print them all, but here are some of the most common: abdomen, actor, administrator, agenda, altar, antenna, apostrophe, apparatus, aquarium, area, aroma, basis, biceps, character, cinnamon, color, coma, conductor, confine, crisis, deficit, diploma, doctor, echo, ego, exit, exterior, favor, geranium, gymnasium, horizon, hyphen, index, instructor, junior, lens, major, minor, maximum, monitor, motor, murmur, narrator, neuter, odor, opera, pathos, pelvis, plasma, plus, pollen, professor, propaganda, quota, rabies, ratio, recipe, rhododendron, rumor, saliva, sector, senior, simile, siren, species, spectator, spectrum, sponsor, stadium, status, tenor, terror, thesis, thorax, translator, trio, tuba, tumor, ulterior, vapor, veto, vice versa, video, vigor, virus, and vortex.

Review. Lists 17–20

I. Antonyms

1. (c) loquacious	5. (d) open statement	8. (c) status quo
2. (a) establish	6. (c) reticence	9. (d) indulge
3. (b) disapprove	7. (e) judicious statement	10. (a) concur
4. (b) spurious		

II. Truth or Fiction

1. F	5. F	9. T
2. T	6. F	10. F (Remember that the verb is
3. T	7. T	determined by the subject
4. F	8. T	nearer to the verb in
		either-or constructions.)

III. Chart Fill-in

1. vociferous	5. moni, premonition	9. insatiable
2. ex-, tempor; unrehearsed, on the spur of the moment	6. a-, morph; lacking definite form or shape, unformed	10. en-, dem; native to a people or country, or restricted to or partic-
3. feasance, malfeasance	7. ex-, extricate	ular to one people or
4. ex-, expurgate	8. loqu, soliloquy	their region

IV. Analogies

1. rootless : vagrant :: glib : spiel [Main characteristic of the type/kind. Answer (a) is grossly understated.]
2. felon : persona non grata :: adjudicator : impartial (Logical characteristic of the type)
3. fondness : sentimentality : talk : prating (Degree)
4. legal code : law of torts :: trees : maple (One of a kind)
5. condescend : stoop :: ascribe : impute (Synonyms)
6. progress : regress :: instigate : discourage (Antonyms)
7. suffice : sate :: suggest : dictate (Degree)
8. sine qua non : essential :: extortion : intimidating (Main characteristic of kind/type)

V. Fill-ins

1. alter ego
2. hyperbole
3. reticent
4. divulging
5. litigation
6. Caveat emptor
7. in extremis
8. pun
9. forensic
10. construed
11. annihilate
12. aphorism
13. ad hoc
14. remonstrated
15. larceny
16. vindicated

VI. Matching

1. (l) retroactively, after the fact
2. (i) exonerate, free
3. (k) surrender to another authority
4. (j) absorb, take in
5. (n) flush, fill, infuse
6. (a) take the place of
7. (o) moderate
8. (d) withdraw, go back
9. (e) continued flow, movement
10. (m) marital
11. (g) clear, sane
12. (f) postulate
13. (b) repentant, contrite
14. (c) low or common
15. (h) urge forward

List 21

I. Definitions

1. staccato
2. patina
3. frieze
4. fresco
5. diva
6. chiaroscuro
7. bravura
8. vignette
9. virtuoso/a
10. aria
11. sonata
12. libretto
13. rhapsody
14. dynamics
15. falsetto
16. concerto

II. Fill-ins

1. dynamics
2. vignette
3. bravura
4. rhapsodize
5. virtuosa
6. aria
7. frieze
8. patina
9. chiaroscuro
10. Diva
11. staccato

III. Logic

1. A *nocturne* might help a baby drift off to sleep because it is dreamy, peaceful music. (Of course, anyone who knows babies realizes that they will go to sleep to any sort of music—or *not* go to sleep until they're darn good and ready.)
2. *Innocuous* means *harmless,* and a rabid dog can be very harmful.
3. *Dynamo* usually has positive connotations when applied to people, as it suggests energy and a desire to accomplish.
4. *Aspirations* are hopes, dreams, plans for the future.
5. *Illegible*—incapable of being read.
6. *Libretto* and *library* share the root LIBR, meaning book.
7. The name Fresca, so close to fresco, suggests a closeness to nature—a freshness and lack of artificiality that appeals to today's diet-conscious consumers.
8. People acting "in concert" are acting together, cooperating as a group. A "concerted effort" is the effort made by people working together in harmony, usually with determination.
9. From softest to loudest: pianissimo, piano, forte, fortissimo. (Think for a moment about our word *fort.* How is it related to *forte, fortissimo,* and *fortitude?*)
10. *Falsetto* and *false* share the root fals, meaning to deceive. Obviously, the Italian *falso* meaning false is derived from this same root.

IV. Analogies

1. wall : fresco :: canvas : oil painting [Implied relationship. Answer (d) is too narrow.]
2. Beethoven : sonatas :: Gilbert and Sullivan : operas (Name related to stock-in-trade or typical product)
3. mountain climbing : bravura :: Windsor family : dynasty (Specific example of a general type, or one of a kind)
4. physics : thermodynamics :: play : vignette (Part of a whole)
5. overture : finale :: onset : expiration (Antonyms)

V. Antonyms

1. (d) bravura
2. (h) full color spectrum
3. (j) bass
4. (a) dampen, discourage
5. (b) sloth
6. (c) harmless
7. (i) unsuitable
8. (f) diurnal (in the daytime)
9. (e) flowing, connected
10. (g) lacking emotion

VI. Word Analysis

1. The suffix *-ette* or *-etta* limits the meaning of the root word in some way, often by giving the idea of little, or perhaps short. A novelette is not as long as a novel, nor a cigarette as large as a cigar, etc. An operetta is less serious, and usually shorter, than an opera.
2. In order, beginning with the lowest (deepest) singing voice: basso, baritone, tenor, alto (contralto), mezzo soprano, soprano.
3. *Staccato* is the opposite of *legato*.
4. De + crescendo = *decrescendo,* gradually decreasing in force or loudness.
5. To different people the phrase "exhibiting the patina of age" may have varied connotations, but in general it would suggest gray or white hair, wrinkles, a less erect carriage, slower movement, and perhaps a general softening or mellowing of appearance.
6. A funeral *dirge* would be somber, and slower and altogether heavier in tone than a rapturous *rhapsody*. It would tend to repeat musical themes, whereas a rhapsody is typically improvisational and may change form at will. (Musically speaking, the two are contrasting terms.)

List 22

I. Multiple Choice

1. (b)
2. (c)
3. (b)
4. (a)
5. (a)
6. (c)
7. (b)
8. (a)
9. (c)
10. (b)
11. (a)
12. (b)
13. (a)
14. (c)
15. (c)
16. (a)
17. (b)

II. Who Said That?

1. a Valkyrie
2. Pandora (or Epimetheus)
3. a myrmidon
4. Tantalus
5. Phaeton
6. centaur
7. Sylvanus
8. Stentor
9. Panacea
10. Procrustes
11. Jove (Jupiter)
12. Iris
13. Pontus
14. Zephyrus
15. Hygeia
16. an amazon

III. Analogies

1. Attic salt : wit :: compensation : emolument (Synonyms)
2. suspense : denouement :: research : panacea (Implied comparison in time/direction; also cause and result.)
3. pleasant : jovial :: bright : iridescent (Degree)
4. amazon : gnome :: stentor : whisperer (Antonyms)
5. manage : conduct :: tantalize : bedevil (Synonyms)

IV. Fill-ins

1. manacled
2. Pandora's box
3. pending
4. hygienic
5. myrmidon
6. Attic
7. sylvan
8. intangible
9. pontoons
10. zephyr
11. agnostic
12. centaur

V. Word Analysis

1. The obvious parallel is that one, at most two, persons were burdened with the guilt of letting evil loose in the world. Most Christians blame Eve for tasting the forbidden fruit, just as the Greeks thought that Pandora was

their troublemaker. In Christian belief, Eve was the first mortal woman, just as Pandora was the first for the Greeks. Both were fashioned by a male god. Both were warned not to do something that they promptly went ahead and did anyway.

2. Either *brilliant* or *glittering* might be substitutes for iridescent in the Ingalls quote, but neither word is a precise equivalent of iridescent, which suggests the shimmering ethereal quality possessed by the rainbow.

3. The major reason for the continued existence of the words in List 22 is that we have no exact equivalent in English for any of them. Because each carries myriad associations with its myth, each is unique. Most of these words lack synonyms in English, and when some are suggested, they are weak.

4. A Valkyrie was an awesome maiden because she chose which warriors were to die in battle, and the image of a life-threatening female still clings to this word. An amazon is supposed to be tougher, taller, and stronger, but the threat of death is not implicit in her.

5. The American Indian warriors went to the Happy Hunting grounds. I can find no mention of where their women went after death but would love to hear from anyone who knows. The Christian equivalent of the Elysian Fields is heaven, a concept much vaguer than that of other religions, but where women are welcome to show up if they wish.

6. Aurora was the goddess of dawn, and Boreas, god of the north. Thus, the words literally mean "northern dawn."

List 23

I. Synonyms and Definitions

All synonyms and definitions shown in Word Study are acceptable as answers, plus those agreeable to each teacher.

II. Antonyms

1. (b) dutiful
2. (a) eternal
3. (b) wasteful
4. (c) immaterial
5. (e) imperceptible
6. (e) insignificant
7. (d) readily comprehensible
8. (e) lukewarm
9. (a) gelid [Answer (d) tepid is close but not an exact opposite.]
10. (b) easily swayed
11. (c) open and easily understood
12. (d) upper

III. Famous Descriptions

1. evanescent
2. frugal
3. prodigious
4. intransigent
5. nether
6. sardonic
7. inscrutable
8. piety

IV. Know Those Roots.

1. (g) sticky
2. (f) a course or route
3. (j) babbling, illogical
4. (k) to send back
5. (a) false, assumed name
6. (i) going from place to place, roving, wandering
7. (c) drive, enterprise
8. (e) follower, believer
9. (l) to name, suggest, propose
10. (h) name derived from a paternal ancestor or father
11. (d) projectile
12. (b) inborn, innate

V. Analogies

1. warm : torrid :: difficult : recondite (Degree)
2. unctuous : sincerity :: sardonic : sympathy (Implied relationship)
3. palpable : touch :: audible : hear (Implied relationship)
4. irreverent : pious :: remiss : attentive (Antonyms)
5. annoyed : vehement :: frugal : miserly (Degree)

VI. Word Analysis

1. *To scrutinize* is to examine carefully. It shares the root scrutari (to search) with *inscrutable*.

2. In Arnold's poem, *dumb* merely means without speech, as a cat certainly would be.

3. Over time the meaning of *pious* has come in some contexts to suggest false or hypocritical devotion to religion, whereas originally it meant devout in an honest sense. Today we are more apt to think of a pious person as one who displays religion or thrusts it upon us, one who is religious above all else. Any word whose meaning changes toward the negative is said to have *degenerated*.

4. A *misnomer* is literally a false name. Usually, misnomers are names that are grossly inappropriate.

5. A *palpable spleen* is one that can be felt, or palpated, by the physician. Normally, the spleen is an organ that is tucked up under the ribs for protection, but in some people it is situated far enough below the rib cage to be felt.

6. At teacher's discretion. This may sound silly, but it is an enjoyable class discussion and may encourage some to participate who typically are silent. Also, students may wish to judge which extenuating circumstances are logical or acceptable and which ones simply ridiculous.

List 24

I. Knowing the Words

1. *Antonyms.*
   a. life, or continuation
   b. honesty, openness, candidness
   c. energy, liveliness, verve, vivacity, etc.
   d. generosity, extravagance, or perhaps philanthropy
   e. cleanliness
2. *Synonyms.*
   a. ghost, specter, or phantom
   b. boor or lout
   c. wail, moan, or cry
   d. villain, criminal, or wrongdoer
   e. harm, damage, or injury
3. *Explanations*
   a. one who enjoys hurting others and witnessing their pain
   b. a twinge of conscience or pang of unease, worry
   c. utter disgrace, usually as a result of a profound wrong or evil
   d. one who believes that mankind is motivated by self-interest
   e. worry or concern about what the future will bring
   f. amazement often mixed with dismay

II. Switcheroo

1. (g) fearful of something ahead
2. (j) notorious
3. (i) stingy, niggardly
4. (a) to understand or to seize
5. (f) boorish
6. (b) wantonly cruel
7. (d) sadly regrettable
8. (l) distrustful of human nature
9. (e) innocent, free of artifice
10. (k) harmful
11. (h) to please by charming
12. (c) to bemoan, regret exceedingly

III. Fill-in Chart

1. example
2. prehens, prehend; tending to take from others for your gain at their expense
3. motive; motion, emote, emotion, mobile, mobility, move, immobile, etc.
4. abysmal; maleficent, maladroit, malfunction, dismal, malady, maladjusted, etc.
5. dol; to sympathize in time of sorrow or grief
6. infamy; famous, infamous, defame, fame, etc.
7. cynic; one who distrusts mankind
8. demise; missile, remit, submit, emit, missive, intermittent, commit, etc.
9. squalidus; utter filth/degradation
10. reprehensible; apprehend, apprehensive, apprehension, comprehend, comprehension, prehensile, etc.

IV. Substitution

1. qualms
2. miscreant
3. detrimental
4. consternation
5. apparitions
6. lassitude
7. demise
8. parsimoniously
9. sadist
10. squalor

V. Find the Oddball.

1. (c) appreciate — Others share the same root.
2. (d) fool — Others refer to churl.
3. (a) impious — Others relate to miscreant.
4. (b) wound — Others relate to qualm.
5. (b) unease — Others relate to lassitude.
6. (a) terror — Others relate to consternation. [Answer (e) belongs in the group because it lacks the intensity of (a), the oddball.]
7. (e) motley — Others share the same root.
8. (c) satiated — Others are negative in meaning.

9. (d) dismal   Only one with a negative connotation. (The name Dolores
                                  does not have a negative connotation, in spite of its
                                  etymology.)

10. (c) medical   Others define malady.

VI. Word Analysis

1. Anyone wearing a "determinedly guileless smile" could be suspected of duplicity. Innocence should be natural to be believed.
2. The suspect is apt to be at the police station, possibly in jail.
3. At teacher's discretion. Some well-known homophones are to, two, and too; right and write; boil (v.) and boil (n.); horde and hoard; bored and board.
4. A maladroit individual is typically clumsy—may drop things, bump into furniture, miss hitting the ball, etc. He or she is physically inept, in other words.
5. This definition is often termed an *epigram,* and Wilde was known for his epigrams. (See List 8.) The class might be interested in briefly discussing the truth, or lack of it, that they see in Wilde's definition of a cynic. What does he mean by someone who knows the price of everything and the value of nothing?

Review. Lists 21–24

I. Antonyms

1. (c) lethargic
2. (b) philanthropy
3. (e) apathy
4. (a) scrupulously attentive
5. (c) tractable
6. (d) irrelevant
7. (b) lingering
8. (e) dulcet
9. (d) choleric
10. (a) flexible

II. Logic

1. apparition
2. amazon
3. laments
4. guile
5. falsetto
6. frieze
7. sonata
8. staccato
9. sardonic
10. consternation
11. infamy
12. arias
13. hygiene
14. panacea
15. demise

III. Synonyms and Definitions

1. (f) pang
2. (h) lower
3. (g) difficult to decipher
4. (k) steamy
5. (d) evildoer
6. (l) abstruse
7. (b) a brief scene
8. (c) injurious
9. (j) holier-than-thou
10. (e) brilliant, scintillating
11. (a) uncouth, rude
12. (i) talk or write in an ecstatic manner

IV. Truth or Fiction

1. F
2. T
3. F
4. F
5. T
6. F
7. F
8. T
9. T
10. F

V. Using the Roots

1. We make *condolence* calls to express our sympathy and friendship to people who are grieving, usually after a death.
2. A *suspension* bridge is suspended in air from cables swung over towers between two banks. It has no pilings for support along its length, which makes it look more precarious than it really is.
3. *Contiguous* pieces of property are situated next to each other, touching along a common border.
4. The *respiratory* tract conducts air (breath) in and out of the body. It includes the nose, mouth, windpipe (trachea), and lungs.
5. A *prognosticator* is one who foretells the future, who claims to know ahead of time what will happen.
6. A *cohesive* argument hangs together, somewhat in the way an *adhesive* bandage sticks to skin. In a debate, only a well-organized, *coherent,* and cohesive argument can stand up to examination by the opponents.
7. *Exit, circuitous, itinerant, initiate,* and *transit* share the root IT meaning *to go.*
8. *Noxious* fumes may be merely harmful, or actually deadly, like the carbon monoxide exhaust from a car.
9. The best antonym of diurnal is *nocturnal.*
10. The root in *denominator* is *nomin* meaning name.

VI. Decoding with Roots

1. Circle MAL; note prefix dis-; bad or badly; gloomy, depressing, or poor, as *dismal prospects*.
2. Circle LEG; note legum-, meaning pea or bean; to choose, select, read; referring to peas or beans.
3. Circle MIT; note prefix e-; to send; to give off or out, as a noise or odor is emitted.
4. Circle MOT; note prefix re-; to move; moved or set away or apart, as *a remote village*.
5. Circle ONYM; note prefix homo-; root = name, prefix = same; homonyms are words spelled exactly the same but with different meanings, as *quail* (n.) and *quail* (v.); *bear* (v.) and *bear* (n.).
6. Circle PREHENS; note prefix mis-; to seize or grasp; a misunderstanding or misconception.
7. Circle TEN; note prefix ex-; to stretch, extend; referring to a reason or excuse that mitigates or lessens the severity of an occurrence, as *extenuating circumstances may convince me to accept a late assignment*.
8. Circle PHON; note prefix homo-; sound; words that sound the same but are spelled differently, as *bear* and *bare, horse* and *hoarse*.

VII. Commonsense Connections

1. (c) mural
2. (a) prima donna
3. (b) James Bond
4. (b) W. S. Gilbert
5. (b) contrast
6. (c) Tchaikovsky
7. (a) metals
8. (b) nature trail
9. (c) Valhalla
10. (b) gentle
11. (a) economy
12. (a) professional
13. (c) cowboy
14. (b) henchman
15. (b) devil

Unit IV. Your Best on the Test

1. Practice Analogies

1. bee : honey :: goat : cheese (Implied relationship)
2. transistor : radio :: spark plug : car (Part of a whole)
3. lace : gown :: frosting : cake [Implied relationship. Answers (b) and (d) cannot be correct as neither functions as an embellishment.]
4. captain : team :: skipper : crew (Implied relationship)
5. client : lawyer :: patient : physician (Implied relationship)
6. quibble : fight :: glance : inspect (Degree)
7. trespass : property :: intrude : privacy (Implied relationship)
8. dancer : lithe :: bookkeeper : meticulous (Person related to major/logical trait or skill)
9. fat : congeal :: blood : coagulate (Implied relationship)
10. strength : debility :: meaning : incoherence (Implied relationship and antonyms)

Note: The note in the text stresses that the currently favored variety of analogy question is implied relationships. If you examine past PSATs and SATs, you will see that the analogy questions have become more demanding in the past five years than in preceding years, when simpler relationships made up the bulk of analogy questions.

2. Practice Analogies

1. beam : support :: shingle : shield (Noun related to logical purpose)
2. monarchy : government :: sonata : music (One of a kind)
3. article : newspaper :: scene : play (Part of a whole)
4. orchestra : pit :: skaters : rink (Relationship of location)
5. hotelier : rooms :: merchant : wares (Implied relationship)
6. eager : zealous :: generous : prodigal (Degree)
7. clumsy : movement :: convoluted : writing (Implied relationship)
8. malign : vilification :: satirize : mockery (Cause and effect/result)
9. connoisseur : discrimination :: monk : asceticism (Person related to logical trait/characteristic)
10. novel : review :: court case : adjudication (Implied relationship)

3. Practice Analogies

1. kernel : ear :: curd : cottage cheese (Part of a whole)
2. vixen : fox :: bitch : dog (Implied relationship)
3. pioneer : apathy :: disciple : rebellion (Person related to least likely characteristic)
4. recruit : engage :: air : expose (Synonyms)
5. predator : claws :: frontiersman : musket (Implied relationship)
6. dissension : harmony :: obtuseness : perception (Implied relationship and antonyms)
7. glut : satiation :: work : remuneration (Cause and effect/result)
8. student : savant :: tyro : master (Degree, and also antonyms)
9. toady : sycophant :: storyteller : raconteur (Synonyms)
10. wastrel : dissipation :: recluse : isolation (Person related to logical characteristic/state)

1. Practice Antonyms

1. (c) redundant
2. (b) disperse
3. (a) irritate
4. (e) great
5. (e) lacking experience
6. (d) impartiality
7. (b) paucity
8. (a) subtle
9. (d) laggard
10. (c) balance

2. Practice Antonyms

1. (c) arid
2. (c) instigate
3. (e) sophisticated
4. (a) suitable
5. (b) unite
6. (d) compatible
7. (b) aggravate
8. (a) fondness
9. (c) wither
10. (e) blithe

3. Practice Antonyms

1. (b) release
2. (c) haughty
3. (e) insecure and unsure
4. (a) separate
5. (a) aboveboard
6. (c) inept
7. (d) sweet
8. (e) unobtrusive
9. (b) deterrent
10. (e) disinclination

1. Practice Sentence Completions

1. (c) problem-solving skills [Answer (b) merely repeats *logic* in the sentence and is not as specific as answer (c).]
2. (e) didactic (Definition of required word in sentence.)
3. (a) lackluster ... incapable (Sentence logic requires two negative words.)
4. (b) disregard ... transcribe (Contrast requires that opposing actions take place.)
5. (d) sanguinity ... debacle [Comparison requires a word meaning *optimistic* in the first blank and a word referring to the effect of investments going sour in the second blank. Answer (a) shows a weak word, *process*, in its second slot.]
6. (b) catholic ... demagogue [Contrast requires an antonym of *parochial* (narrow, limited) in the first blank. The second blank is followed by a definition of *demagogue*, pointing to it as the perfect answer choice.]
7. (a) combat ... isolation (Sentence logic and idiomatic usage allow only the word *combat* in the first blank; the words *alone* and *solitary* mandate choosing *isolation*.)
8. (c) reluctant ... inaccurately reflect [The word *although* sets up a sentence with contrasting clauses, further emphasized by the verb *feared*. Answer (c) is the only logical choice.]
9. (e) fortuitous (This word is what the sentence goes on to define.)
10. (d) punctual ... disheveled (Contrast requires that the word in the first blank be an opposite of *unready* and the word in the second blank be an opposite of *well-groomed*.)

2. Practice Sentence Completions

1. (b) freedom [Sentence calls for a word meaning *liberation*, and answer (b) is the only choice.]
2. (d) potential [Logic and comparison to the discovery of fire, plus the phrase *yet to be fully realized* demand answer (d), *potential*.]
3. (b) incongruous [This sentence of stark contrasts joined in one person requires a word that describes this odd state, not a judgment call as offered by answers (c), (d), and (e).]
4. (c) canny ... acumen [Contrast requires that the first blank be filled by an opposite of *young, ingenuous;* the second blank must explain why opponents are often *surprised*. Answer (a) is weak all around.]
5. (a) attest ... unabated [Sentence sense and general knowledge require answer (a).]
6. (d) prehensile ... precocious (The first clause points to a word meaning *to grasp quickly and well,* for which *prehensile* is the perfect choice; the word required in the second blank is extremely similar, and it is defined in the sentence.)
7. (b) dearth ... inundated with [Contrast requires a negative word in the first blank, especially called for by the verb *suffered;* the second blank must complete the meaning of *reams of information.* Answer (e) is weak, off the mark.]
8. (e) altruism ... narcissism (The first blank must be a word that coordinates well with *generosity,* because the two words are joined by *and;* the contrast, however, requires an opposite in the second blank, and *narcissism* is the most specific, given the phrase *in her own name.* Her new charity is an extremely selfish-looking thing to her associates.)
9. (c) ascetic ... avaricious [Only answers (a), (b), and, (c) can be considered for the first blank, and, of those choices, only answer (c) has a negative word in the second blank, and it's the perfect word, as it must be an opposite to *no need of worldly goods*.]
10. (e) obsolescent ... myopic [Logic requires a word meaning *old, outdated,* or *obsolete* in the first blank; only answer (e) is possible. *Myopic,* meaning nearsighted, completes the contrast.]

3. Practice Sentence Completions

1. (d) inestimable (This word is defined after the blank.)
2. (b) ambivalent ... diversity [Everything after the semicolon shows that James is of two minds about joining a fraternity, and the first blank must describe this state; only answer (b) and possibly answer (a) fill this requirement. The second blank must offer a contrast to being with people just like James—like-minded, in other words. The question is of people types, not education, so that answer (a) does not work.]
3. (c) compromise ... disparate [Logic points to *disparate* for the second blank; the first blank must be filled by a word describing how people with differences can meet and solve problems. Answer (d) is way off the mark.]
4. (a) effected ... elicit [Only answers (a) and (c) can be considered, because Louie obviously did escape from jail; of the two, only answer (a) offers a logical second verb.]
5. (b) volatile (The word chosen must be a direct opposite of the name *Patience;* note *at odds with her name,* plus the entire predicate.)
6. (b) incompatible ... witty repartee [Logic requires a negative word for the first blank, because this sentence contrasts the attitude of a serious artist with that of people who give endless parties. Idiomatic usage then requires *witty repartee* for the second blank, as the people are being *regaled* (delightfully entertained).]
7. (c) paradox ... inhibited [This sentence requires an understanding of the word *paradox,* which the sentence goes on to illustrate. The second blank demands a negative word; thus, answer (b) may be tempting, but it is not as precise as answer (c), nor does it work idiomatically.]
8. (d) inarticulate ... divine [The phrase *unable to express* and *silently* point to *inarticulate* for the first blank; while answer (e) may be tempting, *relieve a longing* is not correct idiom. Jane wants someone to divine her desire.]
9. (c) indigent ... demur (The first blank needs a word to complete the phrase *eke out their existence by begging;* the second blank must mean the same as *object.*)
10. (a) terseness ... welter [This sentence contrasts literary styles, the lean versus the fat. Other answers may be momentarily tempting, but none set up the exact contrast except answer (a).]

1. Practice Reading Passage

1. (c) [Answer (d) is too narrow.]
2. (a) (Note last two sentences of second paragraph.)
3. (b) (Note last paragraph.)
4. (e) (Note second paragraph.)

2. Practice Reading Passage

1. (d) (Note the deliberate contrast in sentences 1 and 2.)
2. (e) [No support can be found in the passage for choices III or V. Answer choice (a) is too narrow, as it omits IV, great intelligence.]
3. (d) [Answer choice (a) is correct but not as specific as (d).]
4. (c) (Note third paragraph.)
5. (b) (Note second paragraph, last sentence.)

3. Practice Reading Passage

1. (b) (Note the first sentence.)
2. (e) (If in any doubt, reread the passage.)
3. (c) [Answer (e), while momentarily tempting, cannot be right, because the narrator is involved, not detached.]
4. (a) (Note last paragraph.)

4. Practice Reading Passage

1. (b) (Note last half of paragraph 3.)
2. (a) (Note paragraph 2.)
3. (d) (This is the purpose of the second half of the reading segment.)
4. (e) (Note the first paragraph.)
5. (c) (Note the last half of paragraph 3.)

5. Practice Reading Passage

1. (e) (This is a major theme of the passage.)
2. (b) (This information can be concluded from the first eight lines, using simple arithmetic.)
3. (c) (This is the author's conclusion, last paragraph.)
4. (a) (Note lines 12–15.)
5. (d) (The passage supports only this answer, a correct interpretation here, as well as in the dictionary.)

6. Practice Reading Passage

1. (c) (Note the fifth sentence.)
2. (a) (Note the second paragraph, sentence 5.)
3. (d) (Note the first paragraph.)
4. (b) (Note the last paragraph.)
5. (c) (Note the second paragraph.)

Index

This index lists words that are taught, referred to frequently, or used as synonyms or antonyms. Pages shown in bold type give a definition of the words.

Have You Seen These Other Publications from Peterson's?

SAT Success:
Peterson's Study Guide to English and Math Skills for College Entrance Examinations
REVISED EDITION
Joan Davenport Carris with William R. McQuade and Michael R. Crystal

This proven step-by-step system is an effective self-instruction aid to build both the skills and the confidence of students preparing for college entrance examinations. Quiz-filled verbal and math sections plus mock SATs and actual questions from recent tests are included for practice.

8½ x 11, 380 pages   Item 5803
ISBN 0-87866-580-3   **$9.95** pb

Guide to Four-Year Colleges 1988
EIGHTEENTH EDITION
Editor: Andrea E. Lehman
Data Editor: Eric A. Suber

The largest, most up-to-date guide to the more than 1,900 accredited four-year colleges and universities in the United States and Canada. Contains information-packed college profiles, a directory of approximately 450 majors, a career-planning section, photographs, admissions guidance, including an entrance difficulty chart, and two-page "Messages from the Colleges" that are found in no other guide.

8½ x 11, 2,300 pages   Item 5498
ISBN 0-87866-549-8   **$15.95** pb

Guide to Two-Year Colleges 1988
EIGHTEENTH EDITION
Editor: Andrea E. Lehman
Data Editor: Eric A. Suber

This Guide covers approximately 1,450 accredited U.S. institutions that grant associate degrees. It contains extensive college profiles, two-page in-depth college descriptions written by admissions directors, directories of colleges by geographical area and by major, and advice on financial aid, standardized tests, majors and careers, and the admissions process. Companion volume to the *Guide to Four-Year Colleges 1988*.

8½ x 11, 550 pages   Item 5757
ISBN 0-87866-575-7   **$11.95** pb

Peterson's Competitive Colleges
SIXTH EDITION
Editor: Karen C. Hegener

The only book that determines college selectivity from objective data—and gives you the facts to work with. *Peterson's Competitive Colleges* presents a full page of comparative data for each of over 300 colleges that consistently have more undergraduate applicants—with above-average abilities—than they can accept.

7 x 10, 356 pages   Item 5390
ISBN 0-87866-539-0   **$9.95** pb

Peterson's Guide to College Admissions:
How to Plan Your Admissions Strategy and Get into the College of Your Choice
FOURTH EDITION
R. Fred Zuker and Karen C. Hegener

This helpful book takes students behind the scenes at college admissions offices and gives personal advice and step-by-step instruction about the admissions process. Contains sample essays, worksheets, dozens of campus photos, and capsule profiles of 1,700 accredited four-year colleges.

8½ x 11, 375 pages   Item 4637
ISBN 0-87866-463-7   **$11.95** pb

College 101
Dr. Ronald T. Farrar

The first book to answer the questions college-bound students most often ask—about money, health, social life, sex, and academic concerns. Written with empathy, common sense, and knowledge, this book can serve as a springboard to frank discussions on all college-related topics.

5¼ x 8¼, 187 pages   Item 2693
ISBN 0-87866-269-3   **$6.95** pb

National College Databank
FOURTH EDITION
Editor: Kim R. Kaye

The fourth edition of this innovative reference book helps college-bound students, researchers, and others find out which colleges have particular features and characteristics. It groups over 3,000 colleges by hundreds of characteristics and shows surprising similarities and differences among U.S. institutions.

8½ x 11, 477 pages   Item 5501
ISBN 0-87866-550-1   **$12.95** pb

The College Money Handbook 1988:
The Only Complete Guide to Scholarships, College Costs, and Financial Aid
FIFTH EDITION
Editor: Andrea E. Lehman
Data Editor: Eric A. Suber

The only book that presents the complete picture of costs and financial aid at accredited four-year colleges in the United States. The book is divided into three sections: an overview of the financial aid process and ways to make it work for you; current cost and aid profiles of each college, detailing need-based and non-need scholarship programs available; and directories showing which colleges offer merit awards in more than 70 areas.

8½ x 11, 575 pages   Item 5714
ISBN 0-87866-571-4   **$17.95** pb

Winning Money for College:
The High School Student's Guide to Scholarship Contests
SECOND EDITION
Alan Deutschman

The only guide to national scholarship competitions that award millions of dollars to students each year. This valuable book presents facts, figures, and advice about America's most prestigious—and most financially rewarding—privately offered merit scholarships. Contests cover public speaking, writing, science and math, citizenship, the arts, leadership, and more. Sample winning entries included.

6 x 9, 220 pages   Item 5552
ISBN 0-87866-555-2   **$8.95** pb

How to Order

These publications are available from booksellers, or you may order direct from **Peterson's Guides, Dept. 7620, P.O. Box 2123, Princeton, New Jersey 08543-2123.** Please note that prices are subject to change without notice.

- Enclose full payment for each book, plus postage and handling charges as follows:

Amount of Order	4th-Class Postage and Handling Charges
$1–$10	$1.75
$10.01–$20	$2.75
$20.01–$40	$3.75
$40.01 +	Add $1.00 shipping and handling for every additional $20 worth of books ordered.

Place your order TOLL-FREE by calling 800-EDU-DATA between 8:30 a.m. and 4:30 p.m. Eastern time, Monday through Friday. From New Jersey, Alaska, Hawaii, and outside the United States, call 609-924-5338. Telephone orders over $15 may be charged to your charge card. Institutional and trade orders over $20 may be billed (use your institutional ordering process). You may also use the order form below. After you have completed the form, just tear out this page and send it to us along with your check or charge card information.

- For faster shipment via United Parcel Service (UPS), add $2.00 over and above the appropriate fourth-class book-rate charges listed.
- Bookstores and tax-exempt organizations should contact us for appropriate discounts.
- You may charge your order to VISA, MasterCard, or American Express. Minimum charge order: $15. Please include the name, account number, and validation and expiration dates for charge orders.
- New Jersey residents should add 6% sales tax to the cost of the books, excluding the postage and handling charge.
- Write for a free catalog describing all of our latest publications.

ORDER FORM

Name _____

Address _____

City _____ State _____ Zip _____

Telephone (_____) _____

Quantity	Stock No.	Book Title	Cost Each	Total
____	____	____	____	____
____	____	____	____	____
____	____	____	____	____

Subtotal _____

Sales tax (NJ residents add 6%) _____

Shipping and handling _____

Grand total _____

METHOD OF PAYMENT

☐ Check or money order enclosed.
☐ Charge to MasterCard, VISA, or American Express (minimum order $15).

CHARGE CARD INFORMATION

(Minimum charge order $15)

☐ MasterCard ☐ VISA ☐ American Express

Name _____

Account No. _____

Valid from _____ Valid to _____

Signature _____

Peterson's Guides

Department No. 7620, 166 Bunn Drive, P.O. Box 2123, Princeton, NJ 08543-2123

Key to Abbreviations and Symbols

Abbreviations Used in the Text

adj.	adjective
adv.	adverb
AN	Anglo-Norman
Du.	Dutch
E.	English
e.g.	*exempli gratia*, for example
et al.	*et alia*, and others
F.	French
Ger.	German
Gr.	Greek
ibid.	*ibidem*, in the same place, the same
i.e.	*id est*, that is
It.	Italian
L.	Latin
N.	Norse
n.	noun
N.B.	*nota bene*, note well
OE	Old English
part.	participle
Pg.	Portuguese
Sp.	Spanish
v.	verb
v.i.	verb intransitive
v.t.	verb transitive

Pronunciation Symbols

ə	banana, collide, abut
'ə, ˌə	humdrum, abut
ᵊ	immediately preceding (l), (n), (m), (ŋ), as in battle, mitten, eaten, and sometimes open ('ōp-ᵊm), lock and key (-ᵊŋ-); immediately following (l), (m), (r), as often in French table, prisme, titre
ər	further, merger, bird
'ər-ˌ 'ə-r ⎰	as in two different pronunciations of hurry ('hər-ē, 'hə-rē)
a	mat, map, mad, gag, snap, patch
ā	day, fade, date, aorta, drape, cape
ä	bother, cot, and, with most American speakers, father, cart
a	father as pronounced by speakers who do not rhyme it with *bother;* French patte
au	now, loud, out
b	baby, rib
ch	chin, nature ('nā-chər) [actually, this sound is (t) + (sh)]
d	did, adder
e	bet, bed, peck
'ē, ˌē	beat, nosebleed, evenly, easy
ē	easy, mealy
f	fifty, cuff
g	go, big, gift
h	hat, ahead
hw	whale as pronounced by those who do not have the same pronunciation for both *whale* and *wail*
i	tip, banish, active
ī	site, side, buy, tripe [actually, this sound is (ä) + (i), or (ä) + (i)]
j	job, gem, edge, join, judge [actually, this sound is (d) + (zh)]
k	kin, cook, ache
l	lily, pool
m	murmur, dim, nymph
n	no, own
ⁿ	indicates that a preceding vowel or diphthong is pronounced with the nasal passages open, as in French *un bon vin blanc* (œⁿ-bōⁿ-vaⁿ-bläⁿ)
ŋ	sing ('siŋ), singer ('siŋ-ər), finger ('fiŋ-gər), ink ('iŋk)
ō	bone, know, beau
o	saw, all, gnaw, caught
œ	French boeuf, German Hölle
oi	coin, destroy
p	pepper, lip
r	red, car, rarity
s	source, less
sh	as in shy, mission, machine, special (actually, this is a single sound, not two)
t	tie, attack, late, later, latter
th	as in thin, ether (actually, this is a single sound, not two)
th	then, either, this (actually, this is a single sound, not two)
ü	rule, youth, union ('yün-yən), few ('fyü)
u	pull, wood, book, curable ('kyur-ə-bəl), fury ('fyu[ə]r-ē)
v	vivid, give
w	we, away; in some words having final ([ˌ]ō), ([ˌ]yü), or ([ˌ]ü) a variant (ə-w) occurs before vowels, as in ('fäl-ə-wiŋ), covered by the variant (ə[-w]) or (yə[-w]) at the entry word
y	yard, young, cue ('kyü), mute ('myüt), union ('yün-yən)
z	zone, raise
zh	as in vision, azure ('azhər) (actually, this is a single sound, not two); with a hyphen between, two sounds as in *hogshead* ('hogz-ˌhed, 'hägz-)
'	mark preceding a syllable with primary (strongest) stress: ('pen-mən-ˌship)
ˌ	mark preceding a syllable with secondary (medium) stress: ('pen-mən-ˌship)
	mark of syllable division
[]	indicate that what is symbolized between is present in some utterances but not in others: *factory* ('fak-t[ə-]rē)

The system of indicating pronunciation is used by permission. From *Webster's Ninth New Collegiate Dictionary* © 1985 by Merriam-Webster Inc., publishers of the Merriam-Webster® Dictionaries.